HOAX of Biblical Proportions

God's Inspired King James Holy Bible Exposes Satan's Profane Bibles

Edward Hendrie

[S]tand thou still a while, that I may shew thee the word of God. (1 Samuel 9:27 AV)

For we are not as many, which corrupt the word of God: but as of sincerity, but as of God, in the sight of God speak we in Christ. 2 Corinthians 2:17.

And they shall teach my people the difference between the holy and profane, and cause them to discern between the unclean and the clean. Ezekiel 44:23.

Copyright © 2023 by Edward Hendrie
All Rights Reserved
ISBN: 978-1-943056-18-7
Other books from Great Mountain Publishing®
- 9/11-Enemies Foreign and Domestic
- Solving the Mystery of BABYLON THE GREAT
- The Anti-Gospel
- Bloody Zion
- What Shall I Do to Inherit Eternal Life?
- Murder, Rape, and Torture in a Catholic Nunnery
- Antichrist: The Beast Revealed
- The Greatest Lie on Earth
- The Greatest Lie on Earth (Expanded Edition)
- Rome's Responsibility for the Assassination of Abraham Lincoln
- The Damnable Heresy of Salvation by Dead Faith (Expanded Edition)
- The Sphere of Influence
- Vaccine Danger: Quackery and Sin

Available at:
https://greatmountainpublishing.com
www.antichristconspiracy.com
www.911enemies.com
www.mysterybabylonthegreat.net
www.antigospel.com
https://play.google.com
www.barnesandnoble.com
www.amazon.com

Edward Hendrie rests on the authority of the Holy Bible alone for doctrine. He considers the Holy Bible to be the inspired and inerrant word of God. Favorable citation by Edward Hendrie to an authority outside the Holy Bible on a particular issue should not be interpreted to mean that he agrees with all of the doctrines and beliefs of the cited authority. All Scripture references are to the Authorized (King James) Version of the Holy Bible, unless otherwise indicated.

Table of Contents

Introduction 1

1	Choose You This Day Whom Ye Will Serve	5
2	God Created Through His Word	8
3	God Saves Through His Word.	11
4	God Has Promised to Preserve His Word	16
5	God Has Magnified His Word Above His Name	18
6	The Original Autographs Artifice	21
7	Failed Strategy of Prohibiting God's Word	36
8	Second Prong of Attack - Counterfeit Bibles	43
9	Satan's Circus Barkers.	63
10	Copyrighting Bible Corruptions	75
11	Every Word Is Important	80
12	Whole Verses Deleted From New Bible Versions . . .	83
13	New Bible Versions Say Jesus Lied	92
14	Saved by the Faith of Jesus Christ.	94
15	The Unpardonable Sin.	110
16	Concealing the Deity of Jesus Christ.	113
17	The Only Begotten of the Father	139

18	Flipping the Script	147
19	Jesus Christ Is the Son of the Living God	153
20	The Abominable Catholic Confessional	171
21	New Bibles' Call to Slavery	179
22	Pride Goeth Before Destruction	182
23	The New King James Version	184
24	Giving Themselves over to Fornication	190
25	The Rape of the Church	217
26	The Diabolical Scofield Bible	232
27	Antichrist Zionism in the Churches	244
28	Censoring the Gospel	266
29	New Bibles Undermine Creation by God	275
30	Hiding the Flat Stationary Earth	284
31	The Gospel is the Word of God	292
32	Denying the KJV Is the Inspired Word of God	327
33	All Scripture Is Given by Inspiration of God	345
34	The Arminian Agenda	351
35	Our Heavenly Father's Will Be Done	366
36	They Were Not of Us	374

37	NKJV Hides the Atonement of Jesus Christ	393
38	The Nicolaitans	401
39	Examples of Inspiration	410
40	Revelation 16:5	422
41	New Bible Versions Remove God's Promise	433
42	Proof New Bible Versions Are Not Inspired	437
43	Jehovah (Not Yahweh) Is LORD	443
44	Jesus is Lord	488
45	The Dark Secret of the TNIV	515
Endnotes		527

Introduction

Conspiracy is a concept that has been propagandized into disfavor, much to the delight of Satan and his minions, who are only too happy to push the idea that if one believes there is a world conspiracy against Jesus Christ and his followers, he must be radical on the fringe of society or worse. Most people are afraid of being marginalized and thus avoid speaking of conspiracies. People instead try to construe events as coincidental when, in fact, they can only be adequately explained as the product of prior agreements of conspirators who have combined in coordinated actions. God has revealed that there is a religious conspiracy. See Ezekiel 22:25-28, Jeremiah 11:9-10, and Matthew 26:3-4.

This conspiracy against the LORD and his anointed has been festering since the fall of man in the Garden of Eden and involves the kings and rulers of the earth.

> Why do the heathen rage, and the people imagine a vain thing? The kings of the earth set themselves, and the rulers take counsel together, against the LORD, and against his anointed, saying, Let us break their bands asunder, and cast away their cords from us. He that sitteth in the heavens shall laugh: the Lord shall have them in derision. (Psalms 2:1-4 AV)

While this monstrous conspiracy involves men, it is not headed by a man. The kingpin of this diabolical conspiracy is that terrible dragon, Satan. He is the adversary of Almighty God. He is also an adversary to all of God's creation.

> For we wrestle not against flesh and blood, but against principalities, against powers, against the rulers of the darkness of this world, against spiritual wickedness in high places. Ephesians 6:12.

Satan is leading his minions in a conspiracy against God and man. Satan knows that the word of God is the way to salvation. From the beginning, the chief priests and elders tried to stop the spread of the gospel. "And they called them, and commanded them not to speak at all nor teach in the name of Jesus." (Acts 4:18 AV)

After being admonished to stop preaching the gospel, the disciples, by the inspiration of the Holy Spirit, quoted the very passage from Psalms 2:1-4 that declares the conspiracy against the Lord Jesus Christ. By doing so, God reveals that the attack on the gospel is the core objective of the conspiracy "against the LORD, and against his anointed."

> And being let go, they went to their own company, and reported all that the chief priests and elders had said unto them. And when they heard that, they lifted up their voice to God with one accord, and said, Lord, thou art God, which hast made heaven, and earth, and the sea, and all that in them is: **Who by the mouth of thy servant David hast said, Why did the heathen rage, and the people imagine vain things? The kings of the earth stood up, and the rulers were gathered together against the Lord, and against his Christ.** For of

a truth against thy holy child Jesus, whom thou hast anointed, both Herod, and Pontius Pilate, with the Gentiles, and the people of Israel, were gathered together, For to do whatsoever thy hand and thy counsel determined before to be done. And now, Lord, behold their threatenings: and grant unto thy servants, that with all boldness they may speak thy word. (Acts 4:23-29 AV)

Satan knows he cannot stop the gospel and that God has promised to preserve his words, so it would be futile for him to try to destroy God's words. Thus, Satan's strategy is to obscure God's word by flooding the world with counterfeit Bibles. That way, he can flimflam people into reading his corrupt Bibles instead of God's infallible scriptures. The devil can then lead men astray from God's word. The book will prove that the Authorized (King James) Version of the Holy Bible is inspired by God and reveal how Satan is using profane Bible versions to beguile the world.

The Authorized (King James) Version of the Holy Bible (a.k.a., AV or KJV) is God's word in English. This book will prove that the new Bible versions are the corrupt works of Satan. The changes in God's word in the new Bible versions are not merely cosmetic for ease of reading, as claimed by the publishers. This book will show in Bible passage after Bible passage that the changes being made in the new Bible versions constitute heretical changes in doctrine.

1 Choose You This Day Whom Ye Will Serve

God's word is pure. We are commanded not to add to his words. Those who do so and claim it is the authentic word of God are liars.

> Every word of God is pure: he is a shield unto them that put their trust in him. Add thou not unto his words, lest he reprove thee, and thou be found a liar. (Proverbs 30:5-6 AV)

There is a curse upon all who add or subtract from God's words found in the Holy Bible.

> For I testify unto every man that heareth the words of the prophecy of this book, If any man shall add unto these things, God shall add unto him the plagues that are written in this book: And if any man shall take away from the words of the book of this prophecy, God shall take away his part out of the book of life, and out of the holy city, and from the things which are written in this book. (Revelation 22:18-19 AV)

The new Bible versions have significant additions and subtractions from the Authorized (King James) Version of the Holy Bible. You must choose which is God's word. It is either the King James Bible or one of the new versions. They both cannot be God's word because they say different things. As I will prove in this book, the differences go directly to doctrine. Indeed, in some cases, the new Bible versions say the opposite of what is found in the King James Bible.

Those who promote the new Bible versions fall all over themselves praising the King James Bible. But they think that the new Bibles are superior. There is a problem with their position. If they feel that the new Bible versions are superior, they must necessarily believe that the King James Bible cannot be God's word because it has more words in some verses and fewer words in other verses than in the new version Bibles. In fact, there are whole verses found in the King James Bible that are not in the new Bible versions. If they are to be obedient to God's word, they must necessarily consider the King James Bible to violate the admonition in Revelation 22:18-19. But they don't. Their position is illogical and unbiblical.

Some "prefer" the King James Bible but believe that the new Bible translations are also good translations of God's word in the English language. Those who take that position may be uninformed. But Christians must be informed about this issue because God's word is more dear to him than his name. "[T]hou hast magnified thy word above all thy name." (Psalms 138:2 AV) If a person is informed but still says that both the King James and the new Bible versions are good translations of God's word, that makes him lukewarm. How can one be lukewarm about something that is so dear to God as his word? God has something to say about that. "So then because thou art lukewarm, and neither cold nor hot, I will spue thee out of my mouth." Revelation 3:16.

It gets worse; according to Revelations 22:18-19, those that prefer the new Bible versions must choose which of the many new Bible versions is God's word because all new Bible versions disagree with one another in many verses. But the new Bible advocates will not do that. They will have a "prefered" Bible, but they maintain that they are mostly good English translations. They are double-minded. "A double minded man is unstable in all his ways." (James 1:8 AV)

Dear reader, you must choose whether to abide by the King James Bible or the new Bible versions. There is no middle ground. There can be no compromise. "[I]f the Lord be God, follow him: but if Baal, then follow him." 1 Kings 18:21. You must choose. "[C]hoose you this day whom ye will serve." Joshua 24:15. This book will give you the necessary knowledge to make an informed decision.

2 God Created Through His Word

In the beginning God created the heaven and the earth. How did he create? He created by speaking. **"God said ... and it was so."** *See* Genesis 1:1-2:25. "Through faith we understand that the worlds were framed by the word of God, so that things which are seen were not made of things which do appear." (Hebrews 11:3 AV)

> **By the word of the LORD were the heavens made; and all the host of them by the breath of his mouth.** He gathereth the waters of the sea together as an heap: he layeth up the depth in storehouses. Let all the earth fear the LORD: let all the inhabitants of the world stand in awe of him. **For he spake, and it was done; he commanded, and it stood fast.** (Psalms 33:6-9 AV)

God created by speaking things into existence. For example: "God said, Let there be light: and there was light." (Genesis 1:3 AV)

God's word is so important that one of the monikers for Jesus Christ is **"the Word."**

> In the beginning was **the Word**, and **the Word** was with God, and **the Word was God**. The same was in the beginning with God. All things were made by him; and without him was not any thing made that was made. In him was life; and the life was the light of men." (John 1:1-4 AV)

Jesus Christ is **the Word**. He is the Creator. He made all things.

> For by him were all things created, that are in heaven, and that are in earth, visible and invisible, whether they be thrones, or dominions, or principalities, or powers: all things were created by him, and for him. (Colossians 1:16 AV)

Jesus Christ is called **the word of God**. "And he was clothed with a vesture dipped in blood: and his name is called **The Word of God**." (Revelation 19:13)

Indeed, we can know about God through his creation. The invisible things of God are revealed through his creation, even his eternal power and Godhead.

> For the invisible things of him from the creation of the world are clearly seen, being understood by the things that are made, even his eternal power and Godhead; so that they are without excuse. (Romans 1:20 AV)

God, **the Word**, the Creator, Jesus Christ, came to Earth in the flesh.

> And **the Word** was made flesh, and dwelt among us, (and we beheld his glory, the glory as of the only begotten of the Father,) full of grace and truth.

(John 1:14 AV)

When God reveals the Godhead, he describes Jesus Christ, as "**the Word**."

> For there are three that bear record in heaven, the Father, **the Word**, and the Holy Ghost: and these three are one. (1 John 5:7 AV)

God's word is very essential. It is the very essence of God. Jesus Christ explains how vital every single one of his words is. "It is written, Man shall not live by bread alone, but by **every word** that proceedeth out of the mouth of God." (Matthew 4:4 AV)

3 God Saves Through His Word

God's word is the way to salvation. Salvation comes by faith. "By grace are ye saved through faith." Ephesians 2:8. God's plan for salvation requires that his elect come to him by hearing the gospel.

> For whosoever shall call upon the name of the Lord shall be saved. How then shall they call on him in whom they have not believed? and **how shall they believe in him of whom they have not heard? and how shall they hear without a preacher**? And how shall they preach, except they be sent? as it is written, How beautiful are the feet of them that preach the gospel of peace, and bring glad tidings of good things! But they have not all obeyed the gospel. For Esaias saith, Lord, who hath believed our report? **So then faith cometh by hearing, and hearing by the word of God**. (Romans 10:13-17 AV)

Without faith in Jesus Christ, one cannot be saved. "Without faith it is impossible to please him: for he that cometh to God must believe that he is, and that he is a rewarder of them that diligently seek him." Hebrews 11:6.

The Holy Bible states that God saves through his Word.

Being born again, not of corruptible seed, but of incorruptible, by the word of God, which liveth and abideth for ever. For all flesh *is* as grass, and all the glory of man as the flower of grass. The grass withereth, and the flower thereof falleth away: But the word of the Lord endureth for ever. And this is the word which by the gospel is preached unto you. (1 Peter 1:23-25 AV)

And that from a child thou hast known the holy scriptures, which are able to make thee wise unto salvation through faith which is in Christ Jesus. (2 Timothy 3:15 AV)

The faith comes by the sovereign grace of God. Jesus uses the parable of the sower in Luke 8:4-17 to illustrate his sovereign grace. In the parable, he explains that the seed (the word of God) is sown, and only those whose hearts are honest and good hear the gospel and bring forth the fruit of salvation. Notice that Jesus gives a hint at what it means to have an honest and good heart. At the end of the parable, he cried: "He that hath ears to hear, let him hear." Luke 8:8. What did Jesus mean by that? He explained to his disciples: "Unto you it is given to know the mysteries of the kingdom of God: but to others in parables; that seeing they might not see, and hearing they might not understand." Luke 8:10.

Those who are not saved are not saved because they have not been given spiritual ears to hear the gospel. God has stopped their ears to the truth of the gospel. Jesus made clear that one purpose of the parables is to conceal the spiritual truths of the gospel from those who have been chosen for damnation. God is the one that makes a heart honest and good and able to hear and believe the gospel. God is the husbandman who tills the soil of men's hearts and makes it soft to receive the gospel. The gospel is the means of bringing the hearer to a knowledge of Jesus Christ. Salvation is through faith in Jesus Christ by the grace of God.

> And when much people were gathered together, and were come to him out of every city, he spake by a parable: A sower went out to sow his seed: and as he sowed, some fell by the way side; and it was trodden down, and the fowls of the air devoured it. And some fell upon a rock; and as soon as it was sprung up, it withered away, because it lacked moisture. And some fell among thorns; and the thorns sprang up with it, and choked it. And other fell on good ground, and sprang up, and bare fruit an hundredfold. And when he had said these things, he cried, He that hath ears to hear, let him hear. And his disciples asked him, saying, What might this parable be? **And he said, Unto you it is given to know the mysteries of the kingdom of God: but to others in parables; that seeing they might not see, and hearing they might not understand.** Now the parable is this: The seed is the word of God. Those by the way side are they that hear; then cometh the devil, and taketh away the word out of their hearts, lest they should believe and be saved. They on the rock are they, which, when they hear, receive the word with joy; and these have no root, which for a while believe, and in time of temptation fall away. And that which fell among thorns are they, which, when they have heard, go forth, and are choked with cares and riches and pleasures of this life, and bring no fruit to perfection. But that on the good ground are they, which in an honest and good heart, having heard the word, keep it, and bring forth fruit with patience. No man, when he hath lighted a candle, covereth it with a vessel, or

putteth it under a bed; but setteth it on a candlestick, that they which enter in may see the light. For nothing is secret, that shall not be made manifest; neither any thing hid, that shall not be known and come abroad. (Luke 8:4-17 AV)

It is not for a man of his own free will to choose. Election is completely within the province of God. It is not for man to determine who is chosen by God. It is our responsibility, indeed our duty, to preach the gospel and allow that spiritual seed of God's word to find the soil prepared by God for salvation.

God causes those whom he has chosen for salvation to come in faith to him. "Blessed is the man whom thou choosest, and causest to approach unto thee, that he may dwell in thy courts: we shall be satisfied with the goodness of thy house, even of thy holy temple." Psalms 65:4. God uses his gospel as his means of drawing his elect. In Acts chapter 2, Peter explained the ministry and crucifixion of Jesus Christ. In that passage, we see how God uses his gospel to call those whom he has chosen for salvation. Acts 2:21 states: "And it shall come to pass, that whosoever shall call on the name of the Lord shall be saved." (Acts 2:21 AV) When read in context, however, we find out that it is only those God has chosen for salvation who will understand the gospel and call on the name of the Lord and be saved.

In Acts chapter 2, when the people heard the gospel preached by Peter, they "were pricked in their heart" and asked, "what shall we do?" Peter told them to repent and be baptized. What is revealing is what Peter said next about those who would receive the gift of the Holy Ghost. It was only those whom God had chosen for salvation that would receive the promise of salvation. God called them to salvation by the preaching of the gospel. The entire passage in context explains that the promise of salvation is only for those whom God shall call to salvation.

> Therefore let all the house of Israel know assuredly, that God hath made that same Jesus, whom ye have crucified, both Lord and Christ. **Now when they heard this, they were pricked in their heart, and said unto Peter and to the rest of the apostles, Men and brethren, what shall we do?** Then Peter said unto them, Repent, and be baptized every one of you in the name of Jesus Christ for the remission of sins, and ye shall receive the gift of the Holy Ghost. For the promise is unto you, and to your children, and to all that are afar off, even as many as the Lord our God shall call. (Acts 2:36-39 AV)

It is the Lord who adds to the church those whom he has decided should be saved. Salvation is all of God, who chooses those who will believe in him. Men are powerless to believe in Jesus without the sovereign election of God giving them a spiritual rebirth, whereby they are imbued with spiritual eyes to see and ears to hear.

> And they, continuing daily with one accord in the temple, and breaking bread from house to house, did eat their meat with gladness and singleness of heart, Praising God, and having favour with all the people. **And the Lord added to the church daily such as should be saved.** (Acts 2:46-47 AV)

"Jesus Christ the same yesterday, and to day, and for ever." Hebrews 13:8. God is sovereign and, as always, will continue to exercise his sovereignty in electing his chosen. "For thou art an holy people unto the LORD thy God: **the LORD thy God hath chosen thee to be a special people unto himself, above all people that are upon the face of the earth.**" Deuteronomy 7:6. God has chosen his church, which is spiritual Israel. See Galatians 3:28-29, 6:16.

4 God Has Promised to Preserve His Word

God would not leave us without the means for our salvation—his word. The following scripture passages testify that God has promised that he will forever preserve his word.

> For verily I say unto you, Till heaven and earth pass, one jot or one tittle shall in no wise pass from the law, till all be fulfilled. (Matthew 5:18 AV)
>
> **Heaven and earth shall pass away, but my words shall not pass away.** (Matthew 24:35 AV)
>
> **[T]he word of the Lord endureth for ever.** And this is the word which by the gospel is preached unto you. (1 Peter 1:25 AV)
>
> The grass withereth, the flower fadeth: but **the word of our God shall stand for ever.** (Isaiah 40:8 AV)
>
> **For ever, O LORD, thy word is settled in heaven.** (Psalms 119:89 AV)

Satan's new Bible versions try to obscure God's promise to preserve his words forever by changing the object of the preservation in Psalm 12:6-7 from referring to God's words to something else. Thus, the English Standard Version (ESV) changes the words "preserve them," referring to preserving the words of the LORD forever to "guard us" forever. "Guard us" is a non-sequitur. The words of the LORD are the topic of the sentences and the object of the preservation. Changing the topic to "guard us" makes no sense unless you are trying to edit out God's promise to preserve his words forever.

AV	ESV
The words of the LORD are pure words: as silver tried in a furnace of earth, purified seven times. Thou shalt keep them, O LORD, thou shalt **preserve them** from this generation for ever. (Psalms 12:6-7 AV)	The words of the Lord are pure words, like silver refined in a furnace on the ground, purified seven times. You, O Lord, will keep them; you will **guard us** from this generation forever. (Psalms 12:6-7 ESV)

5 God Has Magnified His Word Above His Name

Indeed, God considers his word even more important than his name. **"[F]or thou hast magnified thy word above all thy name."** Psalm 138:2. Consider the importance of God's word, which is above his name, when his third commandment prohibits taking his name in vain. *See* Exodus 20:7. God has placed a terrible curse on those who would add to or take away from his word. *See* Revelation 22:18-19.

God's name is so precious that the biblical penalty for blaspheming his name is death. Leviticus 24:16. However, God holds his word above even his name. Why? Because God's word is God's revelation of him to man. The Holy Bible states that:

> In the beginning was the Word, and the Word was with God, and **the Word was God**. The same was in the beginning with God. **All things were made by him**; and without him was not any thing made that was made. (John 1:1-3)

> In whom we have redemption through his blood, even the forgiveness of sins: Who is the image of the invisible God, the firstborn of every creature:

> **For by him were all things created, that are in heaven, and that are in earth, visible and invisible, whether they be thrones, or dominions, or principalities, or powers: all things were created by him, and for him: And he is before all things, and by him all things consist**. (Colossians 1:14-17)

The gospel found in John states that God (the Word, the Creator) came to Earth in the flesh: Jesus Christ.

> And the **Word was made flesh**, and dwelt among us, (and we beheld his glory, the glory as of the only begotten of the Father,) full of grace and truth. (John 1:14)

In the Holy Bible God the Father makes it clear that his Son, Jesus, is God.

> But unto the **Son** he saith, Thy throne, **O God**, is for ever and ever: a sceptre of righteousness *is* the sceptre of thy kingdom. (Hebrews 1:8)

The Holy Bible is not like any other book; it is unique; it was written by God through men.

> **All scripture is given by inspiration of God**, and is profitable for doctrine, for reproof, for correction, for instruction in righteousness: (2 Timothy 3:16)

> Knowing this first, that no prophecy of the scripture is of any private interpretation. For the prophecy came not in old time by the will of man: but **holy men of God spake as they were moved by the Holy Ghost**. (2 Peter 1:20-21)

Which things also **we speak, not in the words which man's wisdom teacheth, but which the Holy Ghost teacheth**; comparing spiritual things with spiritual. But the natural man receiveth not the things of the Spirit of God: for they are foolishness unto him: neither can he know *them*, because **they are spiritually discerned**. (1 Corinthians 2:13-14)

6   The Original Autographs Artifice

The serpent was the most subtle of the beasts. Genesis 3:1. That serpent, the devil, and his minions have used all manner of subtlety to undermine God's word. One method is to deny by implication that God has preserved his word. For example, the statement of faith for the Congregational Methodist Church indicates that, while the scripture we have today is authoritative, only the original autographs of the scriptures were infallible and inerrant.

> We believe that the Bible is the word of God, written by holy men of old as they were enabled to communicate God's truth without error. We believe that the scripture is **infallible and inerrant in its original autographs.** The Bible is our rule of faith and practice, and a revelation of God Himself and His will for all people. Written over 1,500 years by as many as 40 authors, the scripture is **authoritative** in matters of faith, doctrine, and practice.[1] (emphasis added)

The teaching institutions that turn out pastors for churches make sure that those pastors have no confidence in the Bible. One example is Dallas Theological Seminary, which is a non-denominational evangelical seminary in Dallas, Texas, with satellite campuses all over the world. It is the seventh-largest seminary in the U.S.² Its statement of faith limits divine inspiration to the "original manuscripts."

> We believe that "all Scripture is given by inspiration of God," by which we understand the whole Bible is inspired in the sense that holy men of God "were moved by the Holy Spirit" to write the very words of Scripture. We believe that this divine inspiration extends equally and fully to all parts of the writings—historical, poetical, doctrinal, and prophetical—**as appeared in the original manuscripts.** We believe that the whole Bible **in the originals** is therefore without error. We believe that all the Scriptures center about the Lord Jesus Christ in His person and work in His first and second coming, and hence that no portion, even of the Old Testament, is properly read or understood until it leads to Him. We also believe that all the Scriptures were designed for our practical instruction.³ (emphasis added)

By limiting the divinely inspired scripture to the original manuscripts, Dallas Theological Seminary implicitly excludes the Bible we have today from being divinely inspired and without error. We find the same equivocation in the Moody Bible Institute Doctrinal Statement.

> The Bible, including both the Old and the New Testaments, is a divine revelation, the **original autographs** of which were verbally inspired by the Holy Spirit.⁴

There is similar language in the Wheaton College Statement of Faith and Educational Purpose.

> WE BELIEVE that God has revealed Himself and His truth in the created order, in the **Scriptures**, and supremely in Jesus Christ; and that the **Scriptures** of the Old and New Testaments are **verbally inspired by God and inerrant in the original writing**, so that they are fully trustworthy and of supreme and final authority in all they say.[5]

Wheaton College considers the original writings of scriptures to be inspired, inerrant, fully trustworthy, and the final authority. There is one problem: the original writings no longer exist. No copies of the originals nor any English translation meet that definition. That means that, according to Wheaton College, there are no scriptures they can point to as their final authority for doctrine. The college states that "God has revealed Himself and His truth in the created order, in the Scriptures." But the college does not know God's truth because, according to its Statement of Faith, the Scriptures can only be found in the "original writing." How can one trust a college allegedly based on Christian principles when its Statement of Faith claims that the inspired scriptures do not now exist?

Allegedly conservative Christian groups have also fallen for the "original autograph" deception. For example, *Creation Ministries International* has a statement of faith that, in pertinent part, states: "The 66 books of the Bible are the written Word of God. The Bible is divinely inspired and inerrant throughout. Its assertions are factually true **in all the original autographs**."[6] (emphasis added). Notice the words: "in all the original autographs." What the *Creation Ministries International* implies by that statement is that they only stand by the "original autographs."

The *Creation Research Society* (CRS) also uses the devil-inspired artifice of textual criticism whereby it subtly attacks the authority of the Bible by the same method used by the *Creation*

Ministries International. The CRS statement of belief is that "the account of origins in Genesis is a factual presentation of simple historical truths."[7] However, the CRS guts the authority of scripture by limiting the inspired word of God to only being "historically and scientifically true in the **original autographs**."[8]

With this artifice of looking for his biblical authority to "the original autographs," which is a Bible that no longer exists, religious charlatans can embark on the duplicity of ignoring the clear meaning of Bible passages by engaging in textual criticism of the English (Authorized King James Version) translation.

Let us follow the logic of the statement of faith for many "Christian" denominations and organizations. Doing so would bring us to the ineluctable conclusion that there is no inerrant word of God to which one can point because the original autographs no longer exist. They assert allegiance to something that does not exist and has not existed for almost two millennia.

But God has promised to preserve his word forever. Even though the original autographs no longer exist, God's word has been supernaturally preserved. God's word is the way to salvation. God would not leave us without the means for our salvation.

Jack McElroy in his book, *Which Bible Would Jesus Use?*, pointed out that scriptures referenced in the Bible have always been available to read. They were necessarily copies of the originals; they were not the original autographs. Yet, God called those readily available holy writs, "scripture," which by definition are inspired by God.

For example, we read in Matthew 21:42 how Jesus asked the chief priests and the elders, "Did ye never read in the scriptures?" The scriptures to which Jesus referred were the then-existing Old Testament scriptures, which were copies; they were not the original autographs. In John 5:39, Jesus told the Jews to "search the scriptures." Those scriptures they were to search were copies. The original signatures were long gone. When, in Acts 17:11, the Bereans searched the scriptures daily, whether those things were so," they were searching copies. And God commended them for it. God described the Bereans as more noble than those in Thessalonica because they searched the scriptures; those scriptures were not the original autographs. The copies were called scriptures. Those copies, being scripture, were by definition inspired because "All scripture is given by inspiration of God, and is profitable for doctrine, for reproof, for correction, for instruction in righteousness:" (2 Timothy 3:16 AV) In Luke 4:17-21 when Jesus read aloud from the book of the prophet Isaiah at 61:1-2, Jesus was reading from a copy. The original book of Isaiah was written about 700 years earlier and no long existed. Jesus fulfilled the scriptures in Psalms 118:22, which was extant only in copies. The copies were inspired. The inspired copies contained the prophecy of Jesus. "And **have ye not read this scripture**; The stone which the builders rejected is become the head of the corner." (Mark 12:10 AV)

The Bible proves that those who limit inspiration to the original autographs are wrong. Timothy had the scriptures from a child. Timothy had only copies; he did not have the originals. Those copies were called "the holy scriptures."

> And that **from a child thou hast known the holy scriptures**, which are able to make thee wise unto salvation through faith which is in Christ Jesus. All scripture is given by inspiration of God, and is profitable for doctrine, for reproof, for correction, for instruction in righteousness: That the man of God may be perfect, throughly furnished unto all good works." (2 Timothy 3:15-17 AV)

The scriptures made Timothy wise unto salvation because the copies were given by inspiration of God. God's word is living;

it gives life. The KJV gives life.

> It is the spirit that quickeneth; the flesh profiteth nothing: the words that I speak unto you, they are spirit, and they are life." (John 6:63 AV)

God's Word abides forever. "Being born again, not of corruptible seed, but of incorruptible, by **the word of God, which liveth and abideth for ever."** (1 Peter 1:23 AV)

God prophesied he will use other tongues. "In the law it is written, **With men of other tongues and other lips will I speak unto this people**; and yet for all that will they not hear me, saith the Lord." (1 Corinthians 14:21 AV) God has made his inspired scriptures known to "all nations." That can only be done through translations into their native tongues. We have God's inspired word available in English in the KJV.

> Now to him that is of power to stablish you according to my gospel, and the preaching of Jesus Christ, according to the revelation of the mystery, which was kept secret since the world began, But now is made manifest, and by the **scriptures of the prophets**, according to the commandment of the everlasting God, made known to **all nations** for the obedience of faith:" (Romans 16:25-26 AV)

We are called on to search the scriptures. "Search the scriptures; for in them ye think ye have eternal life: and they are they which testify of me." (John 5:39 AV) All scripture is given by inspiration of God. 2 Timothy 3:15-16. Jesus commands us to search the scripture we have. We do not have the original autographs. We only have copies. God would not tell us to search in something that no longer exists (original autographs). If only the original autographs are inspired, that means that we do not have scripture today and thus cannot obey God's command to search the scriptures.

Going further, how can we search in a language we do not speak? God's inspired Greek word is purified by the English inspired translation. God does not put his trust in saints. "Behold, he putteth no trust in his saints; yea, the heavens are not clean in his sight." (Job 15:15 AV) God does the inspiration and preservation of his word.

God has preserved his words throughout the ages in Greek, Hebrew, and Aramaic. Faithful translations into other languages are also God's word. Indeed, that was the point of the gift of tongues at Pentecost. It was so all nations could hear the gospel in their own language. The crowd was amazed "how hear we every man in our own tongue, wherein we were born?" Acts 2:8.

The Holy Scriptures testify that both copies and translations of scripture are inspired. For example, in Ezra 4:7-11 we read that the "adversaries of Judah and Benjamin" sent a letter of accusation "against the inhabitants of Judah and Jerusalem" to King Artaxerxes. That letter is quoted in Ezra 4:12-17, which is Holy Scripture. Notice in Ezra 4:7 that the letter to Artaxerxes, king of Persia, "was written in the Syrian tongue, and interpreted in the Syrian tongue." But the letter was quoted in the inspired scriptures in Hebrew in Ezra 4:12-17. That means that the inspired scriptures were translations of the original Syrian language. In addition, the passage found in Exra 4:12-17 quoting the letter sent to the king is a "copy of the letter." So, in Ezra 4:12-17 we have inspired holy scripture that is both a copy and a translation of the original writing.

> And in the days of Artaxerxes wrote Bishlam, Mithredath, Tabeel, and the rest of their companions, unto ArtaCxerxes king of Persia; and **the writing of the letter was written in the Syrian tongue, and interpreted in the Syrian**

> **tongue.** Rehum the chancellor and Shimshai the scribe wrote a letter against Jerusalem to Artaxerxes the king in this sort: Then wrote Rehum the chancellor, and Shimshai the scribe, and the rest of their companions; the Dinaites, the Apharsathchites, the Tarpelites, the Apharsites, the Archevites, the Babylonians, the Susanchites, the Dehavites, and the Elamites, And the rest of the nations whom the great and noble Asnappar brought over, and set in the cities of Samaria, and the rest that are on this side the river, and at such a time. **This is the copy of the letter** that they sent unto him, even unto Artaxerxes the king; Thy servants the men on this side the river, and at such a time. (Ezra 4:7-11 AV)

Proof that copyists are inspired by God is found in Proverbs 25:1. The verses are introduced as being the proverbs of Solomon that "the men of Hezekiah king of Judah copied out." The men of Hezekiah who copied those verses in Proverbs were inspired by God. God has no objection to considering copies of his word inspired.

> These are also proverbs of Solomon, which the men of Hezekiah king of Judah **copied out**. (Proverbs 25:1 AV)

We find the holy scriptures in Ezra 7:12-26 to be a copy. In Ezra 7:11, the edict of King Artaxerxes is introduced as "**the copy of the letter**" that the king gave to Ezra. God was satisfied with a copy.

> Now this is **the copy of the letter** that the king Artaxerxes gave unto Ezra the priest, the scribe, even a scribe of the words of the commandments of the LORD, and of his statutes to Israel. (Ezra

7:11 AV)

God put it on the king's heart to write the proclamation. God inspired King Artaxerxes to write the edict. Ezra reveals: "Blessed be **the LORD God of our fathers, which hath put such a thing as this in the king's heart,** to beautify the house of the LORD which is in Jerusalem:" (Ezra 7:27 AV). God has nothing against copies. God was satisfied to quote "**the copy of the letter**," and that copy is the inspired word of God.

Famous Textual critics Bruce Metzger and Bart Ehrman coauthored a book, *Text of the New Testament: Its Transmission, Corruption, and Restoration*, wherein they claim that God did not preserve his words. They disagree with what God says in his Holy Bible. Metzger and Ehrman state regarding the letters of Paul;

> [I]t is difficult—some would say impossible—to talk about the original text of the Pauline epistles.[9]

Metzger and Erhman claim that what we have today cannot be copies of the original letters of Paul:

> A further complication presents itself in the case of the letters of Paul, in that many scholars have come to think that all of our surviving manuscripts derive ultimately not from the "originals" that Paul produced but from a collection of Paul's writings that was made sometime near the end of the first century. If that is the case, it would be difficult to get behind the texts presented in that collection to the original texts produced some 40 years earlier.[10]

Metzger and Ehrman state that at least part of Mark's gospel we have today is not what Mark originally wrote.

How did Mark end his Gospel? Unfortunately, we

> do not know; the most that can be said is that four different endings are current among the manuscripts but probably none of them represents what Mark originally intended.[11]

Metzger and Ehrman do not see God's hand in preservation at all. They claim that the entire New Testament contains errors that the earliest copyists injected. Those errors were perpetuated, and that is what we have today. They claim that we do not have God's inspired and inerrant word today, but rather error-filled writings of fallible men.

> The earliest copies of each of the books of the New Testament would no doubt have been made either in the community in which the book was first produced. ... Since most, if not all, of them would have been amateurs in the art of copying, a relatively large number of mistakes no doubt crept into their texts as they reproduced them. It is possible that after the original was placed in circulation it soon became lost or was destroyed, so all surviving copies may conceivably have derived from some single, error-prone copy made in the early stages of the book's circulation.[12]

As just one example of Metzger and Ehrman's doubt about God's promise to preserve his word, they state, flat out, that from the textual evidence that is extant today, they do not know what Luke originally wrote in Acts 12:25. "Here, we must acknowledge that we simply do not know what the author originally wrote."[13] But God has promised that his word would be preserved for every generation—forever.

> As for me, this is my covenant with them, saith the LORD; My spirit that is upon thee, and my words which I have put in thy mouth, shall not depart out

of thy mouth, nor out of the mouth of thy seed, nor out of the mouth of thy seed's seed, saith the LORD, from henceforth and for ever. (Isaiah 59:21 AV)

Bart D. Ehrman came to the ineluctable conclusion that limiting the claim of inerrancy of scripture to the original autographs is an implicit admission that God did not keep his promise to preserve his word. Satan's minions have floated the "original autographs" construct with the aim of convincing people that we do not have the inspired word of God today. Thus, if the copies handed down by scribes are not themselves preserved infallible texts, then all we have today are "error-ridden copies." Under the "original autographs" doctrine, the thing we call the Holy Bible is not, and cannot be, the inerrant word of God. Dr. Ehrman said:

> I kept reverting to my basic question: how does it help us to say that the Bible is the inerrant word of God if in fact we don't have the words that God inerrantly inspired, but only the words copied by the scribes—sometimes correctly but sometimes (many times!) incorrectly? What good is it to say that the autographs (i.e., the originals) were inspired? We don't *have* the originals! We have only error-ridden copies.[14] (italics in original)

Ehrman wrote that in 2007. Ehrman's conclusion that the scriptures we have today are not inerrant caused him to go from being a nominal "Christian" to being what he calls an "agnostic atheist."

Who is Bart D. Ehrman? He is one of the most respected authorities against the doctrine that God has preserved his word. He is the James A. Gray Distinguished Professor of Religious Studies at the University of North Carolina at Chapel Hill. He has served as both the Director of Graduate Studies and the Chair of the Department. Professor Ehrman completed his M.Div. and Ph.D. degrees at Princeton Seminary, where he graduated *magna cum laude*. He is considered an expert on the New Testament and the history of Early Christianity. He has written or edited thirty books, numerous scholarly articles, and dozens of book reviews. Dr. Ehrman has also written several textbooks for undergraduate students. Six of his books have been on the New York Times Bestseller list: *Misquoting Jesus; God's Problem; Jesus Interrupted; Forged; and How Jesus Became God.* His books have been translated into twenty-seven languages.[15] The worldly accomplishments of Dr. Ehrman do not stop there. He has a long list of academic accomplishments and awards. "Professor Ehrman has served as President of the Southeast Region of the Society of Biblical literature and chair of the New Testament textual criticism section of the Society. ... Professor Ehrman has been the recipient of numerous academic awards, grants, and fellowships."[16]

Dr. Ehrman has been deceived by the god he serves, Satan.

> In whom the god of this world hath blinded the minds of them which believe not, lest the light of the glorious gospel of Christ, who is the image of God, should shine unto them. (2 Corinthians 4:4)

Satan is using Dr. Ehrman's "pride of life" against him to encourage his obedient service. *See* 1 John 2:16-17. Satan has ensured that Dr. Ehrman receives earthly accolades for his dark spiritual service. For all his highfalutin worldly academic accomplishments and honors, Dr. Ehrman is an ignoramus. "The fear of the LORD is the beginning of knowledge: but fools despise wisdom and instruction." Proverbs 1:7. Dr. Ehrman does not fear God and so does not have the capacity to gain wisdom. He is a fool who despises the wisdom and instruction in the Bible. God speaks of such men as Dr. Ehrman:

Let no man deceive himself. If any man among you seemeth to be wise in this world, let him become a fool, that he may be wise. For the wisdom of this world is foolishness with God. For it is written, He taketh the wise in their own craftiness. 1 Corinthians 3:18-19.

The tricks of the Devil have hoodwinked Dr. Erhman. In this book, I will refute Dr. Ehrman's conclusion and prove that God has kept his promise to preserve his word today. God's word in English is found in the Authorized (King James) Version of the Holy Bible.

How did Dr. Ehrman go from being a "Christian" to being an atheist who rejected the inerrancy of today's Bible. The answer is that he studied higher criticism under the tutilage of Professor Bruce Metzger (1914-2007) at Princeton University. Dr. Metzger was a world-renowned expert on the Greek New Testament manuscripts. He was an editor of the United Bible Societies' UBS standard Greek New Testament. That Greek text was largely based on corrupt Alexandrian manuscripts. The UBS Alexandrian Greek text is the basis for almost all the modern New Testaments. The King James Version (AV or KJV), however, is based on the Textus Receptus (Recieved Text), which is in turn based on the Byzantine Greek Text (a.k.a., the majority text).

Michael Holmes reveals that Dr. Metzger contributed to the corrupt Revised Standard Version (RSV) of the Bible. And from 1977-1990 Metzger "was Chair of the Committee of Translators for the NRSV [New Revised Standard Version], and was largely responsible for seeing it through the press. ... He took great satisfaction in the expansion of the NRSV to include all the texts viewed as canonical by Roman Catholic, Greek Orthodox, and Protestant Christians, and was pleased to present copies of it to both Pope John Paul II and His All Holiness Demetrios."[17]

It is not surprising that Dr. Metzger would present a copy of his impious NRSV to the Pope of Rome, who is the Antichrist.[18] "Can two walk together, except they be agreed?" Amos 3:3. Dr. Metzger was also a member of the Catholic Biblical Association and the American Philosophical Society.

Dr. Ehman heaps effusive praise on his mentor, Bruce Metzger:

> I don't think there's anyone in the known universe who would disagree that Bruce Metzger was the greatest NT textual scholar ever to come out of North America. I first heard about him when I was an undergraduate at Wheaton College. I was taking Greek there and began to be interested in pursuing the study of Greek manuscripts. I knew that Metzger had been one of the five editors who had produced the standard Greek New Testament that everyone used.
>
> He was the only American on the committee. When I told my Greek professor that I was interested in doing graduate work in the field, he enthusiastically told me that I should try to go to Princeton Theological Seminary to study with Metzger.[19]

It was from the misguided tutelage of Dr. Metzger that Dr. Ehrman concluded that the Bible is full of errors and, thus, God does not exist. The plight of Dr. Ehrman is predictable. If one can be convinced that God only inspired the original autographs and then left his word to the carelessness of fallible and uninspired copyists, it is not hard to conclude that errors crept into the copies of scripture. Once the seed that the Bible is full of mistakes is planted in the unregenerate mind, such one will doubt the existence of God. And that is why Satan works so hard to attack the preservation and inerrancy of the Holy Bible.

7 Failed Strategy of Prohibiting God's Word

Satan knows that the word of God is the way to salvation. Satan also knows that God has promised to preserve his words, and so it would be futile for him to try to destroy God's words. Therefore, instead of trying to destroy God's words, Satan instituted a two-prong strategy to keep the Holy Scriptures from the people. The first prong of the strategy was to outlaw the possession and reading of the Holy Bible. When, over the years, that strategy proved ineffective, Satan instituted his second prong, which is to deny that God has preserved his words and offer counterfeit Bibles to the world and to deceive people into believing his counterfeits are the closest that they can get to God's genuine word.

The Roman Church knows that if the people are able to read for themselves God's word, they will discover that the Catholic traditions and doctrines are not just in addition to the Scriptures, they violate the Scriptures. The Catholic Church has a long history of trying to keep God's word from the people. For example, at the *Council of Terragona* in 1234 A.D., the Roman Catholic Church prohibited anyone from possessing any part of the Old or New Testaments in any of the Romance languages (Portuguese, Spanish, Catalan, Provencal, French, Rhaeto-

Romance, Italian, Sardinian, and Romanian). The council ruled that anyone owning a Bible was to turn it over to the local Catholic bishop to be burned. In 1229, at the *Council of Toulouse* (Pope Gregory IX presiding), the Catholic Church prohibited "laymen" from having the Holy Scriptures or translating them into the "vulgar tongue" (common language of the country). In 1551, the Catholic *Inquisitional Index of Valentia* forbade the Holy Bible to be translated into Spanish or any other "vernacular." In 1559, the Roman Catholic *Index Librorum Prohibitorum* (Index of Prohibited Books) required permission from the Catholic Church to read the Catholic version of the Bible; all Christian Bible versions were simply prohibited. On September 8, 1713, Pope Clement XI issued his Dogmatic Constitution, *Unigenitus,* which in part condemned as error the teaching that all people may read the Sacred Scripture. On May 5, 1824, Pope Leo XII issued his encyclical *Ubi Primum* which exhorted the bishops to remind their flocks not to read the Bible. On May 24, 1829, Pope Pius VIII issued the encyclical *Traditi Humilitati,* which exhorted Catholics to check the spread of Bibles translated into the vernacular, because those Bibles endangered the "sacred" teachings of the Catholic Church. On May 8, 1844, Pope Gregory XVI issued his encyclical *Inter Praecipuas* in which he described Bible societies as plotting against the Catholic faith by providing Bibles to the common people, whom he referred to as "infidels." On January 25, 1897, Pope Leo XIII issued his Apostolic Constitution *Officiorum ac Munerum* which prohibited all versions of the Bible in the vernacular tongue. The 1918 Catholic Code of Cannon Law, Index of Prohibited Books, Cannon 1385, § 1 prohibited publishing any edition of the Holy Scriptures without previous Catholic "ecclesiastical censorship." The 1983 Catholic Code of Cannon Law, Cannon 825, § 1 prohibits the publishing of the Sacred Scriptures without the permission of the Apostolic See or the Conference of Bishops.

The official doctrines of the Catholic Church prohibiting the publication, possession, or reading of the Holy Bible, were not mere suggestions, they were enforced. For example, on October 6, 1536 at Vilvorde (outside Brussels, Belgium) William Tyndale was burned at the stake.[20] His crime was that he translated the Holy Scriptures into English and was making copies available to the people in violation of the rules of the Roman Catholic Church.[21]

The progenitors of the Catholic Church were around in the time of the apostles, wresting the Holy Scriptures from the people.

> And account *that* the longsuffering of our Lord *is* salvation; even as our beloved brother Paul also according to the wisdom given unto him hath written unto you; As also in all his epistles, speaking in them of these things; in which are some things hard to be understood, **which they that are unlearned and unstable wrest, as they do also the other scriptures, unto their own destruction.** Ye therefore, beloved, seeing ye know these things before, beware lest ye also, being led away with the error of the wicked, fall from your own stedfastness. (2 Peter 3:15-17 AV)

There has probably not been a person more maligned by the powerful forces of the Roman Catholic Church than Maria Monk. In 1836 she published the famous book, Awful Disclosures of the Hotel Dieu Nunnery of Montreal. In that book, she told of murder, rape, and torture behind the walls of the cloistered nunnery. Because the evidence was verifiably true, the Catholic hierarchy found it necessary to fabricate evidence and suborn perjury in an attempt to destroy the credibility of Maria Monk. The Catholic Church has kept up the character assassination of Maria Monk now for over 175 years. In the book, *Murder, Rape, and Torture in a Catholic Nunnery*, this author examined the evidence and set it forth for the readers to decide for themselves whether Maria Monk was an impostor or a brave victim. An objective view of the evidence leads to the ineluctable conclusion that Maria Monk told the truth about what happened behind the walls of the Hotel Dieu Nunnery of Montreal. The Roman Catholic Church, which is the most powerful religious and political organization in the world, has engaged in an unceasing campaign of vilification against Maria Monk. Its crusade against Maria Monk, however, can only affect the opinion of the uninformed. It cannot change the evidence. The evidence speaks clearly to those who will look at the case objectively. The evidence reveals that the much maligned Maria Monk was a reliable witness who made awful but accurate disclosures about life in a cloistered nunnery. Maria Monk gives the following account of her Catholic instruction when she was a student at the congregational nunnery, regarding the reading of the Holy Bible:

> Among the instructions given us by the priests, some of the most pointed were those directed against the Protestant Bible. They often enlarged upon the evil tendency of that book, and told us that but for it many a soul now condemned to hell, and suffering eternal punishment, might have been in happiness. They could not say any thing in its favour: for that would be speaking against religion and against God. They warned us against it, and represented it as a thing very dangerous to our souls. In confirmation of this, they would repeat some of the answers taught us at catechism, a few of which I will here give. We had little catechisms ("Le Petit Catechism") put into our hands to study; but the priests soon began to teach us a new set of answers, which were not to be found in our books, and from some of which I received new ideas, and got, as I thought, important light on religious subjects, which confirmed me more and more in my belief in the Roman Catholic doctrines. These questions and answers I can still recall with tolerable accuracy, and some of them I will add

here. I never have read them, as we were taught them only by
word of mouth. ...

_Q_. "Why did not God make all the commandments?"

_A_. "Because man is not strong enough to keep them."

And another.

_Q_. "Why are men not to read the New Testament?"

_A_. "Because the mind of man is too limited and weak to understand what God has written."

These questions and answers are not to be found in the common catechisms in use in Montreal and other places where I have been, but all the children in the Congregational Nunnery were taught them, and many more not found in these books.[22]

The truth of Maria's account regarding the Catholic doctrinal biblio-animus is found in the official encyclicals issued by the mythically infallible popes, both before and after Maria Monk was catechized.

The catechism to which Maria Monk referred was consistent with the official catholic doctrine of the Vatican. That is because at the turn of every page in the bible one finds an impeachment of Catholic dogma, and it is therefore clearly not in the Vatican's interest to see the word of God spread.

During a debate with a Protestant minister in the 19th

century, a Catholic priest stated that "certain Protestants repeat that the [Catholic] Church forbids the reading of the Holy Bible by the people. That is a cowardly lie, and it is only the ignorant or the silly amongst Protestants who at present believe this ancient fabrication of heresy."[23] That priest called the pastors who made such allegations "unscrupulous" and their believing flocks "dupes." He gave the example of the availability of the Catholic versions of the bible in bookstores throughout Canada, the United States, and Europe as proof that the allegation that the Catholic Church suppresses the bible is not true.

The Catholic priest quoted in the debate above was Charles Chiniquy. He later left the Catholic priesthood and became one of the most famous Protestant preachers of the 19th century. Charles Chiniquy admitted that as a Catholic priest he had engaged in misleading statements like those in the above quoted debate. After Chiniquy left the Catholic Church, he explained that while Catholics are allowed to have bibles in Protestant countries, that is not the wish of the Catholic Church. The Catholic Church only permits such sales, because without political hegemony over a country, the Catholic Church must allow Catholics to possess Catholic bibles. However, Catholics are admonished by their priests never to interpret the scriptures according to their own understanding. A Catholic must always look to the "infallible" Church of Rome in all spiritual matters.

One major distinction between a Catholic mass and a Protestant service is that almost every Protestant can be seen carrying his bible to the service, whereas almost all Catholics will be walking into the Catholic Church building with empty hands. If a Catholic is carrying anything, it is usually a book called a Catholic missal. The missal looks like a bible, but it only contains the instructions, chants, and rituals of the Catholic Mass. Catholics will often say that the fact that they have in their home a Catholic Douay bible is evidence that it is a slanderous lie that the Catholic Church suppresses the bible. Chiniquy responds to that claim, and in doing so impeaches the position he took as a Roman Catholic priest; his response reveals the subtlety of his prior Catholic deception:

> To whom do they owe the privilege [of possessing a bible]? Is it the Church of Rome? Not at all. It is their Protestant friends, to the Protestant countries in which they live. Were they at Rome, they would be put in jail for the same thing allowed to them here. Then, if the Church of Rome permits the reading of the Scriptures, it is not because she likes that, but because she cannot help herself. The light is so near the eyes of the Roman Catholics of this country that it can't be entirely put out from them.[24]

In 1832, Rebecca Reed, as a candidate to be a nun, spent six months in the Ursuline Convent in Charlestown, Massachusetts, before escaping and exposing the cruelty and oppression of the nunnery. Miss Reed never saw a bible the entire time she was in the convent. All requests made by her to obtain a bible were ignored. She recalls the bishop stating that the laity were not qualified to expound on the scriptures and that only the successors of the apostles were authorized to interpret them.[25]

8 Second Prong of Attack - Counterfeit Bibles

With the advent of the printing press (circa 1455) making Bibles available to the ordinary man, it became evident to Satan that he could not keep God's word from the masses, so he instituted the second prong of his attack on God's word in earnest. He offered counterfeit Bibles.

The KJV translators noted this strategy of obfuscation by many and varied translations. The KJV translators criticized the corrupt translations published by the Vatican. The translators viewed them as the very works of Satan. The translators noted the Catholic Bible published in Latin by Pope Sixtus (Sixtine Latin Vulgate Bible 1590) was decreed by a papal bull to be the authentic Bible. But Sixtus' successor, Pope Clement VIII, published another Bible (Clementine Latin Vulgate Bible 1592) also declared to be the authentic Bible. But the KJV translators revealed Pope Clemenitne's Bible contained "infinite differences from that of Sixtus (and many of them weighty and material)."[26]

Both Catholic Bibles were published under the separate imprimatur of each of the two Popes, claiming them both to be the authentic Bible. But the two Bibles contained material differences from one another. The KJV translators explained:

> Satan taking occasion by them [the Vatican], though they thought of no such matter, did strive what he could, out of so uncertain and manifold a variety of Translations, so to mingle all things, that nothing might seem to be left certain and firm in them...our adversaries [Roman Catholics] do make so many and so various editions themselves, and do jar so much about the worth and authority of them.[27]

The KJV translators understood that they were being inspired by the Holy Spirit in their translation. They said: "[W]e have at the length, through the good hand of the Lord upon us, brought the work to that pass that you see."[28]

The KJV translators understood that they were perfecting out of many good translations, one final perfect translation.

> [N]othing is begun and **perfited [an obsolete word meaning 'perfected']** at the same time, and the later thoughts are thought to be the wiser: so, if we building upon their foundation that went before us, and being holpen by their labours, do endevour to make that better which they left so good; no man, we are sure, hath cause to mislike us; they, we persuade our selves, if they were alive, would thank us.[29]

The KJV translators viewed their mission: "[T]to make a good one better, or out of many good ones, **one principal good one**, not justly to be excepted against; that hath been our endeavor, that our mark."[30] They were polishing what was already precious "the same will shine as gold more brightly, being rubbed and polished." They got to work polishing the many good translations (Wycliffe, Tyndale, Coverdale, Great, Bishops, Geneva) to make one "principal good one" shine.

The modern Bible versions are not polishing anything. They are counterfeiting what is precious. They are following the plan of Satan, altering the words of God as has been done by the Vatican in centuries past. Like their god, Satan, the modern Bible translators typically delete passages. For example, you will find that the New International Version (NIV) Bible will have about 10% less text in the New Testament than in the AV Bible. We can see the method of Satan in full view in Luke 4:10, where Satan quotes from Psalms 91:11. Notice how Satan leaves off the last four words, "in all thy ways," from the verses in Psalms 91:11 when quoting it.

> For he shall give his angels charge over thee, to keep thee **in all thy ways.** (**Psalms 91:11** AV)

> For it is written, He shall give his angels charge over thee, to keep thee. (**Luke 4:10** AV)

The Holy Scriptures reveal a pattern by Satan from the beginning to tamper with God's word. God commanded Adam not to eat from the tree of the knowledge of good and evil.

> And the LORD God commanded the man, saying, **Of every tree of the garden thou mayest freely eat: But of the tree of the knowledge of good and evil, thou shalt not eat of it: for in the day that thou eatest thereof thou shalt surely die**. (Genesis 2:16-17 AV)

In Genesis 3:1-5 the serpent misquotes God, changing God's words; he tricks Eve into eating from the tree of knowledge of good and evil by asking her if God commanded that they not eat of any of the trees in the garden. When Eve responds, she also misquotes God, saying that he commanded that they should not touch the fruit, when God merely prohibited the eating of the fruit. God told Adam that if he ate from the tree "thou shalt surely die."

Once Satan perceived that Eve was ignorant of God's true words he felt confident that he could convince Eve to disobey God by subtly misquoting what God had said. Satan took the warning by God and added one word. Satan said to Eve: "Ye shall **not** surely die." What Satan said sounded authoritative. It sounded almost like what God had said; but that one word corrupted God's word and turned it from the words of God to the words of Satan. The result of the corruption by Satan of God's word was the greatest tragedy in history, the fall of Adam and Eve!

> Now the serpent was more subtil than any beast of the field which the LORD God had made. And he said unto the woman, Yea, hath God said, **Ye shall not eat of <u>every</u> tree of the garden**? And the woman said unto the serpent, We may eat of the fruit of the trees of the garden: But of the fruit of the tree which is in the midst of the garden, God hath said, Ye shall not eat of it, **neither shall ye touch it**, lest ye die. And the serpent said unto the woman, **Ye shall not surely die**: For God doth know that in the day ye eat thereof, then your eyes shall be opened, and ye shall be as gods, knowing good and evil. (Genesis 3:1-5 AV)

In apparent reference to Satan's corruption of God's word in the Garden of Eden, Jesus admonished Satan: "That man shall not live by bread alone, but by **every word** of God." (Luke 4:4 AV) Just as Satan did in the Garden of Eden, he now tries to confuse people about what God has said: "Yea, hath God said . . . ." Pediatrician Dr. Lawrence Dunegan attended a lecture on March 20, 1969, at a gathering of pediatricians at a meeting of the Pittsburgh Pediatric Society. The lecturer at that meeting was a Dr. Richard Day (who died in 1989). At the time of the lecture Dr. Day was Professor of Pediatrics at Mount Sinai Medical School in New York. Previously, Dr. Day had served as Medical Director of Planned Parenthood Federation of America. Dr. Dunegan was well acquainted with Dr. Day and described him as an insider in the "order." Dr. Dunegan did not explain what the "order" was, but from the lecture it was clear that it was a very powerful secret society made up of minions in service to Satan. During the lecture Dr. Day revealed many of the satanic plans that the members of the "order" had agreed upon that would change the United States from a Christian society to a pagan society. One of the strategies was to introduce new Bible versions. By the time of the lecture in 1969, that strategy had long previously been implemented. Dr. Day was indicating that the final success of that strategy was in sight as henceforth it would be implemented with new vigor. Dr. Dunegan explains:

> Another area of discussion was Religion. This is an avowed atheist speaking. And he [Dr. Day] said, "Religion is not necessarily bad. A lot of people seem to need religion, with it's mysteries and rituals - so they will have religion. But the major religions of today have to be changed because they are not compatible with the changes to come. The old religions will have to go. Especially Christianity. Once the Roman Catholic Church is brought down, the rest of Christianity will follow easily. Then a new religion can be accepted for use all over the world. It will incorporate something from all of the old ones to make it more easy for people to accept it, and feel at home in it. Most people won't be too concerned with religion. They will realize that they don't need it.
>
> In order to [do] this, the Bible will be changed. It will be rewritten to fit the new religion. Gradually, key words will be replaced with new words having various shades of meaning. Then the meaning attached to the new word can be close to the old word - and as time goes on, other shades of

meaning of that word can be emphasized. and then gradually that word replaced with another word." I don't know if I'm making that clear. But the idea is that everything in Scripture need not be rewritten, just key words replaced by other words. And the variability in meaning attached to any word can be used as a tool to change the entire meaning of Scripture, and therefore make it acceptable to this new religion. Most people won't know the difference; and this was another one of the times where he said, "the few who do notice the difference won't be enough to matter."[31]

In accordance with the aforementioned conspiracy, Satan and his minions now offer people a whole assortment of different Bible versions, which change and twist God's word. God's word is with us today in the Authorized (King James) Version (referred to as AV or KJV). All other Bible versions are tainted by the hands of Satan and his minions, including the New King James Version (NKJV). "Ye have perverted the words of the living God, of the LORD of hosts our God." Jeremiah 23:36. The corrupted Bible versions are essentially Roman Catholic Bible versions.[32] Sadly, most of the so called church leaders of today have accepted Satan's counterfeit Bibles.

Many who promote the modern Bible versions claim that there are no doctrinal changes resulting from the changes in the Bible text. For example, Dr. James White claims:

> The simple fact of the matter is that no textual variants in either the Old or New Testaments in any way, shape, or form materially disrupt or destroy any essential doctrine of the Christian faith. That is a fact that any semi-impartial review will substantiate.[33]

Dr. Edward F. Hills conducted the impartial review advised by Dr. White. Dr. Hills thoroughly studied the new Bible versions and concluded that the claim by White and the modern Bible promoters is hogwash bluster.

> It is *NOT* true that there are no various readings which involve cardinal Christian doctrines. On the contrary, in the handful of dissenting manuscripts ... there are a HOST of *CORRUPT* READINGS (2 Cor. 2:17) which ALL bring into question such doctrines as the essential GODHEAD of Christ. ... [L]et them say with conviction: 'No important doctrine is affected by various readings.' How GULLIBLE CAN THE CHRISTIAN PUBLIC BE TO SWALLOW SUCH A PALPABLE LIE?"[34] (all capital letters in original)

The following is a partial list of the fraudulent Bible versions: New International Version (NIV), Today's New International Version (TNIV), New Living Translation (NLT), Contemporary English Version (CEV), New Century Version (NCV), New World Translation (NWT), American Standard Version (ASV), English Standard Version (ESV), New American Standard Bible (NASB), Revised Version (RV), Revised Standard Version (RSV), New Revised Standard Version (NRSV), Amplified Version (AMP), New King James Version (NKJV), 21st Century King James Version (KJ21), Third Millennium Bible (TMB), Douay-Rheims Bible (DRB), Good News for Modern Man (GNB), Today's English Version (TEV), The Living Bible (TLB), Darby Translation (DBY), Jerusalem Bible (JB), New Jerusalem Bible (NJB), Literal Standard Version (LSV), and Legacy Standard Bible (LSB).

The Authorized (King James) Version is an English translation of the Masoretic (traditional) Hebrew Old Testament, whereas the new Bible versions are taken from an inferior and corrupted mixture of the Septuagint (Greek Old Testament), Samaritan Pentateuch, Dead Sea Scrolls, and a variety of other transcripts. The corrupt Septuagint used today was translated by Origen (185-254 A.D.), who was a unitarian evolutionist.[35] Origen believed in reincarnation and denied the existence of hell.[36]

The modern Bible versions are based on corrupted Greek tests that originated in Alexandria, Egypt. These corrupted texts were altered by those who believed in the Arian heresy. They changed the Greek text to comport with their heretical theology.

Arius considered only God the Father to be the only eternal God. He viewed Jesus Christ as emanating from God, as a creation of God, but not being God Almighty.[37] Arius opined that the Son was begotten before the world was created, and because he emanated from God the Father, he is not eternal nor coeternal with God the Father.[38] This is known as the Arian heresy. This book will explain how the followers of the Arian heresy tampered with the Greek New Testament to undermine the deity of Jesus.

There are approximately 4,489 Greek New Testament manuscripts known to be extant today.[39] Of these, 170 are papyrus fragments dating from the second to the seventh centuries; there are 212 uncial (capital letter) manuscripts, dating from the fourth to the tenth centuries; there are 2,429 minuscule (small letter) manuscripts, dating from the ninth to the sixteenth centuries; and there are 1,678 lectionaries, which are lesson books for public reading that contain extracts from the New Testament.[40] The vast majority of these manuscripts are in agreement and are the basis for what is known as the *Textus Receptus* (received text). There has been a recent discovery of a small fragment of the earliest known New Testament manuscript not included in the above tally, which was dated to 66 A.D. and is in agreement with the *Textus Receptus*. The King James New Testament is based upon the Greek *Textus Receptus*, whereas the new translations are based upon a very few number of corrupt manuscripts including the

Roman Catholic Greek texts *Vaticanus* and *Sinaiticus*, and a few other texts, the origins of which are a mystery.

The manuscript *Sinaiticus*, which is often referred to by the first letter of the Hebrew alphabet, *Aleph*, is written in book form (codex) on velum.[41] It contains many spurious books such as the Shepherd of Hermes, the Didache, and the Epistle of Barnabas.[42] *Sinaiticus* was allegedly discovered by Constantine Tischendorf (1815-1874) in a wastebasket in St. Catherine's monastery on Mount Sinai in February of 1859.[43] The monks of St. Catherine's denied Tischendorf's wastebasket story. The wastebasket story seems to have been a tale spun by Tischendorf to explain his mutilation of the codex and destruction of some leaves to conceal acrostics that would identify the author of the codex. *Sinaiticus* is covered with alterations that are systematically spread over every page and were made by at least ten different revisors.[44] The alterations are obvious to anyone who examines the manuscript.[45]

Tischendorf was a nominal Protestant who had very close ties with the Roman Catholic hierarchy. He was welcomed at the Vatican by the pope in a private audience. Tischendorf also had meetings in the Vatican with the Vatican Librarian, Cardinal Angelo Mai (1782-1854), who, incidentally, wrote an 1838 edition of the *Codex Vaticanus*.[46] *Sinaiticus* is not an ancient fourth century codex, as alleged by Tischendorf. Indeed, the author of *Sinaiticus* came forward and stated publically that it was in the early nineteenth century that he authored what became known as *Sinaiticus*.[47] When Constantine Simonides (1820-1867), a renowned Greek scholar and paleographer, found out that the Greek manuscript of the Bible that he wrote when he was at the Monastery of Saint Catherine was being promoted by Constantine Tischendorf as a fourth century manuscript, he refuted that claim. Simonides invited Tischendorf to a debate on the issue and challenged Tischendorf to bring *Sinaiticus* with him so that Simonides could demonstrate, with the public watching, where he had made unique markings that only the author of the document would know. Tischendorf agreed to the debate, but never showed up for the planned debate and never explained his absence. Tischendorf instead chose to use the media organs controlled by the Roman Catholic church to attack Simonides' character. To this day, Simonides is libelously accused of forgery, always with qualifiers like "allegedly" and "claimed to be," etc. What is almost never mentioned is that the allegations of forgery were actually litigated and Simonides was exonerated in a court of law.

It is a matter of public record, however, that a Greek Archimandrite (superior abbot) named Kallinikos, who was a resident of the St. Catherine's Monastery, came forward and verified that he witnessed, with his own eyes, Simonides writing *Sinaiticus* at Mount Athos in Greece.[48] Furthermore, Kallikos stated that he was at St. Catherine's Monastery and saw Tischendorf in possession of the manuscript that he recognized as being the work of Simonides.[49] Kallinikos accused Tischendorf of guile. Kallinikos stated that *Sinaiticus* was not an ancient text but was washed with lemon juice and herbs to lighten the text and make it appear to be an ancient text. He further accused Tischendorf of mutilating the codex written by Simonides.

The manuscript *Vaticanus*, often referred to by the letter "B," originated in the Vatican Library, hence the name.[50] *Vaticanus* was first revealed in 1841; where the transcript had been prior to that date is unclear.[51] One thing this is clear is that the manuscript omits many portions of scripture which explain vital Christian doctrines. *Vaticanus* omits Genesis 1:1 through Genesis 46:28; Psalms 106 through 138; Matthew 16:2,3; Romans 16:24; the Pauline Epistles; Revelation; and everything in Hebrews after 9:14.[52] It should not be surprising that the Vatican would produce a manuscript that omits the portion of the book of Hebrews which exposes the mass as completely ineffectual and deletes Revelation chapter 17, which reveals Rome as the seat of "MYSTERY, BABYLON THE GREAT, THE MOTHER OF HARLOTS AND ABOMINATIONS OF THE EARTH." Notice that the two primary manuscripts used by the new Bible versions were found in the care and custody of the Roman Catholic Church.

The *Vaticanus* and *Sinaiticus* manuscripts, which make up less than one percent of the existing ancient manuscripts, differ significantly from the Received Text. *Vaticanus* omits at least 2,877 words; it adds 536 words; it substitutes 935 words; it transposes 2,098 words; and it modifies 1,132 words; making a total of 7,578 verbal divergences from the Received Text. *Sinaiticus* is an even worse corruption, having almost 9,000 divergences from the Received Text.[53]

The corrupt codices *Vaticanus* and *Sinaiticus* are the primary Greek manuscripts for the modern Bible versions. Expert linguist John William Burgon (1813-1888) was Dean of Chichester and a master of classical Greek. After extensive study of the *Vaticanus* and *Sinaiticus* codices, Dean Burgon pronounced them "scandalously corrupt."[54] Dean Burgon stated: "I ... insist, and am prepared to prove, that the text of these two Codexes [B and Aleph known as Vaticanus and Sinaiticus] is very nearly the foulest in existence."[55]

John Burgon, the preeminent Greek textual scholar of his time, documented the many errors in the *Vaticanus* and *Sianaiticus* manuscripts.

> The impurity of the text exhibited by these codices is not a question of opinion but of fact. . . . In the Gospels alone Codex B (Vatican) leaves out words or whole clauses no less than 1,491 times. It bears traces of careless transcription on every page. Codex Sinaiticus abounds with errors of the eye and pen to an extent not indeed unparalleled, but happily rather unusual in documents of first-rate importance. On many occasions, 10, 20, 30, 40 words are dropped through very carelessness.

> Letters and words, even whole sentences, are frequently written twice over, or begun and immediately cancelled; while that gross blunder, whereby a clause is omitted because it happens to end in the same words as a clause preceding, occur is no less than 115 times in the New Testament.[56]

The Vaticanus and Sinaiticus manuscripts are so clearly corrupt that Dean Burgon was at a loss to explain textual scholars accepting them as valid. He concluded that those manuscripts have "established a tyrannical ascendancy over the imagination of the critics which can only be fitly spoken of as blind superstition."[57] The following is Dean Burgon's assessment of the new Greek text, which was produced largely from the *Vaticanus* and *Sinaiticus* manuscripts, and which underlies the new Bible versions.

> [T]he Greek Text which they have invented proves to be hopelessly depraved throughout . . . [I]t was deliberately invented . . . [T]he underlying Greek . . . is an entirely new thing, is a manufactured article throughout. . . . The new Greek text was full of errors from beginning to end. . . . Shame on [those] most incompetent men who - finding themselves in a evil hour occupied themselves . . . with falsifying the inspired Greek Text . . . Who will venture to predict the amount of mischief which must follow, if the 'New' Greek Text . . . should become used.[58]

The Latin translation of the Bible is called the Latin Vulgate. Incidently, the Catholic Church pulled a switch. The Latin text that is today called the Latin Vulgate is very different from the traditional Latin Vulgate. Jerome used corrupted Greek texts from Alexandria, which he translated into Latin, he then added 14 apocryphal books; the Catholic Church called Jerome's new Latin translation the Latin Vulgate.[59] This corrupted Latin

Vulgate text is the official Bible text for the Catholic Church and was the source text for the Jesuit Douay-Rheims English translation of the Bible.

How did the new versions of the Bible become so corrupted? The personalities behind the new texts have an occult new age agenda. The compilers and translators of the new editions aren't just unchristian they are antichristian. The compilers of the corrupted Greek text used in virtually all of the new Bible versions were Brooke Foss Westcott and Fenton John Anthony Hort. They were nominal Protestants, but they were defacto Roman Catholics. Hort denied the infallibility of the Holy Scriptures, he did not believe in the existence of Satan, he did not believe in eternal punishment in Hell, nor did he believe in Christ's atonement.[60] Hort, however, did believe in Darwin's theory of evolution; he believed in purgatory; and he also believed in baptismal regeneration.[61] Hort hated the United States and wished for its destruction during the civil war, because he was a communist who hated all things democratic.[62]

Westcott was equally Romish in his beliefs.[63] He, like Hort, rejected the infallibility of the Holy Scriptures.[64] He viewed the Genesis account of creation as merely an allegory.[65] He did not believe the biblical account of the miracles of Jesus.[66] He did, however, believe in praying for the dead and worshiping Mary.[67] Politically, Westcott was a devout Socialist.[68]

Westcott and Hort were both necromancers who were members of an occult club called the "Ghostly Guild."[69] Westcott also founded another club and named it "Hermes."[70] According to Luciferian H.P. Blavatsky, Hermes and Satan are one and the same.[71] Hort viewed evangelical Christians as dangerous, perverted, unsound, and confused.[72] Westcot and Hort's Greek text was largely based on the fraudulent Catholic texts *Vaticanus* and *Sinaiticus*.[73]

Assisting Westcott and Hort in their revision was Dr. G. Vance, a Unitarian, who denied the deity of Christ, the inspiration of the Holy Scriptures, and the Godhead (Jesus Christ, God the Father, and the Holy Ghost).[74] Jesuit Roman Catholic Cardinal Carlo Maria Martini, the prelate of Milan, was the editor of the corrupted Greek text.[75] Martini believed the occult new age philosophy that man can become divine.[76] Remember, that is the very lie that Satan used to deceive Eve into eating the forbidden fruit: "ye shall be as gods." *Genesis* 3:5.

Westcott and Hort had a fondness for the corrupt Alexandrian Greek texts and an animus and prejudice against the Textus Receptus. The Greek Textus Receptus (Received Text) was derived from the majority of the Greek texts. The King James Bible was principally based on the Textus Receptus. The Hort considered the Textus Receptus a "vile" text.[77]

The publishers of the new Bible versions claim that their Bibles are based on the oldest available manuscripts. First, the oldest available manuscripts are available because they were not used. The reason they were not used is because they were obviously corrupt, and God's church refused to use them. The manuscripts during the early church era were used, and consequently, they wore out, necessitating that they be freshly recopied. Because they were needed by the early church, they were duplicated and disseminated. Accurate manuscripts are oft-used and duplicated. Thus, the number of the available accurate New Testament transcripts outnumber the corrupt version by approximately 100 to 1.

There has been a recent discovery of a small fragment of the earliest known New Testament manuscript. That manuscript was dated 66 A.D. using a high magnification device and the epifluorescent confocal laser scanning technique. The fragment contains Matthew 26:22 with the Greek phrase *"kekastos auton"* which is accurately translated into English in the King James Holy

Bible as "every one of them."[78] The NIV and NASB Bibles used a corrupt Greek manuscript that has the Greek phrase *"heis hekastos,"* which is translated "each one" in the NASB or "one after the other" in the NIV.[79] Again, the evidence proves the accuracy of the King James Holy Bible.

In addition, the new Bible versions use a method of translation known as dynamic equivalence, rather than the formal equivalence used in the Authorized Version (AV), which is also known as the King James Version (KJV). Formal equivalence is a word-for-word translation, whereas dynamic equivalence is a thought-for-thought translation. A translator using dynamic equivalence is less a translator and more an interpreter. Thus, the new versions of Bibles should more accurately be called interpretations, rather than translations. The dynamic equivalent interpreters of the new Bible versions have often made unfounded assumptions as to the meaning of particular passage. Rather than translate what God wrote, they have, with some frequency, twisted passages by injecting their own personal bias. Some of these interpreters have displayed malicious intent and caused great mischief.

The subjective bias of the interpreters has caused changes in the new version English Bibles that are not supported by any of Greek or Hebrew texts. For example, dynamic equivalencies caused 6,653 English word changes in the New International Version (NIV), approximately 4,000 word changes in the New American Standard Bible (NASB), and approximately 2,000 word changes in the New King James Version (NKJV), none of which are supported by the words in any of the Greek or Hebrew texts.[80]

Those word changes reflect the subjective bias of the interpreters. The combined effect of having a corrupted text and then having that text interpreted using dynamic equivalence has been that the NIV has 64,098 fewer words than the AV.[81] That is a 10% loss in the Bible. That means that an NIV Bible would have

170 fewer pages than a typical 1,700 page AV Bible.[82] The new versions of the Bible are materially different; they are the product of the imaginations of interpreters who have applied their personal prejudices to slant already corrupted texts to comport with their own ideas. They are truly counterfeit Bibles.

The Holy Bible is a legal document prepared by God. It contains the Old and New Testaments of Jesus Christ. A testament is a memorialization of the will of a testator. It only has legal effect once the testator has died. The New Testament, in reality, is the last will and testament of Jesus Christ.

> And for this cause he is the mediator of the new testament, that by means of death, for the redemption of the transgressions that were under the first testament, they which are called might receive the promise of eternal inheritance. For where a testament is, there must also of necessity be the death of the testator. **For a testament is of force after men are dead: otherwise it is of no strength at all while the testator liveth.** (Hebrews 9:15-17 AV)

A testator is free to change the testament and add to it. That is what Jesus did when he added the New Testament to the Old Testament. "By so much was Jesus made a surety of a better testament." (Hebrews 7:22 AV) However, it is only the testator who is allowed to change or add to a testament. If anyone else adds to or changes a testament, the changes make the resulting document a forgery.

When trying to determine the meaning of a last will and testament, courts always try to interpret what is the will of the testator. That is why a person's testament is called a will. If a will is to be translated from one language to another, because the heirs or the court speak a different language, courts always use formal equivalence because it is important that the heirs know precisely what the testator said. In fact, a translator must take an oath to faithfully translate the will of the testator. It is important not to allow any bias from a translator to affect what is the meaning of the words used.

If a court allowed dynamic equivalence to be used when translating a last will and testament then the court would not be interpreting the will of the testator; the interpretation would have already been done by the translator of the document when he interpreted the meaning of each passage. The judge would be stuck with a document that has been injected with meaning by the translator. The judge would, in effect, be interpreting the intent of the testator intermixed with the intent of the translator. The bias or errors of the translator would corrupt the final verdict regarding the testator's intent.

In the case of the Holy Bible, it is the New and Old Testaments of God Almighty. They are the most important legal documents ever written. God Almighty is the testator. He wrote both testaments. In addition, he created the languages into which his original testaments would be written. He also created the languages into which those testaments would be translated. Genesis 11:7-9. He has supernaturally controlled the process from beginning to end. **"All scripture *is* given by inspiration of God**, and is profitable for doctrine, for reproof, for correction, for instruction in righteousness." (2 Timothy 3:16 AV)

In addition, God has promised to supernaturally preserve his testaments. **"[T]he word of the Lord endureth for ever**. And this is the word which by the gospel is preached unto you." (1 Peter 1:25 AV) The heirs of Christ are Christians. "The Spirit itself beareth witness with our spirit, that we are the children of God: And if children, then heirs; heirs of God, and joint-heirs with Christ; if so be that we suffer with him, that we may be also glorified together." (Romans 8:16-17 AV)

In order for Christ's heirs to understand his will, they must have a faithful translation. If his heirs try to interpret God's will by using a translation that contains not the pure intent of God, but instead the intent of the translator, then they can no longer determine God's will. A will that has been rewritten and corrupted with the thoughts of one other than the testator, it is considered a forgery and a fraud. So also are the new translations of the Bible forgeries and frauds.

Defenders of the new Bibles claim that the essential doctrines of the Christian Faith are expressed in the new Bibles, even though they have been deleted or changed in many passages. James H. Son, author of *The New Athenians,* likened the logic of that argument to removing a stop sign from a busy street intersection and then justifying the removal because the other traffic signals in the city were left intact. Even though the sign only contained one word, that word is of critical importance to those who arrive at the intersection, just as each word in the Holy Bible is of critical importance to those who are reading it.

The claim that the doctrine from a deleted passage can be found elsewhere in the Bible is simply not true. The claim is refuted by the new Bible version deletion of the clause at the end of the verse at John 3:13, "which is in heaven."

> And no man hath ascended up to heaven, but he that came down from heaven, even the Son of man **which is in heaven**. (John 3:13 AV)

That is the only passage in the Holy Bible that explains the omnipresence of Jesus Christ. The new Bible versions delete the truth that Jesus Christ was in heaven and on Earth at the same time. The omnipresence of Jesus Christ as Lord God Almighty is deleted from the new Bible versions. Deleting that truth, as do the modern Bible versions, deletes that truth from the gospel. It is found nowhere else in the Bible.

God has made the point in the Holy Bible that **every word of God** is important. "And Jesus answered him, saying, It is written, That man shall not live by bread alone, **but by every word of God**." (Luke 4:4 AV)

Incidently, the doctrine of Luke 4:4 is missing in the new Bible versions. The NASB, for example, leaves out the last clause and simply states: "And Jesus answered him, 'it is written, MAN SHALL NOT LIVE ON BREAD ALONE.'" (Luke 4:4 NASB). The NASB is not alone. We can see that omission in almost all new Bible versions.

> Jesus answered, "It is written: 'Man shall not live on bread alone.'" Luke 4:4 NIV.

> And Jesus answered him, "It is written, 'Man shall not live by bread alone.'" Luke 4:4 RSV.

> And Jesus answered him, "It is written, 'Man shall not live by bread alone.'" Luke 4:4 ESV.

The new versions leave the reader in ignorance as to what it is other than bread by which man lives.

> And he humbled thee, and suffered thee to hunger, and fed thee with manna, which thou knewest not, neither did thy fathers know; that he might make thee know **that man doth not live by bread only, but by every word that proceedeth out of the mouth of the LORD doth man live**. (Deuteronomy 8:3 AV)

> **Every word of God is pure**: he is a shield unto them that put their trust in him. (Proverbs 30:5 AV)

The modern Bible versions are not pure; they are profane. God admonishes against mixing holy things with profane things. It is the very error of Israel that profaned the holy things of God by putting no difference between the holy and the profane.

> Her priests have violated my law, and **have profaned mine holy things: they have put no difference between the holy and profane, neither have they shewed difference between the unclean and the clean,** and have hid their eyes from my sabbaths, and I am profaned among them. Ezekiel 22:26.

God uses parallelism in Ezekiel 22:26 to explain what he means by profane and holy. Profane things are unclean things. Holy things are clean things. We are commanded by God to **"touch not the unclean thing."** 2 Corinthians 6:17. The modern Bibles are not Holy Bibles. They are unclean. We are not to touch the profane modern Bibles. It seems that most churches today are not discerning between the holy and the profane, the unclean and the clean.

> And they shall teach my people the difference between the holy and profane, and cause them to discern between the unclean and the clean. Ezekiel 44:23.

9 Satan's Circus Barkers

The promoters of the new bible versions claim that they are merely updating the archaic English in the King James Bible. They are being disingenuous. The Holy Bible is a legal document. The English of the King James Bible is not archaic, it is precise. The precise language used has eternal importance. Thee, thou, thy, and thine are singular pronouns. Thou is the subjective second-person singular, thee is the objective second-person singular, and thy and thine are possessive second-person singular. Ye is a is subjective second-person plural pronoun. Grammatically, you is the dative or objective second-person plural pronoun. Your is the possessive of you. In everyday English usage, you and your have taken on all cases and numbers.

Modern Bible hucksters claim that the English of the King James Bible is Elizabethan English, and we don't speak that way anymore. Gail Riplinger explains they did not speak that way in 1611 Elizabethan England either. King James Bible is not archaic English, as alleged by many; it is biblical English. Biblical English carries important theological and grammatical distinctions not found in the vernacular English of 1611.

"We don't speak that way any more." The fact is — neither did those living in 1611. Shakespeare's plays, written during the same period, did not use the 'eth' and 'est' endings. Read the 'Preface to the KJV,' written before 1611 by the translators. It does not sound like the King James Bible. It says "your very name," not 'thy very name.'[83]

The KJV translators used 'thee,' 'ye,' 'thy,' 'thine,' and 'eth' and 'est' endings (on verbs) because these are the only way to show important grammatical and theological distinctions, clearly seen in the Greek and Hebrew text, and seen in other foreign vernacular Bibles. KJV English is Biblical English, not archaic English. It is much easier to learn than truly archaic koine Greek.

"[The] translator saw half of his task as reshaping English so that it could adapt itself to Biblical languages."[84]

In the King James text, the precision of the language puts the reader in the midst of the narrative. The reader is able to tell whether the person is the object of the action or the subject causing the action. The reader can also tell if the subject or object is a group or an individual. The new versions use either the pronouns "you" or "your" for all of the narratives and the reader is not able to know anything about the setting of the narrative. All one need do is read Galatians 3:16 to know that singularity and plurality are important to God.

Jesus, when speaking to Nicodemus (**thee**), explained that everyone (**ye**) must be born again, not just Nicodemus. "Marvel not that I said unto **thee**, **Ye** must be born again." (John 3:7 AV) That vital doctrine of the gospel required the plural "**ye**."

The writers of the Authorized (King James)Version (AV) did not use the more precise pronouns because that was the customary language of the 16th century; they purposely used those words because they wanted to accurately and faithfully translate God's word into English. To prove the point, all one need do is read the dedicatory at the beginning of the Holy Bible (AV); the dedicatory was written at the completion of the AV Holy Bible in 1611 A.D., not once was thee, thou, thy, thine, or ye used in the dedicatory. Below is an excerpt from the dedicatory, which the translators wrote to King James of England:

> The Lord of heaven and earth bless **Your** Majesty with many and happy days, that, as his heavenly hand hath enriched **Your** Highness with many singular and extraordinary graces, so **You** may be the wonder of the world in this latter age for happiness and true felicity, to the honour of that great GOD, and the good of his Church, through Jesus Christ our Lord and only Saviour.

The same translator who wrote the dedicatory translated the following prophetic passage in the book of Psalms.

> I will speak of the glorious honour of **thy majesty**, and of thy wondrous works. (Psalms 145:5 AV)

Notice that **"Your Majesty"** in reference to King James is now **"thy majesty"** when referring to God. And where they referred to their earthly King James as **"You,"** the translators faithfully translate Luke 3:22 to give us the very words of God who referred to Jesus Christ using pronoun **"Thou."**

> And the Holy Ghost descended in a bodily shape like a dove upon him, and a voice came from heaven, which said, **Thou** art my beloved Son; in thee I am well pleased. (Luke 3:22 AV)

The King James translators were precise and formal when

translating the precious word of God that came down to them from their heavenly King. They were faithful to use the very language of God. But they used the common English vernacular in there own dedicatory to their earthly king.

In her book, *In Awe of Thy Word*, Gail Riplinger explains how the word endings used in the King James Bible are essential to God's revelation to us in his Holy Bible. The endings cannot be willy-nilly purged from the Bible, as in modern Bible versions, without changing the meaning of passages.

> Most languages, including Hebrew and Greek, are types that linguists call 'synthetic.' A single word (love) blends its meaning with an ending (called an inflected ending, e.g. lovest) which indicates that it is a verb (an action or being word) and shows what it modifies (thou). These endings make reading and studying smooth and easy.
>
> First person: I love
> Second person: thou lovest
> Third person: he, she, or it loveth
>
> Modern English and new English bibles are not 'synthetic.' They are what linguists call 'analytical.' The reader must analyze them, hoping for clues from the word order, to determine what part of speech a word is and what word it modifies.
>
> First person: I love
> Second person: you love
>
> Who does 'love'? Such subjective conclusions do not suite the Bible, where "private interpretation" is forbidden (2 Peter 1:20). The word of God is a legal document. Jesus said, "...the words that I have

spoken, the same shall judge him in the last day" (John 12:48). Modern language substitutes are not precise enough.

God purposely put inflected endings on verbs to prevent any confusion or private interpretation. The King James Bible retains these inflected endings. God has never blessed any English Bible that does not make these fine, but important distinctions. It is imperative that these endings be retained because a verb is sometimes separated from its subject. For example, in Romans 2:4, 5 the verb "treasurest up" (v. 5) is separated from its subject, "thou" (v. 4) by twenty-eight words. Likewise, in Romans 2 the subject "thou" is in verse 17, while its verb "knowest" is in verse 18; again, "thou" is in verse 19, while its verb "hast" is in verse 20. In Acts 24:4, 8 "thou wouldest...mayest" is separated by 4 verses!

Doctrinal error is seen in the NKJV, NASB, and most new versions in Matt. 23:37 and Luke 13:34 because they always omit the 'est' ending. The scribes and Pharisees are rebuked in these chapters. The Bible uses the second person, "killest," indicating that Jesus is addressing individually those (thou) who killed the prophets; he is not addressing an impersonal third person (it) city (I kill, thou killest, Jerusalem killeth). If Jesus had been addressing Jerusalem, a city, he would have used the singular third person verb "killeth." The NKJV and NASB incorrectly use the third person singular "kills," instead of the second person "kill" (I kill, you kill, it kills). They move the indictment away from those present individuals to whom Jesus was speaking and move it on to a city. The word "thou" is a part of the English second person verb ending and must be added in English to accurately communicate the person to whom the verb is addressed. The context refers to those present, using the singular second person, "thee" and "thy" to refer to the ones who killed Jesus.[85]

Matt. 23:37		
NKJV	**NASB**	**KJV**
"O Jerusalem, Jerusalem, the one who kill**s** the prophets and stone**s** those who are sent to her! How often...your"	"O Jerusalem, Jerusalem, who kill**s** the prophets and stone**s** those who are sent to her! How often...your"	"O Jerusalem, Jerusalem, *thou* that kill**est** the prophets, and ston**est** them which are sent unto **thee**, how often...**thy**"

Luke 13:34		
"O Jerusalem, Jerusalem, the one who kill**s** the prophets and stone**s** those who are sent to her! How often...your"	"O Jerusalem, Jerusalem, *the city* that kill**s** the prophets and stone**s** those sent to her! How often...your"	"O Jerusalem, Jerusalem, which kill**est** the prophets, and ston**est** them that are sent unto **thee**; how often...**thy**"

Annotated Graphic from Gail Riplinger's *In Awe of Thy Word*

Riplinger explains that removing the endings of the words subjected the redactor to the curses found in Revelation 22:18-19.

> The KJV always retains "the ending." It is not carried over into modern bibles. They "take away" the endings on words like 'lovest' and 'cometh' and change them to 'love' and 'comes.' The editors of the NKJV, so-called Easy Reading KJV-ER, NIV, TNIV, ESV, HCSB, and NASB disobey Rev. 22:19 which warns,
>
> "And if any man shall take away from the words of the book...God shall take away his part out of the book of life..." R
>
> ***
>
> Study the sentence structure in Rev. 22:19. It does not say, "...if any man shall take away words from the book..." Rather, it says, "if any man shall take away from the words..." Examine a parallel if you will. "If any man shall take away the wallet from my pocket..." refers to the wallet being stolen. However, the statement, "If any man shall take away from the wallet...," refers to the contents of the wallet, that is, individual items in the wallet . money!
>
> The warning in Revelation 22 seems to forbid taking away letters "from the word" which affect the meaning. This iswhy the Jewish scribes count every letter when transcribing the Old Testament . lest they should "diminish ought from" a "word" (Deut. 4:2) removing even "one jot [letter] or one tittle" (Matt. 5:18).

*When seeking confirmation about the interpretation of a verse, look nearby for its parallel. (See chapter entitled "Every Word.") Substitute the parallel word and see how that word would be interpreted. Here in Rev. 22, the parallel reconfirms the interpretation that the thing being taken away includes a "part" of a word. The matching parallel peg words are "take away" and "the book of." The word "part" is given as a parallel. A letter is a "part out of" a word.

"<u>take away</u> **from the words of** <u>the book</u> of this prophecy..." Rev. 22:19

"<u>take away</u> **his part out of** <u>the book of</u> life..." Rev. 22:19

One of the arguments used by the promoters of the new versions is that the new versions are easier to read than the King James Bible. Some Bible passages are hard to understand, but that is no excuse to change the meaning of the passages just to make them more readable. Dr. Donald Waite said it best:

> Some people say they like a particular version because they say it's more readable. Now, readability is one thing, but does the readability conform to what's in the original Greek and Hebrew language? You can have a lot of readability, but if it doesn't match up with what God has said, it's of no profit. In the King James Bible, the words match what God has said. You may say it's difficult to read, but study it out. It's hard in the Hebrew and Greek and, perhaps, even in the English in the King James Bible. But to change it around just to make it simple, or interpreting it, instead of translating it, is wrong.

You've got lots of interpretation, but we don't want that in a translation. We want exactly what God said in the Hebrew and Greek brought over into English.[86]

Besides, it is not true that the new bible versions are easier to read. According to a readability study the AV reads at the 5th grade level, whereas the NKJV and NASB read at the 6th grade level and the NIV reads at the 8th grade level.[87] When reading the Holy Bible one should understand that "the natural man receiveth not the things of the Spirit of God: for they are foolishness unto him: neither can he know them, because they are spiritually discerned." (1 Corinthians 2:14 AV) If a passage is hard to understand pray for understanding and study the Bible for the answer. Let God's word explain God's word.

God has promised to preserve his word forever (Psalms 12:6-7), that not one jot nor one tittle will pass from his law (Matthew 5:18), and that heaven and earth will pass away but his words will never pass away (Matthew 24:35). The promoters of the new bible versions call God a liar. They assert that God's word has not been preserved. They admit that they don't know which version is truly God's word. If you ask them to present God's word, they will tell you that parts of his word are lost forever, but that they can come up with a text that they will try to convince you comes close to God's word. But God has stated emphatically: "[T]he word of the Lord endureth for ever. And this is the word which by the gospel is preached unto you." (1 Peter 1:25 AV) "[L]et God be true, but every man a liar." (Romans 3:4 AV)

S. Franklin Longsdon was assigned by Dewey Lockman of the Lockman Foundation to write the guidelines for the translation of the NASB. Longsdon prepared the guidelines, but after much study and prayer, he wrote to Lockman that the NASB was terribly wrong and renounced any attachment to the NASB version of the bible.[88]

The most popular version of the new bibles is the New International Version (NIV). Dr. Virginia Mollenkott, the textual style editor for the NIV, is an admitted lesbian.[89] The Chairman of the NIV Old Testament Committee, Dr. Woudstra, was considered to be sympathetic to the interests and practices of sodomites. The NIV chief editor vaunted the fact that the NIV showed that it is a great error to believe that in order to be born again, one has to have faith in Jesus as Savior. He also thought that few clear and decisive Bible texts express that Jesus is God.[90]

Recall that from the beginning it was the Jewish hierarchy, the chief priests and elders, who tried to stop the spread of the gospel. "And they called them, and commanded them not to speak at all nor teach in the name of Jesus." (Acts 4:18 AV) Having failed in that, they have tried to conceal God's word like a needle covered by a haystack of corrupt Bible versions, the NIV being one of them.

Rupert Murdoch owns the exclusive rights to the NIV.[91] The NIV is published by Zondervan, which is owned by Murdoch's News Corporation.[92] Murdoch's News Corporation also owns Harper Collins, the publisher of Anton La Vey's Satanic Bible. La Vey is the founder of The Church Of Satan. He is reputed to have been a Jew, whose real name was Howard Levey. Both the Satanic Bible and the NIV Bible are featured on the Harper Collins sales website.[93] "Can two walk together, except they be agreed?" (Amos 3:3 AV) La Vey's book is an exoteric Satanic Bible, whereas the NIV is an esoteric Satanic Bible.

Murdoch has been described as an internationalist and a pornographer.[94] *Time* magazine called Murdoch one of the four most powerful people in the world, and for good reason; he has a media empire that includes Twentieth Century Fox, Fox Television, cable television providers, satellites, and newspapers and television stations throughout America, Europe, and Asia.[95] Investigative journalists, however, have discovered that Murdoch, who has a gentile public persona, is in fact a Jew, who is a front man for other much more powerful Zionist Jews: Michel Fribourg, Armand Hammer, and Edgar Bronfman, who prefer to remain out of the spotlight.[96] This author's book, *Solving the Mystery of Babylon the Great*, explains the synergism between Jewish and Catholic interests. The Pope bestowed upon Murdoch the title of "Knight Commander of St. Gregory" for promoting the interests of the Roman Catholic Church.[97]

There is both a Catholic version and a Protestant version of the NIV. The notable difference between the two is the Catholic version contains the apocryphal books that are considered part of the biblical canon by the Vatican. The apocryphal books are rejected and considered non-canonical by Protestant Christians.

10 Copyrighting Bible Corruptions

The New King James Version (NKJV) and the 21st Century King James Version (KJ21) are particularly misleading. They try to trade on the accuracy of the Authorized (King James) Version of the Holy Bible (AV) by putting King James in their titles. They claim that their bibles are simply updates of the King James. Their copyright, however, gives them away. What they don't tell the public is that in order to obtain a copyright on a book that is in the public domain, as is the King James Bible, they are required to make substantial revisions to the text, such that it can be clearly distinguishable from the original. Essentially, it must be a new literary work. Otherwise, the publisher of the revision cannot claim a copyright. The NKJV and the KJ21 are both copyrighted books; which means they must be substantially different from the King James Bible. Yet, in order to sell the new Bible they tell the public that it is really the same as the old King James Bible, that they have simply updated the archaic language in order to make it more readable.

Copyright© Requires a substantial difference from public domain such that it is considered an original work in order to get a copyright as a derivative work. 17 U.S.C. § 101 defines a derivative work as "[a] work consisting of editorial revisions, annotations, elaborations, or other modifications which, as a whole, represent an **original work of authorship**."

U.S. Copyright Office: "To be copyrightable, a derivative work must incorporate some or all of a preexisting "work" and **add new original copyrightable authorship to that work.**"[98] That means that the new bible versions must necessarily change God's word in order to obtain a copyright. All the new bible versions are published under copyright. They have all added "new original copyrightable authorship" to God's word. The U.S. Copyright Office explains:

> A work that has fallen into the public domain, that is, a work that is no longer protected by copyright, is also an underlying 'work' from which derivative authorship may be added, but the copyright in the derivative work will not extend to the public domain material, and the use of the public domain material in a derivative work.[99]

The publishers of the NKJV and the KJ21 versions are being disingenuous when they claim that their new versions are not new at all, but just easier to read updates of the original Authorized (King James) Version (AV). The NKJV made over 100,000 word changes from the AV, deleting 2,289 words from the New Testament alone. The NKJV removed the word "Lord" 66 times, removed the word "God" 51 times, and removed the word "Heaven" 50 times. Yet, Nelson Publications has the nerve to advertise that "Nothing has been changed except to make the original meaning clearer."[100]

The KJ21 publishers claim that:

> *The 21st Century King James Version (KJ21®)* is neither a new translation nor a revision, but an updating of the King James Version (KJV) of A.D. 1611. While no attempt has been made to

"improve" the timeless message or literary style of the KJV, words which are either obsolete or archaic, and are no longer understood by literate Bible readers, have been replaced by carefully selected current equivalents.[101]

The KJ21 publishers state that in order to maintain the accuracy and keep the KJ21 faithful to the original AV they even kept the thees and thous, etc. They have, in fact, made many unnecessary changes to the text, which make their bible less clear and understandable. If one reads the text of the KJ21, one sees that conjunctions are added when unnecessary and the word order is changed in passages, not to make the passages clearer, but so that the revision is considered substantially different from the King James Bible. They had to make substantial changes in order to obtain a copyright on the publication. It must be an "original work of authorship" to be copyrighted.

The KJ21 is, quite simply, about creating an original work of authorship (i.e., a new Bible) and making money. The publishers are not telling the truth when they claim that the KJ21 is not a revision but only an update. George Shafer did a computer check of the verses in the four Gospels, comparing the KJ21 with the original AV. He discovered that the KJ21 modified 2,200 of the 3,779 verses.[102] That is a change in approximately 60% of the verses in the four gospels. Why did they make so many changes, when they claimed to have only updated it? Remember, they must make substantial changes in order to get a copyright, but they also want to sell their corrupted bibles.

The KJ21 claims in their preface: "The *KJ21*® is unique among modern Bibles in that it is closer in language to the original King James Version than any other Bible copyrighted in the twentieth century. Unlike all other modern Bibles, it alone retains the power, beauty, and poetic language of the glorious King James Version."[103] The KJ21 publishers are saying that they have changed the powerful and beautiful King James Bible to a lesser degree than other copyrighted new bible versions. The KJ21 publishers seem to be admitting that the leaven of changes to the King James Bible are for the worse, so they made fewer of them. "A little leaven leaveneth the whole lump." (Galatians 5:9 AV) All it takes is a little poison to poison a well. These new bible versions are spiritual poison.

The KJ21 Bible publishers claim that they maintained the faithfulness of the King James Bible and only changed some archaic words. But that is not true. For example, in 2 Samuel 18, a messenger named Cushi is introduced. The KJ21 translators changed the proper name of the messenger from "Cushi" to a description of his supposed ethnicity, "the Cushite."

AV	KJ21
And the king said unto **Cushi**, Is the young man Absalom safe? And **Cushi** answered, The enemies of my lord the king, and all that rise against thee to do thee hurt, be as that young man is. (2 Samuel 18:32 AV)	And the king said unto **the Cushite**, "Is the young man Absalom safe?" And **the Cushite** answered, "The enemies of my lord the king, and all who rise against thee to do thee hurt, be as that young man is." (2 Samuel 18:32 KJ21)

That translation is clearly wrong because Cushi is the name of a person whose lineage is given in the Bible.

> The word of the LORD which came unto Zephaniah the son of **Cushi**, the son of Gedaliah, the son of Amariah, the son of Hizkiah, in the days of Josiah the son of Amon, king of Judah. (Zephaniah 1:1 AV)

It is no more easy for a person to understand the passage to read "The Cushite" than it is for him to read "Cushi." Changing "Cushi" to "the Cushite" is wrong. It is change for change's sake and is an error.

The publishers of both the KJ21 and the NKJV fall all over themselves praising the accuracy and literary beauty of the King James Bible. If it so accurate and beautiful, why change it? The answer is that they are in service of Satan to draw people away from God's word and at the same time make a lot of money. "For the love of money is the root of all evil: which while some coveted after, they have erred from the faith, and pierced themselves through with many sorrows." (1 Timothy 6:10 AV) The new bible versions are evil.

11 Every Word Is Important

Every word of God is essential. "[M]an shall not live by bread alone, but by every word of God." Luke 4:4. Look at the passage in Galatians 3:16, wherein God points out the importance of every one of his words. In that passage, God explains the significance of the distinction between the singular word "seed" and the plural word "seeds."

> Now to Abraham and his **seed** were the promises made. **He saith not, And to seeds**, as of many; but as of one, And to thy seed, which is Christ. (Galatians 3:16 AV)

If one looks at the AV passages that refer to the promises made to Abraham, one sees that in fact God refers to Abraham's "seed," singular. In the NIV, however, the passages that prophesy the blessings that were to flow from Abraham's seed, Jesus Christ, are changed and obscured. If one were to try to find the passages referred to in Galatians 3:16 in the NIV one would not be able to do so, because the NIV does not use the word chosen by God but has substituted words chosen by man as inspired by Satan.

AV	NIV
And in thy **seed** shall all the nations of the earth be blessed; because thou hast obeyed my voice. (Genesis 22:18 AV)	[A]nd through your **offspring** all nations on earth will be blessed, because you have obeyed me. (Genesis 22:18 NIV)

AV	NIV
And I will establish my covenant between me and thee and thy **seed** after thee in their generations for an everlasting covenant, to be a God unto thee, and to thy **seed** after thee. (Genesis 17:7 AV)	I will establish my covenant as an everlasting covenant between me and you and your **descendants** after you for the generations to come, to be your God and the God of your **descendants** after you. (Genesis 17:7 NIV)

God's heirs need to know who they are. His heirs are those who have the faith of Abraham, not those who have the flesh of Abraham.

> Even as Abraham believed God, and it was accounted to him for righteousness. Know ye therefore that they which are of faith, the same are the children of Abraham. And the scripture, foreseeing that God would justify the heathen through faith, preached before the gospel unto Abraham, *saying*, In thee shall all nations be blessed. **So then they which be of faith are blessed with faithful Abraham.** (Galatians 3:6-9 AV)

This point is understood by the passage in Galatians 3:16 that explains what is meant by the precise word "seed" used in the

Old Testament. **"And if ye be Christ's, then are ye Abraham's seed, and heirs according to the promise."** (Galatians 3:29 AV)

Without the precise word "seed," the meaning of the will of God can be misinterpreted to support false doctrines like the pretribulation rapture fraud, which makes Christ's church a mere parenthesis in history. Under the pretribulation rapture corruption, fleshly Israel is to inherit the promises of God; contrary to God's express intent that it is those who are chosen and justified by his sovereign grace who are his heirs and not those who are born of the flesh of Abraham. **"That being justified by his grace, we should be made heirs according to the hope of eternal life."** (Titus 3:7 AV)

> Not as though the word of God hath taken none effect. For they *are* not all Israel, which are of Israel: Neither, because they are the seed of Abraham, *are they* all children: but, In Isaac shall thy seed be called.   That is, **They which are the children of the flesh, these are not the children of God: but the children of the promise are counted for the seed."** (Romans 9:6-8 AV)

That is one example of a false doctrine that is supported by the change of just one word. There are other false doctrines that have sprung from other corrupt changes to God's word in the new bible versions.

12 Whole Verses Deleted From New Bible Versions

Many new Bible versions delete whole verses. The following is a partial list of some of the deleted passages.

Matthew 12:47
Matthew 17:21
Matthew 18:11
Matthew 23:14
Mark 7:16
Mark 9:44
Mark 9:46
Mark 11:26
Mark 15:28
Luke 17:36
Luke 23:17
John 5:4
Acts 8:37
Acts 15:34
Acts 24:7
Acts 28:29
Romans 16:24
1 John 5:7

To illustrate how it looks to come across a missing verse in the new Bible versions, below are screenshots from the Bible Gateway website showing some of the disappeared passages in different Bible versions. Mark 18:11 is missing from most new Bible versions. The new Bibles have deleted the very mission of Jesus Christ, to save the lost.

> For the Son of man is come to save that which was lost. (Matthew 18:11 AV)

> **10** "See that you do not despise one of these little ones. For I tell you that in heaven their angels always see the face of my Father who is in heaven.[d] **12** What do you think? If a man has a hundred sheep, and one of them has gone astray, does he not leave the ninety-nine on the mountains and go in search of the one that went astray? **13** And if he finds it, truly, I say

Above is a screenshot of the missing Bible verse in the English Standard Version (ESV) at Matthew 18:11. The numbers skip from 10 to 12. There is no verse 11. The footnote [d] states: "Some manuscripts add verse 11: *For the Son of Man came to save the lost.*"

Many charlatans try to excuse the deletions by arguing that the doctrines that are deleted are found in other passages. For example, Allen Parr tries to excuse the deletion of Matthew 18:11 in the New International Version (NIV).[104] "For the Son of man is come to save that which was lost." Matthew 18:11 (AV). Parr argues that no harm is done by deleting the verse in the NIV because the doctrine in the deleted passage can still be found in Luke 19:10. The NIV states in Luke 19:10: "For the Son of Man came to seek and to save the lost." Luke 19:10 (NIV).

But the reader will miss that doctrine when reading Matthew. Parr's argument is like someone who takes down a stop sign at an intersection. Parr would argue that taking down the stop sign will cause no harm because plenty of stop signs remain at other intersections. I don't think that the motorcyclist who is broadsided by a car at the intersection will appreciate Parr's logic, nor will those spiritually broadsided by the missing passage.

Below is yet another example of a missing Bible verse; this time, it is from the New Living Translation (NLT), wherein Mark 7:16 is seen missing. In each instance where the NLT has deleted a verse, it has put a paragraph break between the missing verse and the following verse so that the missing verse would not be so noticeable. The disappeared verse is:

If any man have ears to hear, let him hear. Mark 7:16.

> 15 It's not what goes into your body that defiles you; you are defiled by what comes from your heart.[h]"
>
> 17 Then Jesus went into a house to get away from the crowd, and his disciples asked him what he meant by the parable he had just used. 18 "Don't you

Above is a screenshot of the missing Bible verse in the NLT at Mark 7:16. The numbers skip from 15 to 17. There is no verse 16. The footnote [h] states: "Some manuscripts add verse 16, Anyone with ears to hear should listen and understand."

Prior to Matthew 7:16, Jesus was explaining that "[t]here is nothing from without a man, that entering into him can defile him: but the things which come out of him, those are they that defile the man." That was a spiritual truth that needed to be spiritually discerned. Indeed, in verse 17 "his disciples asked him concerning the parable." Jesus states time and again throughout the Bible: "If any man have ears to hear, let him hear." Mark 4:23. What does he mean by that? In Matthew 13:9-17 Jesus explains that he speaks in parables because not all who hear his words will understand. Those who are chosen by him will hear his voice and understand with their hearts and be converted. The parables are spiritual and can only be understood by those whom God has chosen for salvation. God must give them knowledge; he must "inspire" his elect to understand his word. Revelation 3:20 is completely explained in Matthew 13:9-17. Those who are chosen by God will hear his voice and open the door, those that are not chosen will not hear his voice, because they cannot hear his voice. In fact, Jesus explained that he used parables not only to reveal the gospel to those chosen for salvation but also to hide the gospel from those chosen for destruction.

> **Who hath ears to hear, let him hear**. And the disciples came, and said unto him, Why speakest thou unto them in parables? He answered and said unto them, **Because it is given unto you to know the mysteries of the kingdom of heaven, but to them it is not given.** For whosoever hath, to him shall be given, and he shall have more abundance: but whosoever hath not, from him shall be taken away even that he hath. Therefore speak I to them in parables: because they seeing see not; and **hearing they hear not**, neither do they understand. And in them is fulfilled the prophecy of Esaias, which saith, **By hearing ye shall hear, and shall not understand**; and seeing ye shall see, and shall not perceive: For this people's heart is waxed gross, and **their ears are dull of hearing**, and their eyes they have closed; **lest at any time they should see with their eyes, and hear with their**

ears, and should understand with their heart, and should be converted, and I should heal them. But blessed are your eyes, for they see: and your ears, for they hear. For verily I say unto you, That many prophets and righteous men have desired to see those things which ye see, and have not seen them; and to hear those things which ye hear, and have not heard them. (Matthew 13:9-17 AV)

And when he was alone, they that were about him with the twelve asked of him the parable. And he said unto them, Unto you it is given to know the mystery of the kingdom of God: but unto them that are without, all these things are done in parables: That seeing they may see, and not perceive; and hearing they may hear, and not understand; lest at any time they should be converted, and their sins should be forgiven them. (Mark 4:10-12 AV)

The unsaved will not believe in Christ because they cannot believe in him. Only the chosen sheep, who have been born again from heaven, can believe in the good shepherd. **"But ye believe not, because ye are not of my sheep."**(John 10:26 AV)

The Old Testament is an example; it is an allegorical pattern of the spiritual reality that is God's kingdom. See Galatians 4:22-26; Hebrews 8:5. God hardened Pharaoh's heart which is an example of how he hardens the hearts of unbelievers. "For the scripture saith unto Pharaoh, Even for this same purpose have I raised thee up, that I might shew my power in thee, and that my name might be declared throughout all the earth. **Therefore hath he mercy on whom he will have mercy, and whom he will he hardeneth**." Romans 9:17-18.

Those who do not believe in Jesus cannot believe because

God has blinded their eyes and stopped their ears, just as he hardened Pharaoh's heart. Only the elect of God are saved. "What then? Israel hath not obtained that which he seeketh for; but **the election hath obtained it, and the rest were blinded (According as it is written, God hath given them the spirit of slumber, eyes that they should not see, and ears that they should not hear**;) unto this day." (Romans 11:7-8 AV)

Looking back at Pharaoh, we see that Pharaoh had no choice in the matter. God was in complete control. God hardened Pharaoh's heart so that he would not let the children of Israel go. God also hardened the hearts of Pharaoh's servants.

> And when Pharaoh saw that the rain and the hail and the thunders were ceased, he sinned yet more, and hardened his heart, he and his servants. And the heart of Pharaoh was hardened, neither would he let the children of Israel go; as the LORD had spoken by Moses. And the LORD said unto Moses, Go in unto Pharaoh: for **I have hardened his heart, and the heart of his servants**, that I might shew these my signs before him: (Exodus 9:34-10:1 AV)

The new Bible versions do not always just delete a verse with the number and all. Sometimes, they will try to conceal their deletion by borrowing language from an adjoining verse to fill in for the deleted verse to deceive the reader into thinking that the verse has not been deleted. We see that phenomenon with the deletion of 1 John 5:7.

The new Bible versions have launched a direct attack on the deity of Jesus Christ. In 1 John 5:6-8, we find the authoritative statement of the Godhead, "the Father, the Word, and the Holy Ghost: and these three are one." 1 John 5:7. But Satan cannot allow that truth to be authoritatively stated in the Holy Scriptures.

And so he floated his profane Bibles to distract the unwary from that truth. This was first done with the Revised Standard Version Bible (RSV). In the RSV, the translators deleted the verse at 1 John 5:7. By doing so, they had a problem. It would be evident that they deleted that verse. So they took the second clause of verse 6 and made a new verse 7 out of that second clause they borrowed from verse 6. The following comparison shows what the RSV editors did. The borrowed clause from verse 6 is in italics, and the deleted verse verse 7 is in bold in the AV version.

AV	RSV
6 This is he that came by water and blood, even Jesus Christ; not by water only, but by water and blood. *And it is the Spirit that beareth witness, because the Spirit is truth.* 7 **For there are three that bear record in heaven, the Father, the Word, and the Holy Ghost: and these three are one.** 8 And there are three that bear witness in earth, the Spirit, and the water, and the blood: and these three agree in one. (I John 5:6-8 AV)	6 This is he who came by water and blood, Jesus Christ, not with the water only but with the water and the blood. 7 *And the Spirit is the witness, because the Spirit is the truth.* 8 There are three witnesses, the Spirit, the water, and the blood; and these three agree. (I John 5:6-8 RSV)

Later, other new Bible versions decided that the RSV translators' reworking was unacceptable. And so they instead took the first clause from verse 8 to create a new verse 7 to cover for the deletion of the truth that "there are three that bear record in heaven, the Father, the Word, and the Holy Ghost: and these three are one" in verse 7. Below are examples from the ESV and NIV showing how they created a new verse 7 using the first clause of verse 8. That first clause in verse 8 is in italics.

6 This is he who came by water and blood—Jesus Christ; not by the water only but by the water and the blood. And the Spirit is the one who testifies, because the Spirit is the truth. 7 *For there are three that testify*: 8 the Spirit and the water and the blood; and these three agree. (I John 5:6-8 ESV)

6 This is the one who came by water and blood—Jesus Christ. He did not come by water only, but by water and blood. And it is the Spirit who testifies, because the Spirit is the truth. 7 *For there are three that testify:* 8 the Spirit, the water and the blood; and the three are in agreement. (I John 5:6-8 NIV)

The NIV does something unusual. The NIV keeps the verse number in the text but leaves the passage out, replacing it with a footnote. For example, the passage at Acts 8:37 is missing from the NIV, but verse number 37 remains in a bracket, followed by a footnote. That deleted passage addresses the doctrine of believer's baptism. The disappeared passage at Acts 8:37 states:

And Philip said, If thou believest with all thine heart, thou mayest. And he answered and said, I believe that Jesus Christ is the Son of God. (Acts 8:37 AV)

> **36** As they traveled along the road, they came to some water and the eunuch said, "Look, here is water. What can stand in the way of my being baptized?" [37] [c] **38** And he gave orders to stop the

Above is a screenshot of the missing Bible verse in the NIV at Act 8:37. The number for the verese remains but in brackets. The deleted passage is replaced by footnote [c] which states: "Some manuscripts include here Philip said, 'If you believe with all your heart, you may.' The eunuch answered, 'I believe that Jesus Christ is the Son of God.'"

Revelations 22:18-19 tells us that the publishers of the new Bible versions are in serious trouble with God.

> For I testify unto every man that heareth the words of the prophecy of this book, If any man shall add unto these things, God shall add unto him the plagues that are written in this book: And if any man shall take away from the words of the book of this prophecy, God shall take away his part out of the book of life, and out of the holy city, and from the things which are written in this book. (Revelation 22:18-19 AV)

13 New Bible Versions Say Jesus Lied

God's word tells us that "the serpent was more subtil than any beast of the field which the LORD God had made." Genesis 3:1. Indeed, that subtle beast has ever so slightly changed a word here, a word there, in his corrupt Bibles to change the meaning of passages. For example, the new bible versions have deleted a single word, which, in effect, turns Jesus into a liar.

In John 7:8, Jesus explains that he was not **yet** going up to the feast. He was indicating that he would tarry in Galilee for a while before going to the feast. But the corrupt versions delete the word "yet" and thus have Jesus saying that he was not going up to the feast at all. In verse 10 we find out that "when his brethren were gone up, then went he also up unto the feast, not openly, but as it were in secret." John 7:10.

Thus, according to the new bible versions, Jesus lied. They incorrectly allege that Jesus said he was not going up to the feast at all. That rendition has Jesus lying because verse 10 reveals that Jesus, in fact, did later go to the feast. The Authorized (King James) Version (AV) has it correct. Jesus said he was not "yet" going to the feast.

AV	**ESV**
Go ye up unto this feast: **I go not up yet unto this feast**; for my time is not yet full come. John 7:8 (AV)	You go up to the feast. **I am not going up to this feast,** for my time has not yet fully come. John 7:8 (ESV)

14 Saved by the Faith of Jesus Christ

The NIV and the other new Bible versions are ever so subtle in their twisting of the scriptures in order to conceal the sovereign grace of God. The new Bible versions instead put the focus on the decision of man. If the Christian uses a KJV (AV) Bible, it would be difficult to believe the Arminian gospel, unless the reader ignored the plain language of Romans 3:22 and other passages. Satan had to do something, so he decided to alter the Bible. An altered Bible is no longer genuine, it is a counterfeit. Satan has passed off his counterfeit Arminian Bibles, which conceal the sovereign grace of God.

The genuine passage in Romans 3:22 states that our faith comes from Jesus. One cannot have faith **in** Jesus without being given the faith **of** Jesus. The Arminian gospel, which states that man is the source of his own faith, is exposed as a lie in the genuine passage of Romans 3:22. Satan is a devil of subtlety. Notice that the first act of his subtlety in the Garden of Eden was to attack the word of God. "Now the serpent was more subtil than any beast of the field which the LORD God had made. And he said unto the woman, Yea, hath God said, Ye shall not eat of every tree of the garden?" Genesis 3:1. Satan has continued his acts of subtle sabotage of God's word by having his minions change one two letter word "of" to "in," and presto chango, he is able to keep the people who read his new counterfeit Bibles ignorant of the sovereign grace of God.

AV	NIV
Even the righteousness of God which is **by faith of Jesus Christ** unto all and upon all them that believe: for there is no difference: (Romans 3:22 AV)	This righteousness from God comes **through faith in Jesus Christ** to all who believe. There is no difference, (Romans 3:22 NIV)

Notice that the righteousness of God is "by the faith **of** Jesus Christ." The passage explains the source of the faith; faith comes from Jesus Christ, hence it is the "faith **of** Jesus Christ." The NIV conceals the source of the faith and simply states the result of the working of Christ, that the righteousness of God "comes through faith **in** Jesus Christ." The passage is supposed to reveal the source of our faith, instead it is changed to reveal the object of our faith.

The word "**of**" is defined in Webster's American Dictionary of the English Language as:

> **From or out of; proceeding from, as the cause, source, means, author or agent bestowing.** I have received **of** the Lord that which also I delivered to you. 1 Corinthians 11:23. For it was **of** the Lord to harden their hearts. Joshua 11:20. It is **of** the Lord's mercies that we are not consumed. Lamentations 3:22. The whole disposing thereof is **of** the Lord. Proverbs 16:33. Go, inquire **of** the Lord for me. 2 Chronicles 34:21. That holy thing that shall be born **of** thee. Luke 1:35. Hence of is the sign of the genitive case, the case that denotes production; as the son of man, the son proceeding from man, produced from man. This is the primary sense.[105]

Webster's dictionary states that **"of"** is the sign of the genitive case, which is used to show ownership. That means the faith "of" Jesus Christ indicates that Jesus owns the faith; he is the owner and source of saving faith. That is what Hebrews 12:2 means when it explains that Jesus Christ is the author and finisher of our faith. Thus, believers are saved by the faith "**of**" Jesus Christ, who is the source of our faith. Faith does not come by the will of man. *See* John 1:12-13. Faith is a gift "**of**" God. *See* Ephesians 2:8.

The reader of the NIV can quite comfortably fit the Arminian gospel into the watered-down passage. The innocent Christian sheep using an NIV Bible will not have any notice that an Arminian "minister" is preaching a false gospel because the NIV has concealed the word of God from him. Even the supposedly more fundamental and conservative NKJV and NASB make the same subtle switch in their corrupt versions of Romans 3:22. The NKJV states: "even the righteousness of God, through faith **in** Jesus Christ, to all and on all who believe. For there is no difference." The NASB states: "even the righteousness of God through faith **in** Jesus Christ for all those who believe; for there is no distinction."

We see the same Arminian corruption in the NKJV of Galatians 2:20:

AV	**NKJV**
I am crucified with Christ: nevertheless I live; yet not I, but Christ liveth in me: and the life which I now live in the flesh I live **by the faith of the Son of God**, who loved me, and gave himself for me. (Galatians 2:20 AV)	I have been crucified with Christ; it is no longer I who live, but Christ lives in me; and the life which I now live in the flesh I live **by faith in the Son of God**, who loved me and gave Himself for me. (Galatians 2:20 NKJV)

Next, read Galatians 2:16. The KJV passage indicates that Jesus Christ is both the source of our faith and the object of our faith. There is a clear distinction in the passage between the faith "**of**" Jesus and the faith "**in**" Jesus. The passage reveals that the faith "**of**" Christ is the reason we have faith "**in**" Christ. Our Justification is by the faith "**of**" Christ. We believe "**in**" Jesus, because we have the faith "**of**" Jesus.

Jesus is both the object of our faith and the source of our faith. The faith supplied by Jesus is the means of our justification. Jesus has done it all! The passage refers to the source of our faith as being "**of**" Christ in two separate clauses. The editors of the new Bible versions have removed both references to the faith "**of**" Christ; they end up repeating faith "**in**" Christ 3 times. Look at the example below from the NASB:

AV	**NASB**
Knowing that a man is not justified by the works of the law, but **by the faith of Jesus Christ**, even we have **believed in Jesus Christ**, that we might be **justified by the faith of Christ**, and not by the works of the law: for by the works of the law shall no flesh be justified. (Galatians 2:16 AV)	nevertheless knowing that a man is not justified by the works of the Law but **through faith in Christ Jesus**, even we have **believed in Christ Jesus**, so that we may be **justified by faith in Christ** and not by the works of the Law; since by the works of the Law no flesh will be justified. (Galatians 2:16 NASB)

The Galatians 2:16 passage in the NASB, NKJV, and NIV, and other new Bible versions excise Christ as the source of our faith. In the new Bible versions it is all up to man; Christ is out of the picture, except as the object of faith. The object of faith in the new corrupt Bibles is a different Jesus from the true Jesus of the gospel; the Jesus of the new Bible versions is a helpless Arminian

Jesus. He is not the source of faith.

People are being deceived into believing another gospel (an anti-gospel) with a different Jesus from the true omnipotent Jesus. Their counterfeit Jesus is a pathetic helpless imposter, who is reliant upon the weak and enslaved will of man. "For if he that cometh preacheth **another Jesus**, whom we have not preached, or if ye receive another spirit, which ye have not received, or another gospel, which ye have not accepted, ye might well bear with *him*." (2 Corinthians 11:4 KJV) **"I marvel that ye are so soon removed from him that called you into the grace of Christ unto another gospel**: Which is not another; but there be some that trouble you, and would pervert the gospel of Christ. **But though we, or an angel from heaven, preach any other gospel unto you than that which we have preached unto you, let him be accursed.** As we said before, so say I now again, **If any man preach any other gospel unto you than that ye have received, let him be accursed."** (Galatians 1:6-9 KJV) The new Bible versions remove the grace of Christ and replace it with a cursed free will gospel!

Every passage that describes the "faith **of**" Jesus Christ has been changed in almost all the new Bible versions to read "faith **in**" Jesus Christ, or otherwise obscured by other language. *See, e.g.,* Galatians 3:22, 5:22; Ephesians 3:12; Philippians 3:9; James 2:1, and Revelation 14:12.

It is clear that the new Bible versions have an Armenian agenda. For example in Revelation 14:12 we read: "Here is the patience of the saints: here are they that keep the commandments of God, and **the faith of Jesus**." is changed in the NIV to: "This calls for patient endurance on the part of the saints who obey God's commandments and **remain faithful to Jesus**." Notice how nicely the NIV fits in with the Arminian view that salvation can be lost, and so one must "remain faithful to Jesus." The NIV Revelation 14:12 counterfeit passage completely obscures the description of faith as "the faith **of** Jesus."

Collossians 2:12 is clear, faith is by the operation of God. The NIV, however, hides that fact from the reader. According to the NIV, you are raised with Christ through "your" faith. "The faith **of** the operation of God" is changed in the NIV to "**your** faith **in** the power of God." The AV verse reveals that faith is proceeding from the operation of God. Thus, God is the source of the faith. He bestows the faith on his elect. That truth is hidden from the reading in the NIV verse.

KJV	NIV
Buried with him in baptism, wherein also **ye are risen with him through the faith of the operation of God**, who hath raised him from the dead. (Colossians 2:12 KJV)	having been buried with him in baptism and **raised with him through your faith in the power of God**, who raised him from the dead. (Colossians 2:12 NIV)

Will Kinney reveals how the modern Bible versions, dilute the true gospel of grace and promote a devilish Arminian anti-gospel:

> Much of modern Christianity pictures God as a grandfatherly figure wishing so badly that his errant creatures would heed his pleadings and decide of their own free will to choose to believe and cast their vote for God. For those of us who have been granted by our gracious Lord to see the great truths of election and sovereign grace, we should be greatly concerned to see how many of these truths have been diluted in the new bible versions.[106]

* * *

There is a subtle twisting of God's inspired words taking place in many modern versions in how they are rendering the phrase "respecteth not persons". This is so subtle, that I believe most Christians have not noticed it. The change in meaning produced by versions like the NKJV, NIV, and NASB unfortunately fits in with so much of modern, popular theology, that many would actually consider it to be an improvement over the KJB's reading. It fits the philosophy of the natural mind of man.

The concept that "God has created all men equal" does not come from the Holy Bible. God obviously has not created all men equal, nor does He deal[s] with every single individual or nation in what seems to us as a fair and impartial manner. Many have become so influenced in their thinking by the reasoning of the world, that they cannot discern this obvious truth.

God has created, formed and made each of us. Yet He has not given to all equal intelligence, good looks, physical skills, nor spiritual gifts. "He divideth to every man severally as He will." Exodus 4:11 tells us "And the LORD said unto him, Who hath made man's mouth? or who maketh the dumb, or deaf, or the seeing, or the blind? have not I the LORD?".

Not all are born in a country which even has the word of God in its culture, or where it would be openly taught and encouraged. Psalm 147:19,20 "He sheweth his word unto Jacob, his statutes and his judgments unto Israel. He hath not dealt so with any nation: and as for his judgments, they have not known them. Praise ye the LORD." Some are born in abject poverty, disease and ignorance, while others are blessed with abundant crops, education and families that care for them. "The rich and poor meet together: the LORD is the maker of them all." Proverbs 22:2.

The phrase "to accept the persons of men" or "to respect persons" does not mean, as the modern versions have translated it, "to show partiality" or "to show favoritism". One of the chief arguments of the Arminian side against the doctrine of election is: "God does not show partiality or favoritism, so election cannot be true." The new bibles are reinforcing this fallacious argument.

Not to show partiality is to treat all men equally; and this God does not do, as His word clearly testifies. Daniel Webster's 1828 dictionary defines "respecter of persons" as a person who regards the external circumstances of others in his judgment, and suffers his opinions to be biased by them. God's dealings with a man are not based on outward appearance, position, rank, wealth or nationality. Rather, His own sovereign purpose and pleasure of His will are the only deciding factors.

We are told in Deuteronomy 7:6-8 "For thou art an holy people unto the LORD thy God: the LORD thy God hath chosen thee to be a special people unto himself, above all people that are upon the face of the earth. The LORD did not set his love upon you, nor choose you, because ye were more in number than any people: for ye were the fewest of all people: But because the LORD loved you". Deuteronomy 10: 14-17 "Behold, the heaven and the heaven of heavens is the LORD'S thy God, the earth also, with all that therein is. Only the LORD had a delight in thy fathers to love them, and he chose their seed after them, even you above all people, as it is this day." Verse 17 "For the LORD thy God is God of gods, and Lord of lords, a great God, a mighty, and a terrible, which REGARDETH NOT PERSONS, nor taketh reward." Here both election and not regarding persons are used in the same context.

God says He chose only the fathers (Abraham, Isaac and Jacob) and their seed to be His people, and not the others. That He "regardeth not persons" means that He does this, not on the basis of their nationality, nor their good moral character (for they were a stiffnecked and rebellious people), but because it was His good pleasure to do so. . . . [T]he NKJV, NIV and NASB have "shows no partiality". If God chose Israel to be His people, and not the others, is not this showing partiality?

Deut. 14:1,2 "Ye are the children of the LORD your God...and the LORD hath chosen thee to be a peculiar people unto himself, above all the nations that are upon the earth." Why did not God choose the other nations to be his children and to know his laws? Isn't this showing partiality or favoritism?

One verse among the hundreds that have been messed up by the NKJV, NIV and NASB is 2 Samuel 14:14. Here Joab saw that king David's heart was toward his son Absalom. So Joab sends a wise woman to speak to the king. In verse 14 she says: "For we must needs die, and are as water spilt on the ground, which cannot be gathered up again:

NEITHER DOTH GOD RESPECT ANY PERSON: yet doth he devise means, that his banished be not expelled from him." In other words, we all must die, whether rich, poor, Jew, Gentile, man or woman, king or servant; God does not look at our social station and on this basis exclude some from death.

* * *

[M]any bibles, including the NKJV, NIV and NASB have the ridiculous reading of "YET GOD DOES NOT TAKE AWAY LIFE", instead of "neither doth God respect any person". This is a lie and a contradiction. In this very book in chapter 12:15 "the LORD struck the child" of David and Bathsheeba and it died. In I Sam. 2:6 we are told "The LORD killeth, and maketh alive: he bringeth down to the grave, and bringeth up", and in Deuteronomy 32:39 God says "See now that I, even I, am he, and there is no god with me: I kill, and I make alive; I wound, and I heal: neither is there any that can deliver out of my hand."

It is not that the Hebrew will not allow the meaning found in the KJB, that the NKJV, NIV and NASB have so badly mistranslated 2 Samuel 14:14. They all likewise have translated these same words in other places as they stand in the KJB and others.

This phrase "no respecter of persons" is found six times in the New Testament, and every time the modern versions have distorted the true meaning. Romans 2:11, Ephesians 6:9, Colossians 3:25, James 2:1 and 9, and Acts 10:34. In each case it has to do with not receiving the face, outward position, nationality or social rank of another. But God does not treat all people the same, nor are we told to do so either. We are to withdraw from some, avoid, exclude, reject, separate from, and not cast our pearls before others. Most importantly, God Himself chose His elect people in Christ before the foundation of the world and "of the SAME LUMP" makes one vessel unto honour and another unto dishonour - Romans 9:21. This is definitely showing partiality, but it is not respecting persons.

Romans 2:11 says "For there is no respect of persons with God.". . . But the NKJV, NASB say "no partiality" and the NIV says "not show favoritism". The Worldwide English N.T. says: "God does not love some people more than others". Yet this very book declares in Romans 9 "For the children being not yet born, neither having done any good or evil, that the purpose of God according to election might stand, not of works but of him that calleth...Jacob have I loved, but Esau have I hated...I will have mercy on whom I will have mercy...So then it is not of him that willeth, nor of him that runneth, but of God that sheweth mercy...Therefore hath he mercy on whom he will have mercy, and whom he will he hardeneth."

Please consider the true meaning of the phrase "no respecter of persons" and contrast it with the modern rendering. I hope you will see that it is not the same at all. Only the KJB contains the whole truth of the counsel of God.[107]

Supported by the new Bible versions, the modern model of evangelism starts off with a false premise. Modern evangelism is premised on the fact that God loves everyone, and everyone can, of their own free will, believe in Jesus unto salvation. That premise is false. One must have the **faith "of" Jesus** to be saved. God only gives the **faith "of" Jesus** to his elect.

God loves only his elect. If God loves everyone, that would mean that God sends to hell those whom he loves. The Bible is clear that most people are sent to hell. "Enter ye in at the strait gate: for wide is the gate, and broad is the way, that leadeth to destruction, and many there be which go in thereat:" (Matthew 7:13) The false god of modern evangelism is sending most of his loved ones to hell.

In order to enter the kingdom of God, a man must be born again. John 3:3. It is not possible to birth oneself, God must do it. **"Of his own will begat he us with the word of truth**, that we should be a kind of firstfruits of his creatures." (James 1:18) Those who are born again, have been chosen by God before the world was even created. "According as he hath **chosen us in him before the foundation of the world**, that we should be holy and without blame before him in love: Having **predestinated** us unto the adoption of children by Jesus Christ to himself, according to the good pleasure of his will." Ephesians 1:4-5.

Those chosen by God for salvation have done nothing to merit that salvation. We were not good, we were simply chosen, because God decided according to his own purpose to choose us. "Who hath saved us, and called us with an holy calling, **not according to our works, but according to his own purpose and grace**, which was given us in Christ Jesus before the world began." 2 Timothy 1.9. "In whom also we have obtained an inheritance, **being predestinated according to the purpose of him who worketh all things after the counsel of his own will."** (Ephesians 1:11) Jesus made clear to his disciples that they did not choose him, he chose them. "Ye have not chosen me, but I have chosen you, and ordained you, that ye should go and bring forth fruit, and that your fruit should remain: that whatsoever ye shall ask of the Father in my name, he may give it you." John 15:16.

Indeed, God states that he knew and loved and ordained Jeremiah to be a prophet before he was even conceived. That is certainly foreknowledge by God, but it is more than foreknowledge, it is God predestinating Jeremiah to be a prophet.

> Before I formed thee in the belly I knew thee; and before thou camest forth out of the womb I sanctified thee, and I ordained thee a prophet unto the nations. Jeremiah 1:5.

Consider the example of Paul. How did God choose him and save him? Did he use gentle persuasion? No, he knocked him to the ground, changed his heart, and then commenced giving Paul commands as to what he must do. Notice what Paul said immediately after being knocked to the ground. "Lord, what wilt thou have me do?" Acts 9:6. In a split second, Paul went from a persecutor of the church to a member of the church, all according to the will of God, who chose him and changed his heart.

> And as he journeyed, he came near Damascus: and suddenly there shined round about him a light from heaven: And he fell to the earth, and heard a voice saying unto him, Saul, Saul, why persecutest thou me? And he said, Who art thou, Lord? And the Lord said, I am Jesus whom thou persecutest: it is hard for thee to kick against the pricks. And he trembling and astonished said, Lord, what wilt thou have me to do? And the Lord said unto him, Arise, and go into the city, and it shall be told thee what thou must do. (Acts 9:3-6)

How did he select his apostles? He commanded them to

follow him, and they dropped what they were doing and followed him. They immediately obeyed his command to follow him, without hesitation or question. That is the supernatural power of God at work.

> And Jesus, walking by the sea of Galilee, saw two brethren, Simon called Peter, and Andrew his brother, casting a net into the sea: for they were fishers. And **he saith unto them, Follow me, and I will make you fishers of men. And they straightway left their nets, and followed him**. And going on from thence, he saw other two brethren, James the son of Zebedee, and John his brother, in a ship with Zebedee their father, mending their nets; and **he called them. And they immediately left the ship and their father, and followed him**. (Matthew 4:18-22)

Some may ask: "doesn't man have a free will to choose to believe or not believe in Jesus?" The answer is that man has a will, but it is not free. Man is enslaved by sin and death. Sinful man wishes to rule in his own life, his every impulse is in rebellion against God. Indeed, man cannot freely believe in God. God must transform man by the rebirth wrought by the Holy Spirit.

The reality is that man's will is enslaved to sin. Man will not serve God nor seek God, because man is spiritually dead. "As it is written, **There is none righteous, no, not one: There is none that understandeth, there is none that seeketh after God**." (Romans 3:10-11)

Jesus came to set us free from the bondage of sin. "If the Son therefore shall make you free, ye shall be free indeed." (John 8:36) He gives his elect a new spiritual birth and they are set free from sin and death to serve the Lord. By his grace we are spiritually born again. Once born again, our old flesh driven existence comes to an end, and we are led by the spirit, which up to that time was dead, but now is alive. A Christian becomes a new creation, set free from sin to serve the living God.

> Knowing this, that **our old man is crucified with him, that the body of sin might be destroyed, that henceforth we should not serve sin. For he that is dead is freed from sin**. Now if we be dead with Christ, we believe that we shall also live with him: Knowing that Christ being raised from the dead dieth no more; death hath no more dominion over him. For in that he died, he died unto sin once: but in that he liveth, he liveth unto God. Likewise **reckon ye also yourselves to be dead indeed unto sin, but alive unto God through Jesus Christ our Lord.**" (Romans 6:6-11)

A Christian is justified by God. God does the choosing, not man. James 1:18. God does not love us because we first loved him. "We love him, because he first loved us." (1 John 4:19) It is an act of his Grace toward us that frees us from the bondage of sin. Once we are freed from the bondage of sin we can bear the fruit of righteousness. "But now being **made free from sin**, and become servants to God, ye have your fruit unto holiness, and the end everlasting life." (Romans 6:22) *See also,* Romans 5:16-19; 7:1-8:17. However, it is all a work of God, by his grace. **"For all have sinned, and come short of the glory of God; Being justified freely by his grace through the redemption that is in Christ Jesus."** (Romans 3:23-24)

Chapter 6 of John makes clear that salvation is all of God. God "giveth" eternal life to his chosen through faith in his son, Jesus.

> Then Jesus said unto them, Verily, verily, I say unto you, Moses gave you not that bread from

heaven; but my Father **giveth** you the true bread from heaven. For the bread of God is he which cometh down from heaven, and **giveth life** unto the world. Then said they unto him, Lord, evermore give us this bread. And Jesus said unto them, **I am the bread of life: he that cometh to me shall never hunger; and he that believeth on me shall never thirst.** (John 6:32-35)

Many modern evangelists promote the myth that man has a free will and can thwart the will of God. They disregard the very theme of the Bible that man's will is enslaved to sin as a result of the fall. Ephesians 2:1; 1 Corinthians 2:14.

It is impossible for man to actually obtain salvation under the modern evangelical free will theology, because that theology has a mythical, impotent Jesus. If a man believes that his faith is generated from his own free will, which does not in fact exist, and he exercises that faith to believe in an impotent Jesus, who does not in fact exist, that would mean that he has a salvation that does not in fact exist. Paul warned about just such a false gospel and false Jesus. "For if he that cometh preacheth another Jesus, whom we have not preached, or if ye receive another spirit, which ye have not received, or another gospel, which ye have not accepted, ye might well bear with him." (2 Corinthians 11:4)

15 The Unpardonable Sin

The texts of the new Bible versions, such as the NIV, manifest the heathen antichrist agenda of its publishers. In Isaiah, chapter 14, there is a passage about Lucifer that refers to him as "Lucifer, son of the morning." In the NIV, the Isaiah passage is changed.

Notice in the the Bible passage below that the NIV has changed the subject of the passage from "Lucifer" to the "morning star" in Isaiah 14:12-15. What is the significance of that change? In Revelation 22:16, Jesus calls himself the "morning star." Do you see what Satan has done? Jesus is the "morning star" in the NIV Isaiah passage. Satan's minions have taken a passage that refers to Satan's destruction and have twisted it in the NIV to describe the destruction of Jesus, who is Lord God Almighty.

| **AV** | **NIV** |

| How art thou fallen from heaven, O **Lucifer**, son of the morning! *how* art thou cut down to the ground, which didst weaken the nations! For thou hast said in thine heart, I will ascend into heaven, I will exalt my throne above the stars of God: I will sit also upon the mount of the congregation, in the sides of the north: I will ascend above the heights of the clouds; I will be like the most High. Yet thou shalt be brought down to hell, to the sides of the pit.   (Isaiah 14:12-15 AV) | How you have fallen from heaven, O **morning star**, son of the dawn! You have been cast down to the earth, you who once laid low the nations! You said in your heart, "I will ascend to heaven, I will raise my throne above the stars of God: I will sit enthroned on the mount of assembly, in the utmost heights of the sacred mountain. I will ascend above the tops of the clouds; I will make myself like the most High." But you are brought down to the grave, to the depths of the pit. (Isaiah 14:12-15 NIV) |

      The authors of the NIV, who are evil minions of the devil, have committed the unpardonable sin by changing Isaiah chapter 14 in the NIV to blasphemously attribute to God the evil characteristics of Lucifer. In their Satanic NIV, Isaiah chapter 14 has been changed to prophesy that it is not Lucifer who will in the end be cast into hell, but rather the "morning star," who is the Lord God Jesus Christ. Jesus explains in Matthew 12:24-32 that to attribute to God the characteristics of the devil is the unpardonable sin of blaspheming the Holy Spirit.

      But when the Pharisees heard it, they said, **This fellow doth not cast out devils, but by Beelzebub**

the prince of the devils. And Jesus knew their thoughts, and said unto them, Every kingdom divided against itself is brought to desolation; and every city or house divided against itself shall not stand: And if Satan cast out Satan, he is divided against himself; how shall then his kingdom stand? And if I by Beelzebub cast out devils, by whom do your children cast them out? therefore they shall be your judges. But if I cast out devils by the Spirit of God, then the kingdom of God is come unto you. Or else how can one enter into a strong man's house, and spoil his goods, except he first bind the strong man? and then he will spoil his house. He that is not with me is against me; and he that gathereth not with me scattereth abroad. Wherefore I say unto you, All manner of sin and blasphemy shall be forgiven unto men: **but the blasphemy against the Holy Ghost shall not be forgiven unto men. And whosoever speaketh a word against the Son of man, it shall be forgiven him: but whosoever speaketh against the Holy Ghost, it shall not be forgiven him, neither in this world, neither in the world to come.** (Matthew 12:24-32 AV)

In Revelation 20:12 the small and great stand before God, who is seated on a great white throne. However, to add insult to injury, in the NIV, NASB and other corrupted versions Satan accomplishes his ultimate goal of taking God from his throne in his new Bible versions; in those new versions all mention of God sitting on the throne is deleted. The small and great are simply standing before the throne.

16 Concealing the Deity of Jesus Christ

The modern Bible versions undermine the deity of Jesus Christ. For example, in Luke 23:42, the thief on the cross, being born again by God and given the gift of faith, turned to Jesus and called him Lord. The new Bible versions remove the word Lord and have the thief addressing Jesus without indicating that he was recognizing and addressing the Lord God Almighty on the cross.

AV	ESV
And he said unto Jesus, **Lord**, remember me when thou comest into thy kingdom. (Luke 23:42 AV)	And he said, **"Jesus**, remember me when you come into your kingdom." (Luke 23:42 ESV)

These textual alterations began with the 1885 Revised Version (RV) of the Bible, spearheaded by Brooke Foss Westcott and Fenton John Anthony Hort. The corruptions have been incorporated into most of the modern Bible versions. Westcott tried to justify the many alterations of the Holy Bible while working on the committee of the Revised Version of the Bible. In his book, *Some Lessons of the Revised Version of the New Testament*, Westcott alleged that the removed references to the deity of Jesus Christ were not removals at all. He claimed that the inclusion of "Lord" and "Christ" in Jesus' name in the Textus Receptus (Received Text) was simply due to "inattentive scribes." His mission was to accentuate the humanity of Jesus. Thus, the titles "Lord" and "Christ" needed to go. That resulted in a diminution of his deity in the RV.

> The emphasis which is here laid on the human name Jesus, which fixes attention on the fact of the true humanity of the Lord, is implied in many other passages where the inattention of scribes has led to the alteration of the simple name. For example, we read — I John i. 7: the blood of Jesus (Authorised Version, Jesus Christ) his Son cleanseth us from all sin. I John iv. 3: every spirit which confesseth not Jesus (Authorised Version, Jesus Christ; comp. marg.). Heb. iii. i: consider the Apostle and High Priest of our confession, even Jesus (Authorised Version, Christ Jesus). Luke xxiii. 42: he said, Jesus (Authorised Version, said unto Jesus, Lord) remember me when thou comest in thy kingdom. Acts xvi. 31: believe on the Lord Jesus (Authorised Version adds Christ). Acts xix. 4: that they should believe on him which should come after him, that is, on Jesus (Authorised Version, Christ Jesus).[108]

This diminishment of the deity of the Lord Jesus Christ was done as part of a plot wherein slight changes would be made to the text in the Revised Version, the significance of which would go unnoticed. The Revised Version was intended to alter articles of faith through the cumulative effect of the seemingly inconsequential changes. The doctrinal changes would only be discerned when compiled and read together. Westcott explained the strategy in the 1897 book he wrote about his work on the New Testament Committee of the 1885 Revised Version of the Bible.

> But the value of the Revision is most clearly seen when the student considers together a considerable group of passages, which **bear upon some article of the Faith.** The accumulation of small details then produces its full effect. Points on which it might have seemed pedantic to insist in a single passage become impressive by repetition.[109]

Westcott knew that the cumulative effect of changes he was making in the Revised Version would change the articles of the Christian faith. That was the objective. Westcott's cohort in this spiritual crime was Fenton John Anthony Hort. Hort explained how what would appear to be negligible changes, a little here and a little there, cumulatively would significantly impact Christian doctrine. He analogized their work on the Revised Version of the Bible to a forger of paintings who makes the painting so close to the original that the forgery goes unnoticed.

The forgery of an artwork is an apt analogy to what they were doing. They were creating a forgery, a false Bible that was intended to make doctrinal changes and create a falsified new brand of "Christianity." Hort explained in a July 19, 1870, letter to an unknown friend the concept behind the changes in the Revised Version while he was beginning his work along with Wescott on the committee of the Revised Version of the Bible.

> Our work of last week gave even better promise than the former session. The spirit was almost incredibly good. ... **It is quite impossible to judge of the value of what appear to be trifling alterations merely by reading them one after another. Taken together, they have often important bearings which few would think of at first.** There is but one safe rule, to be as scrupulously exact as possible, remembering, of course, that there is a truth of tone as well as of

> grammar and dictionary. The difference between a picture say of Raffaelle and a feeble copy of it is made up of a number of trivial differences.[110]

Seventeen years before beginning work on the committee for the Revised Version of the Bible, Hort was scheming with Westcott to use the corrupt Alexandrian Greek texts to supplant the Majority Byzantine Greek texts that were the basis for the KJV. In his mind, he considered the genuine Byzantine Greek texts to be "corrupt." He was working with the con man Constantin von Tishendorf (1815-1874), who foisted the corrupted Greek Codex Sinaiticus upon the world. Hort and Westcott would use the Codex Sinaiticus to do much mischief in their Revised Version of the Bible, which was later published in 1885. In 1853, Hort wrote the following to John Ellerton.

> He [Wescott] and I are going to edit a Greek text of the N. T. some two or three years hence, if possible. Lachmann and Tischendorf will supply rich materials, but not nearly enough; and we hope to do a good deal with the Oriental versions. **Our object is to supply clergymen generally, schools, etc., with a portable Gk. Test., which shall not be disfigured with Byzantine corruptions.**[111]

Their strategy was first to get their corrupted Bible into seminaries and pulpits to then change the Christian articles of faith into something very different from what is portrayed in the Holy Scriptures as given in the King James Holy Bible.

Despite the express words of the principal conspirators, Westcott and Hort, that they were engaged in a plot to change the Christian doctrine, advocates of the new Bible versions claim that there is no such plot. Mike Leake gives the common argument dismissing concerns over the new Bible versions.

There is no plot to undermine the word of God. These are very conservative scholars that are doing the work of textual criticism to help us have the most accurate translation of the Bible as possible. And lest anyone think, with all this talk of textual variants, that your Bible cannot be trusted heed these words of David Alan Black:

"No biblical doctrine would go unsupported if a favorite reading was abandoned in favor of a more valid variant…a doctrine that is affected by textual variation will always be adequately supported by other passages."[112]

Leake and Black miss the point. The strategy of Westcott and Hort was to make small changes so that the changes would be less noticeable but which, in the aggregate, would change doctrine. Leake's and David Alan Black's argument that no doctrine is undermined by a textual change in the new Bible versions is countered well by James H. Son.[113] His statement was mentioned earlier in this book but is worth repeating. James Son states the logic of the new Bible version defenders is like arguing that there is no harm in removing a stop sign from a busy street intersection because the other traffic signals in the city were left intact. Even though the sign only contained one word, that word is critically important to those who arrive at the intersection. So also is each word in the Holy Bible of critical importance to those reading it. God has made the point in the Holy Bible that **every word of God** is essential, not just some of the words. "[M]an shall not live by bread alone, but by **every word of God**." (Luke 4:4 AV) Disturbingly but unsurprisingly, the last clause, "but by **every word of God**," was deleted from the RV and almost all new Bible versions.

Deleting that clause from Luke 4:4 strips the passage of all spiritual guidance and enlightenment. Jesus's point was that man is given life by his word, but the new Bible versions remove that truth and instead are left only to learn that man needs more than bread to live, like water and meat. It is a different doctrine. It changes a truth about spiritual health into advice about physical health. It changes an article of faith, just as Westcott and Hort said their changes would do.

It seems that Hort accepted the Arian heresy that Jesus Christ was not the eternal God but rather was created by God. Under the Arian theology, Jesus did not always exist and, therefore, is not coeternal with God the Father. We see evidence of Hort's Arianism in his commentary on Revelation 3:14. That Bible passage states: "And unto the angel of the church of the Laodiceans write; These things saith the Amen, the faithful and true witness, the beginning of the creation of God." (Revelation 3:14 AV)

Hort interpreted the statement that the faithful witness, the Amen, Jesus Christ, being the beginning of the creation of God in Revelation 3:14 meant that God created Jesus. Hort states: **"The words might no doubt bear the Arian meaning 'the first thing created.'"**[114] Hort also held out the possibility that Jesus Christ was "antecedent" to all creation and cited Colossians 1:16 and 1:18 for that possibility. But, oddly, Hort used the word "antecedent" to creation. Antecedent simply means to come before something. It is not the same thing as existing in eternity before creation. There is a difference. The gospel is that Jesus is the eternal God and creator of all things. See Colossians 1:16-18. Jesus did not simply come before creation; he is the eternal creator of all things. But Hort puts Jesus only "antecedent" to creation.

Hort suggests that Jesus was not God, the creator, but simply a vehicle through "whom all creation came and comes to pass." Hort has Jesus being something less than fully God. Hort seemed to lean toward the view that the passage in Revelation 3:14 "might no doubt" mean that Jesus was created by God the Father and is, thus, not the eternal Lord God Almighty presented in the inspired scriptures.

The Arian heresy is premised on the misinterpretation of what scripture means when it says that Jesus Christ is "the only begotten Son of God." See John 3:18. Arius, the namesake for Arianism, called God the Father, unbegotten, but Jesus Christ is God's begotten Son.[115] Arius said that the Son was begotten before the world was created. But because he emanated from God the Father, he is not eternal nor coeternal with God the Father.[116]

What Arius got wrong is that he did not understand the point at which Jesus Christ was begotten. Jesus was begotten by God at his resurrection in fulfilment of the prophecy in Psalm 2:7.

> But God raised him from the dead: And he was seen many days of them which came up with him from Galilee to Jerusalem, who are his witnesses unto the people. And we declare unto you glad tidings, how that the promise which was made unto the fathers, **God hath fulfilled the same unto us their children, in that he hath raised up Jesus again**; as it is also written in the second psalm, Thou art my Son, **this day have I begotten thee**. (Acts 13:30-33 KJV)

The importance of that truth is that believers will, in like manner, be resurrected to eternal life as adopted sons of God.

> For if we have been planted together in the likeness of his death, we shall be also in the likeness of his resurrection:" (Romans 6:5 KJV)

The changes made by Westcott and Hort that undermine the eternal character of Jesus Christ are doctrinal. They go to the heart of the gospel. The Lord Jesus Christ is God. Jesus Christ and the Father are one. John 10:30. "For there is one God, and one mediator between God and men, the man Christ Jesus." 1 Timothy 2:5. Indeed, when Jesus was on Earth, he was in heaven simultaneously. "And no man hath ascended up to heaven, but he that came down from heaven, **even the Son of man which is in heaven.**" (John 3:13 AV) God the Father is in heaven. Matthew 23:9. That verse testifies to Jesus Christ being the imnipresent God Almighty. But the Arians could not allow that pasage to remain, and so they removed it from the Greek text. Consequently, the modern Bible versions contain John 3:13 without any indication of the omnipresence of Jesus Christ.

AV	**NIV**
And no man hath ascended up to heaven, but he that came down from heaven, even the Son of man **which is in heaven.** (John 3:13 AV)	No one has ever gone into heaven except the one who came from heaven—the Son of Man. (John 3:13 NIV)

Brooke Foss Westcott's claim that he changed Bible passages (e.g., Luke 23:42) to emphasize Jesus Christ's humanity is a cover for his true motive to undermine the deity of Jesus Christ in accordance with the Arian heresy. Jesus Christ is the eternal God Almighty who came to Earth in the flesh. The gospel of Mark reveals that Jesus is Jehovah, the LORD of hosts. Mark 1:1-3 states:

> The beginning of the gospel of Jesus Christ, the Son of God; As it is written in the prophets, Behold, I send my messenger before thy face, which shall prepare thy way before **thee**. The voice of one crying in the wilderness, Prepare ye the way of **the Lord**, make his paths straight. (Mark 1:1-3 AV)

That passage contains two quotes from two different prophets, Malachi and Isaiah. The first quote is from Malachi 3:1. That passage in Malachi states:

> Behold, I will send my messenger, and he shall prepare the way before **me**: and the Lord, whom ye seek, shall suddenly come to his temple, even the messenger of the covenant, whom ye delight in: behold, he shall come, saith **the LORD of hosts**. (Malachi 3:1 AV)

Notice that Jehovah is speaking in Malachi, and he is prophesying his coming. Jehovah, in Malachi 3:1, prophesies about the messenger that would go before him. The LORD of hosts states that his messenger will prepare the way for him. We learn in Mark 1 that the prophesied messenger referenced in Malachi 3:1 is John the Baptist, who God said would go before "**me**," meaning the LORD of hosts. The word LORD in English is a translation of the Hebrew (Jehovah) in Malachi 3:1. But when the passage is quoted in Mark 1:1-3, the inspired word of God states that the messenger would go before "**thee**," which is second person singular objective pronoun; it is referring to Jesus Christ. But Malachi 3:1 uses the word "**me**," which is also a singular objective pronoun, but it relates to the speaker in first person, who is Jehovah, "the LORD of hosts." Thus, we see that Jesus is Jehovah.

This is confirmed by the passage in Mark 1:1-3 that follows the quote from Malachi 3:1 with a quote from Isaiah 40:3. The Isaiah prophesy is that the crier in the wilderness calls on the people to prepare the way of the LORD. The word LORD in Isaiah 40:3 is, once again, a Hebrew word (Jehovah) translated as the LORD in English. But we know that the prophecy in Isaiah 40:3

is being fulfilled by John the Baptist and refers to him preparing the way for the Lord Jesus Christ.

> The voice of him that crieth in the wilderness, Prepare ye the way of the LORD, make straight in the desert a highway for our God. (Isaiah 40:3 AV)

Thus, the passage in Mark 1:1-3 establishes that the Lord for whom the way was to be made straight is the same LORD prophesied in Isaiah 40:3. That LORD in Isaiah 40:3 is Jehovah, which means that the Lord in Mark 1:1-3 is also Jehovah. Mark 1:1-3 describes the coming of the Lord Jesus Christ. Thus, Jesus Christ is Jehovah, the LORD of hosts, who came in the flesh.

When Jesus said in John 14:9, "he that hath seen me hath seen the Father," he meant that literally. Jesus explained in no uncertain terms that "I and my Father are one." John 10:30. Jesus identified himself as God almighty. God told Moses he is the eternal "I AM." Exodus 3:14. Jesus also identified himself as the eternal "I AM." "Jesus said unto them, Verily, verily, I say unto you, Before Abraham was, **I am**." John 8:58.

Jesus and Jehovah are one. That is because if Jehovah is God and Jesus is God, then they must necessarily be one. "And the LORD shall be king over all the earth: in that day shall there be one LORD, and his name **one**." (Zechariah 14:9 AV) We read in 1 John 5:7 that "there are three that bear record in heaven, the Father, the Word, and the Holy Ghost: and these three are **one**." In Deuteronomy, we learn that God is one. "Hear, O Israel: **The LORD our God is one LORD**: And thou shalt love the LORD thy God with all thine heart, and with all thy soul, and with all thy might." (Deuteronomy 6:4-5 AV) Jesus reinforced that truth by quoting the Deuteronomy passage in Mark:

> And one of the scribes came, and having heard them reasoning together, and perceiving that he had

answered them well, asked him, Which is the first commandment of all? And Jesus answered him, The first of all the commandments is, Hear, O Israel; **The Lord our God is one Lord**: And thou shalt love the Lord thy God with all thy heart, and with all thy soul, and with all thy mind, and with all thy strength: this is the first commandment. (Mark 12:28-30 AV)

JEHOVAH is God; that is his name (Exodus 6:3, Pslams 83:18); he is our salvation. "Behold, God is my salvation; I will trust, and not be afraid: for the LORD JEHOVAH is my strength and my song; he also is become my salvation." (Isaiah 12:2 AV) We read in Luke how Jesus was born Christ the Lord to save his elect from their sins. "For unto you is born this day in the city of David a Saviour, which is Christ the Lord." (Luke 2:11 AV) It was necessary that God save us from our sins because, as God explains, only he can be our savior. "I, even I, am the LORD; and beside me there is no saviour." Isaiah 43:11. The word LORD in Isaiah 43:11 is a Hebrew word (Jehovah) translated as the LORD in English. That means that only Jehovah can be the savior; there can be no other. Thus, Jesus Christ must necessarily be Jehovah. Indeed, God the Father makes it clear that his Son, Jesus, our savior, is God. "But unto the **Son** he saith, Thy throne, **O God**, is for ever and ever: a sceptre of righteousness *is* the sceptre of thy kingdom." (Hebrews 1:8) The birth of Jesus Christ fulfilled the prophecies in Isaiah 9:6 and Micah 5:2, explaining that the everlasting Lord God Almighty would be the savior born in Bethlehem. God was born as a child to save his elect from their sins. Matthew 1:21. That child was Jesus Christ, God manifest in the flesh. *See* 1 Timothy 3:16. God the Father gets the glory when every knee should bow and every tongue should confess that Jesus Christ is Lord because Jesus Christ and God the Father are one Lord.

That at the name of Jesus every knee should bow,
of things in heaven, and things in earth, and things

> under the earth; And that every tongue should confess that Jesus Christ is Lord, to the glory of God the Father. (Philippians 2:10-11 AV)

God is one Lord. Deuteronomy 6:4-5. That means that the child savior born at Bethlehem was the one Lord God Almighty. Jesus Christ is one with the Godhead. *See* 1 John 5:7-8. "For in him dwelleth all the fulness of the Godhead bodily." (Colossians 2:9 AV). That is how Jesus Christ was both on Earth and in heaven simultaneously. *See* John 3:13. Thus, Christ (The Prince of Peace, John 14:27), the Holy Spirit (Wonderful Counsellor, John 14:16-18), and God the Father (the everlasting Father, John 14:9-10) all dwell in Jesus Christ because God is one Lord.

> For unto us a child is born, unto us a son is given: and the government shall be upon his shoulder: **and his name shall be called Wonderful, Counsellor, The mighty God, The everlasting Father, The Prince of Peace.** (Isaiah 9:6 AV)

God left heaven and came to Earth as a man to give himself as a sacrifice to atone for our sins so that his elect could inherit eternal life. That is the heart of the gospel. "Who was delivered for our offences, and was raised again for our justification." Romans 4:25. As Paul said to Timothy:

> And without controversy great is the mystery of godliness: **God was manifest in the flesh**, justified in the Spirit, seen of angels, preached unto the Gentiles, believed on in the world, received up into glory. 1 Timothy 3:16.

Defenders of the modern Bible versions claim that the essential doctrines of the Christian faith are expressed in the new Bible versions, even though they have been deleted in a particular passage. Dr. James White, for example, claims that no textual variant in any modern Bible version in any way, shape, or form materially disrupts or destroys any essential doctrine of the Christian faith.[117] The promoters of the modern Bibles claim a deleted doctrine in the new Bibles can still be found in other Bible passages. That is not true. And John 3:13 reveals the lie. John 3:13 is the only passage in the Holy Bible that explains the omnipresence of Jesus Christ. Deleting that truth, as do the modern Bible versions, deletes that truth from the gospel.

If Jesus is not God then we have no savior. The Holy Bible tells us that only the Lord God can be our savior. **"I, even I, am the LORD; and beside me there is no saviour."** Isaiah 43:11. The new Bible versions that undermine the deity of Jesus Christ undermine the gospel of salvation by his atoning blood through God's grace by the faith of Jesus Christ. Only the Lord can be our savior. If Jesus is not the Lord, we have no savior.

We find the Arian philosophy in subtle ways in the new Bible versions that spring from the Westcott and Hort Greek text. We read in Micah 5:2 about the prophecy of Christ, the eternal God, being born in Bethlehem. Christ is described as being "from everlasting." The definition of everlasting is: "Eternity; eternal duration, past and future. From everlasting to everlasting thou art God. Psalms 90:2."[118] Everlasting means having no beginning and no end.

But the passage in Micah 5:2 that describes Christ in the new Bible versions changes the description of Christ being "from everlasting" to being only "from ancient times." The new Bible versions support the Arian heresy. This is a subtle change, but it is a proof text that identifies Jesus Christ as the eternal Lord God Almighty, born in Bethelem. The new Bible versions render Jesus Christ as only being around a long time, implying that he had a beginning and thus is not the eternal God.

AV	NIV
But thou, Bethlehem Ephratah, though thou be little among the thousands of Judah, yet out of thee shall he come forth unto me that is to be ruler in Israel; **whose goings forth have been from of old, from everlasting**. (Micah 5:2 AV)	But you, Bethlehem Ephrathah, though you are small among the clans of Judah, out of you will come for me one who will be ruler over Israel, **whose origins are from of old, from ancient times**. (Micah 5:2 NIV)

Another example of the removal of language that identifies Jesus Christ as the eternal God Almighty is found in the modern Bible versions of Revelation 1:11. Jesus Christ identifies himself as "Alpha and Omega, the first and the last." But the modern Bibles founded on Westcott and Hort's work remove that truth.

AV	NLT
I was in the Spirit on the Lord's day, and heard behind me a great voice, as of a trumpet, Saying, **I am Alpha and Omega, the first and the last**: and, What thou seest, write in a book, and send it unto the seven churches which are in Asia; unto Ephesus, and unto Smyrna, and unto Pergamos, and unto Thyatira, and unto Sardis, and unto Philadelphia, and unto Laodicea. (Revelation 1:10-11 AV)	It was the Lord's Day, and I was worshiping in the Spirit. Suddenly, I heard behind me a loud voice like a trumpet blast. It said, "Write in a book everything you see, and send it to the seven churches in the cities of Ephesus, Smyrna, Pergamum, Thyatira, Sardis, Philadelphia, and Laodicea." (Revelation 1:10-11 NLT)

There is a reason that the identification of Jesus as the Alpha and Omega is missing from Revelation 1:11. That is because Hort considered the reference to the Alpha and Omega in the preceding passages at John 1:4 and 1:8 to be a reference to God the Father to the exclusion of Jesus Christ.

Hort's view that Alpha and Omega in Revelation 1:4 and 1:8 could not reference Jesus Christ proves that Hort did not believe that Jesus Christ is God Almighty. As discussed in the chapter in this book titled *Revelation 16:5*, the statement that "I am Alpha and Omega, the beginning and the ending, saith the Lord, which is, and which was, and which is to come, the Almighty" in Revelation 1:8 identifies Jesus Christ as Jehovah. Jesus Christ and God the Father are one.

But Hort does not believe in the deity of Jesus Christ as

revealed in the gospel.[119] And so he analyzes Revelation 1:8 to preclude it from referring to Jesus Christ. That means the clear reference to the Alpha and Omega in Revelation 1:11 had to go. That dirty work was done by the Alexandrian Greek text forgers, which Westcott and Hort pressed into action. And so the Revised Version New Testament committee, under the influence of Westcott and Hort, followed the corrupt Alexandrian text and deleted the reference to Alpha and Omega in Revelation 1:11. In the following quote, please note that Hort is analyzing the Greek from the corrupt Alexandrian text of Revelation 1:8. Hort stated:

> This verse [Revelation 1:8] must stand alone. The speaker cannot be our Lord, when we consider Apoc. 1:4, which makes *oJ w]n* & c. distinctive of the Father; and all Scriptural analogy is against the attribution of *Kuvrio" oJ qeov"* [Lord God] with or without *pantokravtwr*, [the Almighty] G4120, to Christ. The verse is thus the utterance of the great fundamental voice of the Supreme God, preceding all separate revelations concerning or through His Son.[120]

Hort is revealing why the modern translations use the title "Lord God" instead of "Lord" in Revelation 1:8. It is a contrivance based on a corrupt theology that "Lord God" can only refer to God the Father to the exclusion of the Lord Jesus Christ. But when read in context, it is clear that Revelation 1:4 and Revelation 1:8 reference the Lord Jesus Christ. But the insertion of "Lord God" in Revelation 1:8 reveals Westcott and Hort's agenda is to undermine the deity of Jesus Christ by claiming that the Alpha and Omega is a reference to God the Father only and not at all to the Lord Jesus Christ.

This seemingly innocuous change from "Lord" to "Lord God" in Revelations 1:8 would go unnoticed as a doctrinal change when seen in isolation. But the stratagem becomes apparent when combined with the deletion of 1 John 5:7, Alpha and Omega in Revelation 1:11, and the many other changes. Hort let the cat out of the bag when he explained his erroneous view that Alpha and Omega in Revelation 1:4 and 1:8 do not refer to the Lord Jesus Christ. Thus, the change in Revelation 1:8 from "Lord" to "Lord God" is given new meaning. It is part of the scheme. All of these small changes have a purpose. They are being done to obscure the deity of the Lord Jesus Christ.

AV	RV
Behold, he cometh with clouds; and every eye shall see him, and **they also which pierced him**: and all kindreds of the earth shall wail because of him. Even so, Amen. I am Alpha and Omega, the beginning and the ending, saith **the Lord**, which is, and which was, and which is to come, the Almighty. (Revelation 1:7-8 AV)	Behold, he cometh with clouds; and every eye shall see him, and **they which pierced him**; and all the tribes of the earth shall mourn over him. Even so, Amen. I am the Alpha and the Omega, saith **the Lord God**, which is and which was and which is to come, the Almighty. (Revelation 1:7-8 RV)

But as we see in Revelation 11:17, the reference to the Lord God Almighty includes the descriptor "which art, and wast, and art to come." That is a parallel passage referring back to Jesus Christ in Revelation 1:4 and 1:8. Westcott and Hort knew that is a descriptor of Jehovah. They could not have the revelation that Jesus Christ is Jehovah known. That would mean that Jesus Christ is the eternal Lord God Almighty. Westcott and Hort did not believe Jesus Christ is Jehovah, Lord God Almighty. In Revelation 11:17, Jesus Christ is titled "Lord God Almighty." But the artifice that Westcott and Hort have created excludes Jesus Christ from the title "Lord God Almighty." They needed to include "Lord God" in Revelation 1:8 and say that only refers to God the Father to the exclusion of Jesus Christ. That completes their theological scheme of stripping Jesus Christ of his deity in the Godhead.

> Saying, We give thee thanks, O **Lord God Almighty**, which art, and wast, and art to come; because thou hast taken to thee thy great power, and hast reigned. (Revelation 11:17 AV)

Westcott and Hort had a strange concept of the Godhead. They largely strip Jesus Christ of his place in the Godhead, which explains their removal of 1 John 5:7 in the RV. That is a practice followed by most of the modern Bible versions. Westcott diminishes the divinity of Jesus Christ by claiming that Jesus only had the "substance" of God but was not actually God in "person." That concept was brought into the Revised Version. Westcott explains:

> The passages which have been just quoted throw light upon the doctrine of the Lord's true Divinity (comp. Heb. i. 3, **the very image of his substance, not person as in Authorised Version)**. At the same time His true humanity stands out with fresh distinctness in the Revised Version.[121]

The Revised Version (RV) rendered the change so that Jesus Christ is no longer the image of God's person but is instead the image of some nebulous concept called substance, whatever that means. Westcott wanted to make Jesus's humanity stand out by diminishing his deity. The Revised Version of Hebrews 1:3 does not mean that Jesus is God Almighty, a "person" in the Godhead. Instead, the RV has Jesus with some kind of godly substance. That is not the gospel.

AV	RV
Who being the brightness of his glory, and the express image of his **person**, and upholding all things by the word of his power, when he had by himself purged our sins, sat down on the right hand of the Majesty on high. (Hebrews 1:3 AV)	[W]ho being the effulgence of his glory, and the very image of his **substance**, and upholding all things by the word of his power, when he had made purification of sins, sat down on the right hand of the Majesty on high. (Hebrews 1:3 RV)

It seems that Hort did not think very much about God's creation account in the Bible. On March 10, 1860, Hort wrote to Westcott that he believed in the theory of evolution as espoused by Charles Darwin. Indeed, he called Darwin's theory "unanswerable."

> Have you read Darwin? How I should like to talk with you about it! In spite of difficulties, I am inclined to think it unanswerable. In any case it is a treat to read such a book.[122]

Hort followed the letter to Westcott with an April 3, 1860, letter to John Fullerton, wherein he reiterated his agreement with Darwin and again expressed his strong feeling that Darwin's theory of evolution was "unanswerable."

> But the book which has most engaged me is Darwin. Whatever may be thought of it, it is a book that one is proud to be contemporary with. I must work out and examine the argument more in detail, but at present my feeling is strong that the theory is unanswerable. If so, it opens up a new period in—I know not what not.[123]

We find that Hort used his influence on the RV committee to transform a creation Bible passage to comport with the theory of evolution. The RV changed God's word in 1 Corinthians 15:45 from saying that Adam "**was made** a living soul" to say that Adam "**became** a living soul." The theory of evolution is not only contrary to God's word. But that is the point of the RV; it was an assault on God's word, as indeed are all modern Bible versions. That evolutionary convention has been followed in all of the new Bible versions.

AV	RV
And so it is written, The first man Adam **was made a living soul**. (1 Corinthians 15:45 AV)	So also it is written, The first man Adam **became a living soul**." (1 Corinthians 15:45 RV)

Westcott and Hort's mischief lives on in the modern Bible versions. Another example of Satan's twisting of God's word is found in Luke in the new versions of the Bible. In the Authorized Version, Mary's and Joseph's relationship to Jesus is described as "Joseph and his mother." Whereas, in the NIV, and virtually every other new version of the bible, Mary's and Joseph's relationship to Jesus is described as "the child's father and mother." We know that Joseph was not Jesus' father, because Mary, when she was still a virgin, conceived Jesus by the Holy Spirit. **God is Jesus' Father. Jesus is the Son of God, not the son of Joseph.** ". . . [T]hat holy thing which shall be of thee shall be called the **Son of God**." Luke 1:35.

AV	NIV
And **Joseph and his mother** marvelled at those things which were spoken of him. (Luke 2:33 AV)	The **child's father and mother** marvelled at what was said about him. (Luke 2:33 NIV)

Throughout the corrupted bible versions, passages that prove the deity of Jesus are removed or changed. The NIV and the other new bible versions delete the word "God" from 1 Timothy 3:16, using the pronoun "He" in its place. 1 Timothy 3:16 clearly reveals that Jesus is God. The new bible versions, however, remove the revelation that Jesus is God from that passage.

AV	NIV
And without controversy great is the mystery of godliness: **God** was manifest in the flesh, justified in the Spirit, seen of angels, preached unto the Gentiles, believed on in the world, received up into glory. (1 Timothy 3:16 AV)	Beyond all question, the mystery of godliness is great: **He** appeared in a body, was vindicated by the Spirit, was seen by angels, was preached among the nations, was believed on in the world, was taken up in glory. (1 Timothy 3:16 NIV)

This notable change reveals the new Bible versions as antichrist Bibles. One of the signs of the antichrist is to "confess not" that Jesus Christ has come in the flesh.

In Isaiah 9:6 we learn that the Christ would be "called Wonderful, Counsellor, **The mighty God**, The everlasting Father, The Prince of Peace." The coming Christ would be God born as a child in the flesh. That means that Christ is God.

When the new Bible versions remove the word "God" from 1 Timothy 3:16, which explains God "was manifest in the flesh," it eliminates the confession that Jesus is God, the Christ, who came in the flesh. The new Bible versions "confess not that Jesus Christ is come in the flesh."

For many deceivers are entered into the world, who confess not that Jesus Christ is come in the flesh. This is a deceiver and an antichrist. 1 John 1:7.

In Ephesians 3:9 the Holy Bible identifies Jesus as the Creator of the universe. However, the NIV removes the reference to Jesus.

AV	NIV
And to make all *men* see what *is* the fellowship of the mystery, which from the beginning of the world hath been hid in God, who created all things **by Jesus Christ**. (Ephesians 3:9 AV)	[A]nd to make plain to everyone the administration of this mystery, which for ages past was kept hidden in God, who created all things. (Ephesians 3:9 NIV)

Even where the new versions do not delete words they change the word order to obscure the clear message. For example in the following passage from 2 Corinthians 5:19 the NIV obscures the message that "God was in Christ"

AV	NIV
God was in Christ, reconciling the world unto himself, not imputing their trespasses unto them; and hath committed unto us the word of reconciliation. (2 Corinthians 5:19 AV)	**God was reconciling the world to himself in Christ**, not counting men's sins against them. And has committed to us the message of reconciliation. (2 Corinthians 5:19 NIV)

Another example of the new versions' attacks on the deity of Jesus is found in the RSV passage in Isaiah 7:14. In the AV

Holy Bible there is a prophecy that God would be miraculously born of a virgin and that he would be called Immanuel (which means God with us). *See* Matthew 1:23. On the translation committee for the RSV was a Jewish scholar (so called), H.M. Orlinsky of the Jewish Institute of New York, who did not believe in the deity of Jesus.[124] It is no wonder that in the RSV the Isaiah passage is changed to having Immanuel born not of a virgin but of a "young woman."

The RSV has mistranslated that passage. The passage explains that the Lord himself shall give us a "sign." It is a sign from God if a "virgin" conceives and bears a son, but it is not a sign if a "young woman" conceives and bears a son. Young woman give birth all the time. It is a common occurrence. Millions upon millions of young women have given birth over the thousands of years since that prophecy. The RSV mistranslation of Isaiah 7:14 is an attack upon the "sign" of the miraculous virgin birth of our Lord God Jesus Christ.

AV	RSV
Therefore the Lord himself shall give you a sign; Behold, a **virgin** shall conceive, and bear a son, and shall call his name Immanuel. (Isaiah 7:14 AV)	Therefore the Lord himself will give you a sign. Behold, a **young woman** shall conceive and bear a son, and shall call his name Immanuel. (Isaiah 7:14 RSV)

Irenaeus, who died in 202 A.D., identified the Jews as the inventors of the Gnostic philosophy that threatened to spin the early church into apostasy. They were the progenitors of what Arius would, 100 years later, popularize as the Arian heresy that Jesus is only a creation of God and is not the eternal God who always was, is, and ever shall be.

Arising among these men, Saturninus (who was of that Antioch which is near Daphne) and Basilides laid hold of some favourable opportunities, and promulgated different systems of doctrine—the one in Syria, the other at Alexandria. . . . These men, moreover, practise magic; and use images, incantations, invocations, and every other kind of curious art. . . . **They declare that they are no longer Jews, and that they are not yet Christians**; and that it is not at all fitting to speak openly of their mysteries, but right to keep them secret by preserving silence.[125]

Irenaeus wrote extensively against the Judaizers who sought to undermine the deity of Jesus. These Judaizers crept into the church, trying to inject one heresy or another. He explains in one of his writings how two Jewish proselytes, Theodotion of Ephesus and Aquila of Pontus, tried to undermine the prophecy regarding the virgin birth of Jesus by changing the passage in Isaiah 7:14.[126] That passage in Isaiah states: "Therefore the Lord himself shall give you a sign; Behold, a **virgin** shall conceive, and bear a son, and shall call his name Immanuel." *Id.* Theodotion and Pontus corrupted the passage to read "Behold, a **young woman** shall conceive, and bring forth a son." This Jewish corruption had never before been manifested in scripture until after the fulfillment of the prophecy in Isaiah by the birth of Jesus Christ was memorialized in the New Testament.

Irenaeus quite properly points out that the change in Isaiah from "virgin" to "young woman" makes no sense. The prophecy in Isaiah is supposed to be a sign from God of the birth of Christ. Matthew explains that Immanuel means God with us. "Behold, a virgin shall be with child, and shall bring forth a son, and they shall call his name **Emmanuel, which being interpreted is, God with us.**" (Matthew 1:23 AV) If the passage states that the sign is to be that a "young woman" is to conceive, it loses all meaning since that is not a "sign," since young women conceive regularly. The sign must be something unusual in order for it to be a sign, the virgin birth of Jesus was that sign as prophesied by Isaiah.

The virgin birth of Christ is fundamental to Christianity. If Jesus was merely a man, born of natural processes, then his death on the cross could not atone for the sins of others. He could not be the perfect unblemished sacrifice. Hence, Jesus could not be the savior. Only the LORD can be the savior. "I, even I, am the LORD; and **beside me there is no saviour**." Isaiah 43:11, Jesus Christ is Lord and savior.

Jews today argue that the correct rendering of the Hebrew word in the passage should be "young woman" instead of "virgin."[127] They are wrong, the Hebrew word is "*alma*" and it means "virgin." The argument of the Jews makes no sense. Since Jews reject Jesus as the Messiah, they are still looking forward to the birth of the Messiah. How can they tell who that Messiah is, since it is not a sign to be born of a "young woman?" The passage specifically states that "the Lord himself shall give you a sign." The virgin birth is the sign that the child born of the virgin is the Messiah. It is very simple. If there is no virgin birth, there is no sign, if there is no sign, there is no Messiah.

The Jews have painted themselves into a corner; if they maintain their position that the prophecy in Isaiah means that a young woman will give birth, then they have lost the sign for the coming of the Messiah. Why would they do that? Because their position is really an attack on Christianity. They cannot have Christ being born of a virgin. Rather than argue whether Jesus was born of a virgin, they change the passage of the prophecy of the virgin birth, thus making the virgin birth irrelevant. If there is a prophecy of a virgin birth and the New Testament records a virgin birth, that means Jesus is the Messiah. They cannot change the account in the New Testament, so they do the next best thing, they remove the prophecy of a virgin birth from the Old Testament.

Crypto-Jews and their Catholic fellow travelers are still pushing this corruption of the bible today. There are corrupt bible versions that maintain this gnostic fiction and corrupt Isaiah 7:14 to remove the virgin birth: Revised Standard Version (RSV), New Revised Standard Version (NRSV), New World Translation (NWT), Jerusalem Bible (JB), New Jerusalem Bible (NJB).

17 The Only Begotten of the Father

This author was with a group of Christians studying Ligonier's publication "The Word Made Flesh."[128] Ligonier is "a fellowship of teachers dedicated to making the deep truths of the Christian faith accessible to growing believers."[129] I was surprised to find a doctrinal error in footnote 1 on page 7. That footnote quotes John 1:14 from the English Standard Version (ESV) of the Bible. The footnote states, in pertinent part: "And the Word became flesh and dwelt among us, and we have seen his glory, glory as of the **only Son from the Father**, full of grace and truth." (emphasis added) That is contrary to the AV and doctrinally wrong.

AV	ESV
And the Word was made flesh, and dwelt among us, (and we beheld his glory, the glory as of **the only begotten of the Father,**) full of grace and truth. (John 1:14 AV)	And the Word became flesh and dwelt among us, and we have seen his glory, glory as of **the only Son from the Father**, full of grace and truth. (John 1:14 ESV)

Other new bible versions contain the same corruption:

The Word became flesh and made his dwelling among us. We have seen his glory, the glory of the **one and only Son**, who came from the Father, full of grace and truth. John 1:14 (NIV)

And the Word became flesh, and dwelt among us; and we saw His glory, glory as of **the only Son from the Father**, full of grace and truth. John 1:14 (NASB)

This author realized immediately that the ESV and the other new Bible versions are doctrinally wrong. Jesus is the "the only begotten of the Father." He is NOT God's only Son. All who are born again also become sons of God, although it is through adoption by the grace of God through faith in Jesus Christ.

Romans 8:14: For as many as are led by the Spirit of God, they are the **sons of God**.

Galatians 4:5: To redeem them that were under the law, that we might receive the **adoption of sons**.

Ephesians 1:5: Having predestinated us unto the **adoption of children** by Jesus Christ to himself, according to the good pleasure of his will.

The Authorized (King James) Version (KJV or AV) of the Holy Bible is correct in the rendering of **"only begotten of the Father"** in John 1:14.

The doctrinal truth that the new Bible versions get wrong is that Jesus was begotten by God when he raised him from the dead.

But God raised him from the dead: And he was seen many days of them which came up with him from Galilee to Jerusalem, who are his witnesses unto the people. And we declare unto you glad tidings, how that the promise which was made unto the fathers, **God hath fulfilled the same unto us their children, in that he hath raised up Jesus again**; as it is also written in the second psalm, Thou art my Son, **this day have I begotten thee**. (Acts 13:30-33 KJV)

The importance of that truth is that believers will, in like manner, be resurrected to eternal life as adopted sons of God.

For if we have been planted together in the likeness of his death, we shall be also in the likeness of his resurrection. (Romans 6:5 KJV)

The Ligonier publication states that all scriptures in the pamphlet are quoted from the ESV. The ESV repeatedly gets the doctrine of sonship wrong. Consequently, so does Ligonier. Footnote 2 on page 7 of the Ligonier publication, *The Word Made Flesh*, cites John 3:16 and 3:18. The ESV of those passages states that Jesus is the only Son of God. Jesus is the only begotten Son of God; He is not the only Son of God. The KJV has it rendered correctly.

KJV	ESV
For God so loved the world, that he gave his **only begotten Son**, that whosoever believeth in him should not perish, but have everlasting life. (John 3:16 KJV)	For God so loved the world, that he gave **his only Son**, that whoever believes in him should not perish but have eternal life. John 3:16 ESV

KJV	KJV
He that believeth on him is not condemned: but he that believeth not is condemned already, because he hath not believed in the name of the **only begotten Son of God**. (John 3:18 KJV)	Whoever believes in him is not condemned, but whoever does not believe is condemned already, because he has not believed in the name of the **only Son of God**. John 3:18 ESV.

The ESV corruption conceals the fulfillment of prophecy and God's sovereign election. We can see that in Hebrews 11:17.

KJV (AV)	ESV
By faith Abraham, when he was tried, offered up Isaac: and he that had received the promises offered up his **only begotten son**." (Hebrews 11:17 KJV)	By faith Abraham, when he was tested, offered up Isaac, and he who had received the promises was in the act of offering up **his only son**. Hebrews 11:17 ESV.

The ESV has it wrong. Isaac was not Abraham's only son; he was Abraham's second son. Ishmael was born to Sarah's maidservant, Hagar, 13 years prior to Isaac being born to Sarah. The King James Bible correctly explains that Isaac was Abraham's **only begotten son**. That shows the parallelism between Abraham's attempted sacrifice of Isaac with the crucifixion and resurrection of Christ. Isaac was the son of promise. He was miraculously begotten by the intervention of God in Abraham's and Sarah's old age. That parallelism is lost in confusing disinformation in the ESV, where Isaac is incorrectly identified as Abraham's "only son."

This author emailed Ligonier about the errors in the ESV that they use in their publication. A representative from "Ask Ligonier" justified the errors in the ESV by claiming in a January

4, 2023, email that the ESV's rendition of "only Son" in John 1:14 is the equivalent of the KJV "only begotten Son."

> Certainly we would warmly agree that Christ is the "only begotten Son" as well. I have no reason to consider the ESV translation decision here to indicate anything to the contrary. In other words, I do not view this suspiciously. But again, this might be a question best posed to the editors of the ESV.[130]

That statement from Ligonier was in response to this author's email sent on December 9, 2022, wherein I gave a detailed explanation of the clear doctrinal difference between the ESV "only Son" and the KJV "only begotten Son" in John 1:14. I explained to Ligonier how the passage in Acts 13:30-33 reveals how God raised Jesus from the dead and pronounced: "Thou art my Son, this day have I begotten thee." I explained how saying that Jesus is the "only Son of God" contradicts the promise of the adoption as sons of God explained in Ephesians 1:5: "Having predestinated us unto the adoption of children by Jesus Christ to himself, according to the good pleasure of his will." Believers are redeemed and become adopted sons of God. Galatians 4:5, Romans 8:14. Ligonier dismissed those truths and claimed that the word "begotten" adds no real meaning to John 1:14. Ligonier's position renders Acts 13:30-33 meaningless surplusage and undermines the promises in Ephesians 1:5, Galatians 4:5, and Romans 814.

I responded to Liginier's January 4, 2023, email by explaining that Jesus being "begotten" at his resurrection is key to the gospel. That is because Jesus "was delivered for our offences, and was raised again for our justification." (Romans 4:25 KJV) Believers take part in his resurrection. "For if we have been planted together in the likeness of his death, we shall be also in the likeness of his resurrection:" (Romans 6:5 KJV) Doing so, we become sons of God "For as many as are led by the Spirit of God, they are the sons of God." (Romans 8:14 KJV) The ESV's claim that Jesus is "the only Son of God" undermines those truths. The Ligonier representative replied in a January 5, 2023, email to the gospel truths I set forth in my email by shamefully sticking his head in the sand and dismissing the issue.

> With respect, I would point you back to my comments and the Ligonier resources. Particularly the part about not engaging in protracted debate about translation decisions. At this point I do not think there is anything constructive to add.[131]

On page 7 of the Ligonier pamphlet, it states: "We affirm that in the unity of the Godhead the eternally begotten Son is cosubstantial (homoousios), coequal, and eternal with the Father and the Holy Spirit." Ligonier provides citations for that statement in footnote 2. But, curiously, it does not cite the principal passage in the Bible at 1 John 5:7-8 that describes the Godhead of God the Father, God the Son, and God the Holy Spirit being one. Why did Ligonier not cite 1 John 5:7-8? The reason is that Ligonier uses the ESV, which eviscerates the Godhead from the Bible at 1 John 5:7-8.

KJV (AV)	ESV
For there are three that bear record **in heaven, the Father, the Word, and the Holy Ghost: and these three are one. And there are three that bear witness in earth,** the Spirit, and the water, and the blood: and these three agree in one. 1 John 5:7-8 KJV.	For there are three that testify: the Spirit and the water and the blood; and these three agree. 1 John 5:7-8 ESV.

That pathetic corruption by the ESV of scripture does not testify to the Godhead. Ligonier knows it, and that is why Ligonier did not cite or quote it. This author emailed Ligonier and asked why Ligonier did not cite 1 John 5:7-8 and raised the issue of the missing verses in the ESV of 1 John 5:7-8. The representative responded to those issues by stating: "I would simply and warmly mention that the fact that the passage you reference is not included does not mean we would disagree that this is certainly an appropriate passage in this context."[132] He then quoted from some Ligonier resources that, once again, did not cite or quote 1 John 5:7-8. His acknowledgment that 1 John 5:7-8 is an appropriate passage was unresponsive to my question as to why Ligonier did not cite or quote that passage. On January 5, 2023, I replied to Ligonier via email:

> I noted that Ligonier did not cite 1 John 5:7 when discussing the Godhead. You did not explain why. I pointed out that the ESV used by Ligonier corrupts that passage and removes the doctrine of the Godhead. I suggested that because the ESV version of 1 John 5:7 does not testify to the Godhead, and that was why Ligonier did not cite 1 John 5:7. You are silent in addressing that matter. Why?[133]

Ligonier again refused to address those issues and simply responded that it would not engage in a protracted debate about translation decisions.[134] In the first email this author sent on December 9, 2022, to Ligonier I sated:

> For more abominations found in the ESV read the ESV renderings of Matthew 12:47; Matthew 17:21; Matthew 18:11; and Matthew 23:14. You will look in vain for those passages in the ESV; they have been deleted by the ESV translators. I could find

similar deletions in Mark, Luke, John, Acts, and Romans, but that sampling from Matthew should be sufficient to make my point. Read Revelation 22:19 to understand what is at stake when you delete words from the Holy Scripture.

"And if any man shall take away from the words of the book of this prophecy, God shall take away his part out of the book of life, and out of the holy city, and from the things which are written in this book." (Revelation 22:19)[135]

That matter was never addressed. Ligonier just refused to disucuss anything about the corruptions in their chosen ESV. No matter how clear the error, how doctrinally erroneous, how corrupt, and how perverted a passage is in Ligonier's chosen Bible version, the ESV, it will not entertain or address the matter. It will continue to use and teach from a Bible with clear errors.

18 Flipping the Script

God condemns idolatry. When Paul tells the people gathered at Mars' Hill that their graven images prove that they are "too superstitious," the NIV, NASB, and NKJV scribes change the rebuke to a compliment; the same passage in the "new improved" versions reads that the people are "very religious." The new maltranslations support the idol worship practiced in the Roman Catholic Church.

God condemns idolatry. When Paul tells the people gathered at Mars' Hill that their graven images prove that they are "too superstitious," the NIV, NASB, and NKJV scribes change the rebuke to a compliment; the same passage in the "new improved" versions reads that the people are "very religious." The new maltranslations support the idol worship practiced in the Roman Catholic Church.

AV	**NKJV**
Then Paul stood in the midst of Mars' hill, and said, *Ye* men of Athens, I perceive that in all things ye are **too superstitious**. (Acts 17:22 AV)	Then Paul stood in the midst of the Areopagus and said, "Men of Athens, I perceive that in all things you are **very religious**. (Acts 17:22 NKJV)

The new Bible versions cannot be the word of God because they often say the very opposite of God's word found in the inspired text of the Authorized (King James) Version of the Bible. One must choose between the KJV (AV) or the new Bible versions. They cannot both be the word of God.

For example, in the KJV (AV), the ways of the wicked are always "grievous." Psalms 10:4-5. The devil cannot have that, so Psalms 10:4-5 in his new Bible versions state the ways of the wicked are always "prospering."

KJV	NKJV
The wicked, through the pride of his countenance, will not seek after God: God is not in all his thoughts. His ways are **always grievous**; thy judgments are far above out of his sight: as for all his enemies, he puffeth at them. (Psalms 10:4-5 AV)	The wicked in his proud countenance does not seek God; God is in none of his thoughts. His ways are **always prospering**; Your judgments are far above, out of his sight; As for all his enemies, he sneers at them. (Pslams 10:4-5 NKJV)

The wicked "were forgotten" in Ecclesiastes 8:10 of God's word in the KJV, but in the NIV Ecclesiastes 8:10 passage the wicked "receive praise."

AV	NIV
And so I saw the wicked buried, who had come and gone from the place of the holy, and **they were forgotten** in the city where they had so done: this is also vanity. (Ecclesiastes 8:10 AV)	Then too, I saw the wicked buried—those who used to come and go from the holy place and **receive praise** in the city where they did this. This too is meaningless. (Ecclesiastes 8:10 NIV)

The Zionist disciples of Satan were able to change their bibles to make Israel a "spreading vine" in the NIV and even a "luxuriant vine" in the NASB and ESV in Hosea 10:1. God, however, states that "Israel is an empty vine" in his KJV Holy Bible at Hosea 10:1.

AV	ESV
Israel is an empty vine, he bringeth forth fruit unto himself: according to the multitude of his fruit he hath increased the altars; according to the goodness of his land they have made goodly images. (Hosea 10:1 AV)	**Israel is a luxuriant vine** that yields its fruit. The more his fruit increased, the more altars he built; as his country improved, he improved his pillars. (Hosea 10:1 ESV)

God states that "the words of a talebearer are as wounds." Proverbs 26:22. However, the new Bible versions say just the opposite. For example, the NIV change agents contradict God by saying in Proverbs 26:22 that "the words of a gossip are like choice morsels."

AV	NIV
The words of a talebearer are as **wounds**, and they go down into the innermost parts of the belly. (Proverbs 26:22 AV)	The words of a gossip are like **choice morsels**; they go down to the inmost parts. (Proverbs 26:22 NIV)

In Proverbs 25:23 God states that "the north wind driveth away rain." The NASB, however, states in Proverbs 25:23 that "the north wind brings rain."

AV	NASB
The north wind driveth away rain: so doth an angry countenance a backbiting tongue. (Proverbs 25:23 AV)	**The north wind brings rain,** And a gossiping tongue brings an angry face. (Proverbs 25:23 NASB)

We find similar language in the other modern Bible versions. The passage is scientific proof that the KJV is God's word and the modern Bibles are counterfeits. It is well established that the north wind is cold.[136] Cold air is dryer than warm air.[137] Thus, the cold, dry air from the north will drive away rain.

In absolute terms, cold air holds less moisture than warm air.[138] For example, assuming 100% relative humidity at a temperature of 30°C/86°F, the atmosphere can hold approximately 30g of water vapor per cubic meter (30g/m3). But if we lower the temperature to 0°C/32°F, the atmosphere can only hold approximately 5g of water vapor per cubic meter (5g/m3).[139] That means that colder air is dryer air. The north wind is colder air.

Thus, when the cold (and thus dry) wind blows out of the north it will drive away the rain from the warmer moister air that it displaces. That proves the King James Holy Bible is true and the modern Bibles are counterfeit lies. The passage in the NASB completely switches the cause and effect. Where God states in the KJV that an angry countenance drives away a backbiting tongue just as the north wind drives away rain, the NASB and the modern Bible versions switch it and say that the gossiping tongue brings an angry face the way the north wind brings rain. But, as we have seen, the north wind drives away rain. That truth exposes the new Bible versions as delusory counterfeits.

The NIV takes away the witness of God to the faith of Sara in Hebrews 11:11 and substitutes Abraham in her place.

AV	NIV
Through faith also Sara herself received strength to conceive seed, and was delivered of a child when she was past age, because **she judged him faithful who had promised**. (Hebrews 11:11 AV)	**By faith Abraham**, even though he was past age--and Sarah herself was barren--was enabled to become a father because **he considered him faithful who had made the promise**. (Hebrews 11:11 NIV)

We see that the NIV contradicts the AV on Hosea 11:12. They say the opposite. In the AV, Judah rules with God, but in the NIV, Judah is unruly against God. They cannot both be true. One is God's word and the other is not.

AV	NIV
Ephraim compasseth me about with lies, and the house of Israel with deceit: but **Judah yet ruleth with God, and is faithful with the saints.** (Hosea 11:12 AV)	Ephraim has surrounded me with lies, Israel with deceit. And **Judah is unruly against God, even against the faithful Holy One**. (Hosea 11:12 NIV)

In Genesis 27:39, Isaac gives his son, Essau, a blessing. But the New Living Translation (NLT) turns the blessing into a curse. Both passages cannot be Holy Scripture. One is genuine, and the other is a counterfeit. The context proves that the AV version is genuine because, in verse 37, Isaac asks Essau what he could do for him. In verse 38, Essau requests a blessing. And Isaac gave him the requested blessing in verse 39.

AV	NLT
And Isaac his father answered and said unto him, Behold, **thy dwelling shall be the fatness of the earth, and of the dew of heaven from above**. (Genesis 27:39 AV)	Finally, his father, Isaac, said to him, "**You will live away from the richness of the earth, and away from the dew of the heaven above.**" (Genesis 27:39 NLT)

19 Jesus Christ Is the Son of the Living God

That diabolical devil has left his unmistakable fingerprint on the new Bible versions. The devil used the "Holy One of God" to describe Jesus in Mark 1:24 and Luke 4:34. In those verses, a devil, who has possessed a man, cries out to Jesus to leave him alone and states: "I know thee who thou art, the **Holy One of God**." (Mark 1:24; Luke 4:34 AV) Jesus immediately rebuked the devil, telling him to "Hold thy peace, and come out of him." Mark 1:25; Luke 4:35. The devil then came out of the man. Notice that many other times, Jesus drove devils from people; in every other instant, the devils identified Jesus as the Son of God. See, e.g., Matthew 8:29 ("Jesus, thou son of God"); Mark 5:7 ("Jesus, thou son of the most high God"); Luke 8:28 ("Jesus, thou son of God most high"); See Luke 4:41 ("Christ the Son of God."). It is only in Mark 1:24 and Luke 4:34 that the devils identify Jesus as the "Holy One of God."

There are two definitive verses in the Holy Bible where the apostle Peter expressly identifies Jesus as the **"Christ, the Son of the living God."** One verse is found in Matthew 16:16, and the other verse is found in John 6:69. The new Bible versions change the language in John 6:69 from "Christ, the Son of the living God." to "Holy One of God." Not only does the change in that verse obscure the fact that Jesus is Christ, the Son of the living God, but it is also unmistakable evidence that the new Bible versions are the work of the devil. The actual authorship of the new Bible versions is exposed when we read the very words used by a devil to describe Jesus (Holy One of God) substituted in place of the revelation of who Jesus is (Christ, the Son of the Living God), which was given by his "Father which is in heaven." See Matthew 16:16. Almighty God told the devil to hold his peace when he first described Jesus as the "Holy One of God," yet the devil thinks nothing of disobeying God by having Peter in his new Bible versions say the very words God ordered him not to repeat.

AV	**NASB**
And we believe and are sure that thou art **that Christ, the Son of the living God**. (John 6:69 AV)	And we believe and have come to know that You are **the Holy one of God**. (John 6:69 NASB)

Jesus is described elsewhere in the Holy Bible as the "Holy One" (*See, e.g.*, Psalms 16:10; Acts 3:14), and the "Holy One of Israel" (*See, e.g.*, Isaiah 30:12; Jeremiah 50:29), but he is called "the Holy One of God" in only two Bible passages (Mark 1:24 and Luke 4:34) and both passages recount the words spoken by the devil. The devil certainly knows that Jesus is "Christ the Son of God." *See* Luke 4:41. Why then would the devil use the title "Holy one of God" to describe Jesus as recounted in Mark 1:24 and Luke 4:34 and then put that title in place of the title "Christ the Son of the living God" in John 6:69 in his new Bibles? Because the devil is the unclean spirit of antichrist, and his change of those passages in his new Bibles is an implicit denial that Jesus is the Christ. *See* 1 John 4:3. "Who is a liar but he that **denieth that Jesus is the Christ**? He is antichrist, that denieth the Father and the Son. Whosoever denieth the Son, the same hath not the Father: (but) he that acknowledgeth the Son hath the Father also." (1 John 2:22-23 AV) Just as the Catholic church has a different Jesus, they also have a different Peter than the Peter of the Holy Bible. By removing the revelation that Jesus is the Christ, the Catholic Peter in John 6:69 of the Catholic Bible versions is implicitly denying that Jesus is the Christ.

According to Catholic folklore, the Catholic Peter is purported to be the first pope of the Catholic church. The Catholic church claims that their Peter is the rock upon which the church is built and not Jesus. In another verse, Matthew 16:13-18, even in the new Bible versions, Peter states that Jesus is the Christ, the Son of the living God. Jesus explains that upon this rock ("the Christ, the Son of the living God") I will build my church. However, the Catholic authorities claim that the rock is their Peter not Jesus. Again, denying that Jesus is the rock is an implicit denial that Jesus is the Christ, hence signifying that the pope is the antichrist in fulfillment of the prophecy in 1 John 2:22-23.

The rock is God Almighty. By claiming that Peter is the rock and that they are the successors of Peter, they are claiming to be God Almighty. It sounds incredible, but read the official pronouncement from the pope: "**I have the authority of the King of kings. I am all in all and above all, so that God, Himself and I, The Vicar of God, have but one consistory, and I am able to do almost all that God can do. What therefore, *can* you make of me but God**." *The Bull Sanctum*, November 18, 1302 (emphasis added).[140]

Pope John Paul II calls Jesus the Holy One of God in his letter *Dominicae Cenae*: "There is a close link between this element of the Eucharist and its sacredness, that is to say, its being a holy and sacred action. Holy and sacred, because in it are the continual presence and action of Christ, **'the Holy One' of God**." LETTER *DOMINICAE CENAE* OF THE SUPREME PONTIFF JOHN PAUL II TO ALL THE BISHOPS OF THE CHURCH ON THE MYSTERY AND WORSHIP OF THE EUCHARIST. One of the passages that is footnoted for the term "holy one of God" in the letter *Dominicae Cenae* is John 6:69. The very passage that in God's word describes Jesus as the "Christ, the Son of the living God," the antichrist uses as authority for calling him "the Holy One of God." The Pope used the very words of the devil, which the devil is trying to insert in John 6:69 in his counterfeit Bibles. *See* Mark 1:24, Luke 4:35.

The antichrist doctrine that Peter is the rock upon which Christ would build his church is summarized in the 1994 Catechism of the Catholic Church, §§ 881-882, which contains the official doctrine of the Catholic Church. The Catholic claim is that the Pope, as the bishop of Rome, is Peter's successor as the vicar of Christ.[141] James Aitken Wylie explains the distinction between the true church of Christ and the false church of antichrist.

> That "Christ is the Son of God," is the corner-stone of the Gospel church. Out of that root the whole Gospel springs. It is the "rock" on which Christ, addressing Peter, said that He would build His Church. That the "Pope is the Vicar of Christ" is the corner-stone of the papal Church. Out of that root does the whole of popery spring. On that "rock" said Boniface III. in the seventh century, and Gregory VII., with yet greater emphasis in the eleventh, will I build my church.
>
> And let us further mark that both churches rest not on a *doctrine*, but on a *person*. The Church of God rests on a Person, even Christ. No one is saved by simply believing a system of truth. The truth is the light that shows the sinner his way to the Saviour. He is united to Christ by his faith which takes hold of the Saviour, and by the Spirit who comes to dwell in his heart. Thus is he a member of the Spiritual Body. The Bible, ministers, and ordinances are the channels through which the life

of the Head flows into the members of the body. Thus are they built up a spiritual house, a holy temple -"built on the foundation of prophets, and apostles, Jesus Christ Himself the chief cornerstone."[142]

There is only one head of the church. To claim to be the rock of the church is to implicitly deny that Jesus is the rock of the church. To deny that Jesus is the rock is to deny that Jesus is Christ. Denying that Jesus is the Christ is a doctrine specifically identified in 1 John 2:22-23 as a teaching of the antichrist.

> Who is a liar but he that denieth that Jesus is the Christ? He is antichrist, that denieth the Father and the Son. Whosoever denieth the Son, the same hath not the Father: (but) he that acknowledgeth the Son hath the Father also. (1 John 2:22-23)

The headship of the church is reserved for Christ alone. "[H]e is the head of the body, the church: who is the beginning, the firstborn from the dead; that in all things he might have the preeminence." (Colossians 1:18) Christ will not share his glory nor his authority nor his station with anyone, Christ has preeminence in all things. "For thou shalt worship no other god: for the LORD, whose name is Jealous, is a jealous God." (Exodus 34:14) The Old Testament prophecies of the coming Christ indicate that the cornerstone of the church is to be a heavenly stone that is cut out without hands, and the church will grow from this stone to become a large spiritual mountain and fill the earth. *See* Daniel 2:34-45. This prophesied rock is Christ. For a man to claim to be the rock of the church is to claim to be Christ, because the Bible makes clear that Christ is the rock, the head of the church. To falsely claim to be Christ, the head of the church, fulfills the prophecies that identify the antichrist.

> Let no man deceive you by any means: for that day

shall not come, except there come a falling away first, and that man of sin be revealed, the son of perdition; **Who opposeth and exalteth himself above all that is called God, or that is worshipped; so that he as God sitteth in the temple of God, shewing himself that he is God.** (2 Thessalonians 2:3-4)

And the king shall do according to his will; and **he shall exalt himself, and magnify himself above every god, and shall speak marvellous things against the God of gods**, and shall prosper till the indignation be accomplished: for that that is determined shall be done. Neither shall he regard the God of his fathers, nor the desire of women, nor regard any god: for **he shall magnify himself above all.** (Daniel 11:36-37)

In Matthew 16:16 Peter said that Jesus is the Christ, the Son of the living God. Jesus said that upon that rock he would build his church. That passage, which is often cited by the Catholic Church to support their claim that the pope rules God's church, is not supportive of Peter as the rock but rather as Christ being the rock. Jesus asks his disciples "whom say ye that I am?" When Peter answered that he is "the Christ, the Son of the living God." That answer reveals the rock upon which God would build his church, Jesus Christ, and not Peter. That is what Jesus was conveying when he said "upon **this** rock I will build my church."

By the pope saying that Peter is the rock, he is denying Jesus is the rock, the Christ, the Son of the living God. That papal denial of Christ is a fulfillment of the prophecy found in 1 John 2:22-23, which identifies the antichrist as one who will deny that Jesus is the Christ. The pope's claim, essentially, is that Peter is the rock and hence the Christ and that he, as Peter's purported successor, is also Christ. The Bible reveals that the pope is the antichrist!

> When Jesus came into the coasts of Caesarea Philippi, he asked his disciples, saying, **Whom do men say that I the Son of man am?** And they said, Some say that thou art John the Baptist: some, Elias; and others, Jeremias, or one of the prophets. He saith unto them, But **whom say ye that I am?** And Simon Peter answered and said, **Thou art the Christ, the Son of the living God**. And Jesus answered and said unto him, Blessed art thou, Simon Barjona: for flesh and blood hath not revealed it unto thee, but my Father which is in heaven. And I say also unto thee, That thou art Peter, and **upon this rock I will build my church**; and the gates of hell shall not prevail against it. (Matthew 16:13-18)

Christ is the head of the church, not Peter! *See* Ephesians 5:23; Colossians 1:18. If Peter is now the rock of God's church, why would Jesus call Peter Satan within moments of making Peter the foundation of the church? The following passage signifies that those who would have Peter as their rock, have someone who savourest the things of man and not of God.

> But he turned, and said unto Peter, **Get thee behind me, Satan**: thou art an offence unto me: for thou savourest not the things that be of God, but those that be of men. (Matthew 16:23)

The Holy Spirit further signified that the pope is antichrist by having Peter, as the Catholic Church's first purported pope, start his alleged reign by denying Christ 3 times in fulfillment of the prophecy in 1 John 2:22-23 that the antichrist (the alleged successors of Peter) "denieth the Father and the Son." *See* Matthew 26:31-75.

The rock of the Catholic Church is not God. Their rock is only a man trying to take God's place.

> **For their rock is not as our Rock**, even our enemies themselves being judges. For their vine is of the vine of Sodom, and of the fields of Gomorrah: their grapes are grapes of gall, their clusters are bitter: **Their wine is the poison of dragons, and the cruel venom of asps**. (Deuteronomy 32:31-33)

Peter, to whom Jesus was talking, clearly understood what Jesus was saying when he said "upon this rock I will build my church." The rock was Jesus. In the following passages Peter repeatedly refers to Jesus as the stone rejected by the builders becoming the head of the corner and the rock of offense. If Peter understood that he was the rock upon which God was to build his church he would have said so. Instead, Peter repeatedly referred to Jesus as the "stone," "corner stone," "stone of stumbling," and "rock of offense." Jesus is the only name under heaven that can save one from the eternal punishment of sin, not Peter and not the pope.

> Be it known unto you all, and to all the people of Israel, that by the name of **Jesus Christ of Nazareth**, whom ye crucified, whom God raised from the dead, even by him doth this man stand here before you whole. **This is the stone which was set at nought of you builders, which is become the head of the corner. Neither is there salvation in any other: for there is none other name under heaven given among men, whereby we must be saved.** (Acts 4:10-12)

> Wherefore also it is contained in the scripture, **Behold, I lay in Sion a chief corner stone**, elect,

precious: and he that believeth on him shall not be confounded. Unto you therefore which believe he is precious: but unto them which be disobedient, the stone which the builders disallowed, the same is made the head of the corner, And **a stone of stumbling, and a rock of offence, even to them which stumble at the word, being disobedient: whereunto also they were appointed**. (1 Peter 2:6-8)

Read through the following passages, and decide for yourself who is the Rock of the Church.

And did all drink the same spiritual drink: for they drank of that **spiritual Rock** that followed them: and **that Rock was Christ**. (1 Corinthians 10:4)

And are built upon the foundation of the apostles and prophets, **Jesus Christ himself being the chief corner stone**. (Ephesians 2:20)

For other foundation can no man lay than that is laid, which is Jesus Christ. (1 Corinthians 3:11)

My soul, wait thou only upon God; for my expectation is from him. **He only is my rock and my salvation**: he is my defence; I shall not be moved. (Psalms 62:5-6)

He is the Rock, his work is perfect: for all his ways are judgment: a God of truth and without iniquity, just and right is he. (Deuteronomy 32:4)

There is none holy as the LORD: for there is none beside thee: **neither is there any rock like our**

God. (1 Samuel 2:2)

And he said, **The LORD is my rock**, and my fortress, and my deliverer; The God of my rock; in him will I trust: he is my shield, and the horn of my salvation, my high tower, and my refuge, my saviour; thou savest me from violence. (2 Samuel 22:2-3)

The LORD is my rock, and my fortress, and my deliverer; my God, my strength, in whom I will trust; my buckler, and the horn of my salvation, and my high tower. (Psalms 18:2)

For who is God save the LORD? or **who is a rock save our God**? (Psalms 18:31)

Unto thee will I cry, **O LORD my rock**; be not silent to me: lest, if thou be silent to me, I become like them that go down into the pit. (Psalms 28:1)

Bow down thine ear to me; deliver me speedily: **be thou my strong rock**, for an house of defence to save me. For **thou art my rock** and my fortress; therefore for thy name's sake lead me, and guide me. (Psalms 31:2-3)

I will say unto **God my rock**, Why hast thou forgotten me? why go I mourning because of the oppression of the enemy? (Psalms 42:9)

From the end of the earth will I cry unto thee, when my heart is overwhelmed: **lead me to the rock that is higher than I**. (Psalms 61:2)

And they remembered that **God was their rock**,

and the high God their redeemer. (Psalms 78:35)

He shall cry unto me, **Thou art my father, my God, and the rock of my salvation**. (Psalms 89:26)

But the LORD is my defence; and **my God is the rock of my refuge**. (Psalms 94:22)

O come, let us sing unto the LORD: let us make a joyful noise to **the rock of our salvation**. (Psalms 95:1)

As it is written, Behold, **I lay in Sion a stumblingstone and rock of offence**: and whosoever believeth on him shall not be ashamed. (Romans 9:33)

He is like a man which built an house, and digged deep, and **laid the foundation on a rock**: and when the flood arose, the stream beat vehemently upon that house, and could not shake it: for it was founded upon a rock. (Luke 6:48)

Therefore whosoever heareth these sayings of mine, and doeth them, I will liken him unto a wise man, which **built his house upon a rock**. (Matthew 7:24)

The stone which the builders refused is become the head stone of the corner. (Psalms 118:22)

And he shall be for a sanctuary; but for **a stone of stumbling and for a rock of offence** to both the houses of Israel, for a gin and for a snare to the inhabitants of Jerusalem. (Isaiah 8:14)

Therefore thus saith the Lord GOD, Behold, **I lay in Zion for a foundation a stone, a tried stone, a precious corner stone, a sure foundation**: he that believeth shall not make haste. (Isaiah 28:16)

Jesus saith unto them, Did ye never read in the scriptures, **The stone which the builders rejected, the same is become the head of the corner**: this is the Lord's doing, and it is marvellous in our eyes? Therefore say I unto you, The kingdom of God shall be taken from you, and given to a nation bringing forth the fruits thereof. And whosoever shall fall on this stone shall be broken: but on whomsoever it shall fall, it will grind him to powder. (Matthew 21:42-44)

The evidence from the Holy Scripture is so clear that even Pope John Paul II has found it necessary to admit that Jesus is the Rock upon which God's Church is built.[143] That is just another of the many contradictory pronouncements of the Roman Catholic Church.

By claiming that Peter is the rock, the pope has denied that Jesus is the rock, which is essentially a denial that Jesus is the Christ. The pope has fulfilled the prophecy in 1 John 2:22-23, which states that the antichrist will deny that Jesus is the Christ. Who then does the pope claim is the Christ? The answer is found when we compare what the Holy Bible says about Christ with what the pope has said. What does it mean when we say that Jesus is Christ? It means that he is the one anointed "God with us." In Matthew 1:23, Jesus is identified as "Emmanuel, which being interpreted is, God with us." The pope, however, claims that he is God with us. **"[W]e hold upon this earth the place of God Almighty."** *Pope Leo XIII* (emphasis added).[144]

Jesus Christ is "an advocate with the Father" for us. 1 John

2:1. In fact, he is the "one mediator between God and men." 1 Timothy 2:5. The pope, however, claims the title of Supreme Pontiff. Pontiff means literally bridge builder; it connotes that the pontiff is one who is a bridge or intermediary between God and man. The pope has stated: "To be subject to the Roman Pontiff is to every human creature altogether necessary for salvation." *The Bull Unum Sanctum*, November 18, 1302. In addition, the Catholic Church teaches that Mary and the saints are advocates before the throne of God for us. "[The saints'] . . . intercession is their most exalted service to God's plan. **We can and should ask them to intercede for us and for the whole world**." *CATECHISM OF THE CATHOLIC CHURCH*, § 2683, 1994.

The pope advises people not to bother going to God for forgiveness of their sins. Pope John Paul II stated: "Don't go to God for forgiveness of sins, come to me."[145] The pope seems to be mounting a blasphemous (and futile) *coup d'etat* against God. He advises his penitents to follow him instead of God.

The pope claims the title of Supreme Pontiff, which means supreme bridge-builder (supreme mediator) between man and God. The subordinate priests are lesser pontiffs and also act as mediators. That priestly authority to mediate between man and God is based upon the Catholic doctrine that the Catholic priests claim to act in the place of the Lord Jesus.

> [T]he priest is constituted an interpreter and **mediator between God and man**, which indeed must be regarded as the principal function of the priesthood. *CATECHISM OF THE COUNCIL OF TRENT.*[146]

God says otherwise. There is only one God and only one mediator between God and man, that is Jesus Christ.

> For there is **one God, and one mediator** between

God and men, the man **Christ Jesus**; (1 Timothy 2:5)

Jesus Christ is the "author and finisher of our faith." Hebrew 12:2. "For by grace are ye saved through faith; and that not of yourselves: it is the gift of God: Not of works, lest any man should boast." (Ephesians 2:8-9) The pope, however, states that faith comes from man and it must be joined with works, i.e. started and finished by man, not Jesus. The Catholic Church even teaches that works done after death by others are effective for the salvation of the deceased.

> [T]he souls . . . are cleansed after death by purgatorial punishments; and so that they may be relieved from punishments of this kind, namely, the sacrifices of Masses, prayers, and almsgiving, and other works of piety, which are customarily performed by the faithful for other faithful according to the institutions of the Church. COUNCIL OF FLORENCE, 1439.[147]

Jesus Christ is the "blessed and only Potentate." 1 Timothy 6:15. Pope Innocent II, however, claimed ownership of the entire universe as the "TEMPORAL SOVEREIGN OF THE UNIVERSE."[148]

Even today the Pope wears a triple crown because he claims to rule as king over Heaven, Hell, and Earth. Jesus Christ is the "great high priest" of God almighty. Hebrews 4:14. The pope claims to be the great high priest. As already mentioned above, the pope claims the title of Supreme Pontiff. He is the successor of the emperors of Rome who were seriatim the Supreme Pontiff (*Pontifex Maximus*),[149] which was the high priest of the pagan religions of Rome.[150] Jesus is higher than the kings of the earth. Psalms 89:27. The pope claims, however, authority over the kings of the earth. "[T]he Roman pontiff possess **primacy over the**

whole world." *The Vatican Council*, Session IV, chapter III, July 18, 1870 (emphasis added). Jesus is "Lord of all." Acts 10:36. The pope, though, claims that all must submit to him: "The Roman Pontiff judges all man, but is judged by no one. We declare, assert, define and pronounce: to be subject to the Roman Pontiff is to every human creature altogether necessary for salvation." *The Bull Unum Sanctum*, November 18, 1302 (emphasis added).[151] The pope has claimed every attribute of Christ for himself. He has essentially denied that Jesus is the Christ and laid claim himself to being Christ. The Holy Bible identifies such a one as antichrist. 1 John 2:20-23.

The Bible says that the antichrist will deny the Son and implicitly deny the Father. 1 John 2:20-23. The pope makes his identity as the antichrist clear by expressly denying the Father. The pope claims the title "Holy Father." *See Catechism of the Catholic Church*, at § 10. Holy Father is a title that appears only once in all the Holy Scriptures and is reserved for God the Father. *See* John 17:11.

Cardinal Giuseppe Sarto, who later became Pope Pius X, wrote: "**The Pope represents Jesus Christ Himself and is therefore a loving Father.**"[152] (emphasis added) Notice how Cardinal Sarto capitalized the word "Father," thus signifying that the pope is considered equivalent to God the Father.

Indeed, since the papacy is founded upon a denial that Jesus is the Christ, it is not surprising to find their dogmatic writings sprinkled with such denials. For example, in 2002, the Vatican published a book by the Pontifical Biblical Commission titled *The Jewish People and Their Sacred Scriptures in the Christian Bible*, with a preface written by Joseph Cardinal Ratzinger (later to become Pope Benedict XVI). The preface by Ratzinger carries the date: "Rome, the feast of the Ascension 2001." The book states:

It may be asked whether Christians should be blamed for having monopolised the Jewish Bible and reading there what no Jew has found. Should not Christians henceforth read the Bible as Jews do, in order to show proper respect for its Jewish origins?

In answer to the last question, a negative response must be given for hermeneutical reasons. For to read the Bible as Judaism does necessarily involves an implicit acceptance of all its presuppositions, that is, the full acceptance of what Judaism is, in particular, the authority of its writings and rabbinic traditions, which **exclude faith in Jesus as Messiah and Son of God**.

As regards the first question, the situation is different, for **Christians can and ought to admit that the Jewish reading of the Bible is a possible one**.[153] (emphasis added)

The above passage is rather cryptic, which is typical of Vatican dogma. In witchcraft, there are often two meanings, which are contrary to one another, expressed in a single passage. That way, an esoteric message can be given to initiates, while concealing that hidden message behind the camouflaged language carrying the opposite meaning that can be used to deceive the uninitiated. That is the case with the above passage. When the text is parsed, it states on the one hand that Christians should not read the Bible as Jews do, because such a reading "exclude[s] faith in Jesus as Messiah and Son of God." On the other hand its states that "Christians can and ought to admit that the Jewish reading of the Bible is a possible one." That possible reading advised by the Vatican's Pontifical Biblical Commission "exclude[s] faith in Jesus as Messiah and Son of God."

The public exoteric meaning of the passage is that Christians should not read the Bible as Jews do, because such a reading "exclude[s] faith in Jesus as Messiah and Son of God." The other language in the passage conveys the esoteric meaning that informs their initiates of the true meaning. The true (but esoteric) meaning of the above passage is intended to appease the Jews, who have always read the Bible to "exclude faith in Jesus as Messiah and Son of God." The true meaning of the passage is that Christians can and ought to admit that a possible reading of the Bible "exclude[s] faith in Jesus as Messiah and Son of God." That instruction by the papacy is a denial that Jesus is the Christ, thus confirming that the papacy is the antichrist in fulfillment of John's prophecy in 1 John 2:22-23.

In addition, the Roman Pontiff could not possibly be a successor to Peter. The Roman church teaches that Peter was the bishop of Rome.[154] There is absolutely no credible evidence to support that claim. In fact it is doubtful that he was ever in Rome. Peter was the apostle to the Jews. *See* Galatians 2:9. Rome was a gentile city. He would have no reason to travel to Rome. Paul, who was an apostle to the gentiles (*see* Romans 11:13), greeted over 25 Christians living in Rome at the end of his letter to the Romans, but he did not greet Peter. *See* Romans 16. If Peter were the Bishop, Paul would certainly have greeted him. He did not greet Peter because Peter was not in Rome. The scriptures, once again, prove the fraud of the papacy; that explains why the Roman Catholic Church want to keep people ignorant of the Bible.

There are numerous other examples of Satan tampering with God's word and trying to pass it off as more accurate than the original. Satan's strategy from the beginning is to "taketh away the word that was sown in their hearts." Mark 4:15. In the NIV, the verse at Matthew 23:14 is missing; it is the verse that criticizes the scribes for making pretentious, long prayers as are made by the Catholic priests of today. "Woe unto you, scribes and Pharisees, hypocrites! for ye devour widows' houses, and for a pretence make long prayer: therefore ye shall receive the greater damnation." Matthew 23:14 AV. The scribes who removed that verse had an interest in removing a verse that promises that they would receive the greater damnation. Mathew 18:11 is deleted from the NIV, that verse states: "For the Son of man is come to save that which was lost." Acts 8:37 is also deleted from the NIV. "And Philip said, If thou believest with all thine heart, thou mayest. And he answered and said, I believe that Jesus Christ is the Son of God." Acts 8:37 AV. In the NIV verse 1 John 5:7, Satan completely removes the reference to the three persons of the Godhead. He tries to cover his tracks by taking part of verse 8 and labeling it verse 7, hoping nobody would notice the missing verse. Verse 7 should read as follows: "For there are three that bear record in heaven, the Father, the Word, and the Holy Ghost: and these three are one." (1 John 5:7 AV) The following verses have been completely removed from the NIV: Matthew 17:21; Mark 7:16; 9:44; 9:46; 11:26; Luke 17:37; 23:17; and Acts 28:29.

The new Bible versions even hide the object of the faith that gains eternal salvation. In John 6:47 the AV passage reads: "Verily, verily, I say unto you, He that **believeth on me** hath everlasting life." The NASB version of John 6:47, however, says: "Truly, truly I say to you, he who **believes** has eternal life." Notice that the NASB simply requires belief. Belief in what? Belief in whom? The NASB passage gives room for the Catholic Church to say that belief in the Catholic Church (plus works) gains salvation. Jesus, however, says that only believing on him attains eternal salvation.

20 The Abominable Catholic Confessional

The NIV and the other new age Bible versions change the word "faults" to "sins" in James 5:16. This is in accordance with the Roman Catholic doctrine of confessing sins to a priest to be forgiven.

AV	NIV
Confess your **faults** one to another, and pray one for another, that ye may be healed. The effectual fervent prayer of a righteous man availeth much. (James 5:16 AV)	Therefore confess your **sins** to each other and pray for each other so that you may be healed. The prayer of a righteous man is powerful and effective. (James 5:16 NIV)

The greatest miracle performed by Jesus is the forgiveness of sins. It is a miracle that is solely within the province of God Almighty. When they brought a person sick of the palsy to Jesus, he performed the greater miracle of forgiving the man's sins. Jesus made the point that forgiving sins is the greatest of miracles by asking the rhetorical question "whether is easier, to say, Thy sins be forgiven thee; or to say, Arise, and walk?" Jesus then told the man to arise, and the man was healed. Jesus healed the man to prove that he was God and thus had the authority to forgive sins.

> And, behold, they brought to him a man sick of the palsy, lying on a bed: and Jesus seeing their faith said unto the sick of the palsy; Son, be of good cheer; thy sins be forgiven thee. And, behold, certain of the scribes said within themselves, This man blasphemeth. And Jesus knowing their thoughts said, Wherefore think ye evil in your hearts? For whether is easier, to say, Thy sins be forgiven thee; or to say, Arise, and walk? But that ye may know that the Son of man hath power on earth to forgive sins, (then saith he to the sick of the palsy,) Arise, take up thy bed, and go unto thine house. And he arose, and departed to his house. (Matthew 9:2-7)

The pope and his minion priests do not have the authority to forgive sins. Their purported miracle of forgiving sin by the Catholic priest is a "lying wonder" indicative of the antichrist. *See* 2 Thessalonians 2:8-10.

Since the Catholic Church claims that the priests are another Christ and another Lord, it should be no surprise that the Catholic Church claims that its priests have the same authority as the Lord to forgive sins. The priests hear confessions from a people seeking absolution for their sins.

> **Indeed bishops and priests, by virtue of the sacrament of Holy Orders, have the power to forgive sins**. CATECHISM OF THE CATHOLIC CHURCH, § 1461, 1994.

Even the Jewish scribes understood that only God has the authority to forgive sins because sin is the violation of God's law.

See, e.g., Exodus 32:33, Numbers 32:33, Deuteronomy 9:16, Joshua 7:20, 2 Samuel 12:13, Psalm 41:4, Jeremiah 3:25, Jeremiah 50:14, and Luke 15:21. The difference between the forgiveness of sin by Jesus and the forgiveness of sin by the Roman Catholic priest is that Jesus is God and thus has the authority to forgive sin (which the Jews did not understand) but the Catholic priests are pretenders and have no authority to forgive sins.

> When Jesus saw their faith, he said unto the sick of the palsy, Son, thy sins be forgiven thee. But there were certain of the scribes sitting there, and reasoning in their hearts, **Why doth this man thus speak blasphemies? who can forgive sins but God only?** And immediately when Jesus perceived in his spirit that they so reasoned within themselves, he said unto them, Why reason ye these things in your hearts? Whether is it easier to say to the sick of the palsy, Thy sins be forgiven thee; or to say, Arise, and take up thy bed, and walk? But **that ye may know that the Son of man hath power on earth to forgive sins, (he saith to the sick of the palsy,) I say unto thee, Arise, and take up thy bed, and go thy way into thine house**. And immediately he arose, took up the bed, and went forth before them all; insomuch that they were all amazed, and glorified God, saying, We never saw it on this fashion. (Mark 2:5-12)

The confessional has been the site of countless seductions of women and young girls by priests.[155] In 1837, Rosamond Culbertson revealed her first-hand knowledge of how the priests use the confessional to seduce and ravish young women. Rosamond Culbertson gave an example she witnessed of a young 14 year old girl named Mariettee, who confessed to a Catholic priest, Manuel Canto. The priest told Culbertson that Mariettee confessed to him that she had stolen two shillings from her mother. Canto told Mariettee that he would not forgive her sin unless she would consent to all his wishes. If she did not obey him, Canto told her that he would be a witness against her and send her to hell. Having sown the fear of eternal damnation in Mariettee's heart, the beastly priest Canto used that trepidation to persuade Mariettee to come to his private abode. Culbertson was present in the house when Mariette arrived. Priest Canto then executed his plan and violated Mariettee.[156] Such was the common practice among the Catholic priests of Cuba and indeed all countries where the Catholic church has hegemony.

In 1892, a former Catholic nun in England, Margaret Shepard, explained the general state of moral degeneracy of the Catholic priests, who use the confessional to seduce women and, when required, arrange abortions to conceal their sin.

> I presume many of my readers will feel shocked when I say that a Roman Catholic priest, as a general rule, will try to have a liaison with a married woman in preference to one unmarried, that in the event of any offspring no scandal will take place. When, however, it is the case of an unmarried woman, priests, who are perfect adepts at malpractice, will see that the girl is supplied with the needful medicine, and where necessary will himself perform an operation for the purpose of hiding the evidence.[157]

The seduction in the confessional is made possible in part by the indoctrination of all penitents that the priest is in the place of Jesus Christ and should be obeyed as though he were God Almighty. For example, Pope Paul VI stated:

> Obey blindly, that is, without asking reasons. Be careful, then, never to examine the directions of

your confessor....In a word, keep before your eyes this great rule, that in obeying your confessor you obey God. Force yourself then, to obey him in spite of all fears. And be persuaded that if you are not obedient to him it will be impossible for you to go on well; but if you obey him you are secure. But you say, if I am damned in consequence of obeying my confessor, who will rescue me from hell? What you say is impossible.[158]

Paul marks the coming antichrist not only with "the working of Satan with all power and signs and lying wonders," but also "with all deceivableness of unrighteousness." Wylie explains the meaning of those words and how they accurately describe the papacy:

> Let us mark the phrase. It is a very remarkable one. It is used in no other place; it is employed to describe no other system; it describes the great apostacy, and it alone. It is not simply "deceivableness," nor is it simply "unrighteousness" -it is the "deceivableness of unrighteousness;" nay, it is the "all-deceivableness of unrighteousness."
>
> Craft and deceivableness were no unknown things before the Papacy entered the world. Priests and statesmen have, in every age, dealt largely in deceivableness. But the deceivableness peculiar to herself -it is the deceivableness of unrighteousness. Not only is it a craft more subtle and more defined than any with which man operated in former ages: it is a craft of a new order. It is a system of unrighteousness so set forth as to seem that system of righteousness which God has revealed for the salvation of the world, and by consequence

accepted as such by all who, not taught of the Holy Ghost, are deceived and destroyed by it.[159]

The papacy is a dark clouded mirror that reflects the gospel of righteousness but in a way that distorts it, resulting in a false gospel of unrighteousness. Wylie perceptively details the distortion:

> Paganism was a system of deceivableness. It was the worship of a false god, under the pretence of being the worship of the true God. But popery is a deceivableness on a scale far beyond that of paganism. The one was a counterfeit of the religion of the Gospel. Popery has a god of its own - him, even, whom the canon law calls the "Lord our God." It has a saviour of its own - the Church, to wit. It has a sacrifice of it own - the Mass. It has a mediator of its own - the Priesthood. It has a sanctifier of its own - the Sacrament. It has a justification of its own - that even of infused righteousness. It has a pardon of its own - the pardon of the Confessional; and it has in the heavens an infallible, all-prevailing advocate unknown to the Gospel - the "Mother of God." It thus presents to the world a spiritual and saving apparatus for the salvation of men, and yet it neither sanctifies nor saves anyone. It looks like a church; it professes to have all that a church ought to have; and yet, it is not a church. It is a grand deception -"the all-deceivableness of unrighteousness."[160]

The papacy is built upon a foundation of deception where evil is celebrated as good. Wylie explains:

> This vast deceivableness is one of the main sources

of the strength of the so-called Church of Rome. She has the art of enlisting all the claims of virtue, and all the sanctions of law, on the side of that by which virtue is outraged and law violated. Where her purpose is the most cruel, her speech is ever the most bland. Where her motive is the most villainous, her profession is ever the most plausible. She always gives the holiest name to the most unholy deed. When she burns a heretic she calls it an *auto-da-fe* -an act of faith. When she ravages a province with fire and sword, she styles it a crusade -that is, an evangelistic expedition. Her torture chamber is styled the "Holy Office." And when she deposes monarchs, stripping them of crown and kingdom, and compelling them, as she did Henry IV of Germany, to stand with naked feet at her gates amid the drifts of winter, it is with the make-believe of a kind father administering salutary chastisement to an erring son. In short, she not only transforms herself into an angel of light, but vice itself she transforms into virtue, decking blackest crime in the white robe of innocence, and arraying foulest iniquity with the resplendent airs of holiness.

What are the sacraments by which she professes to replenish men with grace? What are the Masses by which she professes to impart Christ and his salvation to them? What are the crucifixes, rosaries, and amulets, by which she fortifies men against the assaults of Satan and evil spirits? What are the indulgences by which she shortens the sufferings of souls in purgatory? What are the pardons with which she sends men away into the other world? What are the vows of poverty under which she cherishes a pride the most arrogant, and an avariciousness the most insatiable? What are the vows of celibacy under which she veils an unbridled lewdness? What are the dispensations by she releases men from the obligations of the moral law, and professes to annul oaths, promises, and covenants? Above all, what are her logic and system of ethics by which, as in the hands of Ligouri, she makes vice and virtue falsehood and truth change sides, and shows how one, if he but direct aright his intention, can commit the most monstrous crime and yet contract not a particle of guilt? What are these things, we ask, save the "deceivableness of unrighteousness?" for surely the utmost limits of deception have here been reached, and the Deceiver himself can go no farther. He has produced his masterpiece.[161]

God has placed a curse upon any religion that calls evil good and good evil. "Woe unto them that call evil good, and good evil; that put darkness for light, and light for darkness; that put bitter for sweet, and sweet for bitter!" (Isaiah 5:20)

21 New Bibles' Call to Slavery

God has called us to be servants to one another as Jesus has set the example by giving his life. In the new versions, however, the word "servant" is changed to "slave" in Romans 6:22. Instead of being "servants to God," we have been relegated to be "slaves of God" in the new bible versions.

AV	NLT
But now being made free from sin, and become **servants** to God, ye have your fruit unto holiness, and the end everlasting life. (Romans 6:22 AV)	But now you are free from the power of sin and have become **slaves** of God. Now you do those things that lead to holiness and result in eternal life. (Romans 6:22 NLT)

We are called to be servants; were are not encumbered slaves. *See* Matthew 20:26. God did not call us to slavery but to liberty, but that liberty is not to be used as an occasion for sin but to serve one another. "For, brethren, ye have been called unto liberty; only use not liberty for an occasion to the flesh, but by love serve one another." Galatians 5:13. The theme of the New Testament of Jesus Christ is that those who believe in Jesus are set free from bondage to sin; we are free indeed! He does not want us to go back to the heavy yoke of the regulations of the law and be slaves out of fear, he wants us to serve him out of love. The Catholic position is that the Pope is supreme and submission to him is necessary for salvation.

God warned about such men: "While they promise them liberty, they themselves are the servants of corruption: for of whom a man is overcome, of the same is he brought in bondage." (2 Peter 2:19 AV) We are not God's slaves, for he calls us his "friends." (John 15:15 AV) As the following Bible passages attest, we are adopted not with the spirit of bondage but with the Holy Spirit whereby we cry "Abba, Father." (Romans 8:15-17 AV)

> Come unto me, all *ye* that labour and are heavy laden, and I will give you rest. Take my yoke upon you, and learn of me; for I am meek and lowly in heart: and ye shall find rest unto your souls. For **my yoke is easy, and my burden is light**. (Matthew 11:28-30 AV)

> Then said Jesus to those Jews which believed on him, If ye continue in my word, then are ye my disciples indeed; And ye shall know the truth, and **the truth shall make you free**. (John 8:31-32 AV)

> **If the Son therefore shall make you free, ye shall be free indeed**. (John 8:36 AV)

> But now being made **free from sin, and become servants to God**, ye have your fruit unto holiness, and the end everlasting life. (Romans 6:22 AV)

> For the law of the Spirit of life in Christ Jesus hath made me **free from the law of sin and death**.

(Romans 8:2 AV)

Stand fast therefore in the liberty wherewith Christ hath made us free, and be not entangled again with the yoke of bondage. (Galatians 5:1 AV)

And that because of false brethren unawares brought in, who came in privily to spy out **our liberty which we have in Christ Jesus**, that they might bring us into bondage: (Galatians 2:4 AV)

For, brethren, **ye have been called unto liberty**; only *use* not liberty for an occasion to the flesh, but by love serve one another. (Galatians 5:13 AV)

Because the creature itself also shall be delivered from the bondage of corruption into the **glorious liberty of the children of God**. (Romans 8:21 AV)

As free, and not using your liberty for a cloke of maliciousness, but as the servants of God. (1 Peter 2:16 AV)

22 Pride Goeth Before Destruction

Not only do the new Bibles mislead the readers as to their position with God, they also mislead the readers as to how they should act. For example, the Bible admonishes against being prideful. Read the following passages, and you will learn that God hates pride!

> The fear of the LORD *is* to hate evil: **pride, and arrogancy, and the evil way, and the froward mouth, do I hate**. (Proverbs 8:13 AV)

> When **pride** cometh, then cometh **shame**: but with the lowly *is* wisdom. (Proverbs 11:2 AV)

> In the mouth of the **foolish** is a rod of **pride**: but the lips of the wise shall preserve them. (Proverbs 14:3 AV)

> **Pride goeth before destruction**, and an haughty spirit before a fall. (Proverbs 16:18 AV)

The NIV, however, advises one to be proud by changing the word "rejoice" to "take pride." God has made clear, in the above passages, that pride is a sin which God has admonished against in the strongest terms.

AV	**NIV**
Let the brother of low degree **rejoice** in that he is exalted: (James 1:9 AV)	The brother in humble circumstances ought to **take pride** in his high position. (James 1:9 NIV)
AV	**NIV**
But let every man prove his own work, and then shall he have **rejoicing** in himself alone, and not in another. (Galatians 6:4 AV)	Each one should test his own actions. Then he can **take pride** in himself, without comparing himself to somebody else. (Galatians 6:4 NIV)

23 The New King James Version

The New King James (NKJV) is one of the most nefarious of the new Bible versions because it plays on the established authenticity of the name, King James Bible. The NKJV advises that one should reject a divisive man, whereas God advises in the KJV that it is an heretick who should be rejected.

AV	NKJV
A man that is an **heretick** after the first and second admonition reject. (Titus 3:10 AV)	Reject a **divisive man** after the first and second admonition. (Titus 3:10 NKJV)

According to the NKJV, we should reject Jesus Christ becauase he was divisive.

> Think not that I am come to send peace on earth: I came not to send peace, but a sword. For I am come to set a man at variance against his father, and the daughter against her mother, and the daughter in law against her mother in law. And a man's foes shall be they of his own household.

(Matthew 10:34-36 AV)

The NKJV has a decidedly free-will Arminian slant. For example, the sovereign election of God in moving his elect to confess Jesus Christ is undermined in the NKJV in Proverbs 16:1.

AV	NKJV
The preparations of the heart in man, **and** the answer of the tongue, is from the LORD. (Proverbs 16:1 AV)	**The preparations of the heart belong to man, But** the answer of the tongue is from the Lord. (Proverbs 16:1 NKJV)

The NKJV glorifies witchcraft. It turns the divine words of the king to words of divination.

AV	NKJV
A divine sentence is in the lips of the king: his mouth transgresseth not in judgment. (Proverbs 16:10 AV)	**Divination** is on the lips of the king; His mouth must not transgress in judgment. (Proverbs 16:10 NKJV)

In Proverbs 25:23, the NKJV says the very opposite of God's word in the KJV. God says that just as the north wind drives away rain, so does an angry countenance drive away a backbiting tongue. But the NKJV says something completely different. The meaning is not at all the same. The NKJV says that just as the north wind brings rain, so does a backbiting tongue cause an angry countenance. Rather than an angry countenance driving away a backbiting tongue, as in the KJV (i.e., AV), the NKJV has the backbiting tongue causing an angry countenance. The passages cannot both be true. One is correct, and the other is wrong. One is God's word, and the other is a corruption.

AV	NKJV
The north wind **driveth away rain**: so doth an angry countenance a backbiting tongue. (Proverbs 25:23 AV)	The north wind **brings forth rain**, And a backbiting tongue an angry countenance. (Proverbs 25:23 NKJV)

The NKJV changes the meaning of Proverbs 18:8 to say the very opposite of what is said in God's word in the KJV (AV). The words of a talebearer are transformed in the NKJV from being "wounds" to being "tasty trifles."

AV	NKJV
The words of a talebearer are as **wounds**, and they go down into the innermost parts of the belly. (Proverbs 18:8 AV)	The words of a talebearer are like **tasty trifles**, And they go down into the inmost body. (Proverbs 18:8 NKJV)

In Psalm 10:3, God explains that the ways of the wicked are always grievous. But the devil cannot have that. He wants to convince the world that the ways of the wicked are "always prospering," so he had his minions change Psalm 10:3 in the NKJV to say just that.

AV	NKJV
The wicked, through the pride of his countenance, will not seek after God: God is not in all his thoughts. **His ways are always grievous**; thy judgments are far above out of his sight: as for all his enemies, he puffeth at them. (Psalms 10:4-5 AV)	The wicked in his proud countenance does not seek God; God is in none of his thoughts. **His ways are always prospering**; Your judgments are far above, out of his sight; As for all his enemies, he sneers at them. (Psalms 10:4-5 NKJV)

In Isaiah 9:3, the NKJV changes the passage's meaning to the opposite of God's word. The NKJV translators changed "NOT increased the joy" to "increased its joy." The passages cannot both be true. One is correct, and the other is wrong. One is God's word, and the other is corruption. Indeed, all new bible versions contain the rendering "increased its joy." Those who claim that the King James and the new bible versions are both God's word cannot be correct because they say the opposite of one another. One must abide by either the King James Bible or the new bible versions; you cannot accept both. This is important because God considers his word even more important than his name. "[F]or thou hast magnified thy word above all thy name." Psalm 138:2. Consider the importance of God's word, which is above his name, when his third commandment prohibits taking his name in vain. See Exodus 20:7. God has placed a terrible curse on those who would add to or take away from his word. See Revelation 22:18-19. So you must decide: are the KJV translators under a curse from God, or are the new bible translators under that curse? There is no middle ground here. "Choose ye this day whom ye will serve." Joshua 24:15.

AV	NKJV
Thou hast multiplied the nation, and **not increased the joy**. (Isaiah 9:3 AV)	You have multiplied the nation And **increased its joy**. (Isaiah 9:3 NKJV)

The NKJV has salvation as a process by which the person works toward salvation. For example, in 1 Corinthians 1:18, the NKJV changes "are saved" to "are being saved," making it a process rather than a sovereign election by God before the foundation of the world. See Ephesians 1:4.

AV	NKJV
For the preaching of the cross is to them that perish foolishness; but unto us which **are saved** it is the power of God. (1 Corinthians 1:18 AV)	For the message of the cross is foolishness to those who are perishing, but to us **who are being saved** it is the power of God. (1 Corinthians 1:18 NKJV)

That same doctrine of process implying difficulty is seen in Matthew 7:14, where God provides all that is necessary for salvation. Jesus Christ is the "narrow way" to salvation. Indeed, "Jesus saith unto him, I am the way, the truth, and the life: no man cometh unto the Father, but by me." John 14:6. That is changed in the NKJV to salvation being difficult.

AV	NKJV
Because strait is the gate, and **narrow is the way**, which leadeth unto life, and few there be that find it. (Matthew 7:14 AV)	Because narrow is the gate and **difficult is the way** which leads to life, and there are few who find it. (Matthew 7:14 NKJV)

The NKJV doctrine contradicts the gospel, where Jesus explains that the way to salvation is NOT difficult. Indeed, Jesus' yoke is easy, and his burden is light.

> Come unto me, all ye that labour and are heavy laden, and I will give you rest. Take my yoke upon you, and learn of me; for I am meek and lowly in heart: and ye shall find rest unto your souls. For my yoke is easy, and my burden is light. (Matthew 11:28-30 AV)

Satan wants you to go easy when disciplining your children, and we are seeing the fruit of that false doctrine today. He has changed the admonition to be strident in disciplining children to be easy on them instead.

AV	NKJV
Chasten thy son while there is hope, and **let not thy soul spare for his crying**. (Proverbs 19:18 AV)	Chasten your son while there is hope, And **do not set your heart on his destruction**. (Proverbs 19:18 NKJV)

In Acts 3:13 the NKJV has demoted Jesus from being God's Son to being God's servant.

AV	NKJV
The God of Abraham, and of Isaac, and of Jacob, the God of our fathers, hath glorified **his Son Jesus**; whom ye delivered up, and denied him in the presence of Pilate, when he was determined to let him go. (Acts 3:13 AV)	The God of Abraham, Isaac, and Jacob, the God of our fathers, glorified **His Servant Jesus**, whom you delivered up and denied in the presence of Pilate, when he was determined to let Him go. (Acts 3:13 NKJV)

The NKJV changes Jesus being with us until the end of the world to only being with us to the end of the age. There are many ages demarcated in history. According to the NKJV, Jesus is only with us until the end of the present age.

AV	NKJV
Teaching them to observe all things whatsoever I have commanded you: and, lo, I am with you alway, even unto the **end of the world**. Amen. (Matthew 28:20 AV)	teaching them to observe all things that I have commanded you; and lo, I am with you always, even to the **end of the age**. Amen. (Matthew 28:20 NKJV)

24 Giving Themselves over to Fornication

NOTICE
To adequately address what is meant by fornication requires a detailed discussion of that sensitive topic in this chapter.

The corrupt fruit of the modern Bible versions is manifested in the moral decay and degeneration of society and the doctrinal error that is endemic in so-called "Christian" churches today.

> Even so every good tree bringeth forth good fruit; but a corrupt tree bringeth forth evil fruit. A good tree cannot bring forth evil fruit, neither can a corrupt tree bring forth good fruit. (Matthew 7:17-18 AV)

Moral degeneration germinates from the watered-down ethical standards in modern Bible versions. The modern Bible versions offer an amorphous, ambiguous prohibition against what they call "immorality" or "sexual immorality" in 1 Corinthians 6:18. The problem is that what is immoral is a moving target. As society degenerates, helped along by the new Bible versions, what was once immoral becomes moral. The King James Bible has no such ambiguity. The King James Bible admonishes against fornication in 1 Corinthians 6:18, which has a clear and known meaning. Webster's American Dictionary of the English Language defines fornication thusly:

> The incontinence or lewdness of unmarried persons, male or female; also, the criminal conversation of a married man with an unmarried woman. 2. Adultery. Matthew 5:32. 3. Incest. 1 Corinthians 5:1. 4. Idolatry; a forsaking of the true God, and worshipping of idols. 2 Chronicles 21:11, Revelation 19:2.[162]

AV	RSV
Flee **fornication**. Every sin that a man doeth is without the body; but he that committeth fornication sinneth against his own body. (1 Corinthians 6:18 AV)	Shun **immorality**. Every other sin which a man commits is outside the body; but the immoral man sins against his own body. (1 Corinthians 6:18 RSV)

Most of the modern Bible versions have expanded from the RSV rendering of "immorality" to read "sexual immorality in 1 Corinthians 6:18.

> Flee from **sexual immorality**. Every other sin a person commits is outside the body, but the sexually immoral person sins against his own body. (1 Corinthians 6:18 ESV)

> Flee from **sexual immorality**. All other sins a person commits are outside the body, but whoever sins sexually, sins against their own body. (1 Corinthians 6:18 NIV)

> Flee **sexual immorality**. Every other sin that a

> person commits is outside the body, but the sexually immoral person sins against his own body. (1 Corinthians 6:18 NASB)

When God uses the word fornication, it is a pregnant word that has more than one meaning. It not only means a lack of restraint on sexual appetite and lewd sexual conduct between unmarried persons but also forsaking God and committing idolatry. Notice that the new Bible versions only mention "sexual immorality" and completely miss the concept of leaving the true God and worshiping idols, as described in 2 Chronicles 21:11 and Revelation 19:2.

What does sexual immorality even mean today, when every man is doing what is right in his own eyes? "Every way of a man is right in his own eyes: but the Lord pondereth the hearts." Proverbs 21:2. The degeneration of society has been helped by the ineffectiveness of the churches. They are fruitless because they do not have God's word. They are reading Bibles that prohibit "sexual immorality" rather than "fornication."

Heterosexual fornication has almost been wholly normalized as standard conduct in society today. It is not viewed as "immoral" as long as two people "love" each other. Society is speeding past normalizing heterosexual fornication and is heading to normalizing sodomite fornication. It is almost a mantra today that same-sex intercourse is appropriate because the couple "loves" each other. There is now a privileged class of sodomites. Their conduct is not considered sexually immoral. But nobody can argue what they do is not fornication. And God has spoken clearly about what he thinks of fornication.

> Even as Sodom and Gomorrha, and the cities about them in like manner, giving themselves over to **fornication**, and going after strange flesh, are set forth for an example, suffering the vengeance of

eternal fire. (Jude 1:7 AV)

But when you change the Bible from condemning fornication to condemning sexual immorality, there is no limit to what can be allowed. Churches that use such modern Bible can be expected to conduct themselves accordingly. For example, North Point Community Church, Pastored by Andy Stanley, held a conference wherein they seemingly gave a stamp of approval to sodomite marriage. The objective of the conference was to "support parents and LGBTQ+ children in their churches."[163] The conference featured sodomites "who are either in same-sex relationships or supportive of those who are."[164]

The conference featured the speakers Justin Lee and Brian Nietzel. Stanley described them as "two married gay men" who are also 'Christ-followers today.'" Andy Stanley invited them to speak because he felt that "their stories of growing up in church environments while experiencing same-sex attraction would be 'instructive and inspiring.'"[165] The clear message that is being given by their presence, regardless of what they say, is that Pastor Stanley approves of their sodomite marriage. Stanley explains:

> Some people attracted to the same sex may live "a chaste life," Stanley said, but "for many, that is not sustainable, so they choose same-sex marriage—not because they're convinced it's biblical. They read the same Bible we do. They chose to marry for the same reason many of us do: love, companionship, and family."[166]

Surely, Jesus would not describe married sodomites promoting their lifestyle in a church as "instructive and inspiring." Rather, words like damnable, disgusting, and degenerate come to mind. Notice that Stanley's overriding message is that "love" trumps all. Doctrine be damned; pin the label love on the conduct, and it is okay. Stanley has no idea what love means. Stanley thinks that love is a feeling. It is not. That is the Hollywood version of love. That is infatuation. True love is an action whereby we treat others the way we would like to be treated. An unmarried person using someone else to fulfill his sexual desires is not love. That is fornication. Mutual consent and reciprocation in that sin does not change fornication into love.

Andy Stanley responded to one critic, whom he did not identify, by saying:

> The author is actually accusing me of departing from his version of biblical Christianity. So I want to go on record and say I have never subscribed to his version of biblical Christianity to begin with. So I'm not leaving anything. And if he were here, he would say, "Well, Andy, I've never subscribed to your version of biblical Christianity." And that's okay. We can agree to disagree.[167]

The reason that Stanley has a different version of biblical Christianity is that he has a different bible. Stanley has a skewed view of love because he does not read or preach from God's inspired word. Instead, he uses one of Satan's profane Bible versions. Stanley uses the NIV. Stanley states: "The NIV communicates the message of the original authors of Scripture better than any translation I'm aware of. This is THE translation for our generation."[168] (all capital letters in original)

Andy Stanley's theology is born from the new Bible versions. The new Bible versions give churches leeway to allow the sin of same-sex attraction with the stipulation as long as they don't act on the attraction. The King James Bible condemns the "effeminate" and "abusers of themselves with mankind" in 1 Corinthians 6:9. The RSV opted to change that to "sexual perverts." So, if one normalizes homosexuality and does not think it's a perversion, the RSV would support that reprobate ethic.

The 1984 edition of the NIV changed the passage in 1 Corinthians 6:9 to say "homosexual offenders." The NIV was criticized for that rendering. Dr. Douglas Moo, the of the NIV Committee on Bible Translation and Wessner Chair of Biblical Studies at Wheaton College, stated that "the 1984 NIV rendering ... did not make clear whether homosexual activity per se was being condemned or whether only certain kinds of 'offensive' homosexual activity was being condemned."[169] And so in 2011, the NIV was changed to say "men who have sex with men."

The "men who have sex with men" language of the NIV poses a whole host of ambiguity problems. What does it mean to have sex? Recall that President Bill Clinton, in reference to Monica Lewinski, stated "I did not have sexual relations with that woman, Ms. Lewinsky." He later confirmed that position in a sworn deposition. He was accused of lying when it was established through physical evidence of preserved semen stains on Lewinski's clothing from Clinton that, in fact, Lewinski performed fellatio on Clinton. Clinton later also admitted under oath, during grand jury testimony, that Lewinsky had performed oral sex on him.[170] But Clinton argued that fellatio is not having sexual relations, and therefore, he did not lie when he averred he did not have sexual relations with Lewinski.[171]

As a consequence of Clinton's argument, reportedly, the rates of high school students engaging in oral sex skyrocketed under the Clintion argument that such conduct does not constitute having sex.[172] That finding has been disputed. However, one study found that slightly more than 40% of college students considered oral contact with genitals as having sex.[173] That means, according to that study, 60% of college students did not think that oral contact with genitals constituted having sex. Peter Tiersma, Professor of Law and Joseph Scott Fellow, Loyola Law School, Los Angeles, author of *Legal Language* (1999), and co-author of *Speaking of Crime: the Language of Criminal Justice*, analyzed the issue and agreed with Bill Clinton that "he probably did not commit perjury based on the evidence we have so far examined."[174]

Undoubtedly, the NIV publishers were well aware of the Clinton controversy and that study. They chose the language of "men who have sex with men" to insert into 1 Corinthians 6:9 very carefully and with an eye toward an agenda of excluding oral sex typically performed by sodomites from the condemnation in that verse. The point is that what it means to have sex can be subject to interpretation by nefarious persons bent on changing the mores of society. And that is what the NIV publishers have done.

What we have now in the NIV is condemnation of the act of men having sex with men. We see that in the English Standard Version (ESV), where it changed the AV "effeminate" and "abusers of themselves with mankind" in 1 Corinthians 6:9 to "practice homosexuality." Thus, the ESV with the NIV that it is okay to be an effeminate man attracted to other men as long as he does not "practice homosexuality."

All one needs to do to circumvent the condemnation of those who "practice homosexuality" is to define what is being done as not homosexuality. This is what Muslims do. The Muslim practice is a template Satan will use for nominal Christian countries influenced by the modern Bible versions. The Islamic Sunnah seems to prohibit homosexuality, however, some allege there is an ambiguity in the Quran, giving alternative meanings, one permissive and the other prohibitory. All Muslims needed to do to get around the prohibitions in the Sunah was redefine what it means to engage in homosexual sex, and viola, what was formerly homosexual sex, is no longer.

That same pattern awaits countries that are being flooded with the new profane Bibles. What is happening in Muslim countries with all of the depravity awaits Christian countries that comport their society according to the ambiguous readings of the modern Bibles. It is worthwhile to look closely at what is happening in Muslim countries because they are the canary in the mine for Christian countries.

Muslims engage in all manner of affection between men such as holding hands in public. They do not consider such conduct to be homosexuality. It gets worse, much worse. Pederasty is rampant in Muslim countries. But Muslims justify the practice because they do not consider pederasty to be homosexuality. They claim that they are sodomizing children for sexual gratification, and they have no affectionate feelings toward their victims. Thus, it is not a homosexual act, and they are not homosexuals. That is the same ethic that prison inmates have justifying buggery.

The undercurrent of misogyny in Islamic countries has caused the men to engage in unusual behavior. Because public interaction between the sexes is restricted, it is common to see men walking together holding hands in Islamic countries. Men holding hands with other men is so prevalent in Islamic countries that one Saudi businessman gave a western friend the following advice for blending into Saudi culture and thus avoiding being targeted for violence by Islamic militants: "Stroll like you have nowhere important to go, and if you see a friend's hand next to you, grab it."[175] The act of men holding hands as they walk is practiced by Muslim men who consider themselves heterosexual, and it is not considered a homosexual practice in Islamic countries. Such behavior, however, is symptomatic of a deeper problem in Muslim society. *The New York Times* reported:

> [B]ecause the sexes are segregated, men rarely have the chance to touch or show affection toward a woman. "Arab culture has historically been segregated, so emotions and feelings are channeled to the same sex," said Musa Shteiwi, a sociology professor at the University of Jordan. "Men spend a lot of time together, and these customs grew out

of that." ... "Holding hands is the warmest expression of affection between men," said Samir Khalaf, a sociology professor at American University of Beirut in Lebanon. ... Kissing cheeks, long handshakes and clutching hands are meant to reflect amity, devotion and most important, equality in status, noted Fuad Ishak Khuri, a social anthropologist, in his book, "The Body in Islamic Culture" (2001).[176]

Sodomy is rampant in Islamic countries. Young boys are viewed as prey for the lusts of Muslim men. This sodomite subculture is accommodated in Islamic countries. Nadya Labi explains how the child victim later grows up to become the victimizer:

> However much this may seem like sophistry, it is in keeping with a long-standing Muslim tradition of accommodating homosexual impulses, if not homosexual identity. In 19th-century Iran, a young beardless adolescent was considered an object of beauty—desired by men—who would grow naturally into an older bearded man who desired youthful males.[177]

Muslims have interpreted the prohibition of homosexuality in the Sunnah in such a way that it does not altogether prohibit the practice of sodomy. Muslims have a very narrow definition of what it is to be a homosexual. In the Islamic culture, engaging in sodomy does not necessarily mean that one is a homosexual. Vlad Tepes explains that while homosexuality between men is said by many to be prohibited by Islam, Muslims justify sodomy of children, because there is no affection involved; it is simply a brutal subjugation of a weaker male by a stronger male. That interpretation brings the Sunnah in accord with the Quran. Raping boys is not considered prohibited homosexuality; it is accepted in

Islamic culture. It seems that the above passages in the Quran give Islamic sodomites succor in justifying their conduct.

> Islam may kill 'homosexuals' but homosexuality is regarded as an affectionate/loving relationship between men while the rapes or other abuse of males for means of subjugation or humiliation are not a problem. Islam's text that is filled with loathing for women and the segregation of males and females creates the distorted social, emotional and psychological environment that breeds this unacceptable abuse of young boys or weaker males.[178]

Indeed, many homosexuals find that the Islamic countries offer them the perfect cover for their sodomy. Nadya Labi explains:

> Many gay expatriates say they feel more at home in the kingdom [of Saudi Arabia] than in their native lands. Jason, a South African educator who has lived in Jeddah since 2002, notes that although South Africa allows gay marriage, "it's as though there are more gays here."[179]

Labi states that the prevalence of sodomy in Saudi Arabia is so great that laws against such behavior are rarely or only selectively enforced.

> [T]hey believe the House of Saud isn't interested in a widespread hunt of homosexuals. For one thing, such an effort might expose members of the royal family to awkward scrutiny. "If they wanted to arrest all the gay people in Saudi Arabia," Misfir, my chat-room guide, told me—repeating what he says was a police officer's comment—"they'd have

to put a fence around the whole country."[180]

That is the problem with the ESV condemnation of those who "practice homosexuality." One could just say, as do the Muslims, that he is not practicing homosexuality when he buggers someone. God's standard, as expressed in the AV, is higher and not so easily circumvented. There is no way a bugger could argue he has not violated God's commands when God expressly states that he condemns those who abuse themselves with mankind. God condemns fornication, sodomy and effeminate men. An effeminate man is a weak man resembling the practice or qualities of a woman; he is a man "[h]aving the qualities of the female sex; soft or delicate to an unmanly degree; tender; womanish; voluptuous."[181] Indeed, the popular trend of drag queens would exemplify effeminate men.

AV	ESV
Know ye not that the unrighteous shall not inherit the kingdom of God? Be not deceived: neither fornicators, nor idolaters, nor adulterers, nor **effeminate, nor abusers of themselves with mankind.** (1 Corinthians 6:9 AV)	Or do you not know that the unrighteous[b] will not inherit the kingdom of God? Do not be deceived: neither the sexually immoral, nor idolaters, nor adulterers, nor **men who practice homosexuality.** (I Corinthians 6:9 ESV)

God has unequivocally expressed his abhorrence of sodomy. "Thou shalt not lie with mankind, as with womankind: it is abomination." Leviticus 18:22. "If a man also lie with mankind, as he lieth with a woman, both of them have committed an abomination." Leviticus 20:13.

God was so angry with the abominable sin that "the Lord rained upon Sodom and upon Gomorrah brimstone and fire from the Lord out of heaven." Genesis 19:24. Sodomites to this day avoid calling their sin sodomy in order to conceal the memory of God's judgement upon Sodom and Gomorrah for such deviant conduct. It is common today to call their sinful lifestyle "gay," when there is nothing gay about it.

The sodomite subculture has hit the West. And the modern Bible versions are there to help. Andy Stanley's North Point Community Church is not alone. The Dallas, Texas, Cathedral of Hope, a congregation affiliated with the United Churches of Christ, is said to be the largest LGBTQ-friendly church in the world.[182] That church held a "Drag Sunday" service to bless a drag queen group, the Sisters of Perpetual Indulgence, who make it a practice to dress up as nuns and blasphemously portray the crucifixion of Christ. The Dallas church held the service to protest against a Texas law that protects minors from being exposed to "sexually oriented performances." After the pastor's sermon, "the drag queens came up on stage in front of the congregation, and a blessing was read over them by church leaders."[183] The Cathedral of Hope seems to be salt that has lost its savor. Jesus tells us what happens to such.

> Ye are the salt of the earth: but if the salt have lost his savour, wherewith shall it be salted? it is thenceforth good for nothing, but to be cast out, and to be trodden under foot of men. Matthew 5:13.

The drag queens celebrated by the Cathedral of Hope are the kind of effeminate persons who are condemned in the AV 1 Corinthians 6:9. But that church does not notice that they are violating God's word because they use the lukewarm, profane modern Bible versions that do not contain that condemnation. The Cathedral of Hope uses the New American Standard Bible (NASB) and the English Standard Version (ESV). God thinks that drag queens are an abomination.

> The woman shall not wear that which pertaineth unto a man, neither shall a man put on a woman's garment: for all that do so are abomination unto the Lord thy God. (Deuteronomy 22:5 AV)

Satan has his ambassadors, who are used to popularize the effeminate abomination. For example, Caitlyn Jenner is a famous man who formerly went by the name Bruce Jenner but who dresses as a woman and calls himself Caitlyn Jenner. Bruce Jenner was the 1976 Olympic Decathlon Gold Medalist and set a world record. The Olympic decathlon is typically viewed as an event that establishes the winner as the best all-round track athlete in the world. In 2015, Bruce Jenner announced that he was a woman and would start dressing as such and go by a new name, Caitlyn Jenner.[184]

Jenner has stated that he is not a homosexual.[185] Under his ethics, churches like the Cathedral of Hope could say he does not violate the prohibition against practicing homosexuality found in I Corinthians 6:9 because Jenner does not have sex with men. He only fornicates with women. Because in the new Bible versions, there is no condemnation against being effeminate, and there is no prohibition against fornication, Jenner is in the clear. As long as he is in a loving relationship, he is not engaging in "sexual immorality."

Indeed, such effeminate perversion is not just tolerated; it is celebrated. Caitlyn Jenner is praised as having great courage for being an effeminate man who dresses as a woman. Such behavior is now marketed as "transgender." Jenner was honored with a standing ovation as ESPN awarded him the Arthur Ashe Courage Award.[186] Jenner vowed "to do whatever I can to reshape the landscape of how transgender people are viewed and treated."[187]

Saltless churches, like North Point Community Church and the Cathedral of Hope, have given succor to a sodomite privileged class, a godless generation who have no fear of God. Indeed, they must necessarily reject the God of the Bible, because within the Bible is found God's condemnation of sodomy. "Thou shalt not lie with mankind, as with womankind: it is abomination." (Leviticus 18:22) That sin is so abhorrent to God that he rained fire and brimstone upon Sodom and Gomorrah as punishment for that filthy sin. "Then the Lord rained upon Sodom and upon Gomorrah brimstone and fire from the Lord out of heaven." Genesis 19:24.

Nowadays, however, sodomy is viewed as a protected lifestyle, with the U.S. Supreme Court judging sodomy a good thing, even to the degree of creating a right for same-sex couples to get married. God curses those who call the sin of sodomy good. "Woe unto them that call evil good, and good evil; that put darkness for light, and light for darkness; that put bitter for sweet, and sweet for bitter!" (Isaiah 5:20)

The State and Federal governments in the United States have used the pro-sodomy laws to create a protected class with special government-granted, group privileges, which governments call "civil rights." "Woe unto them that decree unrighteous decrees, and that write grievousness which they have prescribed." (Isaiah 10:1) Those government-granted, group privileges will be used to strike at the God-given, individual rights of Christians. There is no new thing under the sun. God has spoken against such laws contrived to persecute his people. "Shall the throne of iniquity have fellowship with thee, which frameth mischief by a law? They gather themselves together against the soul of the righteous, and condemn the innocent blood." (Psalms 94:20-21)

One might ask, how can granting special privileges to a class of sinners infringe on the God-given, individual rights of Christians? Let us look at the example of the Oregon Equality Act of 2007, which is a law that grants special state privileges to sodomites. In 2013, Christians Aaron and Melissa Klein were fined $135,000 by the Oregon Bureau of Labor and Industries

(BOLI) for declining to bake a cake for a lesbian wedding ceremony in violation of the Oregon Equality Act of 2007.[188] The fine was levied after the lesbian couple, Rachel Cryer and Laurel Bowman, filed a civil rights complaint with BOLI against the bakery, "Sweet Cakes by Melissa," for "emotional, mental, and physical suffering."[189] Tod Starnes reported for Fox News how the couple's small bakery was crushed by the sodomite protests, and as a result they were forced to close their bakery:

> The backlash against Aaron and Melissa Klein, owners of the bakery, was severe. Gay rights groups launched protests and pickets outside the family's store. They threatened wedding vendors who did business with the bakery. And, Klein told me, the family's children were the targets of death threats. The family eventually had to close their retail shop and now operate the bakery out of their home. They posted a message vowing to stand firm in their faith.[190]

Melissa Klein stated: "(I) honestly did not mean to hurt anybody, didn't mean to make anybody upset, (it's) just something I believe in very strongly."[191] After the Kleins were forced to shut down their bakery, Aaron Klein had to find employment as a trash collector to make financial ends meet. The State of Oregon "frameth mischief by a law" against the soul of the righteous. The Klein case in Oregon is not an anomaly.

Christian liberties are being crushed all over the country.[192] New Mexico's Supreme Court ruled unanimously that two Christian photographers, Elaine and Jonathan Huguenin, who declined to photograph a same-sex union violated the state's Human Rights Act.[193] The Attorney General of the State of Washington filed a lawsuit against a florist who refused to provide flowers for a same-sex couple's wedding.[194] Jack Phillips, the owner of Masterpiece Cakeshop in Colorado was ordered by a judge either to serve sodomite couples or face fines.¹⁹⁵ "When the righteous are in authority, the people rejoice: but when the wicked beareth rule, the people mourn." (Proverbs 29:2)

Phillips appealed his persecution all the way to the U.S. Supreme Court, which ruled that the Colorado Civil Rights Commission did not treat the baker fairly and that unfair treatment violated his constitutional rights of free speech and religion.¹⁹⁶ The decision by the U.S. Supreme Court was not a complete victory. The Court did not rule that the Colorado law itself that protected sodomites was an infringement on the baker's constitutional rights to free speech and religion, it was only the unfair way in which the Colorado Civil Rights Commission enforced the law that was unconstitutional.

The *Masterpiece Cakeshop* decision is only the beginning of a long fight. The decision is one step back for the sodomites that will be followed by two steps forward. Justice Thomas pointed that fact out in his concurring opinion. He stated that the *Masterpiece Cakeshop* case is the very type of case that he predicted would surface as a result of the 2015 U.S. Supreme Court decision in *Obergefell v. Hodges*¹⁹⁷ that granted sodomites the constitutional right to marry. That right to marry granted to sodomites, he said, will be used as a lever to persecute Christians and "stamp out every vestige of dissent and vilify Americans who are unwilling to assent to the new orthodoxy."¹⁹⁸ After the *Masterpiece Cakeshop* decision by the U.S. Supreme Court, the agencies of government won't be as overtly evil and stupid as was the Colorado Civil Rights Commission against Phillips. They will try to conceal their animus against Christians, while subtly turning the screws of government against them. As Justice Thomas states, Christians have only lived to fight another day. But it will be a death by a thousand cuts.

The Colorado Civil Rights Commission saw the U.S. Supreme Court decision for what is was: only one step back, which will be followed by two steps forward. Within just two weeks after the U.S. Supreme Court issued its ruling in favor of Phillips, the Colorado Civil Rights Commission was at it again with another prosecution against Phillips for his refusal to make a cake for a transgender customer. The commission alleged that Phillips discriminated against a customer based upon gender identity in violation of Colorado law. No doubt, the commission is going to try to be more subtle in how it handles Phillips this time. But make no mistake about it, their aim is to trample his religious freedom by providing special protections for sodomites.

What did Philips do that violated the laws of Colorado? He refused to make a custom cake with a blue exterior and a pink interior to celebrate the fact that the customer transitioned from male-to-female and had come out as transgender. That transgender customer was a lawyer who had made many previous obscene requests for custom cakes that were refused by Philips. One request by that customer was for Phillips to design a birthday cake for Satan that would feature an image of Satan smoking marijuana. Rod Dreher described the actions of the Colorado Civil Rights Commission in prosecuting Phillips again: "It's as if the state is giving a finger to the Supreme Court."[199]

The promotion and protection of sin acts to degenerate society. One sin begets another sin, as the perversions spiral downward. On July 19, 2016, the U.S. Government announced a new policy of allowing transgender persons to serve in the U.S. Military. A new sexual identity military manual states that "[e]ffective immediately, no otherwise qualified service member may be involuntarily separated, discharged or denied re-enlistment or continuation of service, solely on the basis of their gender identity."[200] The manual goes on to spell out the procedures for service members to obtain sex-change operations at government expense.

The Persecution of Jack Phillips illustrates the militancy of the transgender perversion. The militant transgender movement has infiltrated government agencies, and it will use the force of government to push its Satanic agenda. For example, on the night of January 28, 2018, a drunk and bloodied man, who self-identified as a transgender woman (biologically, he was a man), was ejected from a nearby homeless shelter for fighting. The drunk and bloodied man, wearing a woman's nightgown, sought to stay at Hope Center, which is a shelter for battered women and women escaping from sex-trafficking. He was refused entry, because he was a man, and all of the women in the shelter sleep in a common area. He was given cab fare by the staff at Hope Center so he could go to the emergency room for treatment.

The man returned the next day seeking to stay there, but again he was refused. The man responded by filing a complaint with the Anchorage Equal Rights Commission, under a statute prohibiting discrimination in public accommodations.[201] Essentially, the man (who self-identified as a transgender woman) was suing the women's shelter, claiming it was legally required to allow him (a drunk and violent man) to sleep in a common area among the women it housed, who were fleeing from violent and abusive circumstances. Incidently, in the past, the shelter had provided its services to that very man by serving him meals and allowing him to shower by himself — he simply was not allowed to sleep there. Howard Slugh Aylana Meisel, in an article for the National Review, reported:

> Many of the women had been abused by men and would not feel safe or comfortable sleeping so near a biological man. The lawyer noted that allowing a man to sleep in the room would "traumatize and present unreasonable safety risks for the abused and battered women who are admitted for overnight shelter." If this case alone wasn't disturbing enough, the Anchorage Equal Rights Commission sued Hope's lawyer after he made

comments to a local reporter defending the shelter.²⁰²

The lesbian, gay, bisexual, transgender (a/k/a LGBT) communities have an even more nefarious agenda, which they keep secret from the public at large. Michael Swift's 1987 Gay Manifesto reveals the dirty secret of the LGBT rights movement. The LGBT community wants the right to sodomize children. The Gay Manifesto brazenly states:

> We shall sodomize your sons, emblems of your feeble masculinity, of your shallow dreams and vulgar lies. We shall seduce them in your schools, in your dormitories, in your gymnasiums, in your locker rooms, in your sports arenas, in your seminaries, in your youth groups, in your movie theater bathrooms, in your army bunkhouses, in your truck stops, in your all male clubs, in your houses of Congress, wherever men are with men together. Your sons shall become our minions and do our bidding. They will be recast in our image. They will come to crave and adore us.²⁰³

Former California State Assemblyman Steve Baldwin researched the connection between homosexuality and pederasty. He published his findings in the Spring 2002 Regent University Law Review. Baldwin found that "[s]cientific studies confirm a strong pedophilic predisposition among homosexuals."²⁰⁴ One 1988 study published in the *Archives of Sexual Behavior*, reported that 86% of pedophiles who victimized boys "described themselves as homosexual or bisexual."²⁰⁵ Research statistics further show that homosexuals, as a population, molest children at a rate that is ten to twenty times greater than heterosexuals.²⁰⁶ Those facts are well known in the homosexual community. San Francisco's leading homosexual newspaper, *The Sentinel*, bluntly states that "[t]he love between men and boys is at the foundation of homosexuality."[207]

Homosexual publications openly promote pederasty and are often populated with travel ads for sex tours to Burma, the Philippines, Sri Lanka, Thailand, and other countries infamous for boy prostitution. Baldwin reveals that "[t]he most popular travel guide for homosexuals, Spartacus Gay Guides, is replete with information about where to find boys for sex and, as a friendly warning, lists penalties in various countries for sodomy with boys if caught."

Baldwin found that "the mainstream homosexual culture commonly promotes sex with children. Homosexual leaders repeatedly argue for the freedom to engage in consensual sex with children."[208] He determined that one of the principal aims of the LGBT rights movement is the legalization and promotion of child molestation. Mainstream LGBT organizations such as the International Lesbian and Gay Association (ILGA) and the National Coalition of Gay Organizations have passed many organizational resolutions calling for lowering or eliminating age of sexual consent laws, as a way to legalize pedophilia.[209]

The ILGA represents more than 620 member organizations. In 1995, the UN decertified the consultative status of the ILGA as a Non-Government Organization (NGO), because of political pressure from the U.S. Congress, when it was revealed the several member organizations of the ILGA promoted pedophilia. In an effort to get reinstated, ILGA severed ties with the North American Man Boy Love Association (NAMBLA), whose members practice pederasty. Severing ties with NAMBLA was apparently window dressing, since ILGA refused to expel a half-dozen more powerful (and discreet) pro-pedophile groups.[210] The UN has maintained its ban on the consultative status for ILGA.

The rampant pederasty among sodomites is nothing new. And it is the result of the evil spiritual influence that drives the sodomite perversion. For example, Aleister Crowley was a high Freemason and Satanist who styled himself as "The Beast" and proudly proclaimed himself to be "the wickedest man on earth." Crowley practiced ancient tantric sex magic (a/k/a magick). The core of tantric sex magic is to engage in increasingly cruel and perverse sex acts, gravitating to homosexual acts, and culminating in the rape of a child. The dark masonic secret, known only to the very highest adepts of Freemasonry, is that their way to immortality is to sexually violate a child.[211]

That is the purpose behind the granting of government protected privileges to sodomites. That government-protected privilege is only the first step toward the degenerative goal of the evil occultists who control the governments of the world, which is to legalize sex with children. The powerful elite of the world today secretly engage in all manner of pederasty, which this author details in his book, *Antichrist: The Beast Revealed*.

Indeed, the elite have plans to normalize pedophilia. The first step toward that goal is to convince the populace that pedophilia is simply a sexual preference with which a person is born.[212] Marjan Heine advanced that argument during a 2018 TEDx Talk at the University of Wurzburg. Heine's presentation was titled: *Why Our Perception of Pedophilia Has to Change*.[213] Heine defined pedophilia as a person's inborn sexual preference for pre-adolescent children. She argued that nobody is responsible for their feelings, and so pedophiles are not responsible for their feelings of sexual attraction toward pre-adolescent children.

Heine claimed that it is social isolation that drives pedophiles to sexually abuse children. Heine suggested that if the shame of pedophilia was removed, and pedophiles were welcomed into society, they would not act out their impulses to sexually abuse children. Heine argues that society must overcome its negative feelings toward pedophiles and treat pedophiles with respect, because, after all, they did not choose their sexuality.

Pedophiles should not be blamed for their sexual preference, they should be welcomed for who they are: pedophiles.

Heine uses the evil sophistry that a person's proclivities are dissociated from their actions. She reasons that a pedophile is not necessarily a child molester and a child molester is not necessarily a pedophile. Heine ignores the reality that a person is identified by what he does, not by what he feels or thinks. For example, a football player is a football player because he plays football. He is identified by what he actually does. A person may feel like playing football, but until he actually plays football, he is not a football player. A thief is a thief, because he steals. He is identified as a thief, because of what he does. He is not a thief if he only desires to have someone else's property, but does not take it. A pedophile is a pedophile because he sexually abuses children. He is identified as a pedophile because that is what he does. Heine ignores that reality.

To make a distinction between pedophiles and child molesters is to make a distinction without a difference. It is a false dichotomy. Heine thinks she can get away with making that misleading distinction because most people do not know that recidivism among pedophiles is very high. Show me a pedophile who denies he molests children and I will show you a liar. Research has proven that pedophiles do not control their impulses to sexually molest children. For example, an Emory University Study conducted by a leading child abuse researcher, Dr. Gene Abel, found that the average child molester (i.e., pedophile) claims 380 victims in a lifetime.[214]

The high recidivism of molestation among pedophiles impeaches Heine's statement made during her presentation that "scientific studies indicate that only 20% to 30% of all child molesters are pedophiles."[215] No, 100% of child molesters are pedophiles; just as 100% of those who steal are thieves. All pedophiles sexually abuse children; that is why they are called pedophiles. Pedophiles act on their perverted impulses. The suggestion that they don't is a devilish perversion in-and-of itself. The most disturbing aspect of Heine's speech was that at its conclusion she received applause from the audience in the packed auditorium.

Sin begets sin. Once a sin is legitimized and protected by the force of government, it begins a downward trajectory, where more sin is legitimized and protected. Such sin creates a violent and chaotic society. This chaos gives rise to new restrictive laws, which ultimately brings about a police state to reestablish order. Under the new police powers granted to the state, the exercise of God-given rights is suppressed by the government.

That is not hyperbole. Former U.S. House of Representatives Majority Leader Tom DeLay revealed in an interview on The Steve Malzberg Show that the U.S. Department of Justice plans to expand the "civil rights" granted by the U.S. Government to include a raft of new perversions, including, but not limited to, bestiality, polygamy, and pedophilia. Those abominable "civil rights" to rape children, have polygamous marriages, and have sex with animals will be used as a lever to persecute Christians who exercise their God-given rights, object to those sins, and seek to protect the children. The U.S. Justice Department has been busy strategizing on how to use the force of government to persecute recalcitrant Christians.

> Former U.S. House Majority Leader Tom DeLay claims the Justice Department has drafted a memo that spells out a dozen "perversions," including bestiality and pedophilia, that it wants legalized.
>
> "We've ... found a secret memo coming out of the Justice Department. They're now going to go after 12 new perversions. Things like bestiality, polygamy, having sex with little boys and making

that legal," DeLay said Tuesday on "The Steve Malzberg Show" on Newsmax TV.

"Not only that, but they have a whole list of strategies to go after the churches, the pastors and any businesses that try to assert their religious liberty. This is coming and it's coming like a tidal wave."

The Texas Republican's bombshell claim comes four days after the Supreme Court ruled that same-sex marriage is now legal in all 50 states — a landmark decision DeLay strongly opposes.

When Steve Malzberg repeated to DeLay his assertions that the Justice Department seeks "to legitimatize or legalize" practices such as bestiality — defined as sex acts between humans and animals — DeLay responded:

"That's correct, that's correct. They're coming down with 12 new perversions ... LGBT [short for lesbian gay, bisexual and transgender] is only the beginning. They're going to start expanding it to the other perversions."[216] (bracketed parenthetical in original article)

Satan knows that if man cuts loose his passions without regard to the laws of God, the sinful conduct will necessitate a tyrannical government. How so? The escalating sin is in essence an encroachment upon the God-given rights of another. Jesus explained the concept:

> Jesus said unto him, Thou shalt love the Lord thy God with all thy heart, and with all thy soul, and with all thy mind. This is the first and great

commandment. And the second is like unto it, Thou shalt love thy neighbour as thyself. On these two commandments hang all the law and the prophets. (Matthew 22:37-40)

The love that Jesus speaks of is not an emotional feeling toward another as Hollywood movies would have you believe. Emotions come and go. Love is not an emotion, it is an action. Jesus explained: that "as ye would that men should do to you, do ye also to them likewise." (Luke 6:31). Indeed, doing good for another person has nothing at all to do with how you feel about that person. Jesus stated that you should do good to even your enemies who have treated you badly. Luke 6:27-36. God's word has a built in dictionary where words are defined by the use of parallelism. One can see in Luke chapter 6 at verses 32 and 33 that God uses parallelism to define love, not as a feeling, but rather as an action of "doing good" to another person.

| "For if ye **love** them which **love** you, what thank have ye? for sinners also **love** those that **love** them." (Luke 6:32) | "And if ye **do good** to them which **do good** to you, what thank have ye? for sinners also do even **the same**." (Luke 6:33) |

Doing good to another is not just a suggestion, it is a command from God. Jesus states without equivocation that all of the commands of God are subsumed in the commands to love God and love your neighbor. Love has nothing to do with feelings. You should do nice things for others, whether you "feel" like it or not, because by doing so you are obeying God's command to do good to others. If one loves his neighbor, he will not violate the command, "thou shalt not steal." Exodus 20:15. While the command not to steal is a prohibition, Jesus takes it a step further and commands that we are to affirmatively do good to others (i.e., love).

Doing good often involves putting our needs second to the needs of another. If, however, a person does not regard God and seeks to satisfy the pleasure of his fleshly desires, without regard to the detrimental effect of his conduct on others, it will cause the government to step in to protect the aggrieved party. Sinful behavior brings about more crime in society, which is then used as a justification to bring about more government regulation and control of the masses. As explained by Edmond Burke: "Men are qualified for civil liberty in exact proportion to their disposition to put moral chains on their own appetites. Society cannot exist unless a controlling power upon will and appetite be placed somewhere, and the less of it there is within, the more there is without. It is ordained in the eternal constitution of things that men of intemperate minds cannot be free. Their passions forge their fetters."

That is why Satan wants to drive any thought of God from the minds of men. Indeed, by doing so, a satanically controlled government can impose its tyranny on the people, without much objection from the people, because the people are ignorant that the fetters applied by the government violate the laws of God. For example, the communist collective ideal is based upon larceny. It uses the government to redistribute wealth. The redistribution of wealth is always justified by some purported need, and it usually involves helping children; it is always cloaked in nice sounding labels, like "welfare." There are always powerful corporate interests that are lined up to be on the receiving end of the government forced transaction.

Rather than charity coming willingly from one individual to another, the government uses its force, through taxation, to take money from one group and give it to another. Taking money from one group and giving it to another group cannot be done if the government accepted the existence of God. If God were to be accepted, then necessarily God's commands must be then obeyed. The government would have a hard time justifying taking money from one group of persons for the benefit of another group of persons, when faced with God's command: "Thou shalt not steal." (Exodus 20:15) Using the government as an intermediary does not make the stealing any more justifiable.

Like communism, Darwinian evolution is necessarily atheistic and cannot stand if the authority of the Bible is accepted. The Bible makes it clear that God created man in his image, not after the image of an ape. "So God created man in his own image, in the image of God created he him; male and female created he them." (Genesis 1:27)

25 The Rape of the Church

The NKJV willy-nilly chooses to capitalize pronouns that the translators believe refer to God. The problem is that specific doctrinal errors have crept into passages due to preconceived, unbiblical, systematic theological theories. For example, In 2 Thessalonians 2:7, Paul references a restraining power. The NKJV translators, apparently, believe in the heretical view that a "rapture" will remove the church from the world before the appearance of the antichrist. Consequently, the NKJV capitalizes the pronoun "He" referring to the restraining person, thus indicating the restraining person who is taken out of the way is God the Holy Spirit, who is supposed to be removed when the Holy Spirit indwelt church is allegedly raptured from the world. The NKJV passage displays doctrinal bias; it is the work of men, and it is an error.

AV	NKJV
For the mystery of iniquity doth already work: only **he** who now letteth will let, until **he** be taken out of the way. (2 Thessalonians 2:7 AV)	For the mystery of lawlessness is already at work; only **He** who now restrains will do so until **He** is taken out of the way. (2 Thessalonians 2:7 NKJV)

Those that hold to the pretribulation rapture teaching cite 2 Thessalonians 2:1-12 in support of their doctrine.[217] If one looks at those passages in 2 Thessalonians 2:1-12, it is clear that they refer to the resurrection of believers at the end of the world, and not a rapture.

In verse one, we see that the topic that the Apostle Paul addresses is "the coming of our Lord Jesus Christ" and "our gathering together unto him." The apostle Paul told the Thessalonians that "that day" would not come until there was a falling away first. Notice that Paul refers to "that day," which indicates that the coming of our Lord and our gathering together unto him are to happen contemporaneously. The first thing that happens is the falling away. Then, the man of sin, the son of perdition, is revealed. Verse four indicates that this man of sin will exalt himself above God. Clearly, this is a reference to the antichrist. So we know that the antichrist will be revealed before the coming of Jesus Christ and the resurrection of the Saints. The pretribulation rapturists reverse this sequence and hold that Jesus will return secretly and rapture the saints, and then after the rapture, the antichrist will be revealed.

The pretribulation rapturists hold that the person in verse seven who lets (restrains) the antichrist is the Holy Spirit, who resides in the body of believers. They teach that when the rapture takes place the Holy Spirit will be taken out of the world and the antichrist will then the revealed.[218] If you look at those passages in 2 Thessalonians 2, the apostle Paul told the Thessalonians that "that day" would not come until there is a falling away first. Then, the man of sin, the son of perdition, is revealed. Verse four indicates that this man of sin will exalt himself above God. Clearly, this is a reference to the Antichrist. So we know that the Antichrist will be revealed before the coming of Jesus Christ and the resurrection of the Saints. If, however, he that letteth is the Holy Spirit, verse 3 contradicts verses 6-8. If the Holy Spirit is he that letteth, preventing the Antichrist from being revealed and his being taken out of the way is the resurrection (rapture) of the saints, and it happens first "then" the Antichrist is revealed, that is the reverse of the sequence in verse 3. That contradicts verse 3, which states that the resurrection (rapture) shall not come except if there is a falling away first and the man of sin is revealed. In fact, he that letteth is the Roman Emperor, whom the pope replaced as Pontifex Maximus (Supreme Pontiff), the ruler of all religions. The pope is the Antichrist.

Furthermore, the position that the Holy Spirit will be removed from the earth through the rapture of the saints contradicts the promise that Jesus made. Jesus stated in Matthew 28:20 that he would be with us always, even unto the end of the world. Jesus is with us through the Holy Spirit. We know from 1 John's 5:7 that "there are three that bear record in heaven, the father, the Word, and the Holy Ghost: and these three are one." (1 John's 5:7) So we see that Jesus and the Holy Spirit are one. If you remove the Holy Spirit from the world, then Jesus is removed, and he cannot be with us until the end of the world.

Jesus makes it even more evident in the Gospel of Matthew that the Holy Spirit will abide with us forever: "And I will pray the Father, and he shall give you another Comforter, that **he may abide with you for ever.**" (John 14:16 AV) Who is the comforter that Jesus was referring to? In John 14:26, Jesus states that the comforter is the Holy Spirit. If the Holy Spirit is removed from the world through the rapture, and the rapture is followed by a seven-year tribulation period, how could Jesus keep his promise that the Holy Spirit will be with us forever? The answer is simple: there will not be a pretribulation rapture but a resurrection, which will be at the end of the world when Christ returns. The pretribulation rapture is not supported by Scripture; in fact, it is contrary to Scripture.

The so-called biblical scholars who have adopted the eschatological doctrine of a pretribulation resurrection, but they used the unbiblical term, rapture, instead of resurrection. The term "rapture" is not found anywhere in the Holy Scriptures. It is in fact a derivation of the Latin *Raptus*. *Raptus* is a word that can be found in some of the passages in the Latin translation of the bible, which is known as the Latin Vulgate. *Raptus* is a mistranslation of the Greek word *harpazo*, which literally means "caught up." *See* 2 Corinthians 12:4 in the Latin Vulgate.

Many people believe that rapture is synonymous with resurrection, but that is not true. While rapture does include the idea of being taken away, it is very different from the resurrection promised by Jesus. Rapture means "the act of seizing and carrying off as prey or plunder . . . the act of carrying off a woman . . . rape."[219] The root word for rapture is rapt which means "Rape (abduction or ravishing) . . . . The act or power of carrying forcibly away."[220] Ravish means "[t]o seize and carry away by violence. . . . To have carnal knowledge with a woman by force and against her consent."[221] Both rapture and rape share the same Latin root word, *raptus*.[222] *Raptus* means "a carrying off, abduction, rape."[223] The Holy Scripture describes the church as the chaste bride of Christ who is with Christ at the wedding supper of the Lamb. (Revelation 19:7; 22:17; Matthew 22:1-14; 2 Corinthians 11:2; Ephesians 5:25-33) The wedding supper of the Lamb will take place at the resurrection of the saints when this world ends. By using the term rapture, these "scholars" are blasphemously describing that holy and glorious resurrection of the church as a rape!

One of the tenets of the pretribulation rapture teaching is that once the believers in Christ are raptured out of the world, there will only be unbelievers left behind. The unbelievers will then go through the seven-year period of tribulation, during which the antichrist will make his appearance.[224] The problem with that sequence is that it is contrary to the sequence of events as explained by Jesus.

Another parable put he forth unto them, saying, The kingdom of heaven is likened unto a man which sowed good seed in his field: But while men slept, his enemy came and sowed tares among the wheat, and went his way. But when the blade was sprung up, and brought forth fruit, then appeared the tares also. So the servants of the householder came and said unto him, Sir, didst not thou sow good seed in thy field? from whence then hath it tares? He said unto them, An enemy hath done this. The servants said unto him, Wilt thou then that we go and gather them up? But he said, Nay; lest while ye gather up the tares, ye root up also the wheat with them. **Let both grow together until the harvest: and in the time of harvest I will say to the reapers, Gather ye together first the tares, and bind them in bundles to burn them: but gather the wheat into my barn**. (Matthew 13:24-30 AV) (emphasis added)

Jesus states in his parable in Matthew 13:24-30 that the kingdom of heaven is like a man who sows good seed in this field, but an enemy sows tares. The man allows the tares and the wheat to grow together until the harvest. It is not until the harvest that the tares and the wheat are gathered. The wheat is not gathered some time before the tares. The tares are gathered "first" and burned, then the wheat is gathered into the barn. The parable shows that the tares are gathered first and then the wheat, just the reverse of the pretribulation rapture teaching. One might say "that is just a parable, you can make that mean anything you wish." Jesus himself, however, explained the meaning of that parable later in Matthew.

Then Jesus sent the multitude away, and went into the house: and his disciples came unto him, saying, Declare unto us the parable of the tares of the field.

> He answered and said unto them, He that soweth the good seed is the Son of man; The field is the world; the good seed are the children of the kingdom; but the tares are the children of the wicked one; The enemy that sowed them is the devil; the harvest is the end of the world; and the reapers are the angels. As therefore the tares are gathered and burned in the fire; so shall it be in the end of this world. The Son of man shall send forth his angels, and they shall gather out of his kingdom all things that offend, and them which do iniquity; And shall cast them into a furnace of fire: there shall be wailing and gnashing of teeth. Then shall the righteous shine forth as the sun in the kingdom of their Father. Who hath ears to hear, let him hear. (Matthew 13:36-43 AV)

Notice that Jesus states that both the tares and the wheat are to be left alone to grow up together until the end of the world. He does not say that the wheat should be plucked out ahead of time and the tares will be left behind. He states that he will wait until the end of the world and then his angels will "first" gather out of the field the tares (the children of the wicked one) and they will be bound and cast into a furnace of fire where there shall be wailing and gnashing of teeth. It is after the gathering of the tares that the children of God are gathered together. They are gathered at the end of the world not during some rapture years earlier.

The pretribulation rapturists will cite Revelation 20:5-6 to support their argument that there will be a rapture and then, some time later, a second resurrection. Revelation 20:5-6 does mention a first resurrection, which suggests that there is a second resurrection. Indeed, there is a second resurrection, but that is not a physical resurrection as some have supposed; it is a spiritual resurrection. The pretribulation rapturists ignore Revelation 20:4, where John says: "And I saw thrones, and they sat upon them, and judgment was given unto them: and I saw the souls of them that were beheaded for the witness of Jesus, and for the word of God." Notice he saw the "souls" of the saved; he did not see their bodies. They had been spiritually resurrected (the first resurrection) but not yet bodily resurrected. Before one is born again, he is dead in trespasses and sins. The Holy Spirit quickens the believer, and he is made alive; he is spiritually resurrected from the dead. The spiritual rebirth by the grace of God through faith in Jesus Christ is the first resurrection mentioned in Revelation 20:4-6. The second resurrection is the resurrection of the bodies of the believers at the coming of the Lord Jesus Christ.

And you hath he quickened, who were dead in trespasses and sins. (Ephesians 2:1 AV)

Even when we were dead in sins, hath quickened us together with Christ, (by grace ye are saved;) **And hath raised us up together, and made us sit together in heavenly places in Christ Jesus**: (Ephesians 2:5-6 AV)

And you, being dead in your sins and the uncircumcision of your flesh, hath he quickened together with him, having forgiven you all trespasses; (Colossians 2:13 AV)

If ye then be risen with Christ, seek those things which are above, where Christ sitteth on the right hand of God. (Colossians 3:1 AV)

The pretribulation rapturists believe that Jesus will not return until the end of the seven-year tribulation. They distinguish between the resurrection at Jesus' second coming and the rapture. It would be easy to determine the exact date of Jesus' second coming by simply noting the date of the rapture and adding seven years. The problem is that Jesus stated that the day and hour of his second coming and the end of the world cannot be determined in advance. He stated that only God the Father knows the day, the hour of his return, and the end of the world. He noted that the day would be similar to the great flood. People were eating, drinking, and marrying when suddenly and unexpectedly, a flood came upon the world.

> But of that day and hour knoweth no man, no, not the angels of heaven, but my Father only. But as the days of Noe were, so shall also the coming of the Son of man be. For as in the days that were before the flood they were eating and drinking, marrying and giving in marriage, until the day that Noe entered into the ark, And knew not until the flood came, and took them all away; so shall also the coming of the Son of man be. (Matthew 24:36-39 AV)

Another passage that is directly contrary to the pretribulation rapture teachings is 2 Peter 3:9-15. That passage states that the day of the Lord will come suddenly like a thief in the night. Peter admonishes the saints, therefore, to be "in holy conversation and godliness, looking for and hasting unto the coming of the day of God." In the passage in 2 Peter, Peter referred to the coming of the Lord at the end of the world; he states that on that day, the heavens shall pass away, the elements will melt with fervent heat, and the world will be burned up. Why would Peter admonish the saints to look for the day of God during which the world will be destroyed if the saints are going to the raptured out of the world seven years before it? The answer is simple: the saints will not be raptured seven years before the return of Christ; the saints will be resurrected on that day of the Lord when he returns. On that day, the world will be destroyed, but the saints look forward to that day, for it is the day of promise during which they will be resurrected, and there will be "new heavens and a new earth wherein dwelleth righteousness." See Revelation

21:1; Matthew 13:43.

> The Lord is not slack concerning his promise, as some men count slackness; but is longsuffering to us-ward, not willing that any should perish, but that all should come to repentance. But the day of the Lord will come as a thief in the night; in the which the heavens shall pass away with a great noise, and the elements shall melt with fervent heat, the earth also and the works that are therein shall be burned up. Seeing then that all these things shall be dissolved, what manner of persons ought ye to be in all holy conversation and godliness, Looking for and hasting unto the coming of the day of God, wherein the heavens being on fire shall be dissolved, and the elements shall melt with fervent heat? Nevertheless we, according to his promise, look for new heavens and a new earth, wherein dwelleth righteousness. Wherefore, beloved, seeing that ye look for such things, be diligent that ye may be found of him in peace, without spot, and blameless. And account that the longsuffering of our Lord is salvation; even as our beloved brother Paul also according to the wisdom given unto him hath written unto you; (2 Peter 3:9-15 AV)

The pretribulation rapture advocates state that God has not chosen the church to be the object of his wrath. They claim, therefore, that the church must be raptured out of the world before the tribulation period.[225] Indeed, God's church will never be the object of his wrath. See John 5:24; Romans 5:9, 8:1; 1 Thessalonians 1:10, 5:9. There is, however, a world of difference between God's wrath and the tribulations of this world. The following passages indicate that Christians will, in fact, suffer great persecution and tribulation in this world.

> Then shall they deliver you up to be afflicted, and shall kill you: and ye shall be hated of all nations for my name's sake. (Matthew 24:9 AV)

> These things I have spoken unto you, that in me ye might have peace. In the world ye shall have **tribulation**: but be of good cheer; I have overcome the world. (John 16:33 AV)

> Confirming the souls of the disciples, and exhorting them to continue in the faith, and that we must through much **tribulation** enter into the kingdom of God. (Acts 14:22 AV)

> That no man should be moved by these afflictions: for yourselves know that we are appointed thereunto. For verily, when we were with you, we told you before that we should suffer **tribulation**; even as it came to pass, and ye know. (1 Thessalonians 3:3-4 AV)

If the church of Christ is to be raptured out of the world before the alleged seven-year tribulation period, why did Jesus pray that his church not be taken out of the world? "I pray not that thou shouldest take them out of the world, but that thou shouldest keep them from the evil." (John 17:15 AV) Lest one argue that Jesus was only praying about his then-living disciples, he made it clear that he was praying for all Christians. "Neither pray I for these alone, but for them also which shall believe on me through their word." (John 17:20 AV) Is there any doubt that the prayers of Jesus will be answered?

Jesus did not state that he would rapture his church out of the world seven years before the last day, but to the contrary, he stated that he would raise up all those that the Father had given him **"at the last day."** "And this is the Father's will which hath sent me, that of all which he hath given me I should lose nothing, but should raise it up again at the last day." (John 6:39 AV) Lest there be any confusion about what Jesus meant, he clarified the point in the very next passage. "And this is the will of him that sent me, that every one which seeth the Son, and believeth on him, may have everlasting life: and I will raise him up at the last day." (John 6:40 AV) Notice he does not state that some will be raised up at an earlier time, but rather that he will raise up at the last day everyone who seeth the Son and believeth on him. There is no mention in Bible prophecy of more than one physical resurrection, and that physical resurrection will be on the **last day**, when **every Christian** will be raised to glory. Some will cite the passage in Revelation 20:5 where there is mention of a first resurrection, which suggests a second resurrection. The first resurrection mentioned in that passage is the spiritual resurrection of a Christian when he is born again, it is not the physical resurrection at the end of the world. When one is born again he is spiritually raised from the dead, made alive to be forever spiritually with Christ. "And you hath he quickened, who were dead in trespasses and sins." (Ephesians 2:1 AV) "Even when we were dead in sins, hath quickened us together with Christ, (by grace ye are saved;) And hath raised us up together, and made us sit together in heavenly places in Christ Jesus." (Ephesians 2:5-6 AV) In John 5:24-25 Jesus describes the spiritual resurrection, and then in John 5:28-29, he describes an entirely different physical resurrection; the spiritual resurrection is the first resurrection mentioned in Revelation 20:5.

At this glorious second resurrection, those who are chosen for salvation will be changed in the twinkling of an eye and put on glorified eternal bodies. Those who hold to the pretribulation rapture teaching, however, believe that Christ will return several times, the first being a secret rapture. They extrapolate that because Christ is prophesied to return like a thief in the night, he will stealthily and quietly return. It is true that 1 Thessalonians 5:2 and 2 Peter 3:10 state that the Lord will come as a thief in the night. Those passages, however, point out the suddenness of the Lord's return, not that the Lord will act like a thief and sneak back to Earth. In fact, if one looks at 1 Thessalonians 4:13-17, one sees that the return of Christ will be anything but sneaky. He will come with a shout, with the voice of the archangel, and the trump of God.

> But I would not have you to be ignorant, brethren, concerning them which are asleep, that ye sorrow not, even as others which have no hope. For if we believe that Jesus died and rose again, even so them also which sleep in Jesus will God bring with him. For this we say unto you by the word of the Lord, that we which are alive and remain unto the coming of the Lord shall not prevent them which are asleep. For the **Lord himself shall descend from heaven with a shout, with the voice of the archangel, and with the trump of God**: and the dead in Christ shall rise first: Then we which are alive and remain shall be caught up together with them in the clouds, to meet the Lord in the air: and so shall we ever be with the Lord. (1 Thessalonians 4:13-17 AV)

Those who have been chosen for salvation will be changed and given immortal spiritual bodies. Those saved by the grace of God will be like Christ and shine as the sun in the kingdom of God. See 1 John 3:2 and Matthew 13:43. "Who shall change our vile body, that it may be fashioned like unto his glorious body, according to the working whereby he is able even to subdue all things unto himself." (Philippians 3:21 AV) "[A]s it is written, Eye hath not seen, nor ear heard, neither have entered into the heart of man, the things which God hath prepared for them that love him." (1 Corinthians 2:9 AV) This, however, will not happen until the end of the world at the last trump of God.

But some man will say, How are the dead raised up? and with what body do they come? Thou fool, that which thou sowest is not quickened, except it die: And that which thou sowest, thou sowest not that body that shall be, but bare grain, it may chance of wheat, or of some other grain: But God giveth it a body as it hath pleased him, and to every seed his own body. All flesh is not the same flesh: but there is one kind of flesh of men, another flesh of beasts, another of fishes, and another of birds. There are also celestial bodies, and bodies terrestrial: but the glory of the celestial is one, and the glory of the terrestrial is another. There is one glory of the sun, and another glory of the moon, and another glory of the stars: for one star differeth from another star in glory. So also is the resurrection of the dead. It is sown in corruption; it is raised in incorruption: It is sown in dishonour; it is raised in glory: it is sown in weakness; it is raised in power: It is sown a natural body; it is raised a spiritual body. There is a natural body, and there is a spiritual body. And so it is written, The first man Adam was made a living soul; the last Adam was made a quickening spirit. Howbeit that was not first which is spiritual, but that which is natural; and afterward that which is spiritual. The first man is of the earth, earthy: the second man is the Lord from heaven. As is the earthy, such are they also that are earthy: and as is the heavenly, such are they also that are heavenly. And as we have borne the image of the earthy, we shall also bear the image of the heavenly. Now this I say, brethren, that flesh and blood cannot inherit the kingdom of God; neither doth corruption inherit incorruption. Behold, I shew you a mystery; We shall not all sleep, but **we shall all be changed, In**

a moment, in the twinkling of an eye, at the last trump: for the trumpet shall sound, and the dead shall be raised incorruptible, and we shall be changed. For this corruptible must put on incorruption, and this mortal must put on immortality. So when this corruptible shall have put on incorruption, and this mortal shall have put on immortality, then shall be brought to pass the saying that is written, **Death is swallowed up in victory.** O death, where is thy sting? O grave, where is thy victory? The sting of death is sin; and the strength of sin is the law. But thanks be to God, which giveth us the victory through our Lord Jesus Christ. (1 Corinthians 15:35-57 AV)

The pretribulation rapture contrivance contradicts the Holy Scriptures. The pretribulation rapturists teach that the resurrection described in 1 Corinthians 15:51-57 is, in fact, a description of the rapture before the tribulation period. They teach that Christ will sneak back for his saints seven years before he returns yet a third time. That could not be the case because 1 Corinthians 15:51-57 describes the resurrection of the saints at the end of the world when Christ's saints put on eternal glorified bodies and "[d]eath is swallowed up in victory." "The last enemy that shall be destroyed is death." (1 Corinthians 15:26 AV) See also, Revelation 20:14. If the last enemy destroyed is death, then 1 Corinthians 15:35-57 must be referring to the end of this world. The futurists claim there is a seven-year tribulation period following the rapture of the saints. According to them, death will still reign during this tribulation period, meaning death is not swallowed up in victory. Since death is, in fact, swallowed up in victory at the resurrection referred to in 1 Corinthian 15:51-57, then that passage could not be referring to a rapture that will be followed by a tribulation period. This is further confirmed by 1 Corinthians 15:23-24 which states: "But now is Christ risen from the dead, and become the firstfruits of them that slept. For since by man came death, by man came also the resurrection of the dead. For as in Adam all die, even so in Christ shall all be made alive. But every man in his own order: Christ the firstfruits; afterward they that are Christ's at his coming. Then cometh the end, when he shall have delivered up the kingdom to God, even the Father; when he shall have put down all rule and all authority and power." (1 Corinthians 15:20-24 AV) Notice that the order is first Christ, then second, they that are Christ's at his coming; there is no indication that there will be a sneaky rapture before Christ's coming. This happens just before the end of the world. The next passage says "then" cometh the end. It does not say 7 years later cometh the end as some have "interpreted" it as saying. The passage does not say some of them that are Christ's, it says "they that are Christ's." Who are "they?" They are the "all" who shall be made alive. The Scripture is clear, the resurrection of the saints happens at Christ's coming at the end of the world. Later in verses 51-52, that truth is confirmed. "All" (not some) shall be changed. When shall the "all" be changed? In a moment, at the last trump (not in two installments). Those passages make clear that "all" shall be changed in one moment at one time at the last trump. When is the last trump? At the end of the world. See Matthew 24:31. Once again, we see that the pretribulation rapture teaching contradicts the express language of the prophecies in the Bible.

The false pretribulation doctrine has been nurtured by the militia of the Pope, the crypto-Jewish Jesuits. We see the hidden influence of the Jesuits, starting with Emanuel de Lacunza and Francisco Ribera and continuing through Edward Irving, John Nelson Darby, Cyrus Ingerson Scofield, Billy Graham, and Jerry Falwell. This futuristic interpretation of the bible prophecies was the perfect doctrine to use to hide from the world the fact that the Pope of Rome is the antichrist and the Judaism of today is the same corrupt Judaism that Jesus denounced. Sadly, many have swallowed this sophistry of the Zionist Jews and Rome hook, line, and sinker. The editors of the NKJV corrupted God's word to comport with the pretribulation rapture deception.

26 The Diabolical Scofield Bible

The Scofield bible was funded and nurtured by World Zionist leaders who saw the Christian churches in America as an obstacle to their plan for the establishment of a Jewish homeland in Palestine. These Zionists initiated a program to infiltrate and change the Christian doctrines of those churches. Two tools used to accomplish this goal were Cyrus I. Scofield and a venerable, world-respected European book publisher, The Oxford University Press.[226]

The scheme was to alter the Christian gospel and corrupt the church with a pro-Zionist subculture. "Scofield's role was to re-write the King James Version of the Bible by inserting Zionist-friendly notes in the margins, between verses and chapters, and on the bottoms of the pages."[227] In 1909, the Oxford University Press published and implemented a large advertising budget to promote the Scofield Reference Bible.

The Scofield Reference Bible was a subterfuge designed to create a subculture around a new worship icon, the modern State of Israel. The new state of Israel did not yet exist, but the well-funded Zionists already had it on their drawing boards.[228] C.E. Carlson explains:

Since the death of its original author and namesake, The Scofield Reference Bible has gone through several editions. Massive pro-Zionist notes were added to the 1967 edition, and some of Scofield's most significant notes from the original editions were removed where they apparently failed to further Zionist aims fast enough. Yet this edition retains the title, "The New Scofield Reference Bible, Holy Bible, Editor C.I. Scofield."[229]

The Scoflild Bible's anti-Arab, Zionist "Christian" subculture theology has fostered unyielding "Christian" support for the State of Israel and its barbaric subjugation of the native Palestinians.

Who was C.I. Scofield? Scofield was a young con-artist who engaged in a continual pattern of fraud and deception both before and after his alleged 1879 conversion. Scofield was a partner with John J. Ingalls, a Jewish lawyer, in a railroad scam which led to Scofield being sentenced to prison for criminal forgery.[230] The following was revealed in *The Unified Conspiracy Theory*[231]:

> Upon his release from prison, Scofield deserted his first wife, Leonteen Carry Scofield, and his two daughters Abigail and Helen, and he took as his mistress a young girl from the St. Louis Flower Mission. He later abandoned her for Helen van Ward, whom he eventually married.[232]

Scofield had developed connections with a subgroup of the Illuminati known as the Secret Six.[233] He was taken under the wing of Samuel Untermeyer, an ardent Zionist who later became Chairman of the American Jewish Committee and President of the American League of Jewish Patriots.[234] "Untermeyer introduced Scofield to numerous Zionist and socialist leaders, including

Samuel Gompers, Fiorello LaGuardia, Abraham Straus, Bernard Baruch and Jacob Schiff."[235] These powerful figures financed Scofield's research trips to Oxford and arranged the publication and distribution of his reference bible. He who pays the piper calls the tune.

In 1892 Scofield fraudulently claimed to have a Doctorate of Divinity and began calling himself "Doctor Scofield."[236] In fact, Scofield did not have a doctorate degree from any Seminary or University or any degree of any kind from any college. Below is an excerpt from an article titled "Cyrus I. Scofield in the Role of a Congregational Minister" which appeared on August 27, 1881, in the Topeka newspaper, *The Daily Capital*:

> The last personal knowledge that Kansans have had of this peer among scalawags, was when about four years ago, after a series of forgeries and confidence games he left the state and a destitute family and took refuge in Canada.
>
> For a time he kept undercover, nothing being heard of him until within the past two years when he turned up in St. Louis, where he had a wealthy widowed sister living who has generally come to the front and squared up Cyrus' little follies and foibles by paying good round sums of money.
>
> Within the past year, however, Cyrus committed a series of St. Louis forgeries that could not be settled so easily, and the erratic young gentleman was compelled to linger in the St. Louis jail for a period of six months.
>
> Among the many malicious acts that characterized his career, was one peculiarly atrocious, that has come under our personal notice. Shortly after he

left Kansas, leaving his wife and two children dependent upon the bounty of his wife's mother, he wrote his wife that he could invest some $1,300 of her mother's money, all she had, in a manner that would return big interest. After some correspondence he forwarded them a mortgage, signed and executed by one Chas. Best, purporting to convey valuable property in St. Louis. Upon this, the money was sent to him. Afterwards the mortgages were found to be base forgeries, no such person as Charles Best being in existence, and the property conveyed in the mortgage fictitious.[237]

Scofield abandoned his wife and children and refused to support them. At that time it was difficult for a woman to work and support herself and her children. 1 Timothy 5:8 states: "But if any provide not for his own, and specially for those of his own house, he hath denied the faith, and is worse than an infidel."

When his first wife, Leontine, initially filed for divorce in July 1881, she listed the following reasons: "(he had)…absented himself from his said wife and children, and had not been with them but abandoned them with the intention of not returning to them again… has been guilty of gross neglect of duty and has failed to support this plaintiff or her said children, or to contribute thereto, and has made no provision for them for food, clothing or a home, or in any manner performed his duty in the support of said family although he was able to do so."[238] At that time Scofield was the pastor of Hyde Park Congregational Church in St. Louis.[239] The divorce decree was granted in 1883, with the court finding that Scofield "was not a fit person to have custody of the children."[240]

Scofield's life was marked at every turn by duplicity. J.M. Canfield revealed that Scofield, as a pastor, concealed his abandonment of his family by telling the congregation that he was single before his divorce. In 1912, Scofield sent false biographical information to a publisher for an entry in *Who's Who in America*. Among the many lies and fabrications, Scofield falsely claimed that he was decorated for valor during the Civil War. D. Jean Rushing discovered that, in fact, Scofield was a Confederate deserter. Having been married twice and being a demonstrably covetous and greedy con artist, Scofield did not qualify to be a church leader, let alone a respected commentator of God's word: "A bishop then must be blameless, the husband of one wife, vigilant, sober, of good behaviour, given to hospitality, apt to teach; Not given to wine, no striker, not greedy of filthy lucre; but patient, not a brawler, not covetous; One that ruleth well his own house, having his children in subjection with all gravity;" (1 Timothy 3:2-4)

While Scofield used the King James text, he indicated in his 1909 bible introduction that he viewed favorably the work of Brooke Foss Westcott and Fenton John Anthony Hort, two popular compilers of the corrupt Alexandrian Greek text. Westcott and Hort were nominal Protestants, but they were defacto Roman Catholics. In addition, Westcott and Hort were both necromancers who were members of an occult club called the "Ghostly Guild."[241] Throughout Scofield's Bible, he placed marginal notes that attacked the inerrancy of the Received Text of the Holy Scripture and indicated his preference for the corrupt Alexandrian manuscripts used by the Catholic Church.

The Zionists who funded and directed the Scofield bible knew precisely what they were doing. Their strategy has borne the sour fruit today whereby the ersatz "Christian" churches not only offer no resistance to Zionist aims, but they, in fact, promote Zionism. Incredible as it sounds, the Satanic Zionist conspiracy against Christ and Christians is a cornerstone of many ersatz "Christian" churches. One example is Calvary Chapel, founded by Chuck Smith.

Calvary Chapel has become one of the world's largest and

most influential religious organizations. Calvary Chapel of Costa Mesa, California, where Smith is senior pastor, is a mega-church with a membership of approximately 20,000 people.[242] According to a 2003 article in *Forbes* magazine, Calvary Chapel, Costa Mesa is the third largest non-Catholic church in the United States.[243] In addition, he has a regular radio program, "The Word for Today," which includes edited messages from Smith's sermons at Calvary Chapel, Costa Mesa.. The television version of *The Word for Today* is seen nationwide on the blasphemous Trinity Broadcasting Network.

Calvary Chapel also owns and operates their own radio station (KWVE). Calvary Chapel has a Bible College offering an Associate's Degree in Theology, and a Bachelor's degree in Biblical Studies. It owns a 47-acre campus in Murietta Hot Springs, California. It also owns a castle in Austria. In addition, Calvary Chapel ministries include Calvary Chapel Music, Calvary Chapel Satellite Network International, Calvary Chapel Conference Center, Calvary Chapel Christian Camp, Maranatha Christian Academy, and Calvary Chapel High School. There are over 850 affiliated Calvary Chapels all over the world, including approximately 700 in the United States. Some of the affiliated Calvary Chapels in the United States are mega-churches in their own right, with memberships of more than 5,000 people.[244] *Forbes* magazine lists Calvary Chapel of Fort Lauderdale, Florida, an affiliate of Calvary Chapel, as the ninth largest non-Catholic church in the United States, with an average attendance of 17,000.[245]

Of course, Calvary Chapel promotes and sells the Scofield Study Bible in the NKJV, which is chock full of dispensational Zionist propaganda.[246] "Maranatha! Music," founded by Chuck Smith (allegedly sold in 1988 to Smith's nephew, Chuck Fromm), has branched out to providing NIV (New International Version) bibles. Their website states that "Maranatha! Book Publishing was launched in 1999 as we partnered with Zondervan to create The

NIV Worship Bible." Zondervan is owned by Harper Collins, which is the publisher of *The Satanic Bible*.[247] "Can two walk together, except they be agreed?" Amos 3:3.

In this author's previous book titled *The Anti-Gospel*, I revealed that the initial funding for Calvary Chapel came from the Illuminati.[248] The Illuminati is a powerful Jewish secret society. We see the same Zionist forces behind Smith as were behind Scofield. Smith and his "ministry" are part of a conspiracy for Zionist conquest of Palestine and indeed the world. Smith's Zionist plans parallel the Zionist plans of the Illuminati, which is not surprising in light of the Illuminati funding for Smith. An investigative team from *The Executive Intelligence Review* discovered a group called the "American Jerusalem Temple Foundation," which was an early source of "massive amounts of money from American-based Darbyite Christian fundamentalists"[249] that were poured into "Jerusalem operations, aimed, ultimately, at blowing up the Muslim holy sites at the Temple Mount, and building the Third Temple."[250]

In the middle of this planned bloodfest, we find Chuck Smith, pastor of Calvary Chapel. *The Executive Intelligence Review* discovered the following:

> At the core of the Gnostic "dispensational premillennarianism," advocated by Nineteenth-Century Anglican clergyman John Nelson Darby, is the belief that the extermination of the Jews, in a final battle of Armageddon, brought on by the rebuilding of Solomon's Temple, is the Biblical precondition for the second coming of the Messiah and the Rapture. **Pastor Chuck Smith, Dolphin's mentor at the Calvary Baptist Church, when asked by EIR whether he had any compunctions about unleashing a holy war that would lead to the possible extermination of**

> millions of Jews and Muslims, replied, "Frankly, no, because it is all part of Biblical prophesy."[251]
>
> Smith was also full of praise for the Jewish zealots of the Temple Mount Faithful, and their founder, Goldfoot: "Do you want a real radical?" he asked. "Try Stanley Goldfoot. He's a wonder. His plan for the Temple Mount is to take sticks of dynamite and some M-16s and blow the Dome of the Rock and Al-Aqsa Mosques and just lay claim to the site."[252]

Who is Stanley Goldfoot, upon whom Chuck Smith heaps such praise? He is a psychopathic mass murderer and internationally recognized terrorist! He has admitted he helped plan the 1946 dynamite bombing of the King David Hotel that killed approximately 100 Christian, Jewish, and Muslim civilians.[253] Goldfoot has also admitted that he planned and directed the execution of the United Nations mediator, Count Folke Bernadotte in Jerusalem, in the fall of 1948.[254]

Chuck Smith is so impressed with Goldfoot that he invited that killer to lecture in his Calvary Chapel![255] Smith has also financed Goldfoot's Zionist activities! The Hebrew University of Jerusalem explains:

> Chuck Smith, a noted minister and evangelist whose Calvary Chapel in Costa Mesa, California, has been one of the largest and most dynamic Charismatic churches in America, invited Goldfoot to lecture in his church, and his followers helped to finance Goldfoot's activity.[256]

> Smith secured financial support for exploration of the exact site of the Temple. An associate of Smith,

Lambert Dolphin, a California physicist and archeologist and leader of the "Science and Archeology Team," took it upon himself to explore the Temple Mount. An ardent premillennialist who believed that the building of the Temple was essential to the realization of messianic hopes.[257]

Can we regard Chuck Smith as a faithful minister of the Gospel when he praises and financially supports a terrorist killer? Why would he do such a thing? Because both he and Goldfoot are Zionists who want to bring Palestine under the complete control of Israel. One of the key goals of the Zionist Illuminati is to rule the world. Jewish control of Palestine is one step toward that Zionist goal.

Another Zionist shill was Jerry Falwell. Unsurprisingly, Falwell was on the NKJV overview committee. M. H. Reynolds says this about Falwell and his false claims promoting the NKJV:

> Dr. Jerry Falwell, a member of the NKJV overview committee, gives this new Bible his unqualified endorsement, stating that "It protects every thought, every idea, every word, just as it was intended to be understood by the original scholars." This simply is not true! As already pointed out, words have been changed and with those changed words have come changed thoughts and ideas.[258]

In 1979, Israel gave Falwell a gift of a Learjet.[259] Falwell put the Learjet to good use spreading the dispensational theology that includes a requirement of the Jews to return to Israel as part of God's plan for Christ to return.[260] His purpose was to influence the American Christian audience to favor Israel. Sean McBride explains how it worked:

> When Israel bombed Iraq's Osirak nuclear reactor

in 1981, Begin made his first telephone call to Falwell, asking him to explain to the Christian public the reasons for the bombing. Only later did he call [President] Reagan.[261]

Notice that Israeli Prime Minister Menachem Begin called Falwell before calling the President of the United States. That should give the reader some idea of the political importance of the "Christian" Zionist movement to Israel.

Falwell is now dead, but Israel has many arrows in its Zionist quiver. John Hagee is one of those deadly projectiles. Thomas L. McFadden of the American Free Press explains:

> John Hagee, the megachurch televangelist, is approaching the Washington, D.C. area again, ready to land in his private jet on July 20. An army of politicians and wide-eyed believers will follow this professed "man of God" who outdoes, in a sinister way, televangelists Pat Robertson and the late Jerry Falwell combined. Although Falwell did receive a Lear jet from the Israeli government in 1979, he never had an 8,000-acre luxury ranch loaded with mansions, hotels, barns and a private landing strip. But Hagee, the "corpulent con man," as he is popularly known, does.
>
> This Texas pirate is running a large number of organizations all geared toward spreading the word of the coming rapture and promoting war for Israel.
>
> Cornerstone Church in San Antonio and John Hagee Ministries telecast his national radio and television ministry, carried in America on 160 TV stations, 50 radio stations and eight networks and are heard or seen weekly in 99 million homes. He

is the founder of Christians United for Israel (CUFI).

Hagee spreads misery, destruction and greed wherever his Lear jet lands. He is pumping part of the cash he fleeces from the flock into the illegal settlements in the counterfeit state of Israel, while the child murderers there are aiming to dispose of the remainder of the Christians and Muslims in Palestinian villages with phosphorous bombs received free from America.

Regardless, just like for food, obese Hagee has a bottomless appetite for dead American kids as well, endlessly pushing for a war on Iran to satisfy his Zionist masters and strange followers who jump up and down like so many steroid-loaded basketball players waving their Israeli flags while the cash is collected. He is burning both ends of the candle manufacturing "moral support" for the endless flow of limbless and lifeless bodies that are flown and wheeled back to America to their parents from Iraq and Afghanistan.

But this is not enough for Hagee. At the last Washington conference he said: "[I]t is time for America to embrace the words of Sen. Joseph Lieberman and consider a military pre-emptive strike against Iran to prevent a nuclear holocaust in Israel." Actually jetsetter Hagee and his gang were lobbying Congress for the territorial expansion of Israel and a genocidal American nuclear strike on Iran. These well-financed people seem to be living from holocaust to holocaust just for the excitement of it.

* * *

Hagee is also a frequent guest of Israel. He met Prime Minister Binyamin Netanyahu just recently, a day before Vice President Joe Biden arrived and was humiliated by the Israeli leader.

Hagee also receives extraordinary coverage from the U.S. media, publicity that could not be purchased for tens of millions of dollars. He even appeared as a guest writer for The Washington Post in January 2009 under the title: "My Hopes and Concerns for Obama."

This is a major PR drive to extend the useful life of the "Holocaust" and to serve the Zionist agenda in the United States. There are hundreds of millions of dollars donated by these Israel-worshippers.[262]

I am not suggesting that all who hold to the pretribulation rapture doctrine are agents of Zionists or the Roman Catholic Church. Many in Smith's Calvary Chapel, Hagee's Cornerstone Church, and similar Zionist churches throughout the world have simply been deceived. Like the noble Bereans, let us check the pretribulation rapture teachings against the scriptures. See Acts 17:11. But if one were to look in the NKJV one would be hoodwinked into buying into the pretribulation rapture deception that promotes Zionisma and conceals the Antichris of Rome.

27 Antichrist Zionism in the Churches

The premillennial dispensationalism in the Schofield Bible had a long and sordid history before Scofield was tapped to popularize it. The serpent is ever so subtle. See Genesis 3:1. The devil's subtle change in capitalizing a single letter in 2 Thessalonians 2:7 from "he" in the AV to "He" in the NKJV has formed the foundation of a heathen eschatology invading churches. The groundwork was laid long ago. The pretribulation rapture mythology undermines the grace of the gospel. It includes within it the resurgence of Israel and the extinction of the church during a supposed 1,000 year reign of Christ on Earth from a rebuilt temple in Jerusalem.

The 1,000 year reign of Christ is based on an interpretation of "thousand years" in Revelation 20:2-3 meaning the number, one thousand (1,000) years. But a thousand years in Revelation 20:2-3 does not mean ONE thousand years. Noah Webster explains in his American Dictionary of the English Language that while a thousand can denote "the number of ten hundred," he explains that "thousand can also mean: "Proverbially, denoting a great number indefinitely. It is a thousand chances to one that you succeed."[263] In the context of Revelation 20:2-3, the definition of "thousand" is "an indefinite but very large number: a hyperbolic use."[264] Webster's 1913 Dictionary confirms this. It states that "thousand" means "indefinitely, a great number. A thousand shall fall at thy side, and ten thousand at thy right hand. - Ps. xci. 7."[265]

But Satan wants people to interpret Revelation 20:2-3 to support his mythology that Christ would reinstate animal sacrifices and the Mosaic law and rule Jerusalem for 1,000 years. Of course, he has his corrupt Bible versions to support that heresy. Below is the Contemporary English Version (CEV) wherein "thousand years" is translated as the number, "1,000 years."

AV	CEV
And he laid hold on the dragon, that old serpent, which is the Devil, and Satan, and bound him **a thousand years**, And cast him into the bottomless pit, and shut him up, and set a seal upon him, that he should deceive the nations no more, till **the thousand years** should be fulfilled: and after that he must be loosed a little season. (Revelation 20:2-3 AV)	He chained the dragon for **1,000 years**. It is that old snake, who is also known as the devil and Satan. Then the angel threw the dragon into the pit. He locked and sealed it, so **1,000 years** would go by before the dragon could fool the nations again. But after that, it would have to be set free for a little while. (Revelation 20:2-3 CEV)

The "thousand years" in Revelation is about the binding of Satan for a very long but indefinite period after the crucifixion of Jesus Christ. We read in Revelation 20:7-8 that Satan will be loosed for "a little season" after that "thousand" years. The Literal Standard Version (LSV) Bible, as does the CEV, describes the binding of Satan for exactly "one thousand" numeric years, which plays into the Zionist millennial reign of Christ on Earth mythology.

AV	LSV
And when **the thousand years** are expired, Satan shall be loosed out of his prison, And shall go out to deceive the nations which are in the four quarters of the earth, Gog and Magog, to gather them together to battle: the number of whom is as the sand of the sea. (Revelation 20:7-8 AV)	And when the **one thousand years** may be completed, Satan will be loosed out of his prison, and he will go forth to lead the nations astray, that are in the four corners of the earth—Gog and Magog—to gather them together to war, of whom the number—as the sand of the sea. (Revelation 20:7-8 LSV)

In the 1800s, Zionist Jews needed financial backing from the United States, or their plan for a New Israel would fail. In the 1800s, the United States was a predominantly Christian country. Any attempt to subjugate Palestine and reestablish Israel as a state in that region would be met with resistance from the then politically influential Christian quarter in the U.S. The Christians in the U.S. posed a political roadblock to funding the new state of Israel. The Zionists knew that they had to nullify the anticipated Christian resistance to their Zionist plan. They decided that the Christian theology in the Protestant churches must be changed to favor an Israeli state. They had ready theologians to perform this duty in their Jesuit auxiliary.

The Jesuits decided upon a plan to inject a theology into the Protestant churches whereby the Jews would be restored to their lost prominence via the rebuilding of the Jewish temple in Jerusalem. There would be a reinstatement of animal sacrifices and the ordinances of the Old Testament law. Christ would return and rule from the temple during a millennial reign. Thus, the Christians would look upon reestablishing the Jewish state of Israel in Palestine as a fulfillment of the prophecy. Consequently, they would not offer any political resistance but would be encouraged to support Israel. The pretribulation rapture was part of their premillennial eschatology that included a resurgence of Israel.

The Roman Catholic Church also wanted to steer the Protestant theology away from identifying the Pope as the Antichrist. The idea was to point the attention of Protestants to a future Antichrist and away from the Antichrist sitting on the throne in Rome. So the Jesuits tried to frame a new "Christian" eschatology that accomplished both concealing the Antichrist and reestablishing the Jews to prominence in God's prophetic plan. The Jesuits and their fellow travelers cobbled together a disjointed patchwork of Bible passages to create the pretribulation rapture mythology that served to lay the groundwork for this new futurist/Zionist theology.

Ultimately, this new theology was introduced in the seminary schools controlled by crypto-Jews. The witting and unwitting seminary graduates then taught their new "Christian" theology in the Protestant churches throughout the world. This new theology is the basis for the *Left Behind* series of 16 religious novels, that have sold more than 65 million copies.[266] The *Left Behind* series of books is also very popular series of movies that are heavily promoted in churches worldwide. It called for a rapture followed by a tribulation period, which, in turn, would be followed by the millennial reign of Christ from Jerusalem for 1,000 years.

Tens of millions of Christians were executed by the Roman Catholic Church during the Dark Ages because those brave witnesses for Christ believed that the Pope was the Antichrist. One of the foundational principles of the Protestant Reformation was that the Pope was the Antichrist.[267] The Holy Scriptures amply support this view.

The belief that the Pope is the Antichrist was once a virtually unanimous belief among Protestant denominations. The Westminster Confession of Faith (Church of England) states: "There is no other Head of the Church but the Lord Jesus Christ, nor can the Pope of Rome, in any sense, be head thereof, but is that Antichrist, that man of sin, and Son of perdition, that exalteth himself in the Church against Christ and all that is called God." Other Protestant confessions of faith identified the Pope as the Antichrist, including but not limited to the Morland Confession of 1508 and 1535 (Waldenses) and the Helvetic Confession of 1536 (Switzerland).[268] Today, those who hold such a belief are in the minority. Nowadays, it is viewed as radical and uncharitable for a Christian to say that the Pope is the Antichrist. How did such transformation take place among the Protestant denominations?

The change in the position of the Protestant denominations toward Rome was the direct result of a concerted campaign by agents of the Roman Catholic Church.[269] One of the methods used by the Roman Catholic theologians was to relegate much of the book of Revelation to some future time.[270] In 1590 a Roman Catholic Jesuit priest, Francisco Ribera, in his 500-page commentary on the book of Revelation, placed the events of most of the book of Revelation in a period in the future just prior to the end of the world.[271] He claimed that the Antichrist would be an individual who would not be manifested until very near the end of the world. He wrote that the Antichrist would rebuild Jerusalem, abolish Christianity, deny Christ, persecute the church, and dominate the world for three and half years.[272]

Another Jesuit, Cardinal Robert Bellarmine, promoted Ribera's teachings.[273] Bellarmine was one of the most influential cardinals of his time. In 1930, the Vatican canonized him as a saint and "Doctor of the Church." This Catholic interpretation of the book of Revelation did not become accepted in the Protestant denominations until a book titled *The Coming of the Messiah in Glory and Majesty* was published in 1812, 11 years after the death of its author.[274] The author of that book was another Jesuit by the name of Emanuel de Lacunza.

William Kimball in his book *Rapture, A Question of*

Timing, reveals that de Lacunza wrote the book under the pen name of Rabbi Juan Josaphat Ben Ezra.[275] Kimball attributes the pen name to a motive to conceal his identity, thus taking the heat off of Rome and making his writings more palatable to the Protestant readers.[276] It is as likely that, in fact, the pen name was not a pen name at all, but rather Lacunza'a true identity as a Jewish Rabbi. It is possible that Lacunza was a crypto-Jew, who wrote the book under his true identity as a rabbi. One does not suddenly convert to Judaism and then become immediately so versed in that religion that one takes on the title "rabbi." He must have had the learning of a Rabbi to write a book that contains knowledge of Judaism expected of a Rabbi.

Notably, Lacunza did not publish the book; it was published by someone else eleven years after his death. Why would Lacunza go through such trouble and then not publish the book? Could it be that Lacunza was in a dilemma? The book targeted at a Protestant audience, who would not accept a futurist theory from a Jesuit. So he knew he could not publish it under his actual name. He had to publish under another name. Could it be that he was concerned about publishing the book, which would expose his true identity as a Jewish rabbi and demurred on doing so? While that explains his actions, couldn't he have simply used some other non-Jewish pen name? There is no authoritative answer to that mystery.

Lacunza's status as a rabbi is all the more believable when one considers the fact that he was a Jesuit and the Jesuits are a crypto-Jewish secret society. The first Jesuits were crypto-Jews.[277] Ignatius Loyola himself was a crypto-Jew of the Occult Kabbalah. Jews were attracted to the Jesuit order and joined in large numbers.[278] Ribera[279] was a crypto-Jew. Lacunza would not be out of place as a Jewish Jesuit. Lacunza and Ribera, being Jews, would explain why they introduced the eschatological teaching of a return to the Jewish animal sacrifices. That doctrine gives the Jews primacy in God's plan and relegates Christians to a prophetic parenthetical to be supplanted by the Jews during the supposed one thousand year earthly reign of Christ.

Lacunza wrote that during a millennium, which would be after the tribulation, the Jewish animal sacrifices would be reinstated, along with the Eucharist (the mass) of the Catholic Church.[280] Lacunza followed after Jewish fables and replaced the commandments of God with the commandments of men. See Titus 1:13. "They profess that they know God; but in works they deny him, being abominable, and disobedient, and unto every good work reprobate." (Titus 1:16 AV)

Hebrews 8:1-10:39 explicitly states that Christ fulfilled the requirements of the law by sacrificing himself once for sins for all time. If the blood of animals were sufficient to satisfy God, there would be no need for him to come to the earth and sacrifice himself. "But now hath he obtained a more excellent ministry, by how much also he is the mediator of a better covenant, which was established upon better promises. For if that first covenant had been faultless, then should no place have been sought for the second." (Hebrews 8:6-7 AV)

> So Christ was **once offered** to bear the sins of many; and unto them that look for him shall he appear the second time without sin unto salvation. (Hebrews 9:28 AV)

> By the which will we are sanctified through the offering of the body of Jesus Christ **once for all**. And every priest standeth daily ministering and offering oftentimes the same sacrifices, which can never take away sins: But this man, after he had **offered one sacrifice for sins for ever**, sat down on the right hand of God; From henceforth expecting till his enemies be made his footstool. For **by one offering he hath perfected for ever**

> **them that are sanctified**. (Hebrews 10:10-14 AV)

God would not have us return to the weak and beggarly elements of the Old Testament law. See Galatians 4:9-11. To teach such a thing is to blasphemously state that Christ's sacrifice was imperfect and insufficient and that, therefore, there is a need to reinstate the animal sacrifices. The Old Testament law was to act as a schoolmaster until the promise of Christ. God would have no reason to reinstate something that was intended to be in place only until he came to offer his own body as a perfect sacrifice. In Christ there is neither Jew nor Gentile; we are all one by faith in Christ. He is not going to divide us once again into Jew and Gentile. His church is his body, which cannot be divided. 1 Corinthians 1:13. For a kingdom divided against itself cannot stand. Mark 3:24.

> But before faith came, we were kept under the law, shut up unto the faith which should afterwards be revealed. Wherefore the law was our schoolmaster *to bring us* unto Christ, that we might be justified by faith. **But after that faith is come, we are no longer under a schoolmaster**. For ye are all the children of God by faith in Christ Jesus. For as many of you as have been baptized into Christ have put on Christ. **There is neither Jew nor Greek, there is neither bond nor free, there is neither male nor female: for ye are all one in Christ Jesus**. And if ye *be* Christ's, then are ye Abraham's seed, and heirs according to the promise. (Galatians 3:23-29 AV)

The Bible clarifies that the old covenant is to vanish, replaced by the new covenant of faith in Jesus Christ. "In that he saith, A new covenant, he hath made the first old. Now that which decayeth and waxeth old is ready to vanish away." (Hebrews 8:13 AV) Why would God reinstate something which he has said would vanish away and in which he has had no pleasure? "In burnt offerings and sacrifices for sin thou hast had no pleasure." (Hebrews 10:6 AV)

Christ made his one sacrifice on the cross whereby those who believe in him are made perfect; there will be no more offering of any kind for sin, period.

> But this man, after he had offered one sacrifice for sins for ever, sat down on the right hand of God; From henceforth expecting till his enemies be made his footstool. For **by one offering he hath perfected for ever them that are sanctified**. Whereof the Holy Ghost also is a witness to us: for after that he had said before, This is the covenant that I will make with them after those days, saith the Lord, I will put my laws into their hearts, and in their minds will I write them; And their sins and iniquities will I remember no more. **Now where remission of these is, there is no more offering for sin**. (Hebrews 10:12-18 AV)

Christ has set us free from the law of sin and death in our flesh. Because of the weakness of the flesh, we can't obey God's holy law. God must change our hearts through spiritual rebirth so that we can walk not after the flesh but after the spirit. Our obedience to God's law does not earn salvation; it is a sign of salvation. We fulfill the righteousness of his law through the obedience of Jesus and his final sacrifice. Jesus' righteousness is imputed to those whom God chooses by his grace through faith in Jesus Christ for salvation.

> And therefore it was imputed to him for righteousness. Now it was not written for his sake alone, that it was imputed to him; But for us also, **to whom it shall be imputed, if we believe on him that raised up Jesus our Lord from the**

dead; Who was delivered for our offences, and was raised again for our justification. Therefore being justified by faith, we have peace with God through our Lord Jesus Christ. (Romans 4:22-5:1 AV)

Those who try to use obedience to the law of God as a means to salvation are carnally minded, trying to earn salvation through the works of the flesh. The carnal minds that teach a return to the carnal sacrifices of the law are enmity against God. For more information about that principle, read this author's book, *The Damnable Heresy of Salvation by Dead Faith*.

There is therefore now no condemnation to them which are in Christ Jesus, who walk not after the flesh, but after the Spirit. For the law of the Spirit of life in **Christ Jesus hath made me free from the law of sin and death**. For what the law could not do, in that it was weak through the flesh, God sending his own Son in the likeness of sinful flesh, and for sin, condemned sin in the flesh: That **the righteousness of the law might be fulfilled in us, who walk not after the flesh, but after the Spirit**. For they that are after the flesh do mind the things of the flesh; but they that are after the Spirit the things of the Spirit. For to be carnally minded *is* death; but to be spiritually minded *is* life and peace. Because **the carnal mind *is* enmity against God: for it is not subject to the law of God, neither indeed can be.** So then they that are in the flesh cannot please God. (Romans 8:1-8 AV)

Jesus blotted out the ordinances that were against us and nailed them to the cross. The law was only a shadow of Christ; he fulfilled the law. Having fulfilled the law, Christ will not reinstate it.

And you, being dead in your sins and the uncircumcision of your flesh, hath he quickened together with him, having forgiven you all trespasses; **Blotting out the handwriting of ordinances that was against us, which was contrary to us, and took it out of the way, nailing it to his cross;** *And* having spoiled principalities and powers, he made a shew of them openly, triumphing over them in it. **Let no man therefore judge you in meat, or in drink, or in respect of an holyday, or of the new moon, or of the sabbath** *days*: **Which are a shadow of things to come; but the body** *is* **of Christ**. (Colossians 2:13-17 AV)

The law of God was added after the promise given to Abraham. The law did not void the promise of God given to Abraham. The blessings of Abraham flow to all who believe in Jesus Christ. All who believe in Jesus are heirs of the promise given to Abraham. Galatians 3:23-29. That is, through faith in Jesus Christ, one becomes the spiritual seed of Abraham. Obedience to God is the result of salvation, not the cause of it. Just as Abraham believed in God, and it was accounted to him as righteousness, so too do all others who believe in God; it is also accounted unto them as righteousness.

Even as Abraham believed God, and it was accounted to him for righteousness. Know ye therefore that **they which are of faith, the same are the children of Abraham**. And the scripture, foreseeing that God would justify the heathen through faith, preached before the gospel unto Abraham, saying, In thee shall all nations be blessed. **So then they which be of faith are blessed with faithful Abraham**. For as many as are of the works of the law are under the curse: for it is written, Cursed is every one that continueth not in all things which are written in the book of the law to do them. **But that no man is justified by the law in the sight of God, it is evident: for, The just shall live by faith**. And the law is not of faith: but, The man that doeth them shall live in them. **Christ hath redeemed us from the curse of the law, being made a curse for us: for it is written, Cursed is every one that hangeth on a tree: That the blessing of Abraham might come on the Gentiles through Jesus Christ; that we might receive the promise of the Spirit through faith**. Brethren, I speak after the manner of men; Though it be but a man's covenant, yet if it be confirmed, no man disannulleth, or addeth thereto. Now to Abraham and his seed were the promises made. He saith not, And to seeds, as of many; but as of one, And to thy seed, which is Christ. And this I say, that the covenant, that was confirmed before of God in Christ, **the law, which was four hundred and thirty years after, cannot disannul, that it should make the promise of none effect. For if the inheritance be of the law, it is no more of promise**: but God gave it to Abraham by promise. **Wherefore then serveth the law? It was added because of transgressions, till the seed should come to whom the promise was made**; and it was ordained by angels in the hand of a mediator. Now a mediator is not a mediator of one, but God is one. Is the law then against the promises of God? God forbid: for if there had been a law given which could have given life, verily righteousness should have been by the law. **But the scripture hath concluded all under sin, that the promise by faith of Jesus Christ might be given to them that believe**. (Galatians 3:6-22 AV)

All the law and the prophets are summarized in two commandments.

> Master, which *is* the great commandment in the law? Jesus said unto him, Thou shalt love the Lord thy God with all thy heart, and with all thy soul, and with all thy mind. This is the first and great commandment. And the second *is* like unto it, Thou shalt love thy neighbour as thyself. **On these two commandments hang all the law and the prophets**. (Matthew 22:36-40 AV)

Jesus set us free by fulfilling the requirements of the law for us. Matthew 5:17; John 8:32; Ephesians 2:15; Colossians 2:14. Because we are set free does not mean we are free to sin. He gave us a new heart so that we are free to obey the law of God, which would otherwise have been impossible. God commands us to love one another and love God; upon those two commandments hang all the requirements of the law. Matthew 22:36-40. "For, brethren, ye have been called unto liberty; only use not liberty for an occasion to the flesh, but by love serve one another. For all the law is fulfilled in one word, even in this; Thou shalt love thy neighbour as thyself." (Galatians 5:13-14 AV) The royal law of God is that we should love our neighbors as we love ourselves. James 2:6. In fact, Jesus gave us a new commandment that goes further and tells us to what degree we are to love one another. Our obedience to this new commandment does not earn salvation, but our obedience is a sign that we are his disciples. "A new commandment I give unto you, That ye love one another; as I have loved you, that ye also love one another. By this shall all men know that ye are my disciples, if ye have love one to another." (John 13:34-35 AV)

Righteousness is imputed to those who believe; it is not earned. The deeds of the law will never earn salvation. Salvation is a gift of God through faith in Jesus Christ. Ephesians 2:8-10.

Therefore by the deeds of the law there shall no flesh be justified in his sight: for by the law is the knowledge of sin. **But now the righteousness of God without the law is manifested**, being witnessed by the law and the prophets; **Even the righteousness of God which is by faith of Jesus Christ unto all and upon all them that believe: for there is no difference: For all have sinned, and come short of the glory of God; Being justified freely by his grace through the redemption that is in Christ Jesus**: Whom God hath set forth to be a propitiation through faith in his blood, to declare his righteousness for the remission of sins that are past, through the forbearance of God; To declare, I say, at this time his righteousness: that he might be just, and the justifier of him which believeth in Jesus. Where is boasting then? It is excluded. By what law? of works? Nay: but by the law of faith. **Therefore we conclude that a man is justified by faith without the deeds of the law. Is he the God of the Jews only? is he not also of the Gentiles? Yes, of the Gentiles also: Seeing it is one God, which shall justify the circumcision by faith, and uncircumcision through faith**. Do we then make void the law through faith? God forbid: yea, we establish the law. (Romans 3:20-31 AV)

The true Jews are those who accept their Messiah, Jesus. The kingdom of God is a spiritual kingdom, it is not a kingdom based on race or tribe. Those who are chosen by God to believe in Jesus Christ are the spiritual Israel of God.

Not as though the word of God hath taken none effect. **For they are not all Israel, which are of Israel**: Neither, because they are the seed of

Abraham, are they all children: but, In Isaac shall thy seed be called. That is, **They which are the children of the flesh, these are not the children of God: but the children of the promise are counted for the seed.** (Romans 9:6-8 AV)

For he is not a Jew, which is one outwardly; neither is that circumcision, which is outward in the flesh: But **he is a Jew, which is one inwardly; and circumcision is that of the heart, in the spirit, and not in the letter; whose praise is not of men, but of God.** (Romans 2:28-29 AV)

Being born into a particular tribe or nation is irrelevant to entering God's kingdom. God's kingdom is made up of those whom he has chosen by his grace.

So then it is not of him that willeth, nor of him that runneth, but of God that sheweth mercy. (Romans 9:16 AV)

Therefore hath he mercy on whom he will have mercy, and whom he will he hardeneth. (Romans 9:18 AV)

God has not cast away Israel. His Israel is made up of those whom he foreknew before the foundation of the world who would believe in Jesus unto salvation. Therefore, all Israel shall be saved.

God hath not cast away his people which he foreknew. (Romans 11:2 AV) And so **all Israel shall be saved.** (Romans 11:26 AV)

Part and parcel of the belief in the renewed millennium sacrifices is the belief that the Jewish temple will be rebuilt. Many believe that the supposed future temple will be rebuilt at the location of what is now known as the Wailing Wall. They believe that the Wailing Wall is a remnant of the western wall from the old temple. In fact, the wailing wall is not the western wall of the ancient Jewish temple but is the western wall of the Roman Fort Antonia.[281] Fort Antonia was a permanent Roman fort at the time of Jesus. Fort Antonia was 800 feet north of the temple, and the southern wall of the fort was connected to the northern wall of the temple by double colonnades.

Jesus made it clear that the temple would be destroyed so thoroughly that "[t]here shall not be left here one stone upon another, that shall not be thrown down." Matthew 24:1,2; Mark 13:1,2; Luke 19:43,44; 21:5,6. The Jews are all too happy to deceive the world into believing that Jesus was wrong. In fact, the prophecy of Jesus was fulfilled perfectly. The temple was completely destroyed down to the last stone, the remains that are left standing today are the remains of Fort Antonia, not the temple.

The Dome of the Rock is not as it is supposed the place where Mohamad ascended into heaven. The Dome of the Rock is a pagan Islamic shrine built over the Roman *Praetorium,* which was where Pilate sentenced Jesus.[282] The *Praetorium* was inside Fort Antonia, not the Jewish temple.

Just as Christ repeated throughout his New Testament, so I will repeat: God has abolished the distinction between Jew and Gentile. Romans 3:28-30; 10:11-13. His church has become one spiritual temple and household of God, with Christ being the chief cornerstone. There is no more need for a physical temple, which was merely a shadow of the greater spiritual temple, his church.

> For he is our peace, who hath made both one, and hath broken down the middle wall of partition between us; **Having abolished in his flesh the enmity, even the law of commandments contained in ordinances**; for to make in himself

of twain one new man, so making peace; And that he might reconcile both unto God in one body by the cross, having slain the enmity thereby: And came and preached peace to you which were afar off, and to them that were nigh. **For through him we both have access by one Spirit unto the Father.** Now therefore ye are no more strangers and foreigners, but fellowcitizens with the saints, and of the household of God; And are built upon the foundation of the apostles and prophets, Jesus Christ himself being the chief corner stone; **In whom all the building fitly framed together groweth unto an holy temple in the Lord: In whom ye also are builded together for an habitation of God through the Spirit.** (Ephesians 2:14-22 AV)

Why would the Catholic Church want to deceive the world to follow after the Jewish fable of the reinstitution of the temple sacrifices? We must look to scripture to find the answer. In 2 Thessalonians 2:1-4, God states that the man of sin, the Antichrist, will exalt himself above all that is called God and sit in the temple of God and claim to be God.

Now we beseech you, brethren, by the coming of our Lord Jesus Christ, and *by* our gathering together unto him, That ye be not soon shaken in mind, or be troubled, neither by spirit, nor by word, nor by letter as from us, as that the day of Christ is at hand. Let no man deceive you by any means: for *that day shall not come*, except there come a falling away first, and that **man of sin be revealed, the son of perdition; Who opposeth and exalteth himself above all that is called God, or that is worshipped; so that he as God sitteth in the temple of God, shewing himself that he is God.**

(2 Thessalonians 2:1-4 AV)

What is the temple of God? Each saved Christian individually, and all saved Christians corporately make up the temple of God.

> Know ye not that **ye are the temple of God**, and that the Spirit of God dwelleth in you? If any man defile the temple of God, him shall God destroy; for **the temple of God is holy, which temple ye are**. (1 Corinthians 3:16-17 AV)

> What? know ye not that **your body is the temple of the Holy Ghost** which is in you, which ye have of God, and ye are not your own? For ye are bought with a price: therefore glorify God in your body, and in your spirit, which are God's. (1 Corinthians 6:19-20 AV)

> In whom all the **building fitly framed together groweth unto an holy temple in the Lord**: (Ephesians 2:21 AV)

The Pope has claimed the authority and position of God Almighty. He claims to be the God who rules the universal (catholic) church of God. That is, he claims to rule as God in the temple of God, the church.

> The Roman Pontiff judges all men, but is judged by no one. We declare, assert, define and pronounce: to be subject to the Roman Pontiff is to every human creature altogether necessary for salvation. . . . That which was spoken of Christ . . . 'Thou hast subdued all things under His feet,' may well seem verified in me. **I have the authority of the King of kings. I am all in all**

> and above all, so that God, Himself and I, The Vicar of God, have but one consistory, and I am able to do almost all that God can do. What therefore, *can* you make of me but God. *The Bull Sanctum*, November 18, 1302 (emphasis added).[283]

> **[W]e hold upon this earth the place of God Almighty.** *Pope Leo XIII* (emphasis added).[284]

To conceal the fact that the Pope fulfills the prophecy in 2 Thessalonians 2:1-4 of the Antichrist sitting in the temple of God, the Pope had his minions, the Jesuits, promote the millennium temple fable so that the deceived will be looking for the Antichrist in the distant future and not see the papal Antichrist right beneath their noses. Those who accept this millennium temple, however, have rejected righteousness by faith in Jesus Christ and instead teach a rebuilding of the physical temple, where righteousness will be by the law.

This Zionist/Catholic millennium doctrine is a rejection of Christ, the Chief cornerstone of the spiritual temple of God. The rebuilding of the physical temple with physical stone is a rejection of the rock of salvation, Jesus Christ.

> But Israel, which followed after the law of righteousness, hath not attained to the law of righteousness. Wherefore? Because **they sought it not by faith, but as it were by the works of the law. For they stumbled at that stumblingstone**; As it is written, Behold, I lay in Sion a stumblingstone and rock of offence: and whosoever believeth on him shall not be ashamed. (Romans 9:31-33 AV)

Jesus Christ is the stone that the builders of this false

religion have rejected; to them he is a rock of offense upon whom they will stumble to their ultimate demise. "For if they which are of the law be heirs, faith is made void, and the promise made of none effect." (Romans 4:14 AV) Jesus is the rock of salvation. Psalms 62:6; 89:26; 95:1. Christians are spiritual stones that are incorporated into Jesus Christ to make a holy temple of the Lord.

> As newborn babes, desire the sincere milk of the word, that ye may grow thereby: If so be ye have tasted that the Lord is gracious. **To whom coming, as unto a living stone, disallowed indeed of men, but chosen of God, and precious, Ye also, as lively stones, are built up a spiritual house**, an holy priesthood, to offer up spiritual sacrifices, acceptable to God by Jesus Christ. Wherefore also it is contained in the scripture, Behold, I lay in Sion a chief corner stone, elect, precious: and he that believeth on him shall not be confounded. **Unto you therefore which believe he is precious: but unto them which be disobedient, the stone which the builders disallowed, the same is made the head of the corner,** And a stone of **stumbling, and a rock of offence, even to them which stumble at the word, being disobedient: whereunto also they were appointed**. But ye are a chosen generation, a royal priesthood, an holy nation, a peculiar people; that ye should shew forth the praises of him who hath called you out of darkness into his marvellous light: (1 Peter 2:2-9 AV)

The Pope is a usurper, who is against Christ and claims to take the place of Christ in his temple (the church).

The Spanish edition of Lacunza's book became so popular in England that an English version was published. Edward Irving translated the English version.[285] He completed the translation in 1826, but the book was not published until 1827.[286] In 1830, a journal titled *The Morning Watch* published by Irving and his followers refined the futuristic interpretation and presented a theory that is popular in protestant denominations today known as the "pretribulation rapture."[287] Irving was placed on trial by the Presbyterian Church in 1832 for permitting unauthorized utterances of tongues and prophecies in his London church.[288] He was censored and officially removed as pastor. He then formed the Catholic Apostolic Church.[289] In 1830, Irving wrote a tract suggesting Jesus Christ possessed a fallen human nature. In 1833, he was tried for heresy and deposed from the ministry.[290] Irving died on December 7, 1834 at the age of 42.[291]

Robert Baxter, an associate of Edward Irving, wrote of his experience in Irving's church.[292] Irving would often have meetings that involved subjective spiritual manifestations, such as speaking in tongues that purportedly revealed new doctrines and predicted future events. Baxter was the source of a variant of Irving's pretribulation rapture teaching; Baxter spontaneously uttered a doctrine involving a mid-tribulation rapture. Baxter had so little control over his manifestation of tongues that in some instances he found it necessary to stuff a handkerchief in his mouth so as not to disturb his household.[293] Baxter was mercifully delivered from this power, which he identified as the power of Satan.[294] Baxter later renounced his own utterances and warned of the cunning craftiness of Satan, who can appear as an angel of light to deceive the unwary. *See* 2 Corinthians 11:14-15.

Dispensationalists who believe in a pretribulation rapture try to disassociate the pretribulation rapture doctrine from Edward Irving because of his tainted reputation and connection with the translation of Lacunza's book.[295] They prefer, instead, to attribute the pretribulation rapture origin to John Nelson Darby. Those who ascribe to the pretribulation rapture theory hold that there will be a resurrection of the Saints seven years prior to the return of Jesus

Christ, but they call it a rapture in order to distinguish it from the resurrection that is so clearly prophesied in the Holy Bible. This rapture of the Saints is supposed to be the catalyst for the entry of the Antichrist on the world scene. The appearance of the Antichrist is supposed to take place during a seven-year tribulation period following the rapture of the saints, hence the term "pretribulation rapture."[296] Darby was very familiar with Lacunza's book and wrote about it in 1829, just two years after the publication of Lacunza'a book in English.[297] Irving and Lacunza constructed a theory and then sought biblical support for it (eisegesis), rather than reading the Bible for what it says (exegesis). The publishers of the new Bibler versions are only too happy to help them serve the interests of Satan and his minions.

28 Censoring the Gospel

The Jewish hierarchy and the Vatican are joined in a conspiracy against God and man. The synergism between the two satanic spiritual camps is explored in detail in this author's book, *Solving the Mystery of Babylon the Great*. Their principal target is the Holy Bible. The Jews have gained hegemony over the Vatican. The Jewish influence over the Roman Catholic institution and its doctrines is manifest in *The Document of the Vatican Commission for Religious Relations with Judaism* § 4, which states: **"We propose, in the future, to remove from the Gospel of St. John the term, 'the Jews' where it is used in a negative sense, and to translate it, 'the enemies of Christ.'"**[298]

At a speech at Hebrew University in Jerusalem, Roman Catholic Cardinal Joseph Bernadine stated:

> [T]here is need for . . . theological reflection, especially with what many consider to be the problematic New Testament's texts . . . Retranslation . . . and reinterpretation certainly need to be included among the goals we pursue in the effort to eradicate anti-semitism.

> [T]he gospel of John . . . is generally considered among the most problematic of all New Testament books in its outlook towards Jews and Judaism . . . . this teaching of John about the Jews, which resulted from the historical conflict between the church and synagogue in the latter part of the first century C.E., can no longer be taught as authentic doctrine or used as catechesis by contemporary Christianity . . . Christians today must see that such teachings . . . can no longer be regarded as definitive teachings in light of our improved understanding.[299]

The effort by the Catholic Church to change the gospel in order to remove any mention of the Jewish rebellion against God is just one part of a manifold strategy by Zionist Jews to conceal their antichrist agenda. Zionist Jews view the New Testament as antisemitic hate literature.[300] That is why the Jewish hierarchy prohibits Jews from reading the New Testament. The Talmud at Sanhedrin 90a, 100b, states that those who read the gospels are doomed to hell. Furthermore, Shabbath 116a states that the New Testament is blank paper and should be burned.

    Orthodox Jews consider Shabbath 116a as a command to burn New Testaments. In Israel, they can get away with burning New Testaments, so that is what they do. For example, in 2008 *USA Today* reported that "Orthodox Jews set fire to hundreds of copies of the New Testament in the latest act of violence against Christian missionaries in the Holy Land."[301] When Or Yehuda Deputy Mayor Uzi Aharon heard that Christian missionaries distributed hundreds of New Testaments, he took to the roads in a loudspeaker car. He drove through the city urging people to turn over the New Testaments to Jewish religious students, who were going door to door to collect them. The New Testaments were then dumped into a pile and set afire in a lot near a synagogue. Aharon said it was a commandment to burn books that urge Jews to convert to Christianity.[302]

The Zionist Jews have influenced the United States Government to implicitly agree that the New Testament is antisemitic. The official U.S. Government position on antisemitism is memorialized in a March 13, 2008, report from the U.S. State Department to the U.S. Congress. The U.S. Government thinks that it is antisemitism to tell the truth about Jewish control of global financing, media, the U.S. Government, or Hollywood. The evidence is that Jews, in fact, control global financing, media, the U.S. Government, and Hollywood. The report, however, does not let the evidence get in the way of the Zionist political agenda. The report carries a dedication from two Zionist lackeys, President George W. Bush and Vice President Richard B. Cheney. The report was released by the United States State Department Special Envoy to Monitor and Combat Anti-Semitism, Gregg J. Rickman. The report states:

> The tactics of many anti-Semitic groups include the propagation of conspiracy theories, Holocaust denial, and the attribution to Jews of a satanic and "cosmic" evil. Traditional conspiracy theories claiming Jewish control of global financial systems, the media, the U.S. government, or Hollywood remain widespread. May and July 2007 Anti-Defamation League polls found that 39% of Polish respondents and 26% of Hungarian respondents, respectively, agrees that the Jews are responsible for the death of Christ.[303]

The State Department report cites to the Jewish Anti-Defamation League. That suggests that the government political agenda is being dictated by the Anti-Defamation League, which is under the control of *B'nai Brith*, which is Jewish Freemasonry. Notice that the report implies by the cited Anti-Defamation League survey that to agree "that the Jews are responsible for the death of Christ" constitutes antisemitism. That indicates that the U.S. Government agrees with the Anti-Defamation League position that the New Testament is antisemitic. In fact, in an earlier 2005 Report on Global Anti-Semitism, the U.S. State Department listed the following example of antisemitism: "In April, the pastor of St. Brigid Church in Gdansk told parishioners during services that 'Jews killed Jesus and the prophets.'"[304] The report states that the Archbishop of Gdansk removed the offending priest for saying that and for other alleged "improprieties."[305] In fact, that pastor was merely repeating the truth as stated clearly in the New Testament:

> For ye, brethren, became followers of the churches of God which in Judaea are in Christ Jesus: for ye also have suffered like things of your own countrymen, even as they have of **the Jews: Who both killed the Lord Jesus, and their own prophets**, and have persecuted us; and they please not God, and are contrary to all men. 1 Thessalonians 2:14-15.

That truth stated in the New Testament is considered antisemitic by the ADL and the U.S. Government. Abraham H. Foxman, National Director of the Anti-Defamation League of *B'nai B'rith*, believes that the historical record is that the Roams crucified Jesus, not the Jews. Foxman states:

> Over the last century a growing preponderance of evidence and scholarly study has demonstrated that the execution of Jesus was instigated primarily by the Roman authorities who ruled Palestine in the first century C.E., not by the Jewish people.[306]

Let's see what the inerrant word of God in the New Testament says. We read in the following passage how the Jewish religious leaders conspired to kill Jesus.

> Then assembled together the chief priests, and the scribes, and the elders of the people, unto the palace of the high priest, who was called Caiaphas, And consulted that they might take Jesus by subtilty, and kill him. (Matthew 26:3-4)

Who did Judas go to and arrange to betray Jesus? Did he go to the Romans? Judas did not go to the Romans, he went to the chief priests of the Jewish Sanhedrin.

> And Judas Iscariot, one of the twelve, went unto the chief priests, to betray him unto them. And when they heard it, they were glad, and promised to give him money. And he sought how he might conveniently betray him. Mark 14:10-11.

The inerrant New Testament records that it was the chief priests of the supreme ruling council of the Jews (the Sanhedrin) who were behind the crucifixion of Jesus Christ. The chief priests and the elders persuaded the Jewish mob to demand that Jesus be crucified, despite Pontius Pilate's determination to set Jesus free because he was innocent.

> **But the chief priests and elders persuaded the multitude that they should ask Barabbas, and destroy Jesus.** The governor answered and said unto them, Whether of the twain will ye that I release unto you? They said, Barabbas. Pilate saith unto them, What shall I do then with Jesus which is called Christ? **They all say unto him, Let him be crucified.** And the governor said, Why, what evil hath he done? **But they cried out the more, saying, Let him be crucified.** When Pilate saw that he could prevail nothing, but that rather a tumult was made, he took water, and washed his hands before the multitude, saying, I am innocent

of the blood of this just person: see ye to it. **Then answered all the people, and said, His blood be on us, and on our children.** Then released he Barabbas unto them: and when he had scourged Jesus, he delivered him to be crucified. (Matthew 27:20-26)

There is no question regarding the record contained in the infallible word of God. The Jewish leaders conspired to crucify Jesus, and they persuaded the Jewish mob to demand that the Roman governor, Pontius Pilate, crucify Jesus.

Ye men of Israel, hear these words; Jesus of Nazareth, a man approved of God among you by miracles and wonders and signs, which God did by him in the midst of you, as ye yourselves also know: Him, being delivered by the determinate counsel and foreknowledge of God, **ye have taken, and by wicked hands have crucified and slain**. (Acts 2:22-23)

God states in Acts 2:22-23 that the "men of Israel . . . have taken, and by wicked hands have crucified and slain" Jesus Christ. That fact is repeated in Acts 2:36, which states: "Therefore **let all the house of Israel know** assuredly, that God hath made that same **Jesus, whom ye have crucified**, both Lord and Christ." (Acts 2:36) The U.S. Government and the *B'nai Brith's* Anti-Defamation League think that the truth in God's word is antisemitic. Those are not the only passages that reveal that the Jews crucified Christ.

And when Peter saw it, he answered unto the people, **Ye men of Israel**, why marvel ye at this? or why look ye so earnestly on us, as though by our own power or holiness we had made this man to walk? The God of Abraham, and of Isaac, and of

> Jacob, the God of our fathers, hath glorified his Son Jesus; whom **ye delivered up, and denied him in the presence of Pilate, when he was determined to let him go. But ye denied the Holy One and the Just, and desired a murderer to be granted unto you; And killed the Prince of life**, whom God hath raised from the dead; whereof we are witnesses. (Acts 3:12-15)

God states in Acts 3:12-15 that the "men of Israel . . . delivered up and . . . killed the Prince of life," although Pontius Pilate "was determined to let him go." The truth that the Jews crucified Christ is repeated over and over again in the bible.

> Then Peter, filled with the Holy Ghost, said unto them, **Ye rulers of the people, and elders of Israel** . . . Be it known unto you all, and to all the people of Israel, that by the name of **Jesus Christ of Nazareth, whom ye crucified**, whom God raised from the dead, even by him doth this man stand here before you whole. (Acts 4:8-10)

> For of a truth against thy holy child Jesus, whom thou hast anointed, **both Herod, and Pontius Pilate, with the Gentiles, and the people of Israel, were gathered together**. (Acts 4:27)

> And when they had brought them, **they set them before the council: and the high priest** asked them, Saying, Did not we straitly command you that ye should not teach in this name? and, behold, ye have filled Jerusalem with your doctrine, and intend to bring this man's blood upon us. Then Peter and the other apostles answered and said, We ought to obey God rather than men. **The God of our fathers raised up Jesus, whom ye slew and**

hanged on a tree. Him hath God exalted with his right hand to be a Prince and a Saviour, for to give repentance to Israel, and forgiveness of sins. (Acts 5:27-31)

Which of the prophets have not your fathers persecuted? and they have slain them which shewed before of the coming of the Just One; of whom ye have been now the betrayers and murderers. (Acts 7:52)

And we are witnesses of all things which he did both in the land of the Jews, and in Jerusalem; **whom they slew and hanged on a tree**. (Acts 10:39)

Men and brethren, children of the stock of Abraham, and whosoever among you feareth God, to you is the word of this salvation sent. **For they that dwell at Jerusalem, and their rulers**, because they knew him not, nor yet the voices of the prophets which are read every sabbath day, **they have fulfilled them in condemning him. And though they found no cause of death in him, yet desired they Pilate that he should be slain.** And when they had fulfilled all that was written of him, they took him down from the tree, and laid him in a sepulchre. But God raised him from the dead. (Acts 13:26-30)

Abraham Foxman states that the New Testament inaccurately records that the Jewish hierarchy crucified Jesus.[307] Foxman characterizes the New Testament as antisemitic hate literature.[308] God states that the U.S. Government, the Roman Catholic Church, *B'nai Brith's* Anti-Defamation League, and Abraham Foxman are liars for contradicting God's perfect word.

"He that believeth on the Son of God hath the witness in himself: he that believeth not God hath made him a liar; because he believeth not the record that God gave of his Son." (1 John 5:10) The position of all Christians should be "let God be true, but every man a liar." (Romans 3:4) Just as the Jews persuaded the government of Rome to crucify Jesus Christ, they are now convincing the government of the United States to coverup their roll in that crucifixion. The Jews also work hand in glove with the Roman Catholic Church to censor their misdeeds from Christ's gospel.

29 New Bibles Undermine Creation by God

In 1996, Pope John Paul II announced that evolution is compatible with Christian beliefs. While evolution is compatible with Catholicism, evolution is not compatible with Christianity; evolution is irreconcilable with and antagonistic to Christianity. In 1998, the pope toned down his position by announcing that evolution alone cannot account for human existence. He, however, did not repudiate his pro-evolutionary position. God's word describes Adam as being "**made** a living soul." The NIV, NKJV, NASB, ESV, and virtually all new bible versions, however, follow the evolutionary philosophy of the world and changes God's word to say that Adam "**became** a living being." In the new Bible versions, man was not created, but instead just "became." This evolutionary slant fits in nicely with Roman Catholic teachings.

AV	NKJV
And so it is written, The first man Adam **was made a living soul**. (1 Corinthians 15:45 AV)	And so it is written, "The first man Adam **became a living being**." (1 Corinthians 15:45 NKJV)

The theory of evolution is not only contrary to God's word,

but it is not based on actual science; its origins are from heathen religious beliefs. According to the established laws of science, evolution is an impossibility. The second law of thermodynamics, also known as entropy, is that all matter, living or inanimate, goes from a state of order to disorder. The theory of evolution reverses that sequence and states that over time organisms go from a state of disorder to order; from the simple to the complex.

To illustrate the conflict between evolution and the laws of science, suppose one were to write each letter of one's name on a separate card. If those cards were thrown out a second story they would scatter and fall to the ground in a chaotic display. The scattering of the cards over time as they fall to the ground illustrates the law of entropy. The evolutionist would say that the reason that the cards did not fall to the ground in order, spelling out the person's name, is that they were not given enough time to become orderly. The evolutionist would advise one to get into an airplane and throw the cards out of the plane when it reaches an altitude of 10,000 feet. By the theory of evolution the more time the cards are in the air falling, the more time they have to organize and spell out the person's name when they finally land on the ground.

According to the law of entropy and common sense, giving the cards more time to fall to the ground only increases the disorder. The evolutionist, however, contrary to the laws of science and common sense, would have you believe that the more time the cards have to fall to the ground, the more orderly they will become.

The theory of evolution is the seed that germinated into communism and socialism. Hitler, Lenin, Stalin, and Trotsky, were all converts to the theory of evolution. Evolution was the foundational philosophy for their political actions and their justification for their maniacal brutality. Once one becomes a believer in evolution, it is a small step beyond that to being a believer in a communist revolution. If there is no life giver, there is no law giver, no one made me, no one owns me, and, therefore, there is no right and wrong. Thus, there is nothing intrinsically wrong with stealing, assaulting, torturing, murdering, even murdering millions of people.

The theory of evolution is founded upon racism. To understand this evolutionary racism we must examine what is meant by the term race. Race is simply defined as a group of persons who have a common lineage.[309] Race is not a biblical concept. God in the bible does not once catagorize different people according to race. He distinguishes different people by their tongues, families, nations, and countries. See Genesis 10:5, 20, 31; Revelation 10:11.

Prior to the 1800's, races of people were generally categorized according to their nationality (the German race, the English race, etc.).[310] With the popularity of Charles Darwin's theory of evolution, which was first published in 1859, it eventually became the widespread practice to define race according to physical appearance.

Darwin was a racist who believed that Blacks were closer to apes in the evolutionary process. The liberal humanists don't want the general public to know that the full title of Darwin's seminal 1859 book on evolution was: "The Origin of Species by Means of Natural Selection or the Preservation of Favored Races in the Struggle for Life." Darwin elaborated on his racist views as follows: "At some future period, not very distant as measured by centuries, the civilized races of man will almost certainly exterminate and replace the savage races throughout the world. At the same time the anthromorphous apes will no doubt be exterminated. The break between man and his nearest allies will the be wider, for it will intervene between man in a more civilized state, as we may hope, even that the Caucasian and some ape as low as a baboon instead of as now between the Negro or

Australian and the gorilla."³¹¹

Darwin's racist theory of evolution is refuted by natural science. Many scientists hold that because the physical variations that are used to catagorize people into different races (skin color, eye shape, etc.) are trivial (only .012 percent of human biological variation) and that genetically all humans are fundamentally the same, racial distinctions based upon physical appearance are not founded on biological reality but are in fact a social construct.³¹²

Professor of Epidemiology Raj Bhopal, who is the head of the Department of Epidemiology and Public Health at the University of Newcastle, stated in the British Medical Journal: "Humans are one species: races are not biologically distinct, there's little variation in genetic composition between geographically separate groups, and the physical characteristics distinguishing races result from a small number of genes that do not relate closely to either behaviors or disease."³¹³

In addition, a panel of "scientists, including geneticists and anthropologists meeting at the American Association for the Advancement of Science convention, said that the whole notion of race, based on skin color and hair type, is a social construction that has nothing to do with the genetic makeup of humans. . . . So while society busily tries to classify and reclassify races, the researchers say, it should remember that race is an artificial way to organize and categorize and has nothing to do with humans' fundamental makeup."³¹⁴

Those scientists maintain that it is a misnomer, therefore, to label people with different physical characteristics as being of different races. Because racial distinctions are somewhat arbitrary, there is no standardization of racial categories; in fact, the labels for the various races have changed with some frequency. There has been a recent trend in the United States to categorize races of people according to their perceived national or regional origin, such as African-American, Mexican-American, etc.

In *Saint Francis College et al. v. Al-Khazraji, Aka Allan*,[315] a United States citizen born in Iraq was denied tenure at a private college in Pennsylvania. The professor made a claim under a federal statute, 42 U.S.C. § 1981, alleging that he was discriminated against because of his ancestry. The college argued that § 1981 only prohibits racial prejudice and because the professor was considered a Caucasian under modern "scientific" theory that he could not be subjected to racial discrimination from another Caucasian.

The U.S. Supreme Court examined dictionaries and encyclopedias from the 1800's and discovered that the theory of racial classifications has undergone a significant change since then. It was not until the early 20th Century that dictionaries started defining race according to physical appearance and listing the racial categories: Mongoloid, Caucasoid, and Negroid. The Court recognized the lack of scientific authority for the modern racial classifications and found those classifications to be inadequate to address the issue of racial prejudice that 42 U.S.C. § 1981 was drafted to prohibit. The Court ruled that § 1981 prohibited discrimination based on ancestry or ethnic characteristics, regardless of whether the person has the physical appearance that places him into one of the modern racial categories.

The U.S. Supreme Court in the *Saint Francis College* case stated:

> There is a common understanding that there are three major human races - Caucasoid, Mongoloid, and Negroid. Many modern biologists and anthropologists, however, criticize racial classifications as arbitrary and of little use in understanding the variability of human beings. It is said that genetically homogeneous populations do

not exist and traits are not discontinuous between populations; therefore, a population can only be described in terms of relative frequencies of various traits. Clear-cut categories do not exist. The particular traits which have generally been chosen to characterize races have been criticized as having little biological significance. It has been found that differences between individuals of the same race are often greater than the differences between the "average" individuals of different races. These observations and others have led some, but not all, scientist to conclude that racial classifications are for the most part sociopolitical, rather than biological, in nature. S. Molnar, Human Variation, (2d ed. 1983); S. Gould, The Mismeasure of Man (1981); M Banton & J. Harwood, The Race Concept (1975); A. Montagu, Man's Most Dangerous Myth (1974); A. Montagu, Statement on Race (3d ed. 1972); Science and the Concept of Race (M. Mead, T. Dobzhansky, E. Tobach, & R. Light eds. 1968; A. Montagu, The Concept of Race (1964); R. Benedict, Race and Racism (1942); Littlefield, Lieberman, & Reynods, Redefining Race: The Potential Demise of a Concept in Physical Anthropology, 23 Current Anthropology 641 (1982); Biological Aspects of Race, 17 Int'l Soc. Sci. J. 71 (1965); Washburn, The Study of Race, 65 American Anthropologist 521 (1963).[316]

God "hath made of one blood all nations of men for to dwell on all the face of the earth." Acts 17:26. Racial distinctions are contrary to the commands of God: **"Judge not according to the appearance**, but judge righteous judgement." John 7:24. *See also* 1 Samuel 16:7: "But the LORD said unto Samuel, Look not on his countenance, or on the height of his stature; because I have refused him: for the LORD seeth not as man seeth; for **man looketh on the outward appearance, but the LORD looketh on the heart.**"

Christians should understand that our war is not a carnal war where distinctions are made between races of people as defined by the pagan world system. Christians are in a spiritual war against unseen "spiritual wickedness in high places." Ephesians 6:12. **"For though we walk in the flesh, we do not war after the flesh: (For the weapons of our warfare *are* not carnal,** but mighty through God to the pulling down of strong holds;) Casting down imaginations, and every high thing that exalteth itself against the knowledge of God, and bringing into captivity every thought to the obedience of Christ; And having in a readiness to revenge all disobedience, when your obedience is fulfilled. **Do ye look on things after the outward appearance?** If any man trust to himself that he is Christ's, let him of himself think this again, that, as he *is* Christ's, even so *are* we Christ's." (2 Corinthians 10:3-7 AV)

It is a natural heathen view of the world that judges men after their outward appearance. A Christian, on the other hand, is imbued with the Holy Spirit and does not judge a person based on his skin color or outward physical appearance. A Christian instead has "the mind of Christ."

> **But the natural man receiveth not the things of the Spirit of God: for they are foolishness unto him: neither can he know *them*, because they are spiritually discerned.** But he that is spiritual judgeth all things, yet he himself is judged of no man. For who hath known the mind of the Lord, that he may instruct him? **But we have the mind of Christ.** (1 Corinthians 2:14-16 AV)

The racist carnal mind is enmity against God.

"For they that are after the flesh do mind the things of the flesh; but they that are after the Spirit the things of the Spirit. For to be carnally minded *is* death; but to be spiritually minded *is* life and peace. Because **the carnal mind *is* enmity against God**: for it is not subject to the law of God, neither indeed can be. **So then they that are in the flesh cannot please God.** But ye are not in the flesh, but in the Spirit, if so be that the Spirit of God dwell in you. Now if any man have not the Spirit of Christ, he is none of his." (Romans 8:5-9 AV)

Who do we find in the middle of this evolutionary attack upon man and God? None other than the Militia of the Pope, the Jesuits. It was the Piltdown Man fraud that did the most to embed the evolutionary religion in the minds of scientists and the curricula of schools. In 1913, Piltdown Man was announced to the world as clear evidence of a transition between man and ape. For 40 years it was touted as evidence in support of evolution, until in 1953 it was exposed as a forgery.

It was determined that the skull of Piltdown Man was from a modern man and that the jawbone and teeth were from an orangutan. The teeth in the jaw had been filed down to make them look human. The bones and teeth had been chemically treated to give them the appearance of being prehistoric. The bones were then planted at the burial site in which they were found.

There is a strong belief among those who have investigated the matter that the noted Jesuit Priest Pierre Teilhard de Chardin, was instrumental in perpetrating that hoax. The scientist who helped unmask the forgery, Dr. Kenneth Oakley, formerly of the British Museum, said that a letter written to him by Teilhard in 1954 had given him "strong indications that Teilhard was in collusion with Charles Dawson" in committing the Piltdown Man hoax.[317]

30 Hiding the Flat Stationary Earth

God's word states that the earth is fixed and does not move. "Fear before him, all the earth: the world also shall be stable, that it be not moved." (1 Chronicles 16:30) Indeed, the earth cannot be moved. "The LORD reigneth, he is clothed with majesty; the LORD is clothed with strength, wherewith he hath girded himself: the world also is stablished, that it cannot be moved." (Psalms 93:1).

Notice that the immovable earth is closely associated with the praise and glory of God Almighty. They are inseparable concepts. In Psalms 93:1 we read that the LORD is clothed with majesty and strength, just as the world is stable and cannot be moved. If the earth is movable, then it impeaches the majesty and strength of God. Psalms 104.1-5 makes it clear that God laid the foundations of the earth and stretched forth the heavens just as he is clothed with honor and majesty. The concepts of God's majesty and a stable immovable earth are inseparable. If the earth moves and spins, then the God of the Bible cannot exist. However, a stable immovable earth confirms the existence of God. For more information about God's creation of a flat and stationary earth read this author's book, *The Sphere of Influence*.

So-called scientists, however, have concluded that the earth orbits the sun. Nicolaus Copernicus died in 1543 on the day his book, On the Revolutions of the Celestial Spheres, was published. Most people do not know that Copernicus did not originate the theory that the earth revolves around the sun. Aristarchus of Samos (310 – 230 B. C.) is the first person known to have postulated that the earth rotates on an axis daily and orbits the sun annually. Aristarchus' model had been rejected until Copernicus' book was published.

There was initially strong resistance to Copernicus' heliocentric system. However, over time the heliocentric view, with the earth and the other planets rotating around sun, has won popular acceptance. The heliocentric theory removed the earth as the center of creation and challenged the entire ancient authority of the Bible regarding the universe and its origins. Under the heliocentric model the earth is supposed to be rotating on an axis at approximately 1,000 mph at the equator while at the same time it supposed to be traveling approximately 66,000 mph (which would be 30 times the speed of a rifle bullet) as it revolves around the sun once each year. Heliocentricity is the progenitor of the theory of evolution.

Tycho Brahe (1546 – 1601), who was born three years after Copernicus died, was the most brilliant astronomer in all of history. His observations and models established that the earth is stationary and the sun revolves around the earth, with the other planets revolving around the sun.

Scientists have through objective experiments confirmed Brahe's findings. Today many of the astrophysical equations used to launch and navigate satellites assume a stationary earth. Satan has been successful in suppressing the fact that in 1898, physicists A.A. Michelson (1852 – 1931) and chemist E. W. Morley (1838 – 1923) proved that the earth does not move. The series of Michelson/Morley experiments, using an interferometer, which measured light rays, established that the earth was stationary.[318]

Throughout history scientists have conducted experiments that each time gave results that were not only consistent with a stationary earth but indicative of a stationary earth, from the light polorization experiments of E. Muscart in 1872 to the mutual inductance experiments of Theodore de Coudres in 1889 to the 1903 *Touton-Noble* experiments.[319]

Evidence that the earth is stationary is all around us. For example, assuming the heliocentric model with the earth traveling at over 1000 mph at the equator, if one were to take a plane flight from Buffalo, New York to Miami, Florida, by the time the airplane arrived in Miami over two hours after taking off from New York, due to the Coriolis effect Miami would have rotated over 2000 miles to the East. That would put the plane over the Pacific Ocean, just off the west coast of Mexico's Baja Peninsula. Yet, in reality, the flight arrives in Miami on time and without the pilot having to adjust for the rotation of the earth. The reason that the pilot does not have to adjust for the rotation of the earth is that the earth is not rotating, it is stationary just as God has said in his Holy Bible.

Some who accept that the earth rotates have argued that the atmosphere moves with the earth and therefore it keeps the plane synchronized with the earth. The problem with that argument is that nobody has ever identified or measured this mysterious force that keeps the plane synchronized with the rotation of the earth. The reason that the force has never been discovered is that it does not exist. This mystical (or rather fictional) lateral force does not exist because there is no need or it; the earth is not moving.

Not only is the earth stationary, it is at the center of God's creation. In 1976 Y.P. Varshi did an extensive study of the distribution of Quasars and published his conclusion in the *Astrophysics and Space Science Journal*. Varshi was forced by the evidence to conclude that "the cosmological interpretation for the red shift in the spectra of quasars leads to yet another paradoxical result: namely, that the earth is the center of the Universe."[320] Varshi calculated the odds for of the distribution of Quasars around the earth happening by chance at 3×10^{86} to one.

Satan has tried to muddy the waters so that Christians will not discover the truth of the flat unmovable earth at the center of God's creation. He must do this by having his minions publish corrupt versions of the Bible. For example, corrupt Bible versions like the New International Version (NIV) have been trotted out with corrupt passages that obfuscate the clarity of God's word. Despite the fact that God's word states clearly the earth is immovable, the new Bible versions wish to change God's word to comport with what they believe is the "scientific fact" that the earth is rotating on its axis and at the same time orbiting around the sun. In 2 Kings God reveals a miracle he performed by making the shadow cast by the sun on Ahaz's sundial to reverse and go back ten degrees.

> And Isaiah said, This sign shalt thou have of the LORD, that the LORD will do the thing that he hath spoken: shall the shadow go forward ten degrees, or go back ten degrees? And Hezekiah answered, It is a light thing for the shadow to go down ten degrees: nay, but let the shadow return backward ten degrees. And Isaiah the prophet cried unto the LORD: and he brought the shadow ten degrees backward, by which it had gone down in the dial of Ahaz. (2 Kings 20:9-11 AV)

Now, if you accept what God says in his word as true that the earth cannot be moved, it must have been the sun that went back ten degrees.

In fact, in Isaiah 38:8, God reveals that is exactly what happened; the sun moved back ten degrees by which degrees it had already gone down. In order for the sun to return the ten degrees that it had already gone down, the sun must have been moving across the sky in its ordinary path before its reversal. Hence, the earth is stationary and the sun travels in a circuit above the earth.

The translators of the new bible versions are more concerned with changing and twisting God's words to comport with popular opinion than using God's words to change the world. God's word makes clear that the earth is God's creation and it is fixed and cannot be moved. "Fear before him, all the earth: the world also shall be stable, that it be not moved." (1 Chronicles 16:30 AV) Because the New International Version (NIV) Bible translators do not believe God's word, they have changed the passage in Isaiah 38:8 to state that "sunlight" went back ten steps on the "stairway," rather than what actually happened, that the sun itself returned ten degrees. Simply stated, they have changed the verse to comport with a heliocentric view of the universe.

AV	NIV
Behold, I will bring again the shadow of the degrees, which is gone down in the sun dial of Ahaz, **ten degrees backward. So the sun returned ten degrees, by which degrees it was gone down.** (Isaiah 38:8 AV)	I will make **the shadow cast by the sun go back the ten steps** it has gone down on the stairway of Ahaz. So the **sunlight went back the ten steps** it had gone down. (Isaiah 38:8 NIV)

By changing the passage to say that the sunlight went back instead of the sun, the NIV translators have removed the fact that the sun is moving and have allowed for an explanation that the earth reversed its rotation, thus causing the sunlight to move back. Furthermore, they have removed the miracle of the event entirely by stating that the shadow went back ten steps on a stairway, rather than ten degrees on a sundial. A shadow cast by a pillar can go up and then back down steps due to the ordinary travel of the sun across the sky, however, the shadow cast upon a sundial cannot move backwards unless the sun moves backwards.

The corrupt new Bible versions have concealed from the reader the admonition to avoid the opposition of "**science** falsely so called." God clearly had in mind to warn his flock about heliocentricity and evolution. Instead, the reader of the new Bible versions is told to turn away from "what is falsely called **knowledge**." There is no field of study called "knowledge," but there is a whole discipline of study called "science." The admonition to avoid so-called knowledge, therefore, has no real meaning. That is the point of the new Bible versions: to strip the Bible of any real guidance.

AV	NIV
O Timothy, keep that which is committed to thy trust, avoiding profane and vain babblings, and oppositions of **science** falsely so called. (1 Timothy 6:20 AV)	Timothy, guard what has been entrusted to your care. Turn away from godless chatter and the opposing ideas of what is falsely called **knowledge**. (1 Timothy 6:20 NIV)

Nowhere in the Bible does God state that the earth is a globe. In fact, God expressly states that the face of the earth is a circle. "**It is he that sitteth upon the circle of the earth**, and the inhabitants thereof are as grasshoppers; that **stretcheth out the heavens as a curtain, and spreadeth them out as a tent to dwell in**:" (Isaiah 40:22)

The corrupt Bible versions leave the reader without any warning against so-called science. Bible corruption is a centuries old plan by Satan. One of the early Bible corruptions was the Roman Catholic Douay-Rheims Bible, which was an English translation of the Latin Vulgate. It was published in 1610. In 1750 the Roman Catholic Church published a revision of the Douay-Rheims Bible under the guidance of Roman Catholic

Bishop Richard Challoner (1691–1781). The revision changed the word "compass" in the original 1610 Douay-Reims Bible in the verse at Isaiah 40:22 to "globe" in the 1750 revision, just in time to hop on the heliocentric bandwagon. That Bible is given over entirely to following after "science falsely so called" in direct opposition to God's admonition. In the passage at Isaiah 40:22, the Douay-Rheims Bible changes the word "circle" to "globe," to comport with the godless helicentric model that has since become all the rage in "science falsely so called."

AV	Douay-Rheims
It is he that sitteth upon the **circle** of the earth, and the inhabitants thereof are as grasshoppers; that stretcheth out the heavens as a curtain, and spreadeth them out as a tent to dwell in. (Isaiah 40:22 AV)	It is he that sitteth upon the **globe** of the earth, and the inhabitants thereof are as locusts: he that stretcheth out the heavens as nothing, and spreadeth them out as a tent to dwell in. Isaiah 40:22 (Douay-Rheims Version)

A circle is two-dimensional and flat. That does not mean that the earth is two dimensional, as the earth certainly has depth. Rather, it means that the earth has a face that is a flat circle. Amos 9:6. It is "the circle **of** the earth." A globe, on the other hand, is a three-dimensional ball.

A circle is not the same as a ball. A circle is a flat plane whose circumference is equidistant from the center.[321] Indeed, when people refer to a ball they never call it a circle. Can you imagine a player asking his soccer teammate to pass him the "circle?" Nobody confuses a circle with a ball, and you can be sure that God knows the difference. The earth is described by God as a circle (i.e., a flat plane) in the Bible because it is true. "[L]let God be true, but every man a liar." Romans 3:2.

Isaiah knew the difference between a ball and a circle. *See*

Isaiah 22:18. If Isaiah meant ball in Isaiah 40:22, he would have said ball. He did not say ball, because the earth is not a ball. There can be no confusion here. God is stating that the face of the earth is a flat circle and the heavens are spread like a tent over that circle.

31 The Gospel is the Word of God

Many pastors have a very narrow view of the gospel, which, according to them, does not include God's creation of a flat and stationary earth. The new age pastors limit the gospel to only certain select doctrines that exclude God's creation. That way, they can prevent any discussion of God's creation of a flat and stationary earth by claiming that issue has nothing to do with the gospel. They are assisted in this corruption of the gospel by the new Bible versions.

The corrupters of God's word even change the passage that refers to them. In the NIV they changed the word "corrupt" to "peddle for profit" in 2 Corinthians 2:17. The passage "we are not as many, which **corrupt** the word of God" was changed in the NIV to say "[u]nlike so many, we do not **peddle the word of God for profit**." The passage in the Authorized Version establishes that from the beginning of the church there were those that were corrupting the word of God. Satan simply cannot permit that fact to be established in the scriptures, so he changed the passage for his counterfeit bibles.

Because the new bible publishers do not believe that the Bible is God's word, but merely a book that has a good message, some have replaced the word "gospel" with the words "good news." The word "gospel" literally means "God's word."[322] Yet in passage after passage some new bible versions change "gospel" to "good news."

AV	**RSV**
But the word of the Lord endureth for ever. And this is the word which by the **gospel** is preached unto you. (1 Peter 1:25 AV)	but the word of the Lord abides for ever. That word is the **good news** which was preached to you. (1 Peter 1:25 RSV)

The Bible itself has a built in dictionary, defining terms as they appear. In fact, in Romans 10:14-17 it defines the word "gospel" as the "word of God." This meaning is obscured in the new bible versions.

AV	NIV
How then shall they call on him in whom they have not believed? and how shall they believe in him of whom they have not heard? and how shall they hear without a preacher? And how shall they preach, except they be sent? as it is written, How beautiful are the feet of them that preach the **gospel** of peace, and bring glad tidings of good things! But they have not all obeyed the **gospel**. For Esaias saith, Lord, who hath believed our report? So then faith cometh by hearing, and hearing by the **word of God**. (Romans 10:14-17 AV)	How, then, can they call on the one they have not believed in? And how can they believe in the one of whom they have not heard? And how can they hear without someone preaching to them? And how can they preach unless they are sent? As it is written, "How beautiful are the feet of those who bring **good news**!" But not all the Israelites accepted the **good news**. For Isaiah says, "Lord who has believed our message?" Consequently, faith comes from hearing the message, and the message is heard through the **word of Christ**. (Romans 10:14-17 NIV)

John Calvin offers this retort to the new age pastors who limit the gospel to only portions of the Bible to the exclusion of God's creation and decription of a flat and stationary earth.

> [The Christian is not to compromise so as to obscure the distinction between good and evil, and is to avoid the errors of] those dreamers who have a spirit of bitterness and contradiction, who reprove everything and prevent the order of nature. **We will see some who are so deranged, not only in religion but who in all things reveal their monstrous nature, that they will say that the sun**

does not move, and that it is the earth which shifts and turns. When we see such minds we must indeed confess that the devil posses them, and that God sets them before us as mirrors, in order to keep us in his fear. So it is with all who argue out of pure malice, and who happily make a show of their imprudence. When they are told: "That is hot," they will reply: "No, it is plainly cold." When they are shown an object that is black, they will say that it is white, or vice versa. Just like the man who said that snow is black; for although it is perceived and known by all to be white, yet he clearly wished to contradict the fact. And so it is that they are madmen who would try to change the natural order, and even to dazzle eyes and benumb their senses.[323]

Many pastors want to limit the gospel to only Christ's crucifixion. They cite to the following verse in mind: "For I determined not to know any thing among you, save Jesus Christ, and him crucified." (1 Corinthians 2:2) But they misinterpret the verse to mean that one should only know about the crucifixion of Jesus Christ. They misinterpret that passage to mean that we are to eschew any discussion of a flat and stationary earth. But that is not what the passage states. It states that we are to know "Jesus Christ, **and** him crucified." There are two subjects separated by the conjunction, "and." The first thing that we are to know is Jesus Christ.

Who is Jesus Christ? We find the answer throughout the entire Bible. Jesus Christ is the creator of all things. "In the beginning was the Word, and the Word was with God, and the Word was God. The same was in the beginning with God. **All things were made by him [the Word-Jesus Christ]; and without him was not any thing made that was made**. In him was life; and the life was the light of men." (John 1:1-4) We read in Colossians 1:16 that "by him [Jesus Christ] were all things created, that are in heaven, and that are in earth, visible and invisible, whether they be thrones, or dominions, or principalities, or powers: all things were created by him, and for him." We read that Jesus Christ is revealed through his creation. "[T]hat which may be known of God is manifest in them; for God hath shewed it unto them. For **the invisible things of him from the creation of the world are clearly seen, being understood by the things that are made, even his eternal power and Godhead**; so that they are without excuse. (Romans 1:19-20) We read in the book of Genesis about Jesus Christ's creation of a stationary and flat Earth. We read throughout the Bible the importance of God's creation of a flat and stationary earth. *E.g.*, 1 Chronicles 16:30; Psalms 19:1-6, 33:4-9; 93:1,104:1-5, 104:30, 136:6, 102:25; Isaiah 40:22, 44:24; Proverbs 8:27; Job 28:24, 38:4-13; Amos 9:6; Joshua 10:12-13; 2 Kings 20:9-11. Jesus Christ is both our creator and our savior. And he created a flat and stationary earth.

Jesus Christ is the word of God that became flesh. John 1-14; 1 John 5:7-8. Indeed, the Bible is clear that Jesus Christ is all of the Word of God, not just some of it. "And he was clothed with a vesture dipped in blood: and **his name is called The Word of God.**" (Revelation 19:13) The gospel is not just the New Testament. Jesus commanded us to search the scriptures because they speak of him. Jesus explained: "Search the scriptures; for in them ye think ye have eternal life: and they are they which testify of me." (John 5:39) Those scriptures that were in existence at that time to which he was referring were the Old Testament. The gospel is all of God's word found in both the Old and New Testaments. Indeed, the gospel was preached to the Jews in the Old Testament. Hebrews 4:2. The Bible must be taken as a whole; the gospel is the entire word of God. There is a terrible curse on those who would add to or take away from the words found in the Holy Bible. Revelation 22:18-19.

Indeed, God proves that he is the everlasting LORD by his

creation. All false gods are not the Lord God of the Bible because they are not the creators of the heavens and the earth.

> **But the LORD is the true God**, he is the living God, and an everlasting king: at his wrath the earth shall tremble, and the nations shall not be able to abide his indignation. Thus shall ye say unto them, **The gods that have not made the heavens and the earth, even they shall perish from the earth, and from under these heavens. He hath made the earth by his power, he hath established the world by his wisdom, and hath stretched out the heavens by his discretion.** When he uttereth his voice, there is a multitude of waters in the heavens, and he causeth the vapours to ascend from the ends of the earth; he maketh lightnings with rain, and bringeth forth the wind out of his treasures. (Jeremiah 10:10-13)

The fact that Jesus Christ is the creator is part and parcel of the gospel. Jesus Christ created all things through his word. John 1:1-3, 14; Colossians 1:16. All the host of heaven were made by the breath of Jesus Christ's mouth. Psalms 33:6. His creation of massive bodies of water covering a flat, immovable earth is inextricably linked with his blessing on those whom he has chosen for salvation. Psalms 33:6-12. Jesus Christ watches from heaven above the firmament over all the inhabitants of his flat earth and stationary earth. Psalm 33:13-14. Jesus Christ looks out over his created flat and stationary earth to shed his mercy on his elect. Psalms 33:18. The creator of heaven and the earth saves his elect who hope in his mercy. Psalms 33:22. The words of God in Psalm 33 (and indeed the very theme of the Bible) reveals that the nature of Jesus Christ's creation is associated and identified with Jesus Christ's salvation of his elect. Indeed, God, in his Bible, gives us an understanding of his salvation by explaining his creation of a flat and stationary earth. *See* Romans 1:18; Pslams 33:1-22; 136:1-

26; Jeremiah 10:10-13.

Rejoice in the LORD, O ye righteous: for praise is comely for the upright. Praise the LORD with harp: sing unto him with the psaltery and an instrument of ten strings. Sing unto him a new song; play skilfully with a loud noise. **For the word of the LORD is right; and all his works are done in truth.** He loveth righteousness and judgment: the earth is full of the goodness of the LORD. **By the word of the LORD were the heavens made; and all the host of them by the breath of his mouth. He gathereth the waters of the sea together as an heap**: he layeth up the depth in storehouses. **Let all the earth fear the LORD: let all the inhabitants of the world stand in awe of him. For he spake, and it was done; he commanded, and it stood fast.** The LORD bringeth the counsel of the heathen to nought: he maketh the devices of the people of none effect. The counsel of the LORD standeth for ever, the thoughts of his heart to all generations. **Blessed is the nation whose God is the LORD; and the people whom he hath chosen for his own inheritance. The LORD looketh from heaven; he beholdeth all the sons of men. From the place of his habitation he looketh upon all the inhabitants of the earth.** He fashioneth their hearts alike; he considereth all their works. There is no king saved by the multitude of an host: a mighty man is not delivered by much strength. An horse is a vain thing for safety: neither shall he deliver any by his great strength. **Behold, the eye of the LORD is upon them that fear him, upon them that hope in his mercy**; To deliver their soul from death, and to keep them alive in famine. **Our soul waiteth for**

> **the LORD: he is our help and our shield. For our heart shall rejoice in him, because we have trusted in his holy name. Let thy mercy, O LORD, be upon us, according as we hope in thee.** (Psalms 33:1-22)

If the devil can use the big-bang heliocentric model to convince men that God did NOT create a fixed and flat earth by speaking "and it was done; he commanded, and it stood fast" as explained in Psalms 33:9. The devil can then can convince men that it is NOT true that God "[f]rom the place of his habitation he looketh upon all the inhabitants of the earth," as explained in Psalms 33:14. Once the devil removes God from heaven above and the conscience of men below, it is inexorable that he will then remove men's need for salvation, since there are no rules from God that need to be obeyed. Once the devil removes the need for salvation, the devil can attack the Biblical doctrine that God has a "people whom he hath chosen for his own inheritance," as described in Psalm 33:12. If there are NO special people elected by God for salvation, then it CANNOT be true that "the eye of the LORD is upon them that fear him, upon them that hope in his mercy," as declared in Psalms 33:18. Thus, there is NO basis for anyone to "waiteth for the LORD" as described in Psalms 33:20 because God is NOT "our help and our shield," as described in Psalms 33:20.

Once people are convinced by the devil that God is NOT our help and our shield, there is NO cause for our heart to rejoice in him, "because we have trusted in his holy name," as described in Psalms 33:21. In the end, there is NO reason to pray to God: "Let thy mercy, O LORD, be upon us, according as we hope in thee," as depicted in Psalms 33:20-22. You see, an attack on God's creation of a flat and stationary earth is an attack on the very existence of God and his merciful salvation. Heliocentrism is an attack on the gospel of Jesus Christ. Those who argue that the creation account in the Bible of a flat and stationary earth is not part of the gospel are, at the very least, unwittingly accomplices in the devil's dark rebellion against God.

The commonly accepted narrow definition for the gospel which excludes God's creation is found in churches today. Heliocentric pastors seem to have accepted the definition of the gospel from the profane world. *The Webster's Revised Unabridged Dictionary, 1913 Edition* defines "gospel" as "glad tidings; especially, the good news concerning Christ, the Kingdom of God, and salvation."[324] *The Oxford English Dictionary (Unabridged)* defines Gospel as:

> 'The glad tidings (of the kingdom of God)' announced to the world by Jesus Christ. Hence, the body of religious doctrine taught by Christ and His apostles; the Christian revelation, religion, or dispensation. Often contrasted with the Law, i.e., the Old Testament dispensation ... The record of Christ's life and teaching, contained in the books written by the 'four evangelists.'"[325]

The definitions by Webster's Dictionary and the Oxford Dictionary have the correct premise that "gospel" means "glad tidings;" but they narrow the meaning so that it leaves room for unscrupulous heliocentric pastors, like to define the gospel as something less than the entire Holy Bible. Heliocentric pastors interpret the gospel to exclude God's creation. Such a narrow interpretation of what the gospel means allows heliocentric pastors to cut off any discussion of the biblical flat and fixed earth.

Harper's Bible Dictionary (HBD) defines "gospel" as "good news."[326] HBD limits the gospel entirely to "the good news preached by Jesus that the Kingdom of God is at hand (Mark 1:15) and the good news of what God has done on behalf of humanity in Jesus (Rom.1:3-15)."[327]

The New International Dictionary of the Bible (NIDB) reveals that originally "gospel" denoted "good tidings" and "the story concerning God." As we will see, both of those terms mean God's word as found in the entire Holy Bible. But the NIDB explains that the original definition for "gospel," which included all scriptures, was later supplanted. And now, "gospel" is being defined as only the teachings of Jesus Christ as found in the New Testament.

> The English word *gospel* is derived from the Anglo-Saxon *godspell*, which meant "good tidings" and later the "story concerning God." As now used, the word describes the message of Christianity and the books in which the record of Christ's life and teaching is found.[328]

The Oxford English Dictionary (Unabridged), (OED) which is one of the most authoritative dictionaries in the profane world, has expressly stated that the word "god" in "god-spel" does not mean "God." The OED explained that "godspel" was accepted by ancient people to mean "GOD+spel."[329] But the OED claims that was a mistake: "The form godspel must therefore ... be due to a misinterpretation of the written form before the word had any oral currency."[330] The OED editors are guessing that godspel (with "god" meaning Almighty God) "must" be due to a misinterpretation of the written form of godspel. The OED editors imply that the word "god" should have been given meaning "good" rather than "God."

"Spell," in the context of the words "God spell," means "a story."[331] Since God spell is God's story, gospel was traditionally taken to mean "story concerning God."[332] That means "god-spel" is God's story or God's word. The OED theory that the ancient people misinterpreted "god" in "godspel" to mean Almighty God, implies that "god-spel" does not mean God's story (i.e., God's word). The result of the OED exclusion of God's story (i.e., God's word) as the meaning for "god-spel" is that the gospel can more easily be interpreted narrowly not to encompass the entire Holy Bible. Indeed, the OED expressly limits the gospel to "[t]he record of Christ's life and teaching, contained in the books written by the 'four evangelists.'"[333] and distinguishes the gospel from "the Old Testament dispensation."[334] Armed with this new limited definition of the gospel, heliocentric pastors can avoid addressing God's creation of a flat earth by rendering the topic as a distraction from the gospel.

All dictionaries are imperfect to one degree or another. And the generally accepted definition that renders "gospel" not to mean "God's word" is one example. *The Theological Dictionary of the New Testament,* by Gerhard Kittel, is the standard dictionary used by new bible version translators. The editors of that dictionary admit that it and all other dictionaries are imperfect:

> Dictionaries are incontestably among the most imperfect of human products. Those who are driven by calling or circumstances to seek help in lexical works should realize how inadequate is that which even the best and most comprehensive of dictionaries can offer the user.[335]

God, on the other hand, had this to say about his dictionary, which is built into his Holy Bible:

> "The words of the LORD are pure words" (Psalms 12:6-7)

> "Every word of God is pure:" (Proverbs 30:5)

Gail Riplinger has done extensive research on the meaning of "gospel" as used in the Holy Bible. She concluded that "the form of the first element (god) shows unequivocally that it was identified with 'God' not with 'good.'"[336] She concluded that modern dictionaries have defined gospel too narrowly as meaning only good news or similar such phrases. The word "gospel" does mean glad tidings, and those glad tidings are the word of God. Riplinger bases her conclusion on good authority, God Almighty.

Gail Riplinger is a linguist with both M.A. and M.F.A. degrees. She has done additional postgraduate study at Harvard and Cornell Universities. She was a university professor and authored six college textbooks. She is the best selling author of *New Age Bible Versions*.

The *Oxford English Dictionary (Unabridged)* (OED) gives the standard definition for "gospel" as meaning "good tidings." It is true that the gospel is good tidings. But the "good" in "good tidings" should be understood to be "godly," thus "good tidings" are actually tidings from God. *See* Luke 1:19; 2:9-10. But the OED implicitly sticks with a worldly definition of good. The OED argues that "god" in "god-spel" does not mean Almighty "God." The OED argues that "god" in "god-spel" should be read to only mean "good," and thus the definition of "gospel" should be limited to mean only "good tidings" and, by implication, not mean "God's word."

The editors of the OED base that exclusion of God from being the root of the word "gospel" on their claim that the ancient people who used the word "god" in "god-spel" as meaning "God" got it wrong. The OED stated that "the mistake was very natural."[337] The OED acknowledges that from the earliest development of the English language, the word "gospel" was taken to mean "god-spel," which was traditionally thought to mean "GOD+spel"[338] with "spel" meaning "discourse or story"[339] (i.e., God's story or God's word). The ancient people thought "gospel" meant "God spell" or "God's word." The theory of the OED is that the ancient people were wrong to interpret the "god" in "god-spel" to mean Almighty God, rather than "good."

That is a rather tenuous basis for a dictionary to eschew a definition. It is also a suspicious approach, when a dictionary is supposed to be semasiological. The definitions contained in a dictionary are, in part, descriptive and thus are supposed to reflect the etymology and common usage and meaning given to a word by people. How people use a word is supposed to support, and not undermine, a definition. It is illogical for a dictionary to explain the common usage and understanding of a word and then desconsruct it to explain why that common understanding is **NOT** what the word means. In order for the OED to do that it had to ignore what God says the word "gospel" means. The OED could not say that God was mistaken. The OED simply ignored the fact that the real reason that people thought that "gospel" meant "God spell" or "God's word" is because that is what God said it means in his Holy Bible. The OED had to ignore that elephant in the room in order to undermine the true meaning of the gospel.

Why would the OED go to such effort to undermine "God spell" (i.e. God's word) as the definition for "gospel?" It suggests that the OED has an agenda. The OED seems to be steering people away from a true understanding of the gospel as the whole word of God. Other dictionaries and etymologies have adopted the OED theory. Today, defining "gospel" to mean only "good tidings," to the express exclusion of "God spell," has taken on a life of its own.[340]

The only way to explain the OED editors' efforts to undermine the true meaning of "gospel" is that they have a profane bias and anti-Christian agenda. Indeed, Gail Riplinger reveals that is precisely the case.

> The founder of the Oxford English Dictionary, R.C. Trench, was rabidly against the Holy Bible and its all pervading influence and sociological control. He wanted the dictionary to show that words were being used in society in ways which

differed from the historical Bible usage. He wrote two entire books against the KJB [King James Bible]: *On the Authorized Version of the New Testament*, in connection with some recent proposals for its Revision (New York, 1858) and *Synonyms of the New Testament* (Cambridge, 1854). In these books he set the stage for the watered-down liberal definitions seen in today's new versions. On the title page of one of these books, he placed the same serpent logo used by Luciferian H.P. Blavatsky. Because of his hatred for the KJB, he was asked to be a member of the Westcott-Hort Revised Version Committee. He merits an entire chapter in this book for his vile re-definition of Bible words. As one might expect, *The Shorter Oxford English Dictionary's* definition of 'inspiration' also drops the name "God" for the adjective "Divine." It charges that the inspiration of the Scriptures "are believed by **some**" only. Instead of citing the Bible, it sites Trench's friend and Ghostly Guild founder, "B.F. Westcott" writing what the "early Fathers" believed, instead of what the scripture states. (Other chapters in this book detail the heresies of these ancient Catholic "Fathers." The OED editors, which followed Trench, also believed that they were not compiling prescriptive 'definitions,' but descriptive samples of how a word has been used in different contexts (secular, not always Bible-based contexts). The OED will allow the inclusion of the Biblical definition of words, but merely sets it in the midst of numerous other usages. To take one of its secular definitions and apply it to re-define the Bible's historic usage is to fall squarely into the clutching hands of R.C. Trench, whose official portrait shows him donning the 'X' medallion of the Masonic Grand Scottish Knights of St. Andrew.[341] (bold emphasis in original)

The profane world and heliocentric churches want people to only think of the "gospel" as "good tidings," to the exclusion of "God's word." As we will see, good tidings also means God's word; but because that meaning is not readily apparent, the use of good tidings as a definition for gospel facilitates modern churches accepting a more limited scope of the gospel that excludes God's creation. Expressly excluding "God's word" as a definition for the gospel obscures the reality that the "gospel" is in fact "God's word." That stratagem furthers the modern heliocentric pastors' evasion of what God's word states about God's creation of an immovable and flat earth.

The nature of the earth God created, in most churches today, is a topic considered not part of the gospel. Indeed, heliocentric pastors today argue that whether the earth is a spinning sphere or a stationary and flat earth is irrelevant to the "gospel" as they understand it.[342] Dr. Neelak S. Tjernagel, Ph.D., explains the historical treatment of the two meanings given to the word "gospel."

> Luther's translation of the New Testament appropriated the Greek word *euangelion*, which he used in his work in the form *Evangelium*, hence the words evangel and evangelical. English translators used the Old English term Godspel or, more simply, Gospel. The word signified God's spell, or story, and was identical in significance and meaning to the German adaptation of the Greek original. Unfortunately the word "Gospel" came to be used in two differing senses, one broad, the other narrow in meaning. **In its broad sense the Gospel was synonymous with the term Scripture or the Word of God. It was used in reference to**

the whole counsel and will of God, including both Law and Gospel. In its narrow sense it excluded the law and included only the proclamation of the redemptive work of Christ.[343] (emphasis added)

As much as the OED tried to limit the meaning of "gospel" to only "good tidings," to the exclusion of "God's word," the OED editors ultimately had to admit that "the form of the first element (god) shows unequivocally that it was identified with 'God' not with 'good.'"[344] The OED has to acknowledge that fact because the evidence is clear. Gospel traditionally meant God spell (i.e., God's word). The OED reveals that even the old high German used *gotspell*, which can only mean one thing: God's word.[345]

One might argue that the original Greek, from which "gospel" is translated, means "glad tidings." That statement is correct. But that contention is inaccurate, to the extent that "glad tidings" is argued to not be a reference to God's word. The Greek word, *euaggelion*, can be interpreted as both gospel and glad tidings. Indeed, we find that to be the case in Romans 10:15, where *euaggelion* was translated as both "gospel" and "glad tidings." The meaning of *euaggelion* is gospel, which in turn carries the primary meaning of "God's word." The meaning of *euaggelion* is also "good tidings." The Greek root *eu* is commonly translated as "good," but it is good in the sense of "godly." And so *euaggelion* is thus properly translated as godly words or more precisely God-spell (i.e., gospel, which is God's word). "Good tidings" and "gospel" mean the same thing. They both mean "God's word." Gail Riplinger explains:

> **The KJV correctly translates the first root *eu*, in other words, with its primary meaning, 'God' (godliness, godly).** The eminent scholar Werner Foerster of Munster points out correctly that words with this root, "in early days, are often provided

with more precise definitions to show to whom the...godliness was directed." He writes, "even later the habit of giving the object {God} did not die out." The second root, *aggello*, has the primary meaning of 'word'. Even Kittel had to admit, "It has developed a logos {word} theology." The word 'English' comes from the word 'Anglo-ish,' meaning 'Word-ish.' As people of the 'word,' the English speaking Christians have excelled, in generations past, in spreading and glorifying the word of God.[346] (emphasis added)

The corrupt new bible versions have used the words "good news," or similar phrases, in place of the word "gospel." They do that to limit in the minds of the readers the scope of the gospel. They want people to only think in terms of what is contained in the New Testament account of the atoning sacrifice of Jesus Christ, to the exclusion of all of the other historical and doctrinal revelations in the Holy Bible. Other things in the Bible, like the account of God's creation of a flat and stationary earth, are not considered by most people part of the gospel. Riplinger explains:

Most new versions, like the NIV, New Living Translation, NRSV, and Good News Bible, and reference works like Vine's Complete Expository Dictionary or Zodhiates Complete Word Study Dictionary, opt for the incorrect rendering "good news." ... Not only was 'God' watered down to 'good,' but 'spell,' meaning 'words,' was changed to 'news' to accommodate liberal textual critics who do not believe that the Bible is God's word, but merely a book which contained a 'good message.' The OED also states that 'spel' means specifically, "To read (a book, etc.) letter by letter." In Macaulay's History of England, he writes, "Not one man in five hundred could have spelled his way through the Psalms."³⁴⁷

The OED comes full circle in its definition of "gospel" and squeezes in the fact that "gospel" includes "[i]n extended sense: The Holy Scriptures"³⁴⁸ Gail Riplinger quotes *The Webster's Encyclopedic Dictionary*, which states that "gospel" is "compounded of Anglo-Saxon god. God and Spell - lit. God's word."³⁴⁹ It seems that the profane dictionaries must acknowledge that the full meaning of "gospel" is "God's word" for them to maintain some semblance of credibility; but they obscure that more complete definition for "gospel" by denigrating it.

The 1828 *Webster's Dictionary of the English Language* lists the first numbered definition of gospel as "God's word."³⁵⁰ Noah Webster cited to Galatians 3:8 to explain the scope of the gospel. That passage refers to the gospel (God's word) being preached to Abraham in the first book of the Bible in the Old Testament, Genesis.

> And the scripture, foreseeing that God would justify the heathen through faith, preached before the **gospel** unto Abraham, saying, In thee shall all nations be blessed. (Galatians 3:8)

The bottom line is that "gospel," in its most complete sense, means "God's word," all of God's word. The gospel spans the entire Holy Bible, from Genesis to Revelation, every single word of it. *Helps Ministries* explains that "[t]he Gospel (2098 /euaggélion) includes the entire Bible, i.e. it is not limited to how a person becomes a Christian."³⁵¹ But there is a devilish conspiracy to conceal that truth.

Satan does not want people to know that "gospel" means "God's word," which includes **every word of God**. Matthew 4:4. God uses parallelism to define words in the Bible. That parallelism defines the gospel as "the word of God" (2 Timothy 2:8-9; 2

Corinthians 4:2-3; Romans 10:16-17), "the word of the Lord" (Acts 8:25; 1 Peter 1:25), and "the word of truth" (Ephesians 1:13).

Please do not misunderstand. Gospel does mean "good tidings." None other authority than God himself explains that gospel means good tidings. We find in Luke 4:18 when Jesus read from Isaiah 61:1 he equated the "good tidings" in that passage in Isaiah with the "gospel."

> The Spirit of the Lord is upon me, because he hath anointed me to preach the **gospel** to the poor; he hath sent me to heal the brokenhearted, to preach deliverance to the captives, and recovering of sight to the blind, to set at liberty them that are bruised," (Luke 4:18)

> The Spirit of the Lord GOD is upon me; because the LORD hath anointed me to preach **good tidings** unto the meek; he hath sent me to bind up the brokenhearted, to proclaim liberty to the captives, and the opening of the prison to them that are bound;" (Isaiah 61:1)

"Tidings" is defined as being primarily an "account of what has taken place, and was not before known."[352] The definition of "tidings" describes to a T God's account in Genesis of the creation of the earth. Tidings includes "news; advice; information; intelligence."[353] Intelligence, in pertinent part, means "an account of things distant or before unknown."[354] The primary sense of intelligence is understanding.[355] We see that concept in the book of Revelation where Jesus told John to "[w]rite the things which thou hast seen, and the things which are, and the things which shall be hereafter." Revelation 1:19. The tidings from God are always good tidings because God is good. Jesus said that "there is none good but one, that is, God." (Mark 10:18)

We find the pertinent part of the definition of "good" in the context of the scriptures means perfect, unblemished, virtuous, incorruptible, and conducive to happiness.[356] Indeed, when God finished his creation he described it as "very good." "And God saw every thing that he had made, and behold, it was very good." Genesis 1:4.

In essence, good tidings means the perfect, unblemished, virtuous, incorruptible, and joyous revelation by God to man of God's love, grace, doctrines, prophecies, and events. Good tidings describes the entire Holy Bible; and it includes God's creation of an immovable and flat earth. Jesus Christ's creation of the stationary, flat earth described in the Bible is an "account of what has taken place, and was not before known."[357] Good tidings in the Bible give us understanding about God's creation, which is "an account of things distant or before unknown."[358] Those good tidings are part and parcel of the gospel. Indeed, all of the word of God contained in the Holy Bible makes up the good tidings (gospel) of Jesus Christ.

Incidently, good tidings means the same thing as glad tidings. Compare Luke 1:19 (glad tidings) with Luke 2:10 (good tidings). God uses those terms interchangeably in the Bible. Paul preached "glad tidings" from the book of Psalms in the synagogue at Antioch. Those same glad tidings were heard by the Gentiles who asked Paul to also preach "these words" to them the next sabbath. God described the **"glad tidings"** that Paul preached to the Gentiles the following sabbath as the **"word of God."**

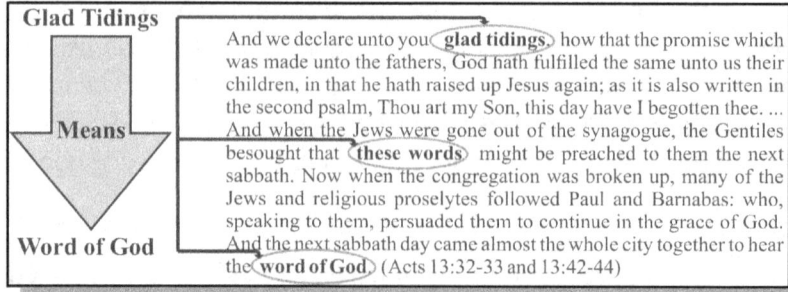

Paul was preaching in Acts 13:32 "glad tidings" from the book of Psalms. God reveals in Acts 13:44 that those "glad tidings" from the book of Psalms are the "word of God." That necessarily means that glad tidings are found in the Old Testament. "Gospel" means "glad tidings." We know that "gospel" is derived from "God spell," which means God's word. Thus, glad tidings = gospel = word of God, all of which span the entire New and Old Testaments.

We also find in Romans 10:17 that the "gospel" that is "glad tidings" is also "the word of God." In Romans 10:16 we learn that the Jews did not obey the gospel (i.e., the word of God) because, as revealed in verse 17, they did not believe the word of God (i.e., the gospel). It is explained in Romans 10:18-11:36, that the Jews did not have the faith required to believe the word of God (the gospel), because faith must be spiritually imparted by the grace of God to the hearer of the word of God (the gospel). Thus, the Jews did not obey the gospel (the word of God) because they could not obey the gospel (the word of God). "God hath given them the spirit of slumber, eyes that they should not see, and ears that they should not hear." (Romans 11:8)

> But they have not all obeyed the **gospel**. For Esaias saith, Lord, who hath believed our report? Romans 10:16.
>
> *Next Verse* ↓
>
> So then faith cometh by hearing, and hearing by the **word of God**. Romans 10:17.

The "gospel" in verse 16 of Romans 10 is equated with the "word of God" in verse 17. Notice in the reference in verse 16 to the Old Testament prophet Esaias (Isaiah 53:1), who prophesied about the preaching of "glad tidings" in Isaiah 52:7. That prophecy in Isaiah comes into view when we read Romans 10:13-15.

> For whosoever shall call upon the name of the Lord shall be saved. How then shall they call on him in whom they have not believed? and how shall they believe in him of whom they have not heard? and how shall they hear without a preacher? And how shall they preach, except they be sent? as it is written, How beautiful are the feet of them that preach the **gospel** of peace, and bring **glad tidings** of good things!" (Romans 10:13-15)

We see that there is parallelism. And that parallelism reveals that "gospel" means "glad tidings." Indeed, Isaiah 52:7 states that "How beautiful upon the mountains are the feet of him that bringeth good tidings, that publisheth peace; that bringeth good tidings of good, that publisheth salvation; that saith unto Zion, Thy God reigneth!" (Isaiah 52:7) Clearly, the gospel is "glad tidings." Heliocentric church authorities want the definition of the gospel to stop there, and go no further, because they do not want the gospel to be understood to be the entire word of God. They seek to limit the definition of the gospel to only be those Bible passages that relate to salvation by grace through faith in Jesus Christ. That is considered the heart of the gospel, but just as the human heart is not the whole body, so also the heart of the gospel is not the whole gospel. The gospel certainly includes the heart of the gospel, but it is much more. The gospel is glad tidings and it includes all of the words of God, including the account of his creation, found in the Holy Bible.

In Romans 10:15, we read that "beautiful are the feet of them that preach the **gospel** of peace and bring **glad tidings** of good things!" The "gospel of peace" and "glad tidings" in verse 15 are the "word of God" in verse 17. The whole point of verses 13 through 15 is to explain that in order for one to call on the name of the Lord, he must believe; in order to believe, he must hear the "gospel;" in order to hear the "gospel," someone must preach the "gospel." In verse 17 we find that same truth, but the gospel in that verse is referred to as the "**word of God.**" "So then faith cometh by hearing, and hearing by the **word of God**." (Romans 10:17) Thus, the **"gospel"** is both **"glad tidings"** and the **"word of God."**

In 2 Timothy 2:8-9 we find that the "**gospel**" preached by Paul, for which he suffered, is the same "**word of God**" that is not bound. The "**gospel**" is the "**word of God.**"

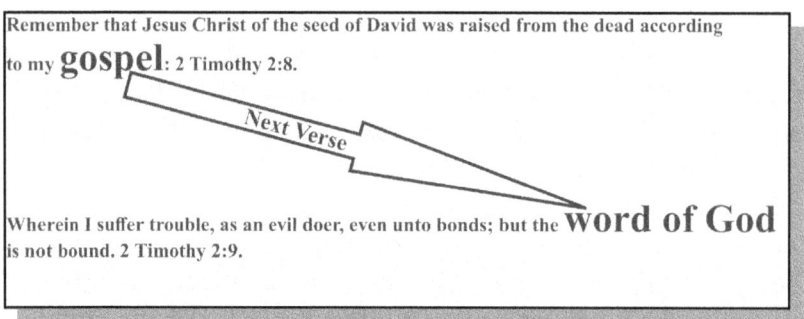

Notice also in Acts 8:25 that the disciples preached the "word of the Lord" at Jerusalem, which was the same "gospel" that they preached in the many villages of the Samaritans.

> And they, when they had testified and preached the **word of the Lord**, returned to Jerusalem, and preached the **gospel** in many villages of the Samaritans. (Acts 8:25)

God explains in Revelation 1:9 that John was a companion with the saints in tribulation while he was in the kingdom. In a parallel phrase John explains that his tribulation was his imprisonment on Patmos Island for the word of God and the testimony of Jesus Christ. We know from that parallelism that the word of God is the testimony of Jesus Christ. John was in tribulation on Patmos while in the kingdom of God and for the word of God. In Matthew 13:18-19 we find Jesus explaining the parable of the sower by revealing that the seed being sown is the "word of the kingdom." That is the same kingdom of which John was a member and for which he was imprisoned in Patmos. John was imprisoned for the word of God, which is the testimony of Jesus Christ, which is the gospel. The testimony of Jesus Christ begins with his creation account in Genesis and ends with his final amen in Revelation. The testimony of Jesus Christ, the gospel, and the word of God are all one and the same.

> I John, who also am your brother, and companion **in tribulation**, and **in the kingdom** and patience of Jesus Christ, was in the isle that is called Patmos, **for the word of God**, and **for the testimony of Jesus Christ**. (Revelation 1:9)

The Genesis account of God's creation is every bit a part of the gospel as is the gospel of John. Moses wrote Genesis. If one does not believe the account of God's creation in Genesis how can one believe the words Jesus spoke? John 5:46-47. One cannot truly know God except through his creation. God makes it clear in his "gospel" that the knowledge of God is revealed through his creation as described in God's word. Romans 1:20.

Jesus is the word that became flesh. John 1:1-14. To be a believer means that you believe all of God's word. If somebody claims to be a believer but rejects some of God's word, that necessarily means that they are not a true believer. The law and the prophets are not to be ignored; Jesus came to fulfill them. He admonished us to do and to teach the commandments in his word. Every word of God is important, right down to the last jot and tittle. We should not exclude any part of God's word from the gospel.

> Think not that I am come to destroy the law, or the prophets: I am not come to destroy, but to fulfil. For verily I say unto you, Till heaven and earth pass, one jot or one tittle shall in no wise pass from the law, till all be fulfilled. Whosoever therefore shall break one of these least commandments, and shall teach men so, he shall be called the least in the kingdom of heaven: but whosoever shall do and teach them, the same shall be called great in the kingdom of heaven. (Matthew 5:17-19)

God commands us not to take his name in vain. Exodus 20:7. But God's word is so precious to God that he exalts his word above even his name. "[F]or thou hast magnified thy word above all thy name." (Psalms 138:2) Each and every word of God is important, we are not to ignore or denigrate any part of God's word. God commands us to preach the gospel (the word of God), which includes the resurrected Jesus Christ sitting on the right hand of the throne of God in heaven, which is above the firmament that Jesus Christ created over the immovable flat earth. Ephesians 1:20; Colossians 3:1; Hebrews 1:3; 8:1; 10:12; 12:2; 1 Peter 3:22. "And he said unto them, Go ye into all the world, and preach the gospel to every creature." (Mark 16:15) Part of that gospel is a command to believers to seek those things that are in heaven. "If ye then be risen with Christ, seek those things which are above, where Christ sitteth on the right hand of God." (Colossians 3:1)

How are we going to explain to the believer who is commanded to "seek those things which are above where Christ sitteth on the right hand of God" where to look if we do not plainly tell him the truth that God's throne is in heaven above the firmament that spans over the immovable flat earth? A believer must know where God's throne is, and he must know its relationship to God's creation. Obviously, God's creation of a stationary and flat earth with a firmament overhead is part and parcel of the gospel.

We find in Acts 8:26-40 that the Ethiopian eunuch had the book of Isaiah explained to him by Philip, which brought the eunuch to a saving knowledge of Jesus Christ. The book of Isaiah is part of the gospel (God's word), just as is the creation account of an immovable and flat earth in Genesis. Just as the book of Isaiah in the Old Testament can bring a person to a saving knowledge of Jesus Christ, so also can the creation account of Jesus Christ in the Old Testament book of Genesis.

Paul explained to Timothy that the holy scriptures that Timothy knew from a child (which were necessarily the Old Testament) were able to bring him to salvation through faith in Jesus Christ. Paul explained that **all** of those scriptures in the Old Testament that made Timothy wise unto salvation by faith in Christ Jesus were inspired by God and are profitable for doctrine, reproof, correction, instruction in righteousness, and perfection. Notice that Paul refers to **all** scriptures, not just some scriptures. Those Old Testament scriptures to which Paul referred included the creation account of a flat and stationary earth in the book of Genesis; and those God inspired scriptures remain just as profitable for all who read them today as they were for Timothy more than 2,000 years ago. All scriptures in both the New and Old Testaments are the inspired word of God; they constitute the gospel.

> And that from a child thou hast known **the holy scriptures**, which are able to make thee wise unto

salvation through faith which is in Christ Jesus. **All scripture** is given by inspiration of God, and is profitable for doctrine, for reproof, for correction, for instruction in righteousness: That the man of God may be perfect, throughly furnished unto all good works. (2 Timothy 3:15-17)

Indeed, Jesus made the point in John 5:45-47 that if one does not believe the account by Moses of Jesus' creation in the book of Genesis in the Old Testament then he will not believe Jesus' words in the New Testament. "For had ye believed Moses, ye would have believed me: for he wrote of me. But if ye believe not his writings, how shall ye believe my words?" (John 5:46-47) There are eternal consequences for the heliocentric pastors who claim that the account in the bible of Jesus' creation of a flat and stationary earth is not part of the gospel.

The Old Testament and New Testament go together; you cannot excise any part of God's word. Indeed, the disciples of Christ held both the words of Jesus and the Old Testament scriptures as having equal authority as foundations for their faith. "When therefore he was risen from the dead, his disciples remembered that he had said this unto them; and **they believed the scripture, and the word which Jesus had said.**" (John 2:22)

The fact that Jesus is the creator of all things, seen and unseen, is a prominent part of the gospel. "For by him were all things created, that are in heaven, and that are in earth, visible and invisible, whether they be thrones, or dominions, or principalities, or powers: all things were created by him, and for him." (Colossians 1:16) If the truth that Jesus is the creator of all things is important, so also then is the nature of his creation important because all things were created for him, and his creation gives us an understanding of Jesus Christ. Romans 1:20. The fact that Jesus created a flat and stationary earth over which he reigns from a throne in heaven, which is above the firmament, gives us an understanding of Christ, and thus it is an important part of the gospel.

Paul, in his first letter to the Thessalonians, explained that the gospel that he preached, which brought salvation to the hearers, was the "word of God."

> For this cause also thank we God without ceasing, because, when ye received the **word of God** which ye heard of us, ye received it not as the word of men, but as it is in truth, the **word of God**, which effectually worketh also in you that believe. (1 Thessalonians 2:13)

Jesus stated that man must live by "every word of God" not just some of them. The gospel is "every" word of God. Jesus emphasized that "[i]t is written, Man shall not live by bread alone, but by **every word** that proceedeth out of the mouth of God." (Matthew 4:4) Pastors cannot pick and choose passages of the Bible to believe. Christian belief is an all or nothing proposition. "**All scripture** is given by inspiration of God, and is profitable for doctrine, for reproof, for correction, for instruction in righteousness." (2 Timothy 3:16) It is improper for a pastor to whittle down the Bible to only those scriptures that he thinks are worthy to be part of the gospel. All scripture is given by inspiration of God. All scripture is profitable for doctrine. All scripture is profitable for reproof. All scripture is profitable for correction. All scripture is profitable for instruction in righteousness. To suggest that any part of scripture is somehow unimportant or insignificant is to imply that God did not inspire those passages.

A claim to be a Christian presupposes faith in Jesus, who is both our savior and our creator. A true Christian believes what Jesus said about both heavenly and earthly things. "If I have told you earthly things, and ye believe not, how shall ye believe, if I tell you of heavenly things?" (John 3:12) God created the flat and stationary earth by his word. Jesus is the Word of God that became flesh. John 1:1-3. Jesus explained that continuing in his word is a sign that one is his true disciple. "If ye continue in my word, then are ye my disciples indeed." John 8:31. To bring forth fruit for Christ, one must hear his word and keep his word. Luke 8:15. The words of Jesus abide in the true believer. John 15:5-8. One who rejects any part of the gospel cannot be a true disciple of Jesus Christ. John 12:48; 14:24.

It bears repeating that Jesus told the Jews that if they did not believe Moses, they would not believe him. "For had ye believed Moses, ye would have believed me: for he wrote of me. But if ye believe not his writings, how shall ye believe my words?" (John 5:46-47) Moses wrote the account of Jesus' creation of an immovable and flat earth in the book of Genesis.

One might ask, where in Genesis did Moses write about Jesus? Understand, Jesus created all things. "For by him were all things created, that are in heaven, and that are in earth, visible and invisible, whether they be thrones, or dominions, or principalities, or powers: all things were created by him, and for him." (Colossians 1:16) We read in Genesis 1:1 that "[i]n the beginning God created the heaven and the earth." The God of creation is Jesus Christ. By Jesus Christ "were all things created." If one does not believe what Moses wrote in Genesis about Jesus Christ as the creator, then they cannot believe in Jesus as savior.

Most pastors seek friendship with the world on heliocentrism to avoid the ridicule of the world. They do not abide by the admonition of God: "[K]now ye not that the friendship of the world is enmity with God? whosoever therefore will be a friend of the world is the enemy of God." James 4:4. Therein lies the impediment to most pastors accepting the truth of the geocentric, flat earth. Fortner is quite frank in saying that belief that the earth is flat is an "idiotic, foolish, absurd, dumb, crazy notion." He does not want to appear to be an idiotic, foolish, absurd, dumb, crazy person. Fortner's enmity for the truth reveals that he has only the wisdom of the fallen world; the true gospel has not been revealed to him. "At that time Jesus answered and said, I thank thee, O Father, Lord of heaven and earth, because thou hast hid these things from the wise and prudent, and hast revealed them unto babes." (Matthew 11:25).

The idea that belief in a flat earth is crazy is reinforced everywhere in mainstream media and academia. For example, Michelle Thaller, NASA Assistant Director for Science Information, dismisses any notion of a flat earth, stating "this is not a viable argument."[359] She feigns puzzlement that anyone would believe the earth is flat and suggests that it is just a passing fancy. "I don't really know what's going on right now with this 'Earth is flat' thing."[360] She goes further and ominously states that "it's not okay to think that the earth is flat."[361] She makes the statement in the midst of an harangue about how nonsensical it is to believe the earth is flat and implies that there is something mentally wrong with anyone who holds to such a belief. That kind of propaganda affected Fortner, and it is why Fortner fears the truth of the flat earth.

It is the fear of ridicule that is born of the "pride of life," which is of the world and is contrary to God. "For all that is in the world, the lust of the flesh, and the lust of the eyes, and the pride of life, is not of the Father, but is of the world." 1 John 2:16. Indeed, the devil knows the weak character of men and thus has conditioned people to have contempt and deride as "idiotic, foolish, absurd, dumb, crazy" anyone who believes the earth is flat. People have been conditioned to have a visceral reaction to any evidence that contradicts the heliocentric model. Such rejection of hard evidence, without a fair hearing, brings folly and shame. "He that answereth a matter before he heareth it, it is folly and shame unto him." (Proverbs 18:13) This folly and shame is manifested in devilish philosophies that permeate society. The deception of a spherical, spinning earth is the foundation for Darwinian evolution, Freudian psychoanalysis, and Marxist communism.

That heliocentric hive environment that zeros in on and attacks a man's pride serves as an impediment to the truth of the geocentric, flat earth being accepted in academic and scientific (and religious) circles. William H. Poole explained: "There is a principle which is a bar against all information, which is proof against all argument, and which cannot fail to keep a man in everlasting ignorance. This principle is, contempt prior to examination."[362] God says it best though. "Blame not before thou hast examined the truth: understand first, and then rebuke." Ecclesiastes 11:7.

Jesus Christ is both savior and creator. Pastors cannot decouple those two facts. Indeed, the character of God, even his eternal power and Godhead, is revealed through his creation.

> For the invisible things of him from the creation of the world are clearly seen, being understood by the things that are made, even his eternal power and Godhead; so that they are without excuse: (Romans 1:20)

One cannot know Jesus Christ as savior without knowing him as the creator. Belief in Jesus Christ presupposes belief in him as both savior and creator. He is the savior of our souls because he is the creator of our souls. He is the creator of all things seen and unseen. The pastors who focus only on God as the savior to the exclusion of God as the creator are eviscerating the gospel. They honor God with their lips, but their hearts are far from him. They, instead, worship a god of their own making.

In Psalms 136, God proclaims that he is our creator and his eternal goodness and mercy are effectual in saving his elect. God created his elect to save them. Ephesians 1:3-11. We are to give thanks to God for his mercy. God created us to dwell on a flat and stationary earth, with the sun to rule by day and the moon and stars to rule by night. God's creation is inseparable from his mercy in saving his elect. Isaiah 42:1-9. Jesus Christ can effectually save us from our sins by his everlasting mercy because he is God Almighty, the creator of all things, and he is sovereign over his creation. Colossians 1:14-17. That God is a merciful redeemer and that God is the sovereign creator are both parts of the gospel. "But now thus saith **the LORD that created thee**, O Jacob, and he that formed thee, O Israel, Fear not: for **I have redeemed thee**, I have called thee by thy name; thou art mine." (Isaiah 43:1) The fact that God "stretched out the [flat] earth above the waters" is as much a part of the gospel as the fact that "his mercy endureth for ever."

> O give thanks unto the LORD; for he is good: for his mercy endureth for ever. O give thanks unto the God of gods: for his mercy endureth for ever. O give thanks to the Lord of lords: for his mercy endureth for ever. To him who alone doeth great wonders: for his mercy endureth for ever. **To him that by wisdom made the heavens: for his mercy endureth for ever. To him that stretched out the earth above the waters: for his mercy endureth for ever. To him that made great lights: for his mercy endureth for ever: The sun to rule by day: for his mercy endureth for ever: The moon and stars to rule by night: for his mercy endureth for ever. ... Who remembered us in our low estate: for his mercy endureth for ever: And hath redeemed us from our enemies: for his mercy endureth for ever.** Who giveth food to all flesh: for his mercy endureth for ever. O give thanks unto the God of heaven: for his mercy endureth for ever. (Psalms 136:1-9, 23-26)

To be a Christian requires one to accept all that God states in his word. Jesus Christ makes it clear that there is no such thing as a partial Christian. "So then because thou art lukewarm, and neither cold nor hot, I will spue thee out of my mouth." (Revelation 3:16) Frank Hall puts it this way: "If you are ashamed of the cross, you are ashamed of the Christ who once hung on it, and if you are ashamed of the circle of the flat earth, you are ashamed of the Christ who sits upon it."

The pastors who are ashamed of the flat earth must understand that the shame cuts both ways. "For whosoever shall be ashamed of me and of my words, of him shall the Son of man be ashamed, when he shall come in his own glory, and in his Father's, and of the holy angels." (Luke 9:26) Read closely what Jesus says in that passage. He says that he who is ashamed of God and his "words," God will also be ashamed of him on judgment day. His words formed his creation, and his words of creation are found in his Bible. Indeed, Jesus is the word who became flesh. John 1:14. By his word, he created a flat, immovable earth over which he reigns. "It is he that sitteth upon the circle of the earth, and the inhabitants thereof are as grasshoppers; that stretcheth out the heavens as a curtain, and spreadeth them out as a tent to dwell in:" (Isaiah 40:22) If one is ashamed of God's expressed words regarding his creation, God will be ashamed of him.

Our salvation is based upon God's grace through faith in Jesus Christ. Ephesians 2:8. Our faith is rooted in God's words; not just some of them, all of them. Frank Hall explains:

> Faith—faith and faith alone—is our only recourse. We must believe God! We must take him at his word in all things. Does God say it? Then let us believe it, come what may and come what will. Does God say that salvation is by grace? Then let us trust him for his grace. Does God say that all men are totally depraved? Then let us own and confess our sin this instant. Does God say that Christ is the end of the law for righteousness to

everyone that believeth? Then let us believe on Christ for righteousness. Does God say that Eve transgressed his commandment by listening to the lies of a talking snake? Then let us submit our reason to God's word. Does God say that the sun is in circuit above the circle of his firm, fixed, flat, and stationary earth? Then let us forsake the devil's globe and submit ourselves to God's revelation.[363]

The church has been infiltrated by the superstitious myth of heliocentrism, which has served to undermine the gospel. The gospel is the entire Holy Bible, not just some of it. Matthew 4:4. Christian belief is an all or nothing proposition. "All scripture is given by inspiration of God, and is profitable for doctrine, for reproof, for correction, for instruction in righteousness." 2 Timothy 3:16.

God's account of his creation is part and parcel of the gospel. A person with genuine faith believes what Jesus said about both heavenly and earthly things. "If I have told you earthly things, and ye believe not, how shall ye believe, if I tell you of heavenly things?" John 3:12.

Jesus is God. Jesus created all things in heaven and on earth. See Colossians 1:16-18. God has revealed himself through his creation.

"[T]hat which may be known of God is manifest in them; for God hath shewed it unto them. For the invisible things of him from the creation of the world are clearly seen, being understood by the things that are made, even his eternal power and Godhead; so that they are without excuse." Romans 1:19-20.

If men have a misunderstanding of God's creation, they will also have a misunderstanding of who God is. If people believe in a creation that does not exist, they consequently also believe in a creator that does not exist. It is essential, therefore, to have an accurate understanding of God's creation. God did not make a movable, spherical earth. If men believe in a heliocentric creation, they will necessarily believe in a heliocentric creator. A heliocentric creation does not exist. So also, a heliocentric creator does not exist. A heliocentric creator is a false god. We have been warned to avoid the preaching of a false gospel, which presents a false Jesus.

> For if he that cometh preacheth another Jesus, whom we have not preached, or if ye receive another spirit, which ye have not received, or another gospel, which ye have not accepted, ye might well bear with him. 2 Corinthians 11:4.

32 Denying the KJV Is the Inspired Word of God

There are a minority of pastors who defend the Authorized (King James) Version of the Holy Bible (a.k.a., AV or KJV) against the corruptions in the new Bible versions. But their defense is ineffectual because they deny the inspiration of the English translation in the AV. For example, Dr Donald A. Waite, Th.D., Ph.D., former President of *The Dean Burgon Society* (DBS) and Director of The Bible for Today, Inc., is one of the foremost Greek scholars who advocates for the authority of the *Textus Receptus*. He is generally viewed as a defender of the Authorized (King James) Version of the Holy Bible. He is the author of *Defending the King James Bible*, which is considered the classic authority on the superiority of the King James Bible. He soundly criticizes the corruptions in the new Bible versions and effectively attacks the Alexandrian Greek texts upon which they are based.

But Dr. Waite's defense of the AV (KJV) is rather tepid. He states that the AV is superior to the new Bible versions. But at the same time, he denies that the AV, itself, is inspired. He states that the English translation found in the AV (KJV) is not the inspired word of God. He dogmatically insists that the statement in 2 Timothy 3:16 that "all scripture is given by inspiration of

God" means that it was "once" given only to the Hebrew, Aramaic and Greek original texts and never to translations.[364] The DBS took that same position. Indeed, if you read the DBS Statement of Faith, you will find that it limits inspiration to the original languages.

> We believe in the plenary, verbal, Divine inspiration of the sixty-six canonical books of the Old and the New Testaments (from Genesis to Revelation) **in the original languages,** and in their consequent infallibility and inerrancy in all matters of which they speak. ... We believe that the Texts which are the **closest** to the **original autographs** of the Bible are the Traditional Masoretic Hebrew Text for the Old Testament, and the traditional Greek Text for the New Testament underlying the King James Version (as found in "The Greek Text Underlying The English Authorized Version of 1611"). We, believe that the King James Version (or Authorized Version) of the English Bible is a **true, faithful, and accurate translation** of these two providentially preserved Texts, which in our time has **no equal among all of the other English Translations.**[365]

Notice that according to the DBS, only the "original languages" are divinely inspired, and the manuscript evidence in copies of the Traditional Masoretic Hebrew Text for the Old Testament and the traditional Greek Text for the New Testament are "closest" to the inspired "autographs." The equivocal word "closest" reveals that the DBS thinks that the copies we have today in the original languages are close to God's word, but those copies are not actually God's word.

Notice also that the DBS thinks that the King James Version of the Bible is the best translation unequaled by any other translation, but it is not divinely inspired. According to the DBS, the AV (KJV) is simply a "true, faithful, and accurate translation" of the original divinely inspired language texts. Lest one thinks that I am misinterpreting the position of the DBS, read what Dr. Waite says.

> Neither the DBS Executive Committee or the DBS Advisory Council will ever call the King James Bible "inspired of God," "given by inspiration of God," "verbally inspired," "inspired," or "God-breathed" at any time or in any place.[366]

Dr. Waite masquerades as a great defender of the King James Bible (AV). But it seems that he is a spy sent behind the lines to undermine the authority of the King James Bible. Dr. Waite is following the age-old strategy of the communists. Vladimir Lenin said: "The best way to control the opposition is to lead it ourselves." Dr. Waite relegates the King James Bible to being merely superior to the new Bible versions, and that is it. He denies that the King James Bible is the inspired word of God. Dr. Waite is rather strident in his condemnation of anyone who says that the AV is the inspired word of God in English. Indeed, he says it is "heresy" to "say that say the 'AV1611' was 'given by inspiration of God.'" Dr. Waite claims:

> Only the Hebrew, Aramaic, and Greek Words were "given by inspiration of God" or "God-breathed." No translation (including the AV1611) was given by verbal plenary inspiration. The "AV 1611" was most definitely not "given by inspiration of God."[367]

God says: "**All scripture** is given by inspiration of God." 2 Timothy 3:16. If the translators of the English Bible were not inspired, and thus their translation into English is not inspired, as claimed by Dr. Waite, that means, by definition, no English Bible can be scripture. God disagrees with Dr. Waite. God states that he has made his scriptures known to "all nations." He has made his inspired words available to them in their native tongues. The KJV is God's inspired word in English.

> Now to him that is of power to stablish you according to my gospel, and the preaching of Jesus Christ, according to the revelation of the mystery, which was kept secret since the world began, But now is made manifest, and by **the scriptures of the prophets**, according to the commandment of the everlasting God, made known to **all nations** for the obedience of faith:" (Romans 16:25-26 AV)

Dr. Waite and the DBS are clearly in a secret war against God's word in the English language while at the same time pretending to be defenders of the King James Bible. While attacking the divine authority of the King James Bible, they portray themselves as great champions of the Greek Textus Receptus and the Traditional Masoretic Text of the Old Testament. But their defense of those texts is not real; it is more of a capitulation. Dr. Waite has stated his belief, in no uncertain terms, that God inspired only the original writers of the scriptures.

> I believe that God inspired and breathed-out the original Hebrew, Aramaic, and Greek Words of the Old and New Testaments. I believe **this miraculous event happened only once and was never repeated**. Especially was this inspiration never repeated in any translation in the past, in the present, or in the future. I believe 2 Timothy 3:16 refers to this once-for-all inspiration by God of those original Hebrew, Aramaic, and Greek Words.[368]

Dr. Waite's once-only inspiration position has a problem. For example, In Luke 4:15-21 Jesus "went into the synagogue on the sabbath day, and stood up for to read. And there was delivered unto him the book of the prophet Esaias." Luke 4:15. Notice that Jesus was handed the book of Isaiah. Jesus then read aloud from Isaiah 61:1-2. The original book of Isaiah was written about 700 years earlier and no longer existed. And so Jesus was reading from a copy. He was not only reading from a copy, he was reading a copy of the Hebrew scripture. The account in Luke quotes the passage in Isaiah at 61:1-2 that was read by Jesus. But the account found in Luke 4:15-21 was originally written in Greek. The account of Jesus's recital of Isaiah given in Luke is a translation from Hebrew to Greek.

Recall that Dr. Waite's view is that inspiration is a one-time event that is never repeated, and consequently, "[n]o translation (including the AV1611) was given by verbal plenary inspiration." Waite's theology means that no quotation in the New Testament Greek of any Old Testament Hebrew scripture can be the inspired word of God. Thus, Matthew 1:22-23, which quotes Isaiah 7:14, which Waite claims was only inspired when it was originally written, is not scripture because the Greek manuscript of Matthew 1:22-23 is a translation of the original once-only-inspired Hebrew.

> Now all this was done, that it might be fulfilled which was spoken of the Lord by the prophet, saying, Behold, a virgin shall be with child, and shall bring forth a son, and they shall call his name Emmanuel, which being interpreted is, God with us. (Matthew 1:22-23 AV)

According to Dr. Waite, the reading of Isaiah in Luke is not, and cannot be, the inspired word of God because inspiration is a miraculous event that happens only once with each piece of scripture and is never repeated. Thus, according to Waite, once the book of Isaiah was written, there could be no further inspiration from copyists or translators. Waite was emphatic on that point. He said: "Especially was this inspiration never repeated in any translation in the past, in the present, or in the future." By Dr. Waite's theology, the passage in Luke where the Isaiah passage appears in Greek is only a translation from Hebrew and thus cannot be the inspired word of God.

Indeed, all of the many quotes of the Hebrew Old Testament prophecies found in the New Testament Greek text, according to Dr. Waite, cannot be the inspired word of God because inspiration only happens once and is never to be repeated. For example, Mark 1:2-3 is not the inspired word of God when translating into Greek the Hebrew language prophecy of John the Baptist found in Malachi 3:1 and Isaiah 40:3. According to Waite, Mark 1:2-3 is only an uninspired translation. Dr. Waite's main attack is aimed at the English translation found in the AV. He relegates the AV translation from Greek into English to the uninspired bin.

A logical conclusion from Dr. Wiate's statement that inspiration is a one-time-only event is that Waite does not believe that copies of the original autographs are inspired but, at best, can only be faithful copies. Under Waite's theory, the copies could have errors, which crept in by the fallible mistakes of men. That conclusion is implied by the DBS, which he headed. The DBS Statement of Faith says that current copies of the Traditional Masoretic Hebrew Text for the Old Testament and the traditional Greek Text for the New Testament are merely **"closest"** to the original autographs. That suggests they are not perfect copies and, thus, not inspired.

Statements by Dr. Waite and the DBS seem to limit inspiration to the original autographs. Their statements suggest that the copies closely reflect the inspired originals. But that is it. According to statements from Waite and the DBS, neither the copies nor the English translation of those copies are the inspired word of God because inspiration happened only once when the original manuscripts were penned. They believe the King James Bible is the best and most accurate translation of the closest copies of the original language texts. They maintain that it is heresy to say that the King James Bible, or indeed any English Bible, is the inerrant and inspired word of God.

The above analysis of the DBS and Dr. Waite was based on their writings. But Dr. Waite is a textual schizophrenic. He realized at some point that his position that inspiration "happened only once and was never repeated" means that we do not have the inspired word of God in any form today because the once inspired manuscripts are long gone. So, like any con artist, he simply amended his position to say that single and unrepeatable event of inspiration extended to the copies of the original autographs, which he calls the "preserved" original words.[369]

Recall that Dr. Waite has dogmatically claimed that inspiration is a one-time, and one-time only, event that applies only to the original autographs. But Dr.Waite wants his cake and eat it too. He claims that only the original writers were inspired to write God's word. But he also wants the copies of the original manuscripts to be God's inspired word. His claim that the copies are the inspired word of God contradicts his statement that inspiration is a one-time event. If the inspiration is a one-time event, as he claims, which only applies to the original writers, inspiration cannot apply to the copyists. If Dr. Waite is to be consistent, he must conclude that the copies cannot be the inspired word of God. But consistency is not Dr. Waite's strong point.

Dr. Waite has not explained how a copyist, who has all of the human frailties and lacks the capacity to be inerrant, can produce an inerrant and perfect copy aside from the inspiration of God. Indeed, he rails against the many errors made by the copyists of the Alexandrian Greek texts. But, according to Waite, the uninspired Byzantine copyists who compiled the majority of Greek text that became what is called the Textus Receptus (Received

Text), which is the Greek text for the AV, did their job flawlessly without the inspiration of the Holy Spirit.

Would God risk his word to the frailties of men and resulting vicissitudes? Certainly not! God puts no trust in his saints. See Job 15:15. "A man's heart deviseth his way: But the LORD directeth his steps." Proverbs 16:9. That is particularly true when God's servants are copying (and translating) his word. "The steps of a good man are ordered by the LORD: and he delighteth in his way." Psalms 37:23. The very theme of the Bible is that God is sovereign over the lives of men. "O LORD, I know that the way of man is not in himself: it is not in man that walketh to direct his steps." Jeremiah 10:23. Men think that they are free of God's will, but they are not. "Man's goings are of the LORD; how can a man then understand his own way?" Proverbs 20:24. Indeed, the very words spoken (and written) are under the sovereign control of God. "The preparations of the heart in man, and the answer of the tongue, is from the LORD." Proverbs 16:1.

Yet Dr. Waite claims that once God memorialized his holy word in writing for men, he was detached from it; he entrusted it to men's weak vicissitudes, offering no continuing inspiration in either copying or translation. But God wants us to "know the certainty of the words of truth." God has inspired them from beginning to end in every language to make us know the certainty of his words of truth.

> Have not I written to thee excellent things in counsels and knowledge, **That I might make thee know the certainty of the words of truth**; that thou mightest answer the words of truth to them that send unto thee? (Proverbs 22:20-21 AV)

Just as Jesus Christ is the "author and finisher of our faith" (Hebrews 12:2), so also is he the author and finisher of his word. God inspired the copyists to faithfully reproduce his perfect word perfectly in the Trextus Receptus and the AV. But Waite does not believe that. Waite squeezed in an exception (more accurately, a contradiction) that says copies of the original Hebrew, Aramaic, and Greek in the Bible are inspired without the copyists themselves being inspired.

The minority spurious Greek texts reveal what happens when copyists are not inspired. The corrupt Alexandrian Greek texts, like the codices Vaticanus and Sinaiticus, form the foundation for the new Bible versions; those corrupt Greek manuscripts are full of false doctrine. They illustrate the mischief that can occur when the copyists act without God's inspiration (i.e., knowledge). "The fear of the Lord is the beginning of wisdom: and the knowledge of the holy is understanding." Proverbs 9:10.

Theodore Beza is an example of God inspiring a copyist. Beza was a gifted linguist, but his work editing and refining the Greek Textus Receptus was more as a compiler and copyist. He was gathering into one text the word of God that was scattered throughout many hundreds of Greek texts. He was inspired by God to faithfully render the Textus Receptus. Proof that God inspired Beza is his rendering of Revelation 16:5. God inspired Beza to give the rendering of Revelation 16:5, in pertinent part, as "which art, and wast, and shalt be." Beza wrote that even though the words "shalt be" did not appear in any extant Greek manuscript he had before him. As explained in a chapter in this book titled "Revelation 16:5," Beza's rendering of Revelation is correct. Beza explained that he "faithfully restored in the good book what was certainly there." And God gave him the knowledge (inspiration) to do that.

Dr. Waite's claim that inspiration is a one-time, never-to-be-repeated event is refuted by chapter 36 of Jeremiah. We read in Jeremiah that the Lord commanded Jeremiah to write a prophecy against Israel, Judah, and all other nations.

> Take thee a roll of a book, and **write therein all the words that I have spoken unto thee against Israel, and against Judah, and against all the nations**, from the day I spake unto thee, from the days of Josiah, even unto this day. It may be that the house of Judah will hear all the evil which I purpose to do unto them; that they may return every man from his evil way; that I may forgive their iniquity and their sin. Then Jeremiah called Baruch the son of Neriah: and Baruch wrote from the mouth of Jeremiah all the words of the LORD, which he had spoken unto him, upon a roll of a book. (Jeremiah 36:2-4 AV)

Jeremiah did what God commanded, and the book from Jeremiah was read to King Jehoiakim. The king was unhappy about what he heard, so he took a penknife, cut out the pages, and threw them into a fire.

> So the king sent Jehudi to fetch the roll: and he took it out of Elishama the scribe's chamber. And Jehudi read it in the ears of the king, and in the ears of all the princes which stood beside the king. Now the king sat in the winterhouse in the ninth month: and there was a fire on the hearth burning before him. And it came to pass, that when Jehudi had read three or four leaves, **he cut it with the penknife, and cast it into the fire that was on the hearth, until all the roll was consumed in the fire** that was on the hearth. (Jeremiah 36:21-23 AV)

The Lord commanded Jeremiah to rewrite the prophecy. God did not repeat the prophecy. Jeremiah rewrote the prophecy that had been previously given to him. God inspired Jeremiah to recreate a copy of his prior prophecy that had been burned in the fire by King Jehoiakim.

> Then the word of the LORD came to Jeremiah, after that the king had burned the roll, and the words which Baruch wrote at the mouth of Jeremiah, saying, Take thee again another roll, and **write in it all the former words that were in the first roll**, which Jehoiakim the king of Judah hath burned. (Jeremiah 36:27-28 AV)

We see God engaged in what many scam artists pejoratively call double inspiration. They mock God's inspiration. God performs double, triple, quadruple, indeed, continuous inspiration. Inspiration by God means something completely different from Dr. Waite's definition. Jeremiah was given inspiration (knowledge) by God to rewrite the exact words. Notice that Jeremiah spoke and Baruch wrote down what was said. Baruch wrote the actual words. Baruch was inspired by God to write down God's words spoken by Jeremiah faithfully. Jeremiah was acting as a sort of copyist who was making a copy of God's prophecy given in the first book that King Jehoiakim burned. Jeremiah and Baruch were acting in much the same capacity as Beza was when he wrote the clause in Revelation 16:5 in theTextus Receptus because we find that Jeremiah and Baruch, in making the copy, were inspired by God to "add[] besides unto them many like words." That means that the copy was not identical. God inspired Jeremiah and Baruch to add "many like words" to the original prophecy. That is proof of progressive revelation by God.

> Then took Jeremiah another roll, and gave it to Baruch the scribe, the son of Neriah; who wrote therein from the mouth of Jeremiah all the words of the book which Jehoiakim king of Judah had burned in the fire: **and there were added besides unto them many like words.** (Jeremiah 36:32 AV)

Waite maintains that translators are not inspired. Thus, no translation can be the inspired word of God. Waite concludes that the Authorized (King James) Version (AV) of the Holy Bible is NOT the inspired word of God. He relegates the AV to being the best uninspired English rendition of scripture available.

The DBS is also suffering from textual schizophrenia. Their Statement of Faith says that the copies are merely the "closest" to the original language signatures. But the DBS Statement of Faith also says those same copies are somehow "providentially preserved." If they are providentially preserved, that would make them perfect copies and not simply close copies as claimed by the DBS. Such inconsistencies can be expected from con artists like Dr. Waite and the DBS.

Sadly, the DBS view has become the orthodox position held by most pastors who defend the AV in churches today. And that poses a real problem for the church today. God states that "all scripture is given by inspiration of God." 2 Timothy 3:16. If the AV translation is not inspired by God, as claimed by DBS and Waite, then by definition, the AV is not, and cannot be, scripture!

It is strange that those who seem to defend the King James Bible, like Dr. Waite and DBS, are actually secret agents in the service of Satan who undermine the authority of the King James Bible. Another example is Bob Jones University, which states: "we continue to use the King James Version (KJV) as the campus standard in the undergraduate classroom and chapel pulpit."[370] However, regarding inspiration, they limit that to the original manuscripts.

> Bob Jones University holds to the verbal, plenary inspiration of the Bible in the original manuscripts and that God has supernaturally preserved His inspired words in the totality of extant manuscript evidence.[371]

Bob Jones University thinks God's word is found in the "totality of extant manuscript evidence." That means it is somewhere in the hundreds of manuscripts in the Greek, Hebrew, and Aramaic languages, and it is a free for all to find it. But one thing that Bob Jones University is clear on is that God's inspired word is NOT found in the King James Bible, the very Bible it requires as the "standard in the undergraduate classroom and chapel pulpit." To even suggest that God's inspired word is found in the King James Bible qualifies you as a heretic and blasphemer at Bib Jones University.

Bob Jones Jr. (1911-1997), who succeeded his father, Bob Jones Sr., as President and Chancellor of Bob Jones University, gives us the generally accepted view among fundamentalist churches and schools regarding the issue of the inspiration of the King James Bible. Bob Jones Jr. considered the King James Bible "a remarkable" and "the loveliest" translation. But he said to consider the KJV the inspired word of God was heresy that is "in a very definite sense, a blasphemy."

> Religiously, I think perhaps **the silliest idea abroad—and one which is calculated to divide the people of God—is the idea that there is some sort of special inspiration attached to the Authorized Version of Scripture commonly called in America "The King James Version."** Many of us, including this writer, believe that the King James Version is by far **the loveliest translation** of the Scripture in the English language. We believe it is a **remarkable translation**. ... To embrace this "King James only" heresy is, in a very definite sense, **a blasphemy**. ... I am sure good men have been taken in by this "King James only" **heresy**, but I do not believe they are logical men. I think that this heresy, like all heresies, will divide the saints, deceive men,

and lead men astray.[372]

William W. Combs, Th.D., Academic Dean and Professor of New Testament at Detroit Baptist Theologic Seminary, agrees with Bob Jones. He states that anyone who claims that God inspired the translators of the King James Bible is "spouting heresy."

> The only way the KJV, or any edition of it, could be infallible and inerrant is if the persons who produced it were under the same superintending ministry of the Holy Spirit as the authors of Scripture. And anyone who makes such an assertion is not just wrong but **spouting heresy**.[373]

God calls on us to search the scriptures. John 5:39. We can only search the scripture we have. If we do not speak Greek or Hebrew and only have an English Bible, which DBS claims is not inspired and is thus not scripture, we cannot obey God's command to search the scriptures. How can we search in a language we do not speak?

If God expected all to learn Greek and Hebrew to be able to search the scriptures, what was the point of the gift of tongues that allowed people from all nations with different languages to understand the gospel? See Acts 2. Notice that the crowd was amazed, "how hear we every man in our own tongue, wherein we were born? Acts 2:8. The miracle was that they heard the gospel in their own tongue; they were not amazed that they understood the Hebrew tongue spoken by the disciples. The miracle of God was that his gospel was to be spread in all the different tongues of the world and not that all the world would learn Greek and Hebrew. Alan James O'Reilly explains, "James 2:26 states that, 'the body without the spirit is dead.' So is the Bible without inspiration."[374]

Jesus commanded us: "Go ye into all the world, and preach

the gospel to every creature. He that believeth and is baptized shall be saved; but he that believeth not shall be damned." Mark 16:15-16. How are we to do that if the only inspired gospel is in the original languages? There is no instruction in the Bible to teach all the world Hebrew, Aramaic, and Greek so that they can receive the inspired word of God. We are to preach the gospel in the people's language so they can understand it. The word of God in other languages, including AV English, is inspired; it is scripture.

When Jesus was crucified, the superscription posted above his head was written in Greek, Latin, and Hebrew. God had no problem sovereignly ensuring that there was a translation in different languages posted over Jesus Christ's head. God was ensuring that everyone knew who was being crucified and that they understood it in their own language.

> And a superscription also was written over him in letters of Greek, and Latin, and Hebrew, THIS IS THE KING OF THE JEWS. Luke 23:38.

All understanding of scripture (not just its writing) is inspired. We are taught the meaning of scripture by the Holy Ghost. 1 Corinthians 2:13-14. The KJV translators had understanding given to them by God to faithfully translate his Bible into English. That is, they were inspired. When God gives you understanding of scripture when you read it, you are inspired. Many pastors denigrate the work of the Holy Spirit in the impartation of understanding of God's word. They claim that only the original autographs were inspired by God. They further allege that the translation from the original tongues into English is not inspired by God. Thus, according to many pastors, the English Bible is not the inspired word of God.

That uninspired position is wrong. In fact, it is by inspiration of God we know that the Authorized (King James) Version of the Holy Bible (a.k.a., AV or KJV) is God's word in

English. The translators were inspired by God in their translation of the Authorized (King James) Version of the Holy Bible.

> Which things also **we speak, not in the words which man's wisdom teacheth, but which the Holy Ghost teacheth**; comparing spiritual things with spiritual. But the natural man receiveth not the things of the Spirit of God: for they are foolishness unto him: neither can he know *them*, because **they are spiritually discerned**. (1 Corinthians 2:13-14 AV)

Notice in 2 Timothy 3:15-16 how all scripture is given by inspiration of the Holy Spirit. The word "is" means presently being given. The context is that Timothy had the scriptures from a child. The scriptures are able to make him wise unto salvation. The parallel statement in the next clause explains how the scripture gave Timothy that wisdom (i.e., inspiration). Thus, inspiration is wisdom given from God.

> "And that from a child thou **hast known the holy scriptures**, which are **able to make thee wise unto salvation** through faith which is in Christ Jesus. **All scripture is given by inspiration of God**, and is profitable for doctrine, for reproof, for correction, for instruction in righteousness:" (2 Timothy 3:15-16 AV)

That means that Timothy's knowledge of the scripture was given to him by inspiration of God. Notice the word "is." That means that scripture is given (presently) by the inspiration of God (the understanding given by God). Notice in Job 3:38 how God explains that it is through inspiration of God that we are given understanding. All who read scripture are given understanding and wisdom unto salvation by the inspiration of God.

> But there is a spirit in man: and the **inspiration** of the Almighty giveth them **understanding**. (Job 32:8 AV)

Paul was given wisdom by God to write scripture. That means that God gave him understanding; Paul was inspired. What Paul wrote was scripture given to him by the inspiration (wisdom) of God.

> And account that the longsuffering of our Lord is salvation; even as our beloved brother Paul also according to the **wisdom given unto him hath written unto you**; As also in all his epistles, speaking in them of these things; in which are some things hard to be understood, which they that are unlearned and unstable wrest, as they do also the other **scriptures**, unto their own destruction. (2 Peter 3:15-16 AV)

God gave Paul the understanding through his revelation to Paul to write what he did.

> But I certify you, brethren, that the gospel which was preached of me is not after man. For I neither received it of man, neither was I taught it, but **by the revelation of Jesus Christ**. (Galatians 1:11-12 AV)

God gives <u>**understanding**</u> of scripture by <u>**inspiration**</u> of God (i.e., revelation).

- **Inspiration of God gives understanding**;
- **"All" Holy scripture "is" given by inspiration of God**;
  - Writers are inspired by God;
  - Copyists are inspired by God;
  - Translators are inspired by God;

- Readers are inspired by God.

Inspiration is not a one-time event that only applies to the writers of the scriptures, as claimed by many. Inspiration is a continual act of God's revelation given to his elect through which he brings understanding of his word unto salvation. God inspired all the writers, copyists, and translators of scripture. Indeed, when one reads the scriptures under the guidance of the Holy Spirit, God inspires the reader to understand what he is reading. "All" scripture "is" given by inspiration of God. *See* 2 Timothy 3:16. The issue is whether the scripture is "given" to a person. Without the guidance and revelation of the Holy Spirit, no man can receive the things of God. That is because "the natural man receiveth not the things of the Spirit of God: for they are foolishness unto him: neither can he know them, because they are spiritually discerned." 1 Corinthians 2:14.

33 All Scripture Is Given by Inspiration of God

The Greek word *theopneustos* is translated as "is given by inspiration of God" in 2 Timothy 3:16. "All [*pasa*] scripture [*graphe*] is given by inspiration of God [*theopneustos*], and is profitable for doctrine, for reproof, for correction, for instruction in righteousness:" (2 Timothy 3:16 AV)

Dr. D. A. Waite is certainly qualified to tell us what *theopneustos* means? Dr. Waite is "a leading spokesman for the authority of the King James Version of the Bible, and author of numerous books explaining this position. He earned a Bachelor of Arts in classical Greek and Latin from the University of Michigan in 1948, a Master of Theology in New Testament Greek Literature and Exegesis from Dallas Theological Seminary in 1952, an M.A. in Speech from Southern Methodist University in 1953, a Doctor of Theology in Bible Exposition from Dallas Theological Seminary in 1955, and a Ph.D. in Speech from Purdue University in 1961. He has been a teacher in the areas of Greek, Hebrew, Bible, Speech, and English for over thirty-five years in nine schools."[375]

Dr. Waite has used his mastery of the Greek language to make the following interpretation of the Greek word *theopneustos*.

> I know and understand what the Greek Words say in 2 Timothy 3:16. PASA ("each," "every," or "all") GRAPHE ("Old Testament Hebrew Words" and "New Testament Greek Words") THEOPNEUSTOS ("God-breathed" or "breathed out by God.") This happened once-for-all when these God-given original Words were given. It has never happened again, including in the King James Bible or in any other translation.[376] (all capital letters in original)

Notice how Dr. Waite has redefined the Greek words. He has taken the Greek word *graphe* and limited it to only "Old Testament Hebrew Words" and "New Testament Greek Words." But that is not what *graphe* means. *Graphe* in this context it means "scripture." Dr. Waite is limiting scripture to only the Old Testament Hebrew and the New Testament Greek. No other language, including English would qualify for his defintion of scripture.

Next, read his defintion of *theopneustos*. He states that *theopneustos* means "God-breathed" or "breathed out by God." Indeed, he exlains that the God-breathed event happened one time only for each scripture. And once God breathed out the original scriptures, there could be no other inspired scripture through translation into English. Dr. Waite expounds on his theme.

> The King James Bible is not **"inspired"**...The word inspired is only used for the Words that God Himself breathed-out, not that which man has merely translated. God did not breathe-out English or any other modern language. God only breathed-out and inspired the Old and New Testament Words of Hebrew, Aramaic, and Greek.[377] (bold emphasis in original)

In order to be scripture it must be inspired. But Dr. Waite thinks that only the original language Old and New Testament writings are scripture. Dr. Waite puts all translations, including English Bibles, outside the definition of scripture.

> I don't like to use the word "inerrant" of any English (or other language) translation of the Bible because the word "inerrant" is implied from the Greek Word, theopneustos (2 Timothy 3:16) which means literally, "GOD-BREATHED." God Himself did NOT "BREATHE OUT" English, or German, or French, or Spanish, or Latin, or Italian. He DID "BREATHE OUT" Hebrew/Aramaic, and Greek. Therefore, ONLY THE HEBREW/ARAMAIC AND GREEK CAN BE RIGHTLY TERMED "GOD-BREATHED" OR "INERRANT," not ANY translation!![378] (all capital letters in original)

Waite's theology is the orthodox view followed in churches today. The problem is that Dr. Waite is wrong. *Theopneustos* in the context of 2 Timothy 3:16 means "is given by inspiration of God" just as the King James translators wrote. Dr.Waite claims to be an expert in the Greek language. He said himself "I know and understand what the Greek Words say in 2 Timothy 3:16." That means that his mistranslation must be intentional.

Dr. Waite's alleged mastery of the Greek language is the basis for changing the translation of *theopneustos* from "is given by inspiration of God" in the King King James Bible to "God-breathed." Alan James O'Reilly points out that Dr. Waite's alleged Greek expertise is rather pedestrian compared to the academic giants on the King James translation committee.

> Noting that the validity of Dr Waite's exposition of "theopneustos" with its centrepiece that "is given

by inspiration of God" should read "God-breathed" is predicated on the extent of Dr Waite's mastery of Koine Greek, it is appropriate to review briefly the expertise of one of the best-known King James translators, John Bois. Bois began to read Hebrew at the age of five and was admitted to St John's College, Cambridge at the age of fourteen, where he distinguished himself as a Greek scholar, customarily studying in the library from 4 a.m. until 8 p.m., during which sessions he studied standing. He became the chief lecturer in Greek at his college, a post he retained for ten years and was one of the six translators chosen to review the whole work on the new Bible after completion of the first draft. This painstaking task took nine months.[379]

Waite is only correct if he were translating the the Greek word *pneustos* by itself. *Pneustos* does mean to breath out. But the King James translators were not translating the word *pneustos* in 2 Timothy 3:16. They were translating the word *theopheustos*. They were inspired (i.e., given understanding by God) to translate *theopneustos* not as "God breathed" but as "is given by inspiration of God." The King James translators correctly translated *theopneustos* in the context of 2 Timothy 3:16 as "is given by inspiration of God."

The King James translators meant to convey that persons writing (and reading) the words in scripture understand what they are writing and reading by the inspiration of God. The English word inspire is a pregnant English word with many meanings. But the overal theme of the word is inhaling, not exhaling as suggested by Waite. One meaning for inspire is "[t]o draw in breath; to inhale air into the lungs; opposed to expire."[380] It also has the meaning of "[t]o infuse into the mind; as, to inspire with new life."[381] and "[t]o infuse or suggest ideas or monitions supernaturally; to communicate divine instructions to the mind. In this manner, we suppose the prophets to have been inspired, and the Scriptures to have been composed under divine influence or direction."[382]

But Waite is an expert in the Greek language. He knows better. This obfuscation of what it means for God to inspire his elect is purposeful. He has an agenda. Dr. Waite portrays himself as a defender of the King Jame Bible. But he seems to play the role as a saboteur of the authority of the King James Bible.

While Dr. Waite claims that the King James Bible is the best English translation. He is not entirely satisfied with it. Dr. Waite criticizes the new Bible version for their reliance on corrupt Alexandrian Greek manuscripts. However, his preferred translation of the Greek word *theopneustos* in 2 Timothy 3:16, contradicts the AV translation and agrees with the new Bible versions. For example, in the English Standard Version ESV of the Bible, we read that all scripture is not "given by inspiration of God," as in the King James Bible. Instead, "[a]ll Scripture is breathed out by God." 2 Timothy 3:16 ESV.

AV	ESV
All scripture **is given by inspiration of God**, and is profitable for doctrine, for reproof, for correction, for instruction in righteousness: (2 Timothy 3:16 AV)	All Scripture **is breathed out by God** and profitable for teaching, for reproof, for correction, and for training in righteousness, (2 Timothy 3:16 ESV)

The ESV limits scripture to only those original manuscripts that were written as God breathed them out in the original languages. It disqualifies translations into other languages as being scripture. But under God's inspired word of God found in the AV, both the writer and reader of scripture are given understanding (inspiration) from God. An English speaker can understand scripture in the AV because "[a]ll scripture is given by inspiration of God, and is profitable for doctrine, for reproof, for correction, for instruction in righteousness." (2 Timothy 3:16 AV)

Inspiration of God means being given knowledge by God. Inspiration is not a one-time event that only happened at the original drafting of scripture. All who write, copy, translate, and read God's word under the guidance of the Holy Spirit are inspired by God. *See* Job 32:8; 2 Peter 3:15-16. Please understand that even those who read the Holy Scriptures under the guidance of the Holy Spirit are inspired by God. That is what God means when he says that "all" scripture "is" given by inspiration of God. *See* 2 Timothy 3:16.

34   The Arminian Agenda

Every false doctrine finds its root in some corruption of the Holy Bible. For example, Dr Ruckman went through 400 Bible verses for 8 hours with an older man who had assimilated the false teachings of the Seventh Day Adventists, the Mormons, the Jehovah's Witnesses, the Church of Christ, the Christian Scientists, the Unity Church, the Catholic Church, the British Israelites, and the Holiness groups. The man claimed that he got those doctrines from reading the King James Bible. Dr Ruckman said that this man could quote from memory every verse that taught every one of the false teachings of those groups from the King James Authorized Text. But, upon closer examination, Dr. Ruckman discovered that the man was ever-so-slightly changing the words in the AV to comport with the false doctrines of each religious sect. Alan James O'Reilly explained what Dr. Ruckman discovered.

> Dr Ruckman observed that every time the man quoted from the Authorized Text to put forward a false doctrine, he would change at least one letter of the King James Text! One example was in John 8:58, where the Lord said "Before Abraham was, I am." The old man insisted that the Lord meant "I was." He took the same approach with every one of

the 400 verses discussed in the 8-hour session. That was how he had assimilated every one of the false teachings of the heretical groups listed above, not by means of the King James Text but by changing a word or a letter in a verse from the King James Text. That is how false doctrine and rogue denominations are hatched, as described and warned of in Isaiah 59:5. "They hatch cockatrice' eggs, and weave the spider's web: he that eateth of their eggs dieth, and that which is crushed breaketh out into a viper."[383]

Indeed, that explains how Dr. Waite and the DBS have come to their false concept that the AV English translation is not the inspired word of God. Dr. Waite changed the meaning of the AV text in 2 Timothy 3:16 from meaning that all scripture "is given by inspiration of God," to all scripture is "God Breathed." By limiting the scriptures to being "God breathed," Dr. Waite could move forward with his heresy that inspiration is a one-time event that applied only to the original language texts. Armed with his corrupted 2 Timothy 3:16 passage, Dr. Waite could move along with his false doctrine that stripped God's word in English (AV) of its authority as the inspired word of God.

Dr. Waite did not stop there with his heresy. Once a person goes down the path of corrupting God's word, there is no stopping his mischief. Dr. D.A. Waite's attack on the inspiration of the Authorized (King James) Version of the Holy Bible has given birth to his rejection of the gospel of grace. Dr. Waite has adopted the heresy of Jacobus Arminius, who was a follower of a Jesuit priest named Luis de Molina. Molina promoted Semi-Pelagianism, which was later known as Molinism, and finally, Arminianism.

Luis de Molina taught the semi-Pelagian view that God predestined believers to salvation, but at the same time, man had free will to choose to be saved. This doctrine became popularly known as Molinism.³⁸⁴ Under Semi-Pelagianism, man has fallen, and his will is hindered by sin, but not totally so. According to Semi-Pelagians, man is not spiritually dead but only spiritually sick. Semi-Pelagians taught that man could utilize his faith to cooperate with God in facilitating his own salvation. Semi-Pelagians accepted that God was sovereign, but at the same time, they promoted the inconsistent view that man had free will to choose whether to believe in Jesus Christ unto salvation. Semi-Pelagianism became the generally accepted doctrine of the Roman Catholic Church. The Catholic Church codified this semi-Pelagian anti-gospel, with accompanying curses, at the Council of Trent (circa 1547).

The Roman Catholic church knew that Protestant Christians would never adopt Molinism if it were known to have sprung from a Jesuit priest, so they decided to use a front man in order to introduce this anti-gospel into the Protestant churches. They used a man named Jacobus Arminius (1560-1609), who was an admirer of Molina, to popularize the free will doctrine of Molina among Protestants. Molinism is now known among Protestants as Ariminianism.

Dr. Waite attacks the inspiration of the AV because he does not believe in the sovereign intervention of God through his grace to impart faith to his elect. Removing God's intervention in translating the Bible into English parallels the Arminian view that God does not intervene to give his elect faith to believe in him. In Waite's view, salvation is man's free choice without the intervention of God, just as the translation is entirely within man's free control without God's intervention.

Dr. Waite cites John 1:12 and alleges that it refutes the biblical doctrine of limited atonement and, by implication, the doctrine of total depravity.

A. THE TERMS OF JOHN 1:12 REFUTE

"LIMITED ATONEMENT"

"But as many as received Him, to them gave He power to become the sons of God, even to them THAT BELIEVE ON HIS NAME."

1. The Goal Of John 1:12

The "goal" spoken of in this verse is the "power to become the sons God." This is another way of saying to be "saved" or to have "eternal life." This is the net result if the requirements in the verse are fulfilled by the individual.

2. The Partakers In That Goal In John 1:12

The verse is quite clear that those who partake in this goal of becoming "the sons of God " by being born again and regenerated by the Holy Spirit through faith, are (1) "as many as received Him" [Christ] and/or (2) "to them that BELIEVE on His Name" [Christ's]. These two synonymous expressions of "receiving" and "believing on His Name" are the only qualifications needed for becoming a "son" or "child" of God. Any others who do NOT meet one or the other of these two qualifications (actually they are the same, but spoken in slightly different words), cannot be the "sons of God" and cannot be saved.

3. The Refutation of "LIMITED ATONEMENT" In John 1:12

There is not a hint in this verse that this INVITATION to sinners to become saints is LIMITED only "to the elect" or that we are to restrict the INVITATION artificially by theological words. We are to preach that "as many" sinners who would "receive" Christ as Savior and "to them that BELIEVE" on His name" whoever they might be- would be guaranteed by God to "become" a "son" or "child" of God! We can make this UNIVERSAL offer, because Jesus Christ died for the SINS OF THE WHOLE WORLD--barring none! They have to "receive" Him and "believe on His Name" to be saved, and to partake of Christ's benefits on their behalf. Not receiving of Him--No benefits!![385] (emphasis in original).

Dr. Waite is very slyly deceiving the reader by isolating John 1:12 from its context. He has wrongly divided God's word and tried to construct an argument by ignoring the whole counsel of God. Those, like Dr. Waite, who would elevate the will of man over the will of God argue that John 1:12 means that a person must be willing to receive that free gift of God by believing in Jesus. Dr. Waite expressly rejects the notion that God has chosen his elect, who will then believe in him.

Dr. Waite argues that Jesus died for the sins of every person in the whole world, and therefore every person in the whole world can be saved, if only they would, of their own free will, believe in Jesus. Under Dr. Waite's interpretation of John 1:12, it is man who chooses God and not God who chooses man. According to Waite's false doctrine, God is passively offering salvation as a gift, but man must receive that gift of his own free will in order to be saved. John 1:12, however, does not say any such thing. John 1:12 simply explains that those who receive Jesus, meaning those who believe in Jesus, will be saved and become adopted sons of God.

When John 1:12 is read in context, we see that the very next passage (verse 13) explains the source of that saving faith through which one is born again. "But as many as received him, to them gave he power to become the sons of God, *even* to them that believe on his name: **Which were born, not of blood, nor of the will of the flesh, nor of the will of man, but of God**." (John 1:12-13 AV) John 1:13 makes it crystal clear that we are saved by the will of God alone, and not by our own will.

Why didn't Dr. Waite quote verse 13 or even try to explain it? Because it completely refutes his Arminian construct that all men of their own free will can believe in Jesus. Dr. Waite portrays himself as a Bible expert (Th.D., Ph.D.). He is head of *The Bible For Today, Inc.*, which has an available resource library of over 2,600 articles. With his expertise in the Bible, we can assume that he is not ignorant of verse 13. He is purposely trying to mislead the reader as to what God means in John 1:12, by taking it out of its context. That is typical of Arminian theologians.

Dr. Waite repeats his strategy of quoting passages out of context as a way to conceal the gospel of grace in his treatment of Matthew 11:28.

> When [in Matthew 11:28] our Savior extended these gracious words, "come unto Me, ALL YE that labour and are heavy laden," I believe that this was an UNLIMITED invitation to an UNLIMITED group of people. This invitation extended, thus, to the ENTIRE WORLD of mankind who would be born . . . His invitation was backed up by his UNLIMITED PROVISION for "REST" in His "UNLIMITED ATONEMENT" at the Cross for the sins of the entire world![386] (all capital letter emphasis in original).

When, however, Matthew 11:28 is read in context, it is clear from the preceding verse (verse 27) that it is only to those whomsoever the Son will reveal the Father who will know the

Father.

> All things are delivered unto me of my Father: and no man knoweth the Son, but the Father; **neither knoweth any man the Father, save the Son, and he to whomsoever the Son will reveal him.** Come unto me, all ye that labour and are heavy laden, and I will give you rest. (Matthew 11:27-28 AV)

Dr. Waite continues with his Arminian strategy of hide the grace by citing Hebrews 2:9 out of context. Dr. Waite states:

> The verse [Hebrews 2:9] clearly teaches that Jesus Christ, in His incarnation, at the Cross of Calvary, "should taste death FOR EVERY MAN." . . . this is another clear and plain verse which teaches Christ's "UNLIMITED ATONEMENT" for everyone, barring none![387] (uncial emphasis in original)

Waite argues that Jesus died for everyone in the world, and therefore, everyone in the world has a chance at salvation if they would only believe in Jesus of their own free will. Waite seems ignorant of the fact that the Epistle to the Hebrews was written by Paul to Jews. Paul was explaining the superiority of Jesus and his New Testament over the Old Testament types, which only foreshadowed the coming of Christ. In writing to the Jews, Paul wanted the Jews to understand that Christ died for both Jews and Gentiles. That is why he said that he "should taste death for every man." Paul meant every kind of man, not just the Jews, but also the Gentiles. Hebrews 9:15 reveals that it is only those Jews and Gentiles who are called by God who are saved.

> And for this cause he is the mediator of the new testament, that by means of death, for the redemption of the transgressions *that were* under

the first testament, **they which are called might receive the promise of eternal inheritance.**" (Hebrews 9:15 AV)

The gospel is that no one can come to Jesus without the calling of the Father. John 6:44,65. God's calling is effectual; all who are called will be saved. John 6:37-39. There is no middle group, as suggested by Waite's theology, that is made up of those whom God called, but are damned to hell, because they decided of their own free will to reject the calling of God.

Furthermore, Waite conceals the fact that only four verses later God explains who are among the "every man" that he referenced in verse 9. God states that Jesus' crucifixion was a way of "bringing many sons unto glory" and those sons are the "children which God hath given me."

> But we see Jesus, who was made a little lower than the angels for the suffering of death, crowned with glory and honour; **that he by the grace of God should taste death for every man.** For it became him, for whom *are* all things, and by whom *are* all things, in bringing many sons unto glory, to make the captain of their salvation perfect through sufferings. For both he that sanctifieth and they who are sanctified *are* all of one: for which cause he is not ashamed to call them brethren, Saying, I will declare thy name unto my brethren, in the midst of the church will I sing praise unto thee. And again, I will put my trust in him. **And again, Behold I and the children which God hath given me.** (Hebrews 2:9-13 AV)

The passage in context proves that Jesus died only for his elect, who were given to him by God the Father. Jesus died on the cross to sanctify his children and Jesus and his children "are all of one." Hebrews 2:9-13 states that Jesus suffered and died to sanctify his children and make them perfect. If, as claimed by Waite, Jesus's sanctified children includes everyone in the entire world, that would mean that God sends to hell most of his sanctified children.

Verse 13 impeaches Waite's claim, by identifying the "every man" for whom Jesus "tasted death" in verse 9 as being only the "children which God hath given me." Who are the children that God hath given to Jesus? The whole counsel of God, which Waite eschews, states that Jesus' children are only those whom the Father draws to the Son, and no others. *See* John 6:37, 39, 44, 65.

Before salvation, we are dead in trespasses and sin such that Jesus must supply the faith for our salvation. That's right, he is not only the object of our faith, but he is also the source of our faith. Everything for our salvation is supplied by and through Christ. **Our faith in Christ is the faith of Christ**. *See e.g.,* Romans 3:22; Galatians 3:22; Revelation 14:12.

> Knowing that a man is not justified by the works of the law, but by the **faith of Jesus Christ**, even we have believed in Jesus Christ, that we might be justified by the **faith of Christ**, and not by the works of the law: for by the works of the law shall no flesh be justified. (Galatians 2:16 AV)

> And be found in him, not having mine own righteousness, which is of the law, but that which is through the **faith of Christ**, the righteousness which is of God by faith. (Philippians 3:9 AV)

All new bible versions change the "faith **of** Jesus Christ" to the "faith **in** Jesus Christ," which conceals the source of the saving faith. That opens the way for the Arminian theology that man can, by his own will, decide whether to believe in Jesus Christ unto salvation.

AV	ESV
But the scripture hath concluded all under sin, that the promise by faith **of** Jesus Christ might be given to them that believe. (Galatians 3:22 AV)	But the Scripture imprisoned everything under sin, so that the promise by faith **in** Jesus Christ might be given to those who believe. (Galatians 3:22 ESV)

Arminianism is a false gospel that was born of Rome. Read one of the many curses the Roman Catholic Church rains down upon those who believe the true gospel: "If anyone saith that the grace of justification is only attained to by those who are predestined unto life; but that all others who are called are called indeed, but bought receive not grace, as being, by the divine power, predestined unto evil; let him be anathema."[388]

The Bible clearly shows one, Judas, being predestined for damnation. As they must, Arminians claim that Judas had the chance, through his own free will, to believe in Jesus unto salvation. The Bible says otherwise. The Bible says that God chose Judas for damnation. Jesus stated: "While I was with them in the world, I kept them in thy name: those that thou gavest me I have kept, and none of them is lost, but **the son of perdition**; that the scripture might be fulfilled." (John 17:12) Jesus said Judas was lost and called Judas the son of perdition before Judas had died, thus indicating that God preordained Judas to perdition.

Judas was sent into perdition as a consequence of his prophesied betrayal. "Yea, mine own familiar friend, in whom I trusted, which did eat of my bread, hath lifted up his heel against me." (Psalms 41:9 AV) Judas had no chance to be saved. He was predestinated to "perdition." Judas' betrayal was preordained by

God: "Him, being delivered by the determinate counsel and foreknowledge of God, ye have taken, and by wicked hands have crucified and slain:" (Acts 2:23 AV)

Some claim that perdition does not mean damnation. But the King James Bible has a built-in dictionary that reveals what perdition means. In John 17:12 Jesus indicates that Judas being the son of perdition means he was lost. Judas was "lost." Jesus said so, and he said so before Judas died. Furthermore, God defines perdition as eternal damnation. In Philippians 1:28, we find that perdition is juxtaposed against salvation. That indicates that perdition is the opposite of salvation. In that passage, damnation in hell is distinguished from salvation in heaven.

> And in nothing terrified by your adversaries: which is to them an evident token of **perdition**, but to you of **salvation**, and that of God. (Philippians 1:28 AV)

Notice how in Hebrews 10:38-39 God states that God has no pleasure in those who draw back. Those are lost. The next sentence states that the saved are not like the lost (those who draw back who go "into perdition"). Thus indicating those who go into perdition are damned to hell. Notice that perdition is the opposite of those who "believe to the saving of the soul."

> Now the just shall live by faith: but if any man draw back, my soul shall have no pleasure in him. But we are not of them who draw back unto perdition; but of them that believe to the saving of the soul. (Hebrews 10:38-39 AV)

The biblical perdition is always a reference to eternal damnation. Noah Webster explains that the biblical definition of perdition is: "The utter loss of the soul or of final happiness in a future state; future misery or eternal death. The impenitent sinner is condemned to final perdition."[389]

Some claim that Judas repented, indicating that he was ultimately saved. The Bible does say that Judas repented. But regarding the repentance of Judas, there is an essential word in Matthew 27:3 that modifies and defines the kind of repentance that Judas had. Judas "repented himself." Judas' repentance was NOT repentance unto salvation. It was NOT repentance from God. It was an enslaved-will repentance. He "repented himself." He regretted his decision to betray Jesus. That is not the same as repentance unto salvation that comes from God.

The fact that repentance comes from God and not from the free will of man was clearly understood by the early church. We see the writer of 2 Timothy expressing God's sovereign rule over the hearts of men; God "gives" repentance.

> And the servant of the Lord must not strive; but be gentle unto all men, apt to teach, patient, In meekness instructing those that oppose themselves; if God peradventure will give them repentance to the acknowledging of the truth. (2 Timothy 2:24-25 AV)

Without God moving the heart of the penitent, there could never be repentance unto salvation. It is Jesus that supplies the faith and the repentance.

> Him hath God exalted with his right hand to be a Prince and a Saviour, for to give repentance to Israel, and forgiveness of sins. (Acts 5:31 AV)

Judas, like the Antichrist, was preordained to damnation. Both Judas (John 17:12) and the antichrit (2 Thessalonians 2:3) are called the "son of perdition." God uses the term "mystery of godliness" and explains in 1 Timothy chapter 3, that the mystery of godliness is, in part, that "God was manifest in the flesh."

> And without controversy great is the **mystery of godliness: God was manifest in the flesh**, justified in the Spirit, seen of angels, preached unto the Gentiles, believed on in the world, received up into glory. (1 Timothy 3:16)

The Antichrist is the opposite of God in character, but he seeks to replace God, then the mystery of iniquity must be the devil manifest in the flesh. It is notable that in the verses following God's explanation of the mystery of godliness in 1 Timothy, he explains that "in the latter times some shall depart from the faith, giving heed to seducing spirits, and doctrines of devils; Speaking lies in hypocrisy; having their conscience seared with a hot iron; Forbidding to marry, and commanding to abstain from meats." 1 Timothy 4:1-2. The Roman Catholic Church has embraced both the doctrine of forbidding Catholic priests to marry and forbidding the eating of meat on Friday during Lent.

So we see that the mystery of iniquity is the manifestation of the devil in the flesh. Are there other verses that support this interpretation? In John 6:70-71, Jesus referred to Judas as a devil. "Jesus answered them, Have not I chosen you twelve, and one of you is a devil? He spake of Judas Iscariot the son of Simon: for he it was that should betray him, being one of the twelve." (John 6:70-71) Was Judas a devil? In looking at the gospel of Luke we see that the devil (Satan) in fact entered into Judas prior to Judas' betrayal of Jesus. "Then entered Satan into Judas surnamed Iscariot, being of the number of the twelve." (Luke 22:3)

We see that the devil was manifest in the flesh when he entered into Judas. This interpretation is confirmed by John 17:12 where Jesus refers to Judas as "the son of perdition" in John 17:12. The term "son of perdition" is the same term used in 2 Thessalonians 2:3 to describe the Antichrist. "Let no man deceive you by any means: for that day shall not come, except there come a falling away first, and that man of sin be revealed, the **son of perdition**." (2 Thessalonians 2:3) The "son of perdition" is also described as "that man of sin" and "the mystery of iniquity" in 2 Thessalonians. They are all descriptions for the Antichrist.

That man of sin, the son of perdition, described in 2 Thessalonians 2:3, can be none other than the pope of Rome. The mystery of iniquity, therefore, must be that the pope of Rome, who, being the son of perdition, is possessed by Satan. Just as Judas, who, also was the son of perdition and was possessed by Satan. As Christ was God manifest in the flesh, and is the "mystery of godliness," so also the Antichrist is the devil manifest in the flesh and is the "mystery of iniquity."

The Roman Church teaches that Peter is the rock upon which God has built his church, and that the Pope, as the bishop of Rome, is Peter's successor, head of the church, and the "Vicar of Christ." The Bible, however, is clear that Jesus Christ is the foundation and head of the church, not the pope. "And he is the head of the body, the church: who is the beginning, the firstborn from the dead; that in all things he might have the preeminence." (Colossians 1:18) So, the pope seeks to replace Christ as he opposes him. He is the Antichrist.

Just as Judas, the son of perdition, pretended to be a loyal follower of Jesus as he worked to betray him (Luke 22:47-48), so the pope, who is also the son of perdition pretends to be a loyal follower of Jesus and is betraying his subjects into the lake of fire. Revelation 20:10, 15. The Antichrist is the very opposite of Jesus; Jesus is the mystery of godliness, who is faithful and true and will never forsake us. Hebrews 13:5, Revelation 19:11. The preordained damnation of Judas and the antirchrist impeaches the claim that Jesus died for every person in the world and that all have the same chance by their own free will to believe unto salvation.

The Bible is in direct contradiction to the free will doctrines of the Catholic Church. If God chooses some for salvation, that means that those not chosen for salvation are in turn chosen for damnation. "Jesus answered them, Have not I chosen you twelve, and one of you is a devil?" John 6:70. For more information about the false Arminian gospel read this author's book, *The Anti-Gospel.*

35 Our Heavenly Father's Will Be Done

In the modern Bible versions, God is stripped of his omnipotence in Luke 11:1-4. In the new Bible versions, God's will is no longer done on earth as in heaven. That fits very nicely into the Arminian free will doctrine whereby the sinner can both choose to be saved and also choose to give up his salvation according to his own will, regardless of the will of God. Under the Arminian theology, God desires that all be saved, but he is helpless to overcome the will of the sinner to reject God's grace. Thus, under Arminianism God's will is not done on earth as in heaven. And so the modern Bible versions delete that passage.

Furthermore, the manner of prayer advised by Jesus Christ in the modern Bible versions changes the object of the prayer from God Almighty, who is in heaven, to an unspecified "Father." Instead of praying to "our Father which art in heaven, the prayer is simply to "Father."

AV	ESV
And he said unto them, When ye pray, say, **Our Father which art in heaven**, Hallowed be thy name. Thy kingdom come. **Thy will be done, as in heaven, so in earth**. Give us day by day our daily bread. And forgive us our sins; for we also forgive every one that is indebted to us. And lead us not into temptation; **but deliver us from evil.** (Luke 11:2-4 AV)	And he said to them, "When you pray, say: "**Father,** hallowed be your name. Your kingdom come. Give us each day our daily bread, and forgive us our sins, for we ourselves forgive everyone who is indebted to us. And lead us not into temptation." (Luke 11:2-4 ESV)

There is no limitation on who that "Father" could be. The Roman Catholic priests are called "Father." They are not in heaven and so could very nicely be the object of the new Bible version prayer. Indeed, the Roman Catholic doctrine is that their priests are intermediaries between God and man. The official doctrine of the Roman Catholic Church is that the Catholic priest is *Alter-Christos* (another Christ).

The priests in the Catholic take the title of God the Father. Jesus warned against calling a person father in the spiritual sense, which is a title reserved for God alone.

> **And call no man your father upon the earth: for one is your Father, which is in heaven.** (Matthew 23:9 AV)

> These words spake Jesus, and lifted up his eyes to heaven, and said, **Father**, the hour is come; glorify thy Son, that thy Son also may glorify thee: (John 17:1 AV)

And now, **O Father**, glorify thou me with thine own self with the glory which I had with thee before the world was. (John 17:5 AV)

That they all may be one; as thou, **Father**, art in me, and I in thee, that they also may be one in us: that the world may believe that thou hast sent me. (John 17:21 AV)

Jesus stated clearly: "That all men should honour the Son, even as they honour the Father. He that honoureth not the Son honoureth not the Father which hath sent him." (John 5:23 AV). Jesus and the Father are one. John 10:30-33. The Catholic church has a priesthood that acts as a mediator between man and God, thus making Jesus' mediation superfluous for that reason. The Catholic priest claims to be the Lord Jesus and to act as mediator between God and man.

> [T]he priest is constituted an interpreter and **mediator between God and man**, which indeed must be regarded as the principal function of the priesthood. *CATECHISM OF THE COUNCIL OF TRENT.*[390]

God says otherwise. There is only one God and only one mediator between God and man, that is Jesus Christ.

> For *there is* **one God, and one mediator** between God and men, the man **Christ Jesus**; (1 Timothy 2:5 AV)

There is only one Christ; however, there are many antichrists. All of the priests, bishops, cardinals, and popes of the Romish church are not christs, they are antichrists.

> Little children, it is the last time: and as ye have

> heard that antichrist shall come, **even now are there many antichrists**; whereby we know that it is the last time. (1 John 2:18 AV)

Catholicism states that the priest is the mediator. Hence, the redacted prayer in the modern Bible versions at Luke 11:2-4 fits nicely into the antichrist theology of the Roman Catholic Church. The Pope even takes the title of God the Father. For example, the *Catechism of the Catholic Church*, at § 10 refers to Pope John II as the "Holy Father, Pope John II." The pope goes by other majestic titles such as "Your Holiness." Pope John Paul II, himself, admitted that such titles are inimical to the gospel. He even cited the Bible passage that condemns such practices. He simply explained that the Catholic traditions of men implicitly authorize this violation of God's commands.

> Have no fear when people call me the 'Vicar of Christ,' when they say to me 'Holy Father,' or 'Your Holiness,' or use titles similar to these, which seem even inimical to the Gospel. Christ declared: 'Call no one on earth your father; you have one Father in heaven. Do not be called 'Master;' you have but one master, the Messiah' (Mt 23:9-10). These expressions, nevertheless, have evolved out of a long tradition, becoming part of common usage. One must not be afraid of these words either. *Pope John Paul II.*[391]

The term "Holy Father" was used in the Holy Scripture only one time, it was used by Jesus the night before his crucifixion to refer to God the Father. Implicit in taking God's name is taking his position and authority. As Jesus said in John 14:28, God the Father is greater than Jesus. By taking the title "Holy Father," the Pope is implicitly presenting himself as greater than Jesus Christ.

> And now I am no more in the world, but these are

> in the world, and I come to thee. **Holy Father**, keep through thine own name those whom thou hast given me, that they may be one, as we *are*. (John 17:11 AV)

> Ye have heard how I said unto you, I go away, and come *again* unto you. If ye loved me, ye would rejoice, because I said, I go unto the Father: for **my Father is greater than I.** (John 14:28 AV)

The very title "Pope" is a Latin word which means papa. It is the term used by small children to refer to their father. It is the Latin equivalent of "dada" or "daddy." In Aramaic Hebrew "papa" would be translated "abba." Abba is used 3 times in the Holy Bible. Each time abba refers to God the Father.

> And he said, **Abba, Father**, all things *are* possible unto thee; take away this cup from me: nevertheless not what I will, but what thou wilt. (Mark 14:36 AV)

> For ye have not received the spirit of bondage again to fear; but ye have received the Spirit of adoption, whereby we cry, **Abba, Father**. (Romans 8:15 AV)

> And because ye are sons, God hath sent forth the Spirit of his Son into your hearts, crying, **Abba, Father**. (Galatians 4:6 AV)

Note the trusting humility connoted in the above passages. The Pope of Rome wants his subjects to humble themselves before him as trusting children. He is the papa of their faith. He has taken the name that is rightfully God's in his attempt to turn men from God to him. The Pope not only desires submission to his authority, but it is not uncommon for the Pope to humiliate his subjects by requiring them to kiss his feet.[392]

The leader of the Roman Catholic organization, the Pope, has claimed that not only is he the leader of the Roman Catholics, but that he is also the head of the true church of God, including Protestant Christians, whom he refers to as "separated brethren." He boldly claims that entrance into Heaven is dependant on submission to his authority.

> **We declare, state and define that it is absolutely necessary for the salvation of all human beings that they submit to the Roman Pontiff.** *Bull Unum Sanctum,* Pope Boniface VIII, 1302.

Such a doctrine reveals the Pope as the antichrist. Pope Bonface VIII implied by the statement in *Bull Unum Sanctum* that he holds the position and authority of God Almighty. The Pope expressly claims the authority of God. Jesus, however, made it clear that he, being God, was the only way to heaven.

> Jesus saith unto him, **I am the way, the truth, and the life: no man cometh unto the Father, but by me.** (John 14:6 AV)

> This is the stone which was set at nought of you builders, which is become the head of the corner. **Neither is there salvation in any other: for there is none other name under heaven given among men, whereby we must be saved.** (Acts 4:11-12 AV)

Not only has the pope claimed the authority to save but he also claims to sit in place of Almighty God with equal authority and infallibility of the Lord Jesus Christ.[393] Not just in spiritual matters but in all matters. The pope claims power over the governments of the earth. During the coronation ceremony the

Pope is crowned with these words: "Take thou the tiara adorned with the triple crown, and know that thou art the father of princes and kings and the governor of the world"³⁹⁴

> The Roman Pontiff judges all man, but is judged by no one. We declare, assert, define and pronounce: to be subject to the Roman Pontiff is to every human creature altogether necessary for salvation. . . . That which was spoken of Christ . . . 'Thou hast subdued all things under His feet,' may well seem verified in me. **I have the authority of the King of kings. I am all in all and above all, so that God, Himself and I, The Vicar of God, have but one consistory, and I am able to do almost all that God can do. What therefore,** *can* **you make of me but God.** *The Bull Sanctum,* November 18, 1302 (emphasis added).³⁹⁵

> **[W]e hold upon this earth the place of God Almighty.** *Pope Leo XIII* (emphasis added).³⁹⁶

> This one and unique Church, therefore, has not two heads, like a monster, but one body and one head, viz., Christ and his **vicar**, Peter's successor. *Bull Unum Sanctum,* Pope Boniface VIII, 1302 (emphasis added).

> [T]he Roman pontiff possess **primacy over the whole world**; and that the Roman pontiff is the successor of Blessed Peter, Prince of the Apostles, and is true **Vicar** of Christ, and Head of the whole Church, and **Father** and Teacher of all Christians; and that full power was given to him in Blessed Peter by Jesus Christ our Lord, to **rule**, feed and govern the universal Church. . . . **This is the**

teaching of Catholic truth, from which no one can deviate without loss of faith and of salvation. And since, by the divine right of Apostolic primacy, one Roman pontiff is placed over the universal Church, We further teach and declare that he is the **supreme judge** of the faithful ... none may reopen the judgment of the Apostolic See, than whose authority there is no greater. *The Vatican Council*, Session IV, chapter III, July 18, 1870 (emphasis added).

[R]oyal power derives from the Pontifical authority.[397] *Pope Innocent III.*

[T]emporal power should be subject to the spiritual.[398] *Pope Boniface VII.*

The doctrines of the Roman Catholic Church puts the redactions in Luke 11:2-4 in a whole new light. The deletion designating the Father "which art in heaven" in Luke 11:1-4 allows for worship and prayer to the earthly "Holy Father," the Pope, the Antichrist. The request to be delivered from evil is deleted from the new Bible versions of Luke 11:2-4 because worshipers of the antichrist embrace evil.

36   They Were Not of Us

Gary Hudson is an example of the what the Arminian gospel does. He became one of Satan's minions who masqueraded as a minister of the gospel while at the same time attacking the authority of God's inspired word in the KJV. Gary Hudson says that he devoted his life to the Bible and to preaching it evangelically when he "gave his life to Christ" after watching a televised Billy Graham "crusade" in 1974.[399] Billy Graham was an ardent free-will Arminian in the service of Satan who used the contrivance of an altar call to deceive many.

To Billy Graham, salvation was a formula to be exercised through the free will of man. Graham was presumptuous enough to write a book titled *How to be Born Again*.[400] He thought man could birth himself again. If man can obtain salvation by the power of his own will, that makes God a passive observer to the extraordinary powers of man. The consequence of that theology goes beyond merely making Jesus a passive observer. Ultimately Jesus becomes unnecessary. Billy Graham views the gospel of Jesus Christ as unnecessary for salvation.

Below is an interview Graham had with Robert Schuller:

<u>Schuller</u>: Tell me, what do you think is the future

of Christianity?

Graham: Well, Christianity and being a true believer - you know, I think there's the Body of Christ. This comes from all the Christian groups around the world, outside the Christian groups. I think everybody that loves Christ, or knows Christ, whether they're conscious of it or not, they're members of the Body of Christ. And I don't think that we're going to see a great sweeping revival that will turn the whole world to Christ at any time. I think James answered that, the Apostle James in the first council in Jerusalem, when he said that God's purpose for this age is to call out a people for his name. And that's what God is doing today - he's calling people out of the world for his name, whether they come from the Muslim world, or the Buddhist world, or the Christian world or the non-believing world, they are members of the Body of Christ because they've been called by God. They may not even know the name of Jesus, but they know in their hearts that they need something that they don't have, and they turn to the only light that they have, and I think that they are saved and that they're going to be with us in heaven.

Schuller: What, what I hear you saying is that it's possible for Jesus Christ to come into human hearts and soul and life, even if they've been born in darkness and have never had exposure to the Bible. Is that a correct interpretation of what you're saying?

Graham: Yes it is, because I believe that. I've met people in various parts of the world in tribal situations, that they have never seen a Bible or heard about a Bible, and never heard of Jesus, but they've believed in their hearts that there was a God, and they've tried to live a life that was quite apart from the surrounding community in which they lived.

Schuller: I'm so thrilled to hear you say this. There's a wideness in God's mercy.

Graham: There is. There definitely is.[401]

Under Billy Graham's unbiblical devilish theology, the word of God is irrelevant. He preaches that people may not even know the name of Jesus or hear the gospel, but they can be saved and go to heaven nonetheless. Contrary to Billy Graham, the bible states: **"So then faith cometh by hearing, and hearing by the word of God."** Romans 10:17. Before one can believe in Jesus, he must have heard the gospel of Jesus. The bible states: "And this is his commandment, That we should believe on the name of his Son Jesus Christ." 1 John 3:23. It is not a suggestion of God, it is a commandment that one believes on the name of Jesus.

Graham believes that Muslims, Buddhists, or even atheists are part of the body of Christ. Jesus, however, states: **"Jesus saith unto him, I am the way, the truth, and the life: no man cometh unto the Father, but by me."** John 14:6. The only way to heaven is by the grace of God through faith in Jesus Christ. All adherents to any other religion in the world are damned to hell. Who are you going to believe, Billy Graham or the Holy Bible?

In a 1978 McCall's Magazine interview Graham stated: "I used to think that pagans in far-off countries were lost -- were going to hell -- if they did not have the Gospel of Jesus Christ preached to them. I no longer believe that ... I believe there are other ways of recognizing the existence of God -- through nature, for instance -- and plenty of other opportunities, therefore, of saying yes to God."

All this apostasy of Graham is quite understandable when one considers that Graham is a Freemason.[402] Indeed, he is likely a 33rd degree Mason. Former 33rd degree Mason, Jim Shaw, has revealed that Billy Graham attended Shaw's 33rd degree induction ceremony. Only other 33rd degree Masons are permitted to attend such ceremonies.

One might ask what is wrong with being a Freemason? Albert Pike, the theological pontiff of Masonry wrote that Lucifer is the god of Freemasonry and that Freemasons look to Lucifer (which means light bearer) to give them light in their struggle against the God of the bible, whom Pike blasphemously calls "the God of Darkness and Evil."[403]

To this day Graham has refused to personally answer the many inquiries whether he is a Freemason. He has left it to his subordinates to deny his membership in Freemasonry for him. His membership in Freemasonry is one reason why Billy Graham has never spoken out against Freemasonry, when God's word states that he should do just that. "And have no fellowship with the unfruitful works of darkness, but rather reprove them." (Ephesians 5:11 AV).

After Gary Hudson saw the televised Billy Graham crusade in 1974, he allegedly "gave his life to Christ." He then taught Sunday school and ultimately decided to attend Bible college, where he obtained a bachelor's degree and a master's degree. He was ordained as a minister in 1983. He engaged in evangelism and Christian revivals. He pastored a church in Georgia. In 2004, Hudson began pastoring *Hope for Life Baptist Church* in Jacksonville, Florida.

At some point, Hudson decided that the KJV was not the inspired word of God. Hudson spent many years as a "Christian" pastor attacking the inspiration and inerrancy of the KJV.[404] He pretended to claim that God's word was in the original Greek and Hebrew somewhere, but it was certainly not in any English translation.

He claimed that there were many errors in the KJV. He was soundly refuted by Peter Ruckman during a debate on July 20, 1990. Ruckman further showed Hudson to be a liar and incompetent.[405] Hudson alleged that he was going to use the Textus Receptus as the standard to prove that the KJV had errors. Hudson began the debate with the following premise upon which he was going to show the allege errors in the King James Bible:

> I would like to begin by making a clear and correct statement on the holy scriptures. ... 2nd Timothy 3:16 tells us that all scripture is given by inspiration of God, and is profitable for doctrine, for correction, for reproof, for instruction in righteousness: that the man of God may be perfect, throughly furnished unto all good works. Now, the languages that God was pleased to give the scripture in were Hebrew in the Old Testament with the exceptions of small portions of Daniel in Aramaic and Greek for the New Testament. And this is why we as Bible-believing Baptists hold to the verbal inspiration and absolute infallibility of the scriptures in these original languages. ... It, therefore, becomes extremely important for us to regard the authority of the original texts as primary in relation to all translations made therefrom, that includes our Authorized King James version.[406]

During his introductory remarks, Hudson spent 5 minutes quoting theologians about the inspiration of the holy scriptures in the original languages. He droned on and on, during his prepared statement that laid the foundation for his attack on the KJV on the authority of the original language texts from which the KJV was translated.

The problem with his argument is that Hudson did not believe what he said. He did not think that the scriptures in the original languages were the inspired words of God, including the Greek Textus Receptus, upon which he principally relied in his attack on the KJV. We know that he lied about what he believed when he made that opening statement because after Hudson made that statement, Dr.Ruckman took the podium and revealed that Hudson wrote to a Christian pastor on October 30, 1989: "I do not believe that the Textus Receptus or the Majority Text are infallible or inerrant, and I never have. I do not believe that an exact inerrant version or text exists."[407]

When Hudson returned to the podium for rebuttal, he did not address the accusation made by Dr. Ruckman. That is considered a tacit admission: "Failure to deny an accusation shows that the accused intended to communicate agreement, and thus adopted the accusation."[408] That means that as of October 30, 1989, Hudson was on record saying he never believed any inerrant scripture text existed. He did not believe the Bible to be true during his Christian ministry. Hudson was only pretending to be a Christian; he was a wolf in sheep's clothing of whom Jesus warned in Matthew 7:15.

Hudson did not believe it when, during the 1990 debate, he said it was a "clear and correct" statement that the original language scriptures are inspired and absolutely infallible. He lied. He was faking it. Hudson is like so many Arminian "Christians" who think that by making a free-will profession of faith, they have been saved. There are many, like Hudson, who fake it. They will one day hear the dreaded words from Jesus Christ: "I never knew you: depart from me." Matthew 7:23.

There is a difference between one who is ignorant about

whether the KJV is the inspired word of God and one who comes out against the KJV and affirmatively rejects it as God's word. Hudson's rejection of the KJV as God's inspired word was evidence that he lacked the unction of the Holy Spirit and was "not of us." 1 John 2:19. Ultimately, the sheep's wool slipped from his shoulders, revealing him as one of Satan's wolves.

Hudson stated he never believed in the infallibility and inerrancy of the Greek Textus Receptus or the Majority Greek Text. He never believed in the infallibility of the KJV English translation or any English translation. Hudson's rejection of the inspired word of God in the KJV is evidence that he never had saving faith.

In 2018 Hudson wrote a book, titled *Surrender to Reason: New Testament Studies that Disputed Faith*.[409] Hudson explains in the book how, as an evangelical pastor, he came to question, and ultimately walk away from, his lifelong Christian faith.[410] He states that in 2007 he "was studying the Bible in preparation for a sermon that started his questioning of the inspiration, inerrancy, and infallibility of the Bible."[411]

According to Hudson's version of events, in 2007, he concluded that the Bible contained errors and, thus, the Christian gospel was untrue. But as we have seen, he was on record as far back as October 30, 1989, saying that he did not believe that an inerrant Bible text existed. That means that he was a minister of the gospel without believing a word of it. He was pretending the entire time. Hudson's version of his rejection of the gospel in 2007 is a made-up legend. In fact, he never believed the gospel.

Hudson said he questioned the resurrection of Jesus Christ. Hudson rejected the book of Romans because of its clear presentation of the sovereign grace of God. Hudson no longer believes in Jesus Christ (actually, he never did believe). He is what the world calls a man who has "left the faith." But we know that he never had saving faith. Hudson states, "absolutely nothing I experienced with believers caused me to question the Bible. It was what I found in the Bible itself and by myself that caused me to question it."[412]

Garry Hudson is like so many pastors who are unbelieving hirelings and care not about the sheep. They have adopted the false Arminian gospel that tickles the ears of men who want to be in control of their salvation. John Wesley is another example of such a man. The only difference between Wesley and Hudson is that Wesley kept up the public charade of being a Christian minister. Wesley was an ardent Arminian and founder of the Methodist Church. Most people are unaware that Wesley admitted privately that he didn't believe in the God of the Bible.

In a 1766 letter to his brother, Charles Wesley, John Wesley bared his soul and revealed to Charles his innermost thoughts. In that letter, which John Wesley never expected to be revealed publicly, he admitted that he preached a faith that he, himself, did not have. John Wesley felt "born along" by some unknown force to do so. God would certainly not compel the preaching of a false gospel. It is, therefore, clear that the unknown force bearing John Wesley along to preach the Arminian gospel was the devil. That is an ineluctable conclusion from Wesley's own words:

> In one of my last [letters] I was saying that I do not feel the wrath of God abiding on me; nor can I believe it does. And yet (this is the mystery), **I do not love God. I never did. Therefore I never believed, in the Christian sense of the word. Therefore I am only an honest heathen**…And yet, to be so employed of God! And so hedged in that I can neither get forward nor backward! Surely there was never such an instance before, from the beginning of the world! If I ever have had that

faith, it would not be so strange. **But I never had any other evidence of the eternal or invisible world than I have now; and that is none at all**, unless such as faintly shines from reason's glimmering ray. **I have no direct witness (I do not say, that I am a child of God, but) of anything invisible or eternal.**

And yet I dare not preach otherwise than I do, either concerning faith, or love, or justification, or perfection. And yet I find rather an increase than a decrease of zeal for the whole work of God and every part of it. I am borne along, I know not how, that I can't stand still. **I want all the world to come to what I do not know.**[413]

Wesley was 63 years old when he wrote that letter. The dirty secret of Wesley is that he was a heathen who did not believe in God. He preached a false gospel about a false god, in whom he did not really believe. How could Wesley so successfully preach a false gospel? Because people had been accustomed to ignoring God's words and accepting a contradictory gloss to those words. The Arminian god appears nowhere in the holy scriptures.

Wesley's Arminianism was only a hair's breadth from atheism. There is little difference between the Arminian god, who minds his own business and leaves his creatures to their own devices, and no god at all. It is no wonder then that Wesley and Hudson did not believe in God. Their Arminian theology created a god in whom it is easy to lose belief. The devil, that subtle beast, could not have designed it any better.

Gary Hudson, has rejected Jesus Christ and now describes himself as **"a very happy peace-loving non-believer."**[414] He regrets having preached the gospel, which he now describes as "B.S." He wrote his book to confess his error. He states his book is "dedicated to all I have influenced to believe in the Christian gospel."[415] Gary Hudson's life illustrates how the rejection of God's inspired word is indicative that the person lacks the unction of the Holy Spirit. *See* 1 John 2:20-29.

This writer does not mean to suggest that all who Arminian preachers deceive are unsaved. There is a difference between ignorance and scienter. If one is presented with the truth of the gospel of grace but rejects it, that is evidence that the person lacks the unction of the Holy Spirit that accompanies salvation. "[Y]e have an unction from the Holy One, and ye know all things." 1 John 1:20. How can one claim to be a Christian when he hears the Christian gospel of grace but nonetheless persists in arguing against it? Jesus said "[h]e that is not with me is against me." Matthew 12:30.

Some pretend to embrace the gospel of grace but reject God's inspired word in the KJV. James White is an example of such a one. On the other side, some accept God's inspired word in the KJV but reject the gospel of election solely by the grace of God through the faith of Jesus Christ. Gail Riplinger and Peter Ruckman are examples of such. Only God knows whether the above are ignorant and innocent or culpable and guilty.

Gary Hudson objects to the argument that he was never a true believer. He thinks that he was once believed, and of his own free will, decided to reject Jesus Christ and the gospel.[416] Now that he has come out as an unbeliever, why would Hudson care about people thinking that he never believed? It seems that he is still working in service of Satan. He wants to be portrayed as an example of one who lost his faith. That myth supports the counterfeit Arminian free will gospel. It is an anti-gospel. It is Satan's gospel. Unsurprisingly, the Roman Catholic Church (the church that was the doctrinal inspiration for Jacobus Arminius) since 1990 has been promoting one of Gary Hudson's other books, *Why I Left Ruckmanism*, which attacks the inspiration of the

KJV.[417] One of the favorite passages for Arminians to read out of context is Hebrews 6:4-6 to support claims that people like Hudson were once saved but later lost their salvation. That passage reads:

> For it is impossible for those who were once enlightened, and have tasted of the heavenly gift, and were made partakers of the Holy Ghost, And have tasted the good word of God, and the powers of the world to come, If they shall fall away, to renew them again unto repentance; seeing they crucify to themselves the Son of God afresh, and put him to an open shame. Hebrews 6:4-6.

Jim McGuiggan tries to explain the Arminian view that Hebrews 6 means that a saved person has the power to reject God and lose his salvation.

> It's true that faith is a gracious work of God in us (Philippians 1:29, Romans 10:17, Acts 18:27 and elsewhere) but God doesn't inject it into us and by its very nature it doesn't exist unless it has our free and vital ongoing consent and commitment. The graciousness of the gift doesn't render us incapable of despising it and throwing it away from us. . . . [T]this relationship has the free consent of our hearts and minds. We aren't zombies or automata. We are friends of God in Jesus Christ. And we can turn from him (2 Peter 2:20-22) and refuse to abide in him (John 15:5-6). To do that is to reject God and the relationship is ended. To say that we're powerless to reject God and the relationship is to ignore the meaning of "reconciliation" and "friendship" with God.[418]

The argument by the Arminians is that Hebrews 6:4-6

contemplates one who once was saved but has fallen away from the grace of God by the power of his own free will. Such an interpretation is directly contrary to the expressed promises of Christ. **"All that the Father giveth me shall come to me; and him that cometh to me I will in no wise cast out."** (John 6:37 AV)

All whom the Father chooses for salvation will be saved. John chapter 6 precludes the possibility of falling away from salvation, the falling away referred to in Hebrews chapter 6 is the falling away from the church, not salvation. There are those like Judas who appear for a time to be part of the church, but in the end, they manifest as enemies of the gospel.

> They went out from us, but they were not of us; for if they had been of us, they would no doubt have continued with us: but they went out, that they might be made manifest that they were not all of us. (1 John 2:19 AV)

Judas and others like him went out, not because they were saved and lost their salvation, but rather because from the beginning "they were not of us." They were pretenders to salvation; they were unsaved tares congregating among the saved wheat. Matthew 13:27-43.

Those who do not believe in Christ are lost because God has not chosen them for salvation. Those who are chosen for salvation cannot lose their salvation. John 10:26-30. There is simply no such thing as a person losing his salvation.

> **But ye believe not, because ye are not of my sheep, as I said unto you. My sheep hear my voice, and I know them, and they follow me: And I give unto them eternal life; and they shall never perish, neither shall any man pluck them**

> **out of my hand. My Father, which gave *them* me, is greater than all; and no *man* is able to pluck *them* out of my Father's hand. I and *my* Father are one.** (John 10:26-30 AV)

There are only two possibilities in the gospel. First, those who are lost cannot believe because God has not chosen them to believe. The other possibility is the flip side of the first; those who are chosen to believe will, in fact, believe, and they cannot ever lose their faith, "no man is able to pluck them out of my Father's hand." There is no category for persons to be first saved and then for them to overrule God's choice by the power of their free will and "unsave" themselves. Such an occurrence is an impossibility. The only way to build such a theology is to ignore the clear message of the gospel.

Furthermore, when we read Hebrews 6:4-6 in context, we can see that it refers to persons who were never saved to begin with. That is evident when one reads the very next passage. That passage refers to the difference between the earth that drinks in the rain and brings forth fine herbs and the parched earth that only tastes of the rain and brings forth thorns and briers. That passage distinguishes between the saved who drink in the word of God and the unsaved who have only tasted the word of God.

> For it is impossible for those who were once enlightened, and have tasted of the heavenly gift, and were made partakers of the Holy Ghost, And have tasted the good word of God, and the powers of the world to come, If they shall fall away, to renew them again unto repentance; seeing they crucify to themselves the Son of God afresh, and put him to an open shame. **For the earth which drinketh in the rain that cometh oft upon it, and bringeth forth herbs meet for them by whom it is dressed, receiveth blessing from God: But**

that which beareth thorns and briers *is* rejected, and *is* nigh unto cursing; whose end *is* to be burned. (Hebrews 6:4-8 AV)

Partaking of the Holy Ghost for the lost soul in Hebrews chapter 6 does not mean a total submersion by the Holy Ghost, which the bible refers to as a baptism of the Holy Ghost. The change in one who is saved goes far beyond the enlightenment attributed to the lost soul in Hebrews chapter 6. The saved person is born again. He becomes a new spiritual creation of God. "Jesus answered and said unto him, Verily, verily, I say unto thee, Except a man be born again, he cannot see the kingdom of God." (John 3:3 AV) The saved person is born again through the baptism of the Holy Ghost. "Then remembered I the word of the Lord, how that he said, John indeed baptized with water; but ye shall be **baptized with the Holy Ghost**." (Acts 11:16 AV)

The baptism of the Holy Ghost is not merely a taste of the spiritual waters. Indeed, the baptism of the Holy Ghost is the total submergence such that God's elect are completely cleansed of their sin in God's sight and are spiritually resurrected with Christ as new creations. "Buried with him in baptism, wherein also ye are risen with him through the faith of the operation of God, who hath raised him from the dead. And you, being dead in your sins and the uncircumcision of your flesh, hath he quickened together with him, having forgiven you all trespasses;" (Colossians 2:12-13 AV)

The word of God is referred to as that spiritual water that cleanses Christ's church from sin. One who is saved does not just taste God's word. He drinks it in; indeed, he immerses himself in God's word and is washed clean thereby. God's church is cleansed by his word, which is the spiritual water of salvation. "That he might sanctify and cleanse it with the **washing of water by the word**, That he might present it to himself a glorious church, not having spot, or wrinkle, or any such thing; but that it should be holy and without blemish." (Ephesians 5:26-27 AV)

Notice how Jesus in John 15 analogizes himself to a vine, with God the Father being the husbandman. In that passage, a saved person does not merely taste the heavenly gift and the word of God; the elect of God "abides" as a branch in the vine of God. That is the only way a person can bring forth the spiritual fruit evidencing salvation. All who do not abide in Jesus are cast from the vine and burned. They are as the thorns and briers referred to in Hebrews 6:8, "whose end is to be burned."

> I am the true vine, and my Father is the husbandman. Every branch in me that beareth not fruit he taketh away: and every *branch* that beareth fruit, he purgeth it, that it may bring forth more fruit. Now ye are clean through the word which I have spoken unto you. Abide in me, and I in you. As the branch cannot bear fruit of itself, except it abide in the vine; no more can ye, except ye abide in me. I am the vine, ye *are* the branches: He that abideth in me, and I in him, the same bringeth forth much fruit: for **without me ye can do nothing. If a man abide not in me, he is cast forth as a branch, and is withered; and men gather them, and cast *them* into the fire, and they are burned.** If ye abide in me, and my words abide in you, ye shall ask what ye will, and it shall be done unto you. Herein is my Father glorified, that ye bear much fruit; so shall ye be my disciples." (John 15:1-8 AV)

The Arminian might say, "Ah, but you still have not presented proof that the decision to abide in the vine of God is not a decision born of man's free will." Jim McGuiggan cited John 15:5-6 to support his argument that man has the power of his own free will to throw away his salvation. When the entire passage in John chapter 15 is read in context, the sovereign grace of God in the election and preservation of the saints becomes clear. In John

15:16-18 Jesus explains the meaning of the metaphor of the vine and branches. Those who are saved are chosen by him. Jesus explicitly states that one does not choose him; rather, Jesus does the choosing. He has chosen his elect branches out of the world and ordained them to bear spiritual fruit.

> **Ye have not chosen me, but I have chosen you, and ordained you, that ye should go and bring forth fruit, and *that* your fruit should remain:** that whatsoever ye shall ask of the Father in my name, he may give it you. These things I command you, that ye love one another. If the world hate you, ye know that it hated me before *it hated* you. If ye were of the world, the world would love his own: but because ye are not of the world, but **I have chosen you out of the world**, therefore the world hateth you. (John 15:16-19 AV)

In John 15:4-5, Jesus also states that the branches he chose can do nothing besides him. He chooses the branches, and they bear fruit because he has purposed that they continue to abide in him. **"[F]or without me ye can do nothing."** (John 15:5 AV) That statement alone impeaches the false notion that man is a free agent in deciding and keeping his salvation. It is not the branches through their free will that support the root, it is the root that supports the branches, and that root is Christ. "Boast not against the branches. But if thou boast, **thou bearest not the root, but the root thee."** (Romans 11:18 AV) Jesus chooses and nourishes the branches, and without him they can do nothing, period.

Notice what God says in 1st Peter. "Being born again, not of corruptible seed, but of incorruptible, by the word of God, which liveth and abideth for ever. For all flesh *is* as grass, and all the glory of man as the flower of grass. The grass withereth, and the flower thereof falleth away:" (1 Peter 1:23-24 AV) We see God using a simile of the earth and the plants springing from the earth.

A saved Christian is born again from the incorruptible seed of the Holy Spirit. All flesh, however, is as grass. Those who have not been reborn and made new spiritual creations remain in the flesh and are like the grass that withers and falls away. The unsaved grass in 1 Peter chapter 1, as the unsaved briers and thorns in Hebrews chapter 6, are good only to be burned.

Read also what Jesus says in Matthew chapter 13 about the unsaved tares that were sown among the wheat. The tares are the "children of the wicked one" sown by the devil. At the end of the world the angels will gather the tares and burn them in the fires of hell, where there will be weeping and gnashing of teeth for eternity. Matthew 13:36-43. The wheat are the children of the kingdom who are born of the good seed of Jesus; they will shine forth as the sun in the kingdom of God.

At the end of the parable of the wheat and the tares in Matthew 13, Jesus repeats, "who hath ears to hear, let him hear." Matthew 13:43. Jesus is indicating that the truths he is revealing can only be understood and accepted by those to whom he has given spiritual ears with which to understand.

Those in Hebrews chapter 6 who only taste the word of God are like the tares in Matthew chapter 13; they are left dry and bring forth spiritual thorns and briers. The thorns and briers are symbolic of their spiritual condition. They are the spiritual weeds in God's kingdom, to be pulled up and burned in the fires of hell. When we read the passages that immediately follow the metaphor of the dry ground that brings forth briers and thorns in Hebrews chapter 6, we read that the good soil that drinks in the rain and brings forth abundant fruit are those who "inherit the promises."

> But, beloved, we are persuaded better things of you, and **things that accompany salvation**, though we thus speak. For God *is* not unrighteous to forget your work and labour of love, which ye

> have shewed toward his name, in that ye have ministered to the saints, and do minister. And we desire that every one of you do shew the same diligence to the full assurance of hope unto the end: That ye be not slothful, but followers of them who through faith and patience **inherit the promises.** For when God made promise to Abraham, because he could swear by no greater, he sware by himself. (Hebrews 6:9-13 AV)

In Hebrews chapter 6, God explains that he makes the referenced promises to Abraham. Hebrews 6:13. The promises were according to the sovereign election of God. That is the whole point of the gospel. It all comes back to the election of God according to his sovereign grace.

> That is, **They which are the children of the flesh, these** *are* **not the children of God: but the children of the promise are counted for the seed.** For this *is* the word of promise, At this time will I come, and Sara shall have a son. And not only *this*; but when Rebecca also had conceived by one, *even* by our father Isaac; (For *the children* being not yet born, neither having done any good or evil, **that the purpose of God according to election might stand, not of works, but of him that calleth**;) (Romans 9:8-11 AV)

Romans 9 clearly states that God's spiritual seed are the object of God's promise and are chosen by God. It is not the children of the flesh that are the children of God (whether by fleshly heredity or fleshly will). Indeed, all flesh is as grass to be burned. God's election is according to his sovereign will and purpose, wherein his elect brings forth the fruit of salvation. The heirs of the promise made to Abraham are chosen by God, not by man. God made the promise, and it is God who fulfills that promise in Christ. "And if ye be Christ's, then are ye Abraham's seed, and heirs according to the promise." (Galatians 3:29 AV)

Once saved, a believer is sealed for eternity by the Holy Spirit. "In whom ye also trusted, after that ye heard the word of truth, the gospel of your salvation: in whom also after that ye believed, ye were sealed with that holy Spirit of promise." (Ephesians 1:13 AV) No one can break God's seal. For more information about the Arminian error, read this author's book, *The Anti-Gospel*.

37 NKJV Hides the Atonement of Jesus Christ

The NKJV conceals the atonement of Jesus Christ. Romans 4:25 in the AV (a.k.a., KJV) reveals that Jesus Christ was delivered **for** our offenses. The NKJV changes the passage to state that Jesus Christ was delivered **because of** our offenses.

AV	NKJV
Now it was not written for his sake alone, that it was imputed to him; But for us also, to whom it shall be imputed, if we believe on him that raised up Jesus our Lord from the dead; Who was delivered **for** our offences, and was raised again **for** our justification. (Romans 4:23-25 AV)	Now it was not written for his sake alone that it was imputed to him, but also for us. It shall be imputed to us who believe in Him who raised up Jesus our Lord from the dead, who was delivered up **because** of our offenses, and was raised **because** of our justification. Romans 4:23-25 NKJV)

Webster's American Dictionary of the English Language defines **"for"** as:

[I]n the place of; as a substitute or equivalent, noting equal value or satisfactory compensation, either in barter and sale, in contract, or in punishment. 'And Joseph gave them bread in exchange for horses, and for flocks, and for the cattle of the herds; ' that is, according to the original, he gave them bread against horses like the Gr. Genesis 48:17. Buy us and our land for bread. Genesis 47:19. And if any mischief follow, then thou shalt give life for life, eye for eye, tooth for tooth, hand for hand, foot for foot. Exodus 21:2.[419]

Thus, AV Romans 4:25 reveals what Jesus accomplished at the cross. He was an atoning sacrifice **for** our sins. An atonement is "[e]xpiation; satisfaction or reparation made by giving an equivalent for an injury, or by doing or suffering that which is received in satisfaction **for** an offense or injury."[420]

Jesus Christ was delivered to satisfy and pay **for** our sins. Indeed, we find that explained in God's word. "Herein is love, not that we loved God, but that he loved us, and sent his Son to be the propitiation **for** our sins." (1 John 4:10 AV) Propitiation is "[t]he act of appeasing wrath and conciliating the favor of an offended person."[421]

The result is that we are redeemed. God's elect, by the grace of God through faith in Jesus Christ, have had their sins paid for. We no longer owe any penalty for our sins. Jesus Christ has paid the price and satisfied the Father. "In whom we have redemption through his blood, even the forgiveness of sins:" (Colossians 1:14 AV) Redemption is:

> [T]he act of procuring the deliverance of persons or things from the possession and power of captors by the payment of an equivalent; ransom; release. ... In theology, the purchase of God's favor by the death

and sufferings of Christ; the ransom or deliverance of sinners from the bondage of sin and the penalties of God's violated law by the atonement of Christ. In whom we have redemption through his blood. Ephesians 1:7.[422]

The NKJV, however, uses the words "**because of**" instead of the word "**for**." The word "because" means "by cause, for the reason that."[423] The NKJV states that Jesus Christ was delivered to execution on the cross for the reason that we sinned. But that is incomplete. It does not reveal what Jesus was accomplishing on the cross. The simple preposition "**for**" explains what Jesus accomplished on the cross. Jesus Christ died as a propitiatory sacrifice in our place **for** our sins, to redeem us and impute us with his righteousness.

There is another problem with the words "**because of**." The clause in the NKJV states Jesus Christ "was delivered up because of our offenses." Everyone born has sinned. Indeed, "[t]here is none righteous, no, not one." Romans 3:10. The NKJV change in Romans 4:25 does not limit the offenses to the elect because both the elect and unelect sin. The implication in the NKJV rendition of Romans 4:25 is that Jesus was delivered up to the cross **because of** all the sins committed by everyone in the word. Even though the clause refers to "our offenses," the words **"because of"** expand the sins to every sin committed. If Jesus Christ was delivered up because of our sin, that would include all sin as the cause of his crucifixion. That would mean that his sacrifice on the cross would be, for the most part, ineffectual.

The gospel is clear that Jesus was an atonement for his elect only. Romans 4:25 when read in the context of the entire gospel indicates that Jesus was delivered **for** the offenses of his elect. But the NKJV changes the passage to state that Jesus Christ was delivered **because of** our offenses. That indicates that Jesus was crucified **because of** sins, without any particularity.

The NKJV passage means that God was punishing Jesus Christ **because** people sin. Hence, he died for all people. What that means is that Jesus was being punished **because of** sins that would later be punished again by people in hell who do not believe in Jesus. Thus, if Jesus was punished **because of** all sin and not **for** the particular sins of his elect, there is a double punishment for sin because Jesus would have breen punished **because of** the sins of those who are being cast into hell. We know that God is perfectly just. "To declare, I say, at this time his righteousness: that he might be just, and the justifier of him which believeth in Jesus." (Romans 3:26 AV) To punish a sin twice is the very opposite of justice.

But the AV passage, in the context of the gospel, means that Jesus only died **for** our sins. Jesus' propitiatory sacrifice was effectual. God's sacrifice was **for** particular sins of particular people, his elect. If Jesus died **because of** all the sins of everyone in the world, his sacrifice would be mostly ineffectual. That is because most will not believe; wide is the gate, broad is the way to hell, and many go therein; narrow is the way to heaven, and few find it.

> Enter ye in at the strait gate: for wide is the gate, and broad is the way, that leadeth to destruction, and many there be which go in thereat: Because strait is the gate, and narrow is the way, which leadeth unto life, and few there be that find it. Matthew 7:13-14.

Notice also that the NKJV version of Romans 4:25 has Jesus being raised **because of** our justification. That makes no sense. Jesus is raised up **for** our justification, meaning to accomplish our justification. He was not raised up **because** we are justified.

Under the NKJV rubric, all sin in the world was punished by Jesus on the cross, and thus, all whose sins were punished are justified. That is because the atonement of Christ was a legal exchange. That means that the sins of the elect were imputed to Christ, and the righteousness of Christ was imputed to God's elect. 2 Corinthians 5:18-21.

A pardon excuses a person from the penalty for a crime. However, the person pardoned is not absolved of the guilt. God does more than just pardon believers; he justifies them. When a person is justified for an alleged wicked act, it means more than a pardon. Justification is a declaration that the person is absolved not only of the punishment but also of the guilt. The person justified is not subject to the punishment for the wicked act, and, in addition, he is not guilty. When the Bible declares that one is justified, though, it does not mean that the person is imparted with actual righteousness of his own because the person is, in fact, guilty of the sin. Rather, justification through Christ means that God imputes the righteousness of Christ to the believer, and thus, God views the person as not guilty of the sin. It is a legal, spiritual exchange; the believer's sins are imputed to Christ, who paid the penalty for them, and Christ's righteousness is imputed to the believer.

A man declaring someone justified for wickedness is an abomination to the Lord. "He that justifieth the wicked, and he that condemneth the just, even they both are abomination to the LORD." Proverbs 17:15. Justification in Proverbs 17:15 is similar to the justification provided for by God in the sense that it is a declaration of justification and not an impartation of actual righteousness. It is the epitome of evil for a man to justify the wicked by declaring them not guilty for their wickedness. That is because a declaration by a man that the wicked is justified is, by definition, an injustice. Even if the sinner were to be punished for his wickedness, he cannot be justified because he is still guilty of the wicked act. Being punished does not justify the act and render him not guilty.

While it is the epitome of unrighteousness for man to justify the wicked, it is the epitome of righteousness for God to do that same thing. That is because God justifies the wicked through the atonement of his Holy Son, Jesus Christ. If God were to punish the sinner directly, the sinner would be punished, but he could never be justified because the guilt for the sin would remain. The only way to justify the sinner is by having Jesus trade places with the sinner. There was a perfect legal exchange at the cross, which accomplished justification. The righteousness of Jesus is imputed to the sinner, and the sins of the sinner are imputed to Jesus.

Without the imputation of the righteousness of Christ to the sinner, justification of the sinner would be an abomination. That is why Jesus had to atone for the sins of his elect. It is only through the grace of God by faith in Jesus Christ that man can be justified. The sacrifice of Jesus accomplished the justification of the wicked because God only sees the righteousness of Christ when he sees a believer. The believer is thus justified in God's eyes. The believer only needs to believe in Jesus. His faith in Jesus will justify him before God. Notice in the parallel passages below that justification is by grace and also by faith. Faith and grace go hand in hand, which indicates that God provides faith through his sovereign grace.

> Being **justified freely by his grace** through the redemption that is in Christ Jesus: Romans 3:24

> Therefore being **justified by faith**, we have peace with God through our Lord Jesus Christ. Romans 5:1.

> That being **justified by his grace**, we should be made heirs according to the hope of eternal life. Titus 3:7.

According to scripture, the universal atonement model

suggested by the erroneous NKJV Romans 4:25 passage is impossible because Jesus's atonement was substitutionary. That means that Jesus took the sins of his elect, and his elect received the righteousness of Christ. If Jesus was an atoning sacrifice for everyone in the world, that means that everyone in the world would have taken on the righteousness of Christ. If everyone took on the righteousness of Christ, then in God's eyes, they would be legally righteous and would not be punished for their sins. The Arminian theology of universal atonement populates hell with those who have the righteousness of Christ.

The Bible tells us that only those chosen by God for salvation by the Grace of God through faith in Jesus Christ are given the righteousness of Christ. All sins for which Jesus was a propitiation were remitted, and all who have had their sins remitted are declared righteous in God's eyes. The Arminian universal atonement allows for only two possibilities: 1) hell is populated entirely with persons who have the perfect righteousness of Christ, or 2) Jesus's sacrifice on the cross was ineffective in atoning for sin. The inerrant word of God does not allow for either possibility.

> For all have sinned, and come short of the glory of God; Being justified freely by his grace through the **redemption** that is in Christ Jesus: Whom God hath set forth to be a **propitiation through faith in his blood, to declare his righteousness for the remission of sins** that are past, through the forbearance of God. (Romans 3:23-25 AV)

All those for whom Jesus died are imputed with Jesus's righteousness. That was the purpose of Jesus's crucifixion. The Arminian universal atonement frustrates God's will and condemns to hell most of those who have been imputed with the righteousness of Jesus.

And all things are of God, who hath reconciled us

to himself by Jesus Christ, and hath given to us the ministry of reconciliation; To wit, that God was in Christ, reconciling the world unto himself, **not imputing their trespasses unto them**; and hath committed unto us the word of reconciliation. Now then we are ambassadors for Christ, as though God did beseech *you* by us: we pray you in Christ's stead, be ye reconciled to God. **For he hath made him to be sin for us, who knew no sin; that we might be made the righteousness of God in him.** (2 Corinthians 5:18-21 AV)

38 The Nicolaitans

If Satan can get people to think that only the original Greek is the inspired word of God, he can have people submit to Nicolaitan preachers who have the answers to what the real scripture means. That is why we have preachers now who do not speak a lick of Greek but will stand up during a church service and explain how the "original Greek" says something completely different from what their AV English translation says. God warned us about those who would come and "corrupt the word of God." 2 Corinthians 2:17. They are the Nicolaitans. They are trying to undo the work of the AV translators. Dr. Miles Smith of the Authorized (King James) Version 1611 translating committee pointed out the the preface to the AV, *The Translators to the Reader*, the importance of a translation in the common tongue to be understood by the people.

> Translation it is that openeth the window, to let in the light; that breaketh the shell, that we may eat the kernel; that putteth aside the curtain, that we may look into the most Holy place; that removeth the cover of the well, that we may come by the water, even as Jacob rolled away the stone from the mouth of the well, by which means the flocks of Laban were watered [Gen 29:10]. Indeed without

translation into the vulgar tongue, the unlearned are but like children at Jacob's well (which is deep) [John 4:11] without a bucket or something to draw with; or as that person mentioned by Isaiah, to whom when a sealed book was delivered, with this motion, "Read this, I pray thee," he was fain to make this answer, "I cannot, for it is sealed." [Isa 29:11].[424]

The Nicolaitan clergy are trying to seal up God's word so that it cannot be known except through their interpretation of the original languages. Who are the Nicolaitans? We read in Revelation 2:6 that God hates the Nicolaitans. "But this thou hast, that thou hatest the deeds of the Nicolaitans, which I also hate." (Revelation 2:6) The very name, Nicolaitans, contains within it the character of those described.

The word Nicolaitans consists of two Greek roots. The first is a Greek word, *nikos,* which is a noun meaning victory or victor; it can also take the form *nike*.[425] The verb form of *nikos* is *nikao*, which means to prevail or overcome.[426] The second half of Nicolaitans is the word *laos*, which means laity or common people.[427] Putting the two words together we understand that Nicolaitans are those in the church who have prevailed over the common people. It points directly to the distinction in the modern church between the clergy and the laity. It denotes those in the clergy who have worldly hegemony over the submissive laity or common church members.

Church members are commanded to practice "[s]ubmitting yourselves one to another in the fear of God." Ephesians 5:21. The church submission is to be in accordance with God's commands and doctrines found in his Holy Bible. It seems, however, that pastors refuse to obey God's command to submit "one to another." The clergy in churches expect to be held in preeminence above the other church members. The clergy requires the laity to submit to them rather than all members submitting "one to another" equally.

The church is a kingdom. That kingdom has a King. And that King is Christ. Christians are to receive the kingdom of God as submissive children not as pastoral autocrats. Indeed, Jesus gives a dire warning to the authoritarian pastors lording over the church. "Verily I say unto you, Whosoever shall not receive the kingdom of God as a little child shall in no wise enter therein." (Luke 18:17)

The office of elder is a spiritual office. Church members may recognize an elder in the church. "Wherefore by their fruits ye shall know them." (Matthew 7:20) But it is an office entered into by the grace of God. Ephesians 4:1-20. The church is the body of Christ. The pastor is NOT the head of the church; Christ is the head of the church. "And he is the head of the body, the church: who is the beginning, the firstborn from the dead; that in all things he might have the preeminence." (Colossians 1:18)

Christ is the "head of the body." Christ has preeminence in "all things." Preeminence means to have superiority over all others. To elevate a pastor above the other members is to give preeminence to the pastor. That violates God's word. Christ is to have preeminence in the church over "all things." Christ will not share his preeminence with a pastor. *See* Isaiah 42:8. Indeed, Jesus could not have made it clearer.

The church is not like any other organization found on earth. That is because, while church members are on earth, the church remains a spiritual assembly. Further, the hierarchy of the church is not like earthly hierarchies, where there is a progressive chain of authority leading to the head of the organization. The hierarchy of the church is that there is one head, Jesus Christ, and the body is made up of "ministers" and "servants." There is no authoritative structure in a chain of authority leading to Christ. To be the chiefest in the church is the opposite of what it means to be the chiefest in an earthly organization. The chiefest in the church is the lowliest and most submissive servant of all other church members.

> But Jesus called them to him, and saith unto them, Ye know that they which are accounted to rule over the Gentiles exercise lordship over them; and their great ones exercise authority upon them. But so shall it not be among you: but whosoever will be great among you, shall be your minister: And whosoever of you will be the chiefest, shall be servant of all. For even the Son of man came not to be ministered unto, but to minister, and to give his life a ransom for many. (Mark 10:42-45)

To be an elder or bishop is a noble office. But it is a spiritual office. And it is an office of service. It is not an authoritarian office of lordship. Jesus is the model for the type of self-sacrificing ministering that a pastor should perform. *E.g.,* John 13:4-17. Jesus washed his disciples feet, and after doing so explained: "I have given you an example, that ye should do as I have done to you." John 13:15. Jesus further explained: "The servant is not greater than his lord." John 13:16. If he, Lord of all, humbled himself to wash their feet, they should do the same for one another. "If I then, your Lord and Master, have washed your feet; ye also ought to wash one another's feet." John 13:14. A pastor is to be a minister of charity and not a despot. Indeed, there is no need for any executive, legislative, or judicial action by a pastor. All of the doctrines and commands have been memorialized by Jesus Christ in his Holy Bible so "that the man of God may be perfect."

> And that from a child thou hast known the holy scriptures, which are able to make thee wise unto salvation through faith which is in Christ Jesus. All scripture is given by inspiration of God, and is

profitable for doctrine, for reproof, for correction, for instruction in righteousness: That the **man of God** may be perfect, throughly furnished unto all good works." (2 Timothy 3:15-17)

By the way, the reference to "the man of God" in 2 Timothy 3:16-17 is a reference to a Christian who is saved by God's grace. It is not a reference to some special person holding an office of a clergyman in the church. The man of God's perfection is to be "thoroughly furnished unto all good works." 2 Timothy 3:17. The church is the body of Christ, and not any part of that body is more important than another. Ephesians 4:1-20; 1 Corinthians 12:11-25; Romans 12:3-8. **"[T]here should be no schism in the body; but that the members should have the same care one for another."** 1 Corinthians 12:25.

A bishop (a.k.a. elder) is an overseer of the church. 1 Timothy 3:1-16; Romans 12:3-8. In 1 Timothy 5:17 we read about elders "that rule well." But an elder's rule is not one of authoritarianism; he is called rather to "take care" of the church. 1 Timothy 3:5. He is to rule by "ensample" and not lording over the church. 1 Peter 5:1-4. An overseer's function is not that of a lord but rather that of a "steward." 1 Corinthians 4:1-2. As a steward, a bishop (or elder) is a minister in the church. But his function is like that of all members of the church, who are called on to be "good stewards" in ministering to the needs of the church. 1 Peter 4:10-11. The bishop is to "work" within the church, as a fellow member of the church. 1 Timothy 3:1. He is not to take on some special title and become the titular head of the church.

Indeed, read what Peter tells the elders. He specifically tells them NOT to lord over the church, which is "God's heritage." Elders are rather to be "ensamples" Ensample is not the same thing as example. Ensample means to exemplify as a model or pattern for imitation or copying. Whereas example means behavior or an event from which to learn. You learn from an example; you don't necessarily copy it. The elders are supposed to be ensamples of good and charitable conduct as a model for the church. They are not to pontificate and harangue the church into submission. The elder is to be submissive himself as a model of meekness.

> The elders which are among you I exhort, who am also an elder, and a witness of the sufferings of Christ, and also a partaker of the glory that shall be revealed: Feed the flock of God which is among you, taking the oversight thereof, not by constraint, but willingly; not for filthy lucre, but of a ready mind; **Neither as being lords over God's heritage, but being ensamples to the flock.** And when the chief Shepherd shall appear, ye shall receive a crown of glory that fadeth not away. (1 Peter 5:1-4)

At no time did any of Christ's disciples take on any title. Paul was simply called "Paul," Peter was simply called "Peter." So it should be in the church today, but sadly it is not. Instead, contrary to Christ's command in Matthew 23:1-12, today we have clergymen who go by titles of "Pastor" so-and-so and "Minister" so-and-so. So audacious are the Nicolaitan wolves in sheep's clothing that they take the title of "Reverend" so-and-so when the Bible states that "holy and reverend is his [God's] name." Psalms 111:9. The Nicolaitans in the Catholic Church contumaciously take the title of "Father" so-and-so, when Jesus Christ commands that we are to "call no man your father upon the earth: for one is your Father, which is in heaven." Matthew 23:9.

The Nicolaitan form of church government, which is endemic in churches today, is a form that God hates. Revelation 2:6. It is a church administration where the common members have little or no say about church doctrine. If a church member disagrees with church doctrine, he has no means of bringing it to a discussion. The Nicolaitan leaders simply show the "trouble maker" the door.

The clergy/laity divide that we see in churches today is antithetical to what Jesus taught. In Matthew we read again what Mark stated (and it bears repeating): there is to be no authoritative reign of the clergy in the church. There is not to be any divide in the church with a class of highfalutin clergy exercising authority over the lowly laity. Indeed, all in the church are one body of Christ. And if any want to be "great" and "chief" in the church they are to serve with charity.

> But Jesus called them unto him, and said, Ye know that the princes of the Gentiles exercise dominion over them, and they that are great exercise authority upon them. But it shall not be so among you: but **whosoever will be great among you, let him be your <u>minister</u>; And whosoever will be chief among you, let him be your <u>servant</u>**: Even as the Son of man came not to be ministered unto, but to minister, and to give his life a ransom for many." (Matthew 20:25-28)

Christ and Christ alone is to have preeminence in the church. Colossians 1:18. The Bible speaks in condemnation of Diotrephes because he sought to have preeminence in the church.

> I wrote unto the church: but Diotrephes, who loveth to have the preeminence among them, receiveth us not. Wherefore, if I come, I will remember his deeds which he doeth, prating against us with malicious words: and not content therewith, neither doth he himself receive the brethren, and forbiddeth them that would, and casteth them out of the church. (3 John 1:9-10)

Notice that Diotrephes sought the preeminence in the

church and in that capacity cast out of the church those who followed the true doctrines of Christ.

When there is mention in the Bible of elders and pastors and bishops and overseers; those terms are virtual synonyms, and they are always mentioned as pluralities. Those terms describe ministers who serve the church, not clergy exercising dominion over the laity.

> And he gave some, apostles; and some, prophets; and some, evangelists; and some, pastors and teachers; For the perfecting of the saints, for the work of the ministry, for the edifying of the body of Christ: Till we all come in the unity of the faith, and of the knowledge of the Son of God, unto a perfect man, unto the measure of the stature of the fulness of Christ. (Ephesians 4:11-13)

When there is mention of elders (Acts 14:23; 20:17) and overseers (Acts 20:28) and bishops (Titus 1:5-9; 1 Timothy 3:1-6) it is regarding their service to the church and not their authoritarian reign over the church members. All church members are kings and priests. "And hast made us unto our God kings and priests: and we shall reign on the earth." (Revelation 5:10) Each church member has the unction of the Holy Spirit and has standing to speak on issues of faith and doctrine. "But ye have an unction from the Holy One, and ye know all things." (1 John 2:20)

Indeed, all who are saved are given the understanding of God's word. "All scripture is given by inspiration of God, and is profitable for doctrine, for reproof, for correction, for instruction in righteousness:" (2 Timothy 3:16) We see in Job that inspiration means understanding. "But there is a spirit in man: and the inspiration of the Almighty giveth them understanding." (Job 32:8) Inspiration through the unction of the Holy Ghost gives all who read God's word "understanding" of his word. His word is given by inspiration of the Holy Spirit to understand it.

The church is made up of members of the body of Christ. "Now ye are the body of Christ, and members in particular." 1 Corinthians 12:27. As such, the church members should be consulted regarding issues of faith and doctrine. There is no place for special officers, called clergy, to be given charge over the members to dictate to them what are to be the faith and doctrines of the church. Issues of faith and doctrine should be brought before the church membership so that they can search out the scripture to see if it is there, just as the noble Berean Christians did in the first century. Acts 17:11. There is no way for the church members to do that if such issues are kept from them by the clergy that exercise lordship over them. The archetypal Nicolaitan church would be the Roman Catholic Church.

39 Examples of Inspiration

The Liddell-Scott-Jones Greek-English Lexicon cites 120,000 Greek words. The "Great Dictionary of the Greek language (Ancient & Modern)" (1964) by Prof. Dimitris Dimitrakos, cites around 200.000 Greek words. According to Nick Nicholas, PhD in Linguistics from Melbourne University, lecturer in historical linguistics, there are 240,000 Greek dictionary words. Koine Greek would be a smaller subset of that. There are approximately 600,000 English dictionary words defined in the Oxford English Dictionary. English is a richer and more refined language than Greek.

The King James translators were inspired by God. One instance of their inspiration is found in their translation of the Greek word, *tupos*. The single Greek word, *tupos*, means both example and ensample. The King James Translators were inspired to correctly translate the one Greek word, *tupos*, according to the context, as alternatively example or ensample as God guided them.

Indeed, the AV translation is more refined than the Greek from which it was translated And the translation of the single Greek word, *tupos*, into two distinct English words, example and ensample, with two distinct definitions is evidence that the English translation is superior to the Greek from which it was translated.

That refinement and precision of the AV translators is by the inspiration of God and fulfilment of the promise in Psalms 12:6-7.

Greek: *Tupos* = Ensample and Example

Ensample means to exemplify as a **model or pattern for imitation or copying**.

Example means **behavior or an event from which to learn**. You learn from it; you don't necessarily copy it.

The Greek word ***tupos*** is used to mean both example and ensample. The King James translators were inspired to sometimes translate it as ensample and other times as example. New Bible versions always use example.

AV	NKJV
Neither as being lords over God's heritage, but being **ensamples** to the flock. (1 Peter 5:3 AV)	nor as being lords over those entrusted to you, but being **examples** to the flock; (1 Peter 5:3 NKJV)
Greek: *tupos*	Greek: *tupos*

Indeed, the newest Bible corruption, the King James Bible 2016 (KJV2016), which is supposed to be a faithful translation (but it is not) mistranslates *tupos* as "example." The KJV2016 passage at 1 Peter 5:3 wrongly states: "nor as being lords over God's heritage, but being **examples** to the flock." Another Bible trading on the good name of King James, 21st Century King James Version (KJ21), similarly mistranslates *tupos* in 1 Peter 5:3, "neither as being lords over God's heritage, but by being **examples** to the flock."

The behavior of the Christian elders is that of "ensamples to the flock" as behavior to be followed, not examples of behavior to merely learn from.

AV	NKJV
Let no man despise thy youth; but be thou an **example of the believers**, in word, in conversation, in charity, in spirit, in faith, in purity. (1 Timothy 4:12 AV)	Let no one [a]despise your youth, but be an **example to the believers** in word, in conduct, in love, in spirit, in faith, in purity. (1 Timothy 4:12 NKJV)
Greek: *tupos*	Greek: *tupos*

Notice that in 1 Timothy 4:12 in the AV Christians are called on to be an **example of the believers**. That means that they are to display a pattern of behavior from which the world made up of believers and unbelievers can learn. The lost part of the world cannot follow the example as they are lost, but they can learn what it means to be a Christian by seeing the "**example of the believers**."

The NKJV gets this wrong. The NKJV erroneously has a believer being an **example to the believers**, which is a completely different meaning. Notice that it is limited only to be an example to believers and not the world. Whereas example of believers is to everyone in the world.

In yet another instance of the inspiration of the King James translators, the two Greek words, *Agape* and *Phileo*, both mean love. The King James translators were inspired to translate those two words correctly into one single English word, love.

Agape = *Phileo* = **Love**

Both *Agape* and *Phileo* mean the same thing. They both mean love.

"So when they had dined, Jesus saith to Simon Peter, Simon, *son* of Jonas, **lovest [*agapao*]** thou me more than these? He saith unto him, Yea, Lord; thou knowest that I **love [*phileo*]** thee. He saith unto him, Feed my lambs. He saith to him again the second time, Simon, *son* of Jonas, **lovest [*agapao*]** thou me? He saith unto him, Yea, Lord; thou knowest that I **love [*phileo*]** thee. He saith unto him, Feed my sheep. He saith unto him the **third time**, Simon, *son* of Jonas, **lovest [*phileo*]** thou me? Peter was grieved because he said unto him the third time, **Lovest [*phileo*]** thou me? And he said unto him, Lord, thou knowest all things; thou knowest that I **love [*phileo*]** thee. Jesus saith unto him, Feed my sheep." (John 21:15-17 AV)

"The Father **loveth [*agape*]** the Son, and hath given all things into his hand." (John 3:35 AV)

"For the Father **loveth [*phileo*]** the Son, and sheweth him all things that himself doeth: and he will shew him greater works than these, that ye may marvel." (John 5:20 AV)

"Husbands, **love [*agape*]** your wives, even as Christ also loved the church, and gave himself for it;" (Ephesians 5:25 AV)

"That they may teach the young women to be sober, to **love [*phileo*]** their husbands, to **love [phileo]** their children," (Titus 2:4 AV)

The Greek word, *Agape*, means both love and charity. The King James translators were inspired to translate that single word in two different ways as the Spirit of God gave them inspiration.

Agape = Love or Charity

Though I speak with the tongues of men and of angels, and have not charity, I am become *as* sounding brass, or a tinkling cymbal. And though I have *the gift of* prophecy, and understand all mysteries, and all knowledge; and though I have all faith, so that I could remove mountains, and have not **charity**, I am nothing. And though I bestow all my goods to feed *the poor*, and though I give my body to be burned, and have not **charity**, it profiteth me nothing. **Charity** suffereth long, *and* is kind; **charity** envieth not; **charity** vaunteth not itself, is not puffed up, Doth not behave itself unseemly, seeketh not her own, is not easily provoked, thinketh no evil; Rejoiceth not in iniquity, but rejoiceth in the truth; Beareth all things, believeth all things, hopeth all things, endureth all things. **Charity** never faileth: but whether *there be* prophecies, they shall fail; whether *there be* tongues, they shall cease; whether *there be* knowledge, it shall vanish away. (1 Corinthians 13:1-8 AV)

Charity is the love a believer shows to another. All other bible versions use the English word, **love**, in 1 Corinthians 13:1-8.

The Geneva Bible is a faithful translation that predated the AV. It is a translation that was part of God's progressive revelation until its perfection in the AV. The AV is more refined than the Geneva Bible; indeed, it is God's perfect revelation of his word to man. We see that illustrated with the translation of the words "patheo," "apatheo," and "pisteuo" into English in the AV.

Patheo and *Apatheo* are Greek words that each have two meanings, depending on the context. The AV translators were inspired by God to give more precision in English than is found in Greek. The English is more refined than the Greek from which it was translated.

Greek: *Patheo* = **Believe or Obey**
Greek: *Apatheo* = **Believe Not or Disobey**
Greek: *Pisteuo* = **Belief or Faith**

AV	Geneva Bible
He that **believeth** [*pisteuo*] on the Son hath everlasting life: and he that **believeth not** [*apatheo*] the Son shall not see life; but the wrath of God abideth on him." (John 3:36 AV)	He that **believeth** [*pisteuo*] in the Son, hath everlasting life, and he that **obeyeth not** [*apatheo*] the Son, shall not see life, but the wrath of God abideth on him. John 3:36 Geneva Bible (1599)

The English translation in the AV is superior to the Greek because the Greek offers two meanings, and the reader must figure it out. The King James translators were inspired by the Holy Spirit to choose "believe not" over "obeyeth not" in John 3:36. The King James Version of the Bible (AV) refined and purified the translation that appeared in the Geneva Bible. The AV is the final refinement of God's progressive revelation to his elect. Just as the New Testament is the final part of God's progressive revelation, so also is the AV the final purification and revelation of God's word.

> The words of the LORD are pure words: As silver tried in a furnace of earth, purified seven times. Thou shalt keep them, O LORD, Thou shalt preserve them from this generation for ever. Psalms 12:6-7.

In this context, there is a close relationship between

"believeth not" and "obeyeth not." Faith is the root of obedience. Because faith is the root of obedience, the better translation for *apatheo* in John 3:36 is "believeth not" as in the AV rather than "obeyeth not" as in the Geneva Bible. One cannot obey without faith. Indeed, obedience is the fruit of genuine faith. "Herein is my Father glorified, that ye bear much fruit; so shall ye be my disciples." John 15:8. Abiding in Christ through faith is necessary to bear fruit by obeying God's command to love one another.

> Abide in me, and I in you. As **the branch cannot bear fruit of itself**, except it abide in the vine; no more can ye, except ye abide in me. I am the vine, ye are the branches: **He that abideth in me, and I in him, the same bringeth forth much fruit**: for without me ye can do nothing. ... If ye **keep my commandments**, ye shall abide in my love; even as I have kept my Father's commandments, and abide in his love. These things have I spoken unto you, that my joy might remain in you, and that your joy might be full. **This is my commandment, That ye love one another, as I have loved you.** ... **Ye are my friends, if ye do whatsoever I command you.** John 15:4-5, 10-12, 14.

We are commanded to "love thy neighbour as thyself." Matthew 22:39. Our obedience to that command requires our faith.

> But without faith it is impossible to please him: for he that cometh to God must believe that he is, and that he is a rewarder of them that diligently seek him. Hebrews 11:6. *See also* John 15:10-12.

Peter reveals that faith, by which we are saved, bears fruit. That fruit is to love on another. Peter explains that the Holy Spirit uses our faith to lead us to obey God and love one another. Thus, our faith bears the fruit of the good works of love.

> Who by him do believe in God, that raised him up from the dead, and gave him glory; that your faith and hope might be in God. Seeing ye have purified your souls in **obeying the truth through the Spirit unto unfeigned love of the brethren,** see that ye love one another with a pure heart fervently." (1 Peter 1:21-22)

James explains: "What doth it profit, my brethren, though a man say he hath faith, and have not works? can faith save him?" (James 2:14) That is when he explains that true, saving faith has works. What works? The works of love. He concludes with the gospel message that "as the body without the spirit is dead, so faith without works is dead also." (James 2:26)

Those good works are the works of Jesus Christ performed through the believer. We are born again through the Holy Spirit as new creations in Christ Jesus to do good works ordained by God for us to walk in them. Works do not save us; our good works in obedience to God's command to love one another are the fruit of our salvation. As Paul explained:

> For by grace are ye saved through faith; and that not of yourselves: it is the gift of God: Not of works, lest any man should boast. **For we are his workmanship, created in Christ Jesus unto good works, which God hath before ordained that we should walk in them.** (Ephesians 2:8-10)

Of course, God sees all, and he sees those works of Christ done through the believer. Indeed, at the judgment seat of Christ, the only good works that are seen are the works of Christ done through the believer. A believer is cloaked with the righteousness of Jesus Christ. The scriptures are clear that it is not necessary for the believer to be de facto righteous (in fact righteous) to be saved. Instead, Jesus imputes his righteousness to the believer, who is consequently made de jure righteous (legally righteous). 2 Corinthians 5:21. Christians are justified by the Lord Jesus Christ, and by virtue of having been made legally righteous, we have peace with God. Romans 5:1. For more information about this read this author's book, *The Damnable Heresy of Salvation by Dead Faith*.

Another proof of the inspiration of the AV translators is their translation of Elohiym in Psalms 8:5. Below is a statistical breakdown of Elohiym in the Old Testament. Notice that only once was Elohiym ever translated as "angels." The AV translators were inspired by God to translate Elohiym as "angels" in Psalms 8:5. That is confirmed by the testimony of Hebrews 2:7-9.

Elohiym

Appears 2700 times in Old Testament.
90% Translated God
200 times gods
5-6 times judge(s)
2 times godess
1 time angels: Psalms 8:5

AV	Geneva Bible
For thou hast made him a little lower than the **angels**, and hast crowned him with glory and honour. (Psalms 8:5 AV)	For thou hast made him a little lower than **God**, and crowned him with glory and worship. (Psalms 8:5 Geneva Bible 1599)

Jesus, who is God, came to Earth as a man. That prophecy is found in Psalms 8:5. The Geneva Bible translation renders Elohiym in Psalms 8:5 as "God," whereas the AV renders Elohiym as "angels." Indeed, Jesus was made a little lower than the angels. We find that truth in Hebrews 2:7-9. It is a quote from Psalms 8:5. Jesus came to Earth as a man, which put him a little lower than the angels. But he remained God. He was not a little lower than God; he was God in the form of a man, but he remained God. *See* John 1:1-14. Indeed, while Jesus Christ was on Earth, he was also in heaven at the same time. *See* John 3:13. The AV is more precise. It is a refinement of the Geneva Bible. Jesus was made a little lower than the angels when he was manifested as a man on Earth. And that is testified by God's word in Hebrews 2:7-19.

> Thou madest him a little lower than the **angels**; thou crownedst him with glory and honour, and didst set him over the works of thy hands: Thou hast put all things in subjection under his feet. For in that he put all in subjection under him, he left nothing *that is* not put under him. But now we see not yet all things put under him. But we see **Jesus**, who was made a little lower than the **angels** for the suffering of death, crowned with glory and honour; that he by the grace of God should taste death for every man. (Hebrews 2:7-9 AV)

Another passage that demonstrates that the AV translators were inspired by God is found at Genesis 22:8. The King James translators provide a further revelation not found in the original Hebrew. No other Bible versions explain that Genesis 22:8 is a prophesy that God would sacrifice himself as the lamb of God. Notice that in Genesis 22:13 it was a **ram** that was found in the thicket **not a lamb**. That indicates that Abraham's statement was not fulfilled at that time.

> "And Abraham said, My son, God will **provide himself a lamb** for a burnt offering: so they went both of them together." (Genesis 22:8 AV)

Read how the original Hebrew is interpreted by the other literal Bible translations that were published prior to the AV. Those English Bibles indicate that God would provide **a** lamb, where the AV translation reveals that "God will provide himself a lamb."

> Abraham said, My son, **God shall purvey to him the beast of burnt sacrifice**. Therefore they went together, (And Abraham said, My son, **God himself shall provide the beast for the burnt sacrifice**. And so they went together,) Genesis 22:8 Wycliffe Bible

> Then Abraham answered, My son, **God will provide him a lamb for a burnt offering**: so they went both together. Genesis 22:8 Geneva Bible

We find the same translation in the alleged literal Bible translations that were published after the AV. Those English Bibles also indicate that God would provide **a** lamb, where the AV translation reveals that "God will provide himself a lamb."

> And Abraham said, "My son, **God will provide for Himself the lamb for a burnt offering**." So the two of them went together. Genesis 22:8 NKJV

> Abraham said, "**God will provide for Himself the lamb for the burnt offering**, my son." So the two of them walked on together. Genesis 22:8 NASB

Jesus is God who provided himself as the "Lamb of God" for a burnt offering.

> And looking upon Jesus as he walked, he saith, Behold **the Lamb of God**! (John 1:36 AV)

> And without controversy great is the mystery of godliness: **God was manifest in the flesh**, justified in the Spirit, seen of angels, preached unto the

Gentiles, believed on in the world, received up into glory. (1 Timothy 3:16 AV)

40 Revelation 16:5

There is a passage in the Authorized (King James) Version of the Holy Bible that has no extant Greek text to support it. James White, a textural critic of the King James Bible, argues that the passage is evidence of an error in the King James Bible. He argues that Revelation 16:5, as it appears in the AV, proves that the King James Bible is not God's inspired word but has been corrupted by men. He states that the substitution of the word "holy" with "shall be" is an emendation by Theodore Beza in his rendition of the Greek Textus Receptus. James White makes his argument thusly,

> Beza did introduce... "conjectural emendations," that is, changes made to the text without any evidence from the manuscripts. A few of these changes made it into the KJV, the most famous being Revelation 16:5, "O Lord, which art, and wast, and shalt be" rather than the actual reading, "who art and who wast, O Holy one."[428]

James White claims that Theodore Beza, who was one of the compilers of the Greek Textus Receptus (Received Text), did not have any Greek manuscript authority for "and shalt be." He claims, therefore, that the AV translation of Beza's Textus

Receptus that reads "and shalt be" is wrong. We see this discrepancy between "and shalt be" and "O Holy One" when comparing the AV to the NASB.

AV	NASB
And I heard the angel of the waters say, Thou art righteous, O Lord, which art, and wast, **and shalt be**, because thou hast judged thus. (Revelation 16:5 AV)	And I heard the angel of the waters saying, "Righteous are You, the One who is and who was, **O Holy One**, because You judged these things; (Revelation 16:5 NASB)

White is correct on one thing. No extant underlying Greek manuscript, be it Byzantine or Alexandrian, says "shalt be." But one contains the Greek word *kai* (and), which poses a real problem for White; it will be discussed below. White's claim that Beza's writing of "and shalt be" was a "conjectural emendation" is wrong. There was no conjecture involved at all. Beza was inspired by the Holy Spirit to write "and shalt be."

First, there is a Greek manuscript, Papyrus 47, discovered in 1930, which is the oldest extant Greek manuscript, dating from 200-250 A.D. It has the Greek word *kai* (and) followed by what appears to be a *nomina sacra* "holy." But White deceptively ignores the *kai* in P47 and instead claims that "[e]very Greek text-not just Alexandrian texts, but all Greek texts, Majority Text, the Byzantine text, every manuscript, the entire manuscript tradition-reads 'Holy One,' containing the Greek phrase ὅσιος ('o hosios.')." White claims that all manuscripts have the rendering "O Holy one." That is not true. P47 contains the phrase "and holy" not "o holy." Often, scribes will use an abreviation for Jesus or Lord, which is called a *nomina sacra*. "Holy" would be an unusual *nomina sacra*. If the word "holy" is a *nomina sacra* for Jehovah, whose name means "shalt be," conveying that he is eternal, then P47 is a fly in the ointment for White's argument. That is because the *nomina sacra* for Jehovah would mean the word "holy" is in place of "shalt be," with a final rendering of "and shalt be."

If the word "holy" is not a *nomina sacra*, the passage in P47 makes no sense. Reading the text at Revelation 16:5 as "which art, and wast, and holy" is a non-sequitur. Based on the readings in Revelation 1:4, 1:8, 4:8, and 11:17, the only proper reading would be "which art, and wast, and shalt be" as it appears in Beza's Greek Textus Receptus and the AV. Nick Sayers explains that Beza understood that principle:

> Beza plainly saw Triadic Declaration [which art, and wast, and shalt be], is the Sacred Name of God in Revelation, not just as a phrase, but as a proper name, describing the eternality of the beginning, middle, and end of Jehovah. The past, present, and future, of the I AM, the 'shalbe.'[429]

Thus, inspired by the Holy Spirit, Beza correctly rendered the Greek text as "which art, and wast, and shalt be" because it is the very definition of Jehovah. E.W. Bullinger explains, "Jehovah means the Eternal, the Immutable One, He Who WAS, and IS, and IS TO COME. The Divine definition is given in Genesis 21:33." (all capital letters in original). We see the clear pattern identifying the Lord who is, was, and is to come in the book of Revelation. It is a reference to Jehovah, whose very name means he who is, was, and is to come.

> John to the seven churches which are in Asia: Grace be unto you, and peace, from him **which is, and which was, and which is to come**; and from the seven Spirits which are before his throne; (Revelation 1:4 AV)

> I am Alpha and Omega, the beginning and the ending, saith the Lord, which is, and **which was,**

and which is to come, the Almighty. (Revelation 1:8 AV)

And the four beasts had each of them six wings about him; and they were full of eyes within: and they rest not day and night, saying, Holy, holy, holy, Lord God Almighty, **which was, and is, and is to come**. (Revelation 4:8 AV)

Saying, We give thee thanks, O Lord God Almighty, **which art, and wast, and art to come**; because thou hast taken to thee thy great power, and hast reigned. (Revelation 11:17 AV)

And I heard the angel of the waters say, Thou art righteous, O Lord, **which art, and wast, and shalt be**, because thou hast judged thus. (Revelation 16:5 AV)

Theodore Beza wrote the notes in the 1599 Geneva Bible. In the notes for Revelation 1:4, Beza states: "By these three times, **Is, Was and shall be**, is signified this word **Jehovah**, which is the proper name of God."[430] Beza understood the importance of ensuring that the triadic declaration was maintained in Revelation 16:5 because it signified the very name of God, Jehovah. Nick Sayers explains the importance of Beza's rendition of "which art, and wast, and shalt be" in Revelation 16:5.

> [...] *Jehovah* is numbered in any modern concordance as H3068. The definition of Jehovah lists the root word as H1961 *hayah*, "to become" which comes from the primitive root H1933 *hava*, "shall be" Take careful notice. Jehovah comes from *hava* which means "shall be" This word in Greek would directly translate as ἐσόμενος (esomenos), which is exactly what Theodore Beza

placed in Revelation 16:5 and which translates as "shalt be"(will be) in English. This is because the word Jehovah means the Existing One, *"who is, and was, and shalt be."* The *Jehovah/hava* link is elementary to Hebraists. For example, the 1814 Elements of Hebrew Grammar below shows us that the name Jehovah stems from *hava*:

Examples of י *prefixed and postfixed.*

י prefixed, commonly forms proper names.

עקב To supplant.	יעקב Jacob.
חנן To show favour.	יוחנן Joannes, Gratiosus.
צחק To laugh.	יצחק Isaac.
הוה To be, to exist.	יהוה Jehovah.

Sometimes common nouns are formed in the same manner.

The example above is revealing that at times, the *Yod* - י is prefixed to proper names, such as to הָוָה *hava* to form Jehovah (Je - hovah). Notice *hava* clearly means "to be, to exist." This clearly shows us that *hava* has a direct link to "ἐσόμενος" "shalt be" "will be."[431]

Dr. Nehemia Gordon, Ph.D., is a Hebraist who explains that Jehovah literally means He who was, He who is, and He who will be.[432] He states in Genesis 3:14 where God said: "I AM THAT I AM," *Ehyah asher Ehyah* reveals what God meant by Jehovah in Genesis 3:15 (translated as "the LORD" in the AV). Dr. Jordan states that "I AM" in Genesis 3:14 explains "the LORD" (Jehovah) in Genesis 3:15. He describes how Jehovah is three forms of the

Hebrew verb "to be." *Hayah* (He was) *Hoveh* (He who is), and *Yihyeh* (He will be).

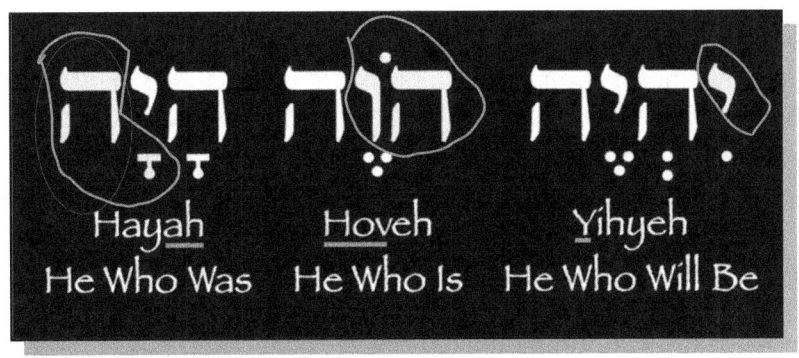

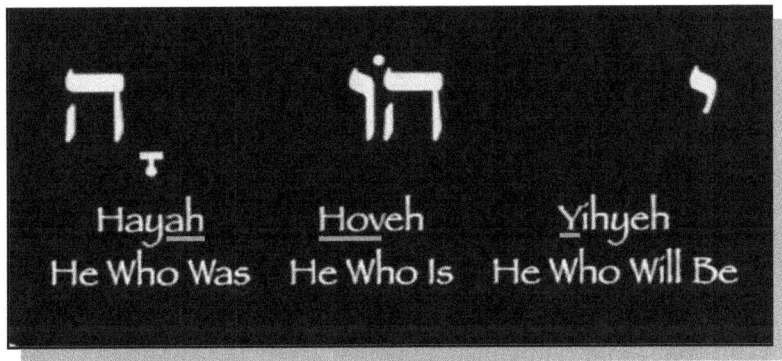

(Hebrew-Right to Left)
JEHOVAH
(English-Left to Right)

Dr. Gordon is a Karaite Jew. Karaite Jews only recognize

the Tanakh (a.k.a., Old Testament) as authoritative in Jewish religious law and theology. In contrast to mainstream Rabbinic Judaism, Karaite Jews eschew other sources like the Talmud and Kabbalah as being authoritative. As a Jew, Dr. Gordon does not believe that Jesus is Christ. Nonetheless, he honestly explains that the same meaning for God's name in Jehovah is found in the book of Revelation, where it says that the Lord is he "which art, and wast, and shalt be" (i.e., the Lord is Jehovah). That confirms that the proper meaning in Revelation 16:5 is as in the AV: "And I heard the angel of the waters say, Thou art righteous, O Lord, **which art, and wast, and shalt be**, because thou hast judged thus." (Revelation 16:5 AV) And we see in Revelations 1:8, Jesus is Jehovah. "I am Alpha and Omega, the beginning and the ending, saith the Lord, **which is, and which was, and which is to come**, the Almighty." (Revelation 1:8 AV)

Nick Sayers explains how the reference to Jesus as Lord means he is Jehovah.

> The authors of the New Testament under inspiration from God translated the Hebrew Jehovah (*Yehovah*) as the Greek *Kurios*, which means "Lord" That is why the KJV translators translated Jehovah as LORD in the Old Testament. One important feature when learning translation methodology is examining how words are carried across (translated) from the Old Testament into the New Testament by the original writers. The King James Version translators knew that if God translated the Hebrew Jehovah (*Yehovah*) as the Greek *Kurios* without any issues, then such methods were also safe to replicate into the English tongue.[433]

God explains this in Philippians 2:11:

Wherefore God also hath highly exalted him, and given him **a name which is above every name**: That at the name of Jesus every knee should bow, of things in heaven, and things in earth, and things under the earth; And that every tongue should confess that Jesus Christ is **Lord**, to the glory of God the Father. Philippians 2:11.

Beza explains why he decided on the "and shalt be" reading in Revelations 16:5 in the absence of any Greek manuscript authority. Beza states that "and holy" is a foolish and distorted rendering. He then explains that John has established a proper pattern of "which art, and wast, and shalt be." It cannot be doubted that John wrote that same rendition identifying Jehovah in Revelation 16:5.

> **[W]ith John there remains a completeness where the name of Jehovah (the Lord) is used, just as we have said before, 1:4; he always uses the three closely together**, therefore it is certainly "καιοεσομενος" for why would he pass over it in this place? And so without doubting the genuine writing in this ancient manuscript, **I faithfully restored in the good book what was certainly there**, "οεσομενος" So why not truthfully, with good reason, write "οερχομενος as before in four other places, namely 1:4 and 8; likewise in 4:3 and 11:17, because the point is the just Christ shall come away from there and bring them into being: in this way he will in fact appear sitting in judgment and exercising his just and eternal decrees.[434]

Nick Sayers explains that Beza was establishing what was there from the beginning. A revelation of God as Jehovah, "which art, and wast, and shalt be."

Beza replaced the illogical language found in earlier Greek texts/manuscripts and knew that "and holy"or "the holy one" interrupts the continuity of reference to God's eternal name of Jehovah/I AM, and omits a predictable logical third verb of "shalt be" Beza' rendering speaks of the eternal God of the past, present & future, as expected of a true reading, and in accord with Revelation 1:4, 8, 4:8, & 11:17. All five of the Revelation verses present the obvious expected future aspect of God's eternality. The "I AM" is the "shalbe." Beza claimed "holy"was *"distorting what is put forth in scripture."*[435]

Daniel Wallace explains the concept of Beza'a rendering of Revelation 16:5.

Imagine we came across an early manuscript copy of the Constitution of the United States, and the preamble said, "We the people of the United States, in order to form a more perfect onion ..." If we were to see that line, we would know that "union" was the original word, not "onion."[436]

Nick Sayers prepared a chart showing the change made by Beza to his 1582 edition of the Textus Receptus to properly render "which art, and wast, **and shalt be**" to properly honor and identify Jehovah.

> Beza saw this erroneous pattern below that disturbed the Triadic Declaration in his previous editions of the Greek New Testament:
>
> | ὁ | ὤν | καί | ὁ | ἦν | καί | ὁ | ἐρχόμενος | Revelation 1:4 |
> |---|---|---|---|---|---|---|---|---|
> | ὁ | ὤν | καί | ὁ | ἦν | καί | ὁ | ἐρχόμενος | Revelation 1:8 |
> | ὁ | ἦν | καί | ὁ | ὤν | καί | ὁ | ἐρχόμενος | Revelation 4:8 |
> | ὁ | ὤν | καί | ὁ | ἦν | καί | ὁ | ἐρχόμενος | Revelation 11:17 |
> | ὁ | ὤν | καί | ὁ | ἦν | καί | ὁ | ὅσιος | Revelation 16:5 |
>
> And he replaced ὅσιος with ἐσόμενος in his 1582 edition:
>
> | ὁ | ὤν | καί | ὁ | ἦν | καί | ὁ | ἐρχόμενος | Revelation 1:4 |
> |---|---|---|---|---|---|---|---|---|
> | ὁ | ὤν | καί | ὁ | ἦν | καί | ὁ | ἐρχόμενος | Revelation 1:8 |
> | ὁ | ἦν | καί | ὁ | ὤν | καί | ὁ | ἐρχόμενος | Revelation 4:8 |
> | ὁ | ὤν | καί | ὁ | ἦν | καί | ὁ | ἐρχόμενος | Revelation 11:17 |
> | ὁ | ὤν | καί | ὁ | ἦν | καί | ὁ | ἐσόμενος | Revelation 16:5 |

A problem with James White's position is that it is premised on the fact that the book of Revelation was originally written in Greek. That is disputable. Indeed, the evidence suggests that the Book of Revelation was written in Hebrew. Old Testament scholar and former Chairman of the Department of Religion at Princeton University said that "[w]e come to the conclusion, therefore, that the Apocalypse [a..k.a., Book of Revelation] as a whole is a translation from Hebrew or Aramaic."[437] Charles Cutler Torrey (1863-1956), was an American historian, archeologist, and scholar who taught Semitic languages at the Andover Theological Seminary and Yale University. He founded the American School of Archeology in Jerusalem. Torrey said that "the book of Revelation was written in a Semitic language and the Greek translation ... is a remarkably close rendering of the original."[438]

If the book of Revelation was written in Hebrew or Aramaic and Greek is a translation, why can we not look at other language translations to see if "and shalt be" is in Revelation 16:5 in those manuscripts? We can. Sure enough, we find the rendition of "which art, and wast, and shalt be" in Revelation 16:5 in Ethiopic and Latin translations.[439]

Remember that Beza was a copyist refining the Textus Receptus as a single authoritative Greek New Testament text from many other Greek manuscripts. He was inspired by God to faithfully render the Textus Receptus. Beza was a gifted linguist, but his work on the Textus Receptus was more as a compiler and copyist. Beza was an inspired copyist who copied from the majority of Greek texts. His rendering of Revelations 16:5 proves that even the copyists are inspired by God. God inspired Beza to give the rendering of Revelation 16:5 as "which art, and wast, and shalt be," although it did not appear in any Greek manuscript he had before him. The Ethiopic and Latin versions confirm that Beza was correct.

What the infidel scholars claim is evidence that the AV is a corrupt Bible with conjectural emendations added by men, instead, turns out to be proof that not only were the translators inspired by God but also the copyists.

41 New Bible Versions Remove God's Promise

God uses the English to refine the Greek. The underlying Greek is inspired but so also is the AV English translation. But the AV English translation refines the Greek, it purifies it. That is what is meant by **"The words of the Lord are pure words: as silver tried in a furnace of earth, purified seven times. Thou shalt keep them, O Lord, thou shalt preserve them from this generation for ever."** Psalms 12:6-7. The inspired AV English translation is more refined than the Greek from which it was translated.

But Satan does not want that to be known. Satan's modern Bible versions take away the promise by God to preserve his word. Instead, they replace the promise to preserve unnamed and unidentified persons. That is no surprise.

> The words of the Lord are pure words: as silver tried in a furnace of earth, purified seven times. Thou shalt keep them, O Lord, thou shalt preserve **them** from this generation for ever. Psalms 12:6-7 KJV

> The words of the Lord are pure words, like silver

refined in a furnace on the ground, purified seven times. You, O Lord, will keep them; you will guard **us** from this generation forever. Psalms 12:6-7 ESV

The words of the Lord are pure words; As silver tried in a furnace on the earth, refined seven times. You, O Lord, will keep them; You will preserve **him** from this generation forever. Psalms 12:6-7 NASB

Dr. John Hinton, Ph.D., an expert in the Hebrew language and grammar, comments:

> Who is "him" supposed to be? Is God supposed to be preserving himself here? This translation is downright stupid, but it does show that they were making a conscious effort to avoid its true meaning.[440]

Dr. Hinton opines that the mistranslation in the new Bible versions of Psalms 12:7 is an inexcusable product of dishonesty and incompetence.

> One of the key verses that assures us that God does preserve His Word is Psalm 12:7, and not surprisingly, it is perverted by most of the modern versions. This mistranslation is often a product of dishonesty, since it is obvious that modern version producers would not want this verse to be known, but it is also a product of incompetence with the Hebrew. It is, above all, an indication of a shocking lack of spiritual discernment.[441]

Dr. Hinton states that there is no excuse for someone familiar with Hebrew to mistranslate Psalms 12:7 as is done in the new Bible versions. The mistranslation was done intentionally. The mistranslation of Psalms 12:7 is evidence that the translators of the new Bible versions have an agenda. "It is clear, as I said above, that the translation committees that had actual Hebraicists knew of the nûn epenthetic, but chose to ignore it. ... What made these translators treat Psalm 12:7 differently? It does not take a whole lot of discernment to be able to answer that question."[442] Dr. Hinton continues:

> It should be noted that the word in question in verse 7 is in pause. It is placed there, and in that form for emphasis. This form is quite common in Classical and Modern Standard Arabic where it also is used as an emphatic, and, as Gesenius points out, is used in Western Aramaic. As a Hebrew form it would certainly go way over the heads of the fake Hebraicists whose entire "knowledge" of Hebrew comes from Strong's Concordance.[443]

The mistranslation is so glaringly obvious and so incriminating Dr. Hinton comes to the ineluctable conclusion that the translators are devil possessed minions of Satan.

> Blaspheming Bible scoffers will continue to attempt to use this verse to attack God's Word, but they do so with no more than hot air. The phrase in question does say that God will preserve them (His Words) just as numerous Hebrew grammars, the Anaytical Hebrew and Chaldee Lexicon of Davidson, and the King James Bible say that it does. The modern version characters will do anything to avoid having to deal with the fact that God has declared to us that he has preserved for us a Final Authority. Why don't they rejoice in that fact and obey it. Would they go out into the woods

with a wild edible plant book that lies and declares poisonous plants to be edible? As a teacher of wild edible plants I could be guilty of murder if I were to intentionally hand out false information. No one who is not completely insane would consider such a thing. Why would anyone then want to intentionally deceive themselves and others at the cost of their very souls by doing the same with the Bible? Demonic possession is the only answer that I can come up with, because logical reasoning does not appear to be a factor.[444]

42 Proof New Bible Versions Are Not Inspired

While the AV Holy Bible is inspired and inerrant, the new bibles are chock full of errors. Those errors prove that they could not be God's word. For example, the NIV, NASB and virtually every new bible version identifies the prophecy in Mark 1:2 as being from Isaiah, when in fact the quote is not from Isaiah but is from Malachi 3:1.

The Isaiah prophecy is not quoted until Mark 1:3. The Authorized Version does not make that mistake; in the AV the two prophecies are correctly introduced in Mark 1:2: "As is written in the prophets."

Incidentally, there is a footnote to Mark 1:1 in the NASB that states that "many" manuscripts do not contain the language "the Son of God." The NASB footnote is misleading, because approximately 99% of the manuscripts have that clause in them. The 1% that do not have that clause are the corrupt Alexandrian manuscripts. That footnote is just another example of Satan attacking the deity of Jesus Christ. The NASB, the NIV and the other new bibles have footnotes like that throughout their corrupt texts attacking the authenticity of scores of bible passages.

AV	NASB
The beginning of the gospel of Jesus Christ, the Son of God; As it is written in the **prophets**, Behold, I send my messenger before thy face, which shall prepare thy way before thee. [*Malachi 3:1*] The voice of one crying in the wilderness, Prepare ye the way of the Lord, make his paths straight. [*Isaiah 40:3*] (Mark 1:1-3 AV)	The beginning of the gospel of Jesus Christ, the Son of God. As it is written in **Isaiah** the prophet, Behold, I send my messenger before your face, who will prepare your way; [*Malachi 3:1*] The voice of one crying in the wilderness, make ready the way of the Lord, make his paths straight. [*Isaiah 40:3*] (Mark 1:1-3 NASB)

Another error in the new Bible versions is found in Luke 4:44. The new versions erroneously have Jesus preaching in the "synagogues of Judea." In fact, Jesus was preaching in Galilee, not Judea. We find that confirmed in the parallel passages in Matthew 4:23 and Mark 1:39.

AV	ESV
And he preached in the synagogues of **Galilee**. (Luke 4:44 AV)	And he was preaching in the synagogues of **Judea**. (Luke 4:44 ESV)

The English Standard Version (ESV) misinforms the reader in 2 Samuel 21:19 that Elhanan slew Goliath. It is well established that David slew Goliath (1 Samuel 17), not Elhanan. The AV in 2 Samuel 21:19 correctly informs the reader that Elhanan "slew the brother of Goliath." The ESV is a counterfeit Bible containing misinformation.

AV	**ESV**
And there was again a battle in Gob with the Philistines, where Elhanan the son of Jaareoregim, a Bethlehemite, slew the **brother of Goliath** the Gittite, the staff of whose spear was like a weaver's beam. (2 Samuel 21:19 AV)	And there was again war with the Philistines at Gob, and Elhanan the son of Jaare-oregim, the Bethlehemite, struck down **Goliath** the Gittite, the shaft of whose spear was like a weaver's beam. (2 Samuel 21:19 ESV)

One of the favorite attacks by the new version advocates is to claim that the word "Easter" in Acts 12:4 is an example of a mistranslation by the King James translators. They assert that the word *pascha* should be translated "Passover" not "Easter."

AV	**NKJV**
Now about that time Herod the king stretched forth his hands to vex certain of the church. And he killed James the brother of John with the sword. And because he saw it pleased the Jews, he proceeded further to take Peter also. (Then were the days of unleavened bread.) And when he had apprehended him, he put him in prison, and delivered him to four quaternions of soldiers to keep him; intending after **Easter** to bring him forth to the people. (Acts 12:1-4 AV)	Now about that time Herod the king stretched out his hand to harass some from the church. Then he killed James the brother of John with the sword. And because he saw that it pleased the Jews, he proceeded further to seize Peter also. Now it was during the Days of Unleavened Bread. So when he had arrested him, he put him in prison, and delivered him to four squads of soldiers to keep him, intending to bring him before the people after **Passover**. (Acts 12:1-4 NKJV)

The so called biblical scholars begin their argument on the right foot but then stumble on man's wisdom. They correctly note that Easter is a word derived from the adoration and worship of the pagan queen of heaven "Astarte" or "Ishtar."[445] Easter was and is a pagan spring festival which involved fertility symbols such as eggs and rabbits.[446] Easter has nothing at all to do with Passover or with the resurrection of our Lord and Savior Jesus Christ.

It is the Roman Catholic Church in mixing the pagan festivals with the Christian history that has seduced people into believing that Christ rose from the dead on Easter Sunday. Because Easter is in fact a pagan holiday, the new versions translate the Greek word *pascha* in Acts 12:4 as "Passover," thinking that God could not possibly mean to refer to a pagan holiday in his Holy Scriptures. In Acts 12:4, however, God is not using the word *pascha* to describe a Christian or Jewish holiday, he is describing the intentions of Herod. Herod was a pagan and it would not be unusual that he would desire to wait until his cherished Easter pagan holiday was over before he brought Peter out before the people.

While Passover is one of the possible English translations for *pascha*, that translation in the context of Acts 12:4 is simply wrong. The more accurate translation is "Easter," which is the translation found in the King James Holy Bible. *Pascha* is a word of Chaldean origin and means either Passover or the pagan festival of Easter. The pedantic and rather sophomoric translation by the modern so called scholars is demonstrably erroneous. They assume that *pascha* must be translated "Passover" in Acts 12:4, based solely on the fact that *pascha* means Passover in all other biblical passages where it appears. They completely disregard the alternative English translation for *pascha* of Easter.

Pascha, however, cannot possibly mean Passover in Acts 12:4, because Herod intended to keep custody of Peter until after *pascha*. *Pascha* in that passage must mean Easter, because Passover had already taken place when Peter was arrested during the days of unleavened bread. The fourteenth day of the first month of the Jewish calendar is the Passover (Leviticus 23:4-5, Genesis 12:17-18). Passover is immediately followed by the seven days of unleavened bread (Leviticus 23:6-7, Genesis 12:15-16). Because Passover is memorialized with unleavened bread (Genesis 12:17-18), it and the seven day feast of unleavened bread are both referred to as the feast of unleavened bread (Matthew 26:17, Mark 14:1, 14:12, Luke 22:1-7, Leviticus 23:6, Exodus 12:17-20). Combining the Passover with the feast of unleavened bread we get eight (8) days of unleavened bread that span from the Fourteenth day (Passover) until the 21st day of the first month in the Jewish calendar (Genesis 12:18).

> These *are* the feasts of the LORD, *even* holy convocations, which ye shall proclaim in their seasons. In the fourteenth *day* of the first month at even *is* the LORD'S passover. **And on the fifteenth day of the same month *is* the feast of unleavened bread unto the LORD: seven days ye must eat unleavened bread.** In the first day ye shall have an holy convocation: ye shall do no servile work therein. But ye shall offer an offering made by fire unto the LORD seven days: in the seventh day *is* an holy convocation: ye shall do no servile work *therein*. (Leviticus 23:4-8 AV)

In Acts 12:1-4 we see that Peter was taken into custody during the days of unleavened bread that follow Passover, Passover had already taken place. Because Passover had already taken place by that time, it makes no sense for the passage to say that Herod intended to hold Peter until after Passover. The pagan holiday Easter, on the other hand, always follows Passover and had not yet occurred. Herod intended to hold Peter until after the pagan holiday of Easter. Therefore, the King James translators were correct when they translated *pascha* as "Easter," and the modern translators are wrong in translating *pascha* as "Passover."

43 Jehovah (Not Yahweh) Is LORD

Many have probably heard people claiming to be "Christians" call God "Yahweh." Many are a little surprised, having never before heard that name for God. The persons using the word take great pride in displaying their understanding of the "true" name of God. The speaker and listener usually don't know that Yahweh is NOT the proper name for God. In reality, Yahweh is the name for a heathen weather god.

God's true name is **Jehovah**. We find in Exodus 6:2-3, that God reveals his proper name, **Jehovah**.

> And God spake unto Moses, and said unto him, I am the Lord: And I appeared unto Abraham, unto Isaac, and unto Jacob, by the name of God Almighty, but by my name **JEHOVAH** was I not known to them. Exodus 6:2-3 (AV)

Jehovah is the proper English translation of the Hebrew Tetragrammaton (יהוה) (YHVH). The minions of Satan in the Hebrew Roots (a.k.a. Sacred Name) movement have hoodwinked their followers into using the name Yahweh in place of Jehovah. They ignorantly think that Yahweh is the correct pronunciation of the Hebrew Tetragrammaton (יהוה) (YHVH), rather than

Jehovah. They are wrong. Yahweh is a satanic trap set for the unlearned and gullible. It subverts people into worshiping a devil, Yahweh, in place of God Almighty, Jehovah. God's name is Jehovah; Yahweh is a heathen tribal god.

Dr. James White, who promotes the corrupt new Bible versions, says Jehovah is a false pronunciation of the Tetragrammaton: "Now, 'Jehovah' is a false pronunciation of the Hebrew word 'YHWH,' correctly pronounced 'Yahweh.' This is God's 'personal' name in the Old Testament."[447] This corruption is finding its way into the modern Bible translations. For example, the New Living Translation (NLT) has changed the passage where God identifies himself as Jehovah to having God identify himself as Yahweh.

AV	NLT
And God spake unto Moses, and said unto him, I am **the LORD**: And I appeared unto Abraham, unto Isaac, and unto Jacob, by the name of God Almighty, but by my name **JEHOVAH** was I not known to them. Exodus 6:2-3 (AV)	And God said to Moses, "I am **Yahweh**—'the Lord.' I appeared to Abraham, to Isaac, and to Jacob as El-Shaddai—'God Almighty'—but I did not reveal my name, **Yahweh**, to them. Exodus 6:2-3 (NLT)

James White promotes the Legacy Standard Bible (LSB) as being more accurate than the King James Bible.[448] The LSB replaces God's name, Jehovah, with the name Yahweh. Using the name Yahweh is not a different way of pronouncing God's name. It is a replacement of God. Indeed, James White is emphatic that God's name is NOT Jehovah. He claims that God's true name is Yahweh, and it is impossible for his name to be Jehovah. "Yahweh is unquestionably the best pronunciation of the Divine name. **Jehovah is not even possible.**"[449] James White and the LSB have rejected the true God, Jehovah, and replaced him with a heathen tribal god, Yahweh.

AV	**LSB**
And God spake unto Moses, and said unto him, I am **the LORD**: And I appeared unto Abraham, unto Isaac, and unto Jacob, by the name of God Almighty, but by my name **JEHOVAH** was I not known to them. (Exodus 6:2-3 AV)	God spoke further to Moses and said to him, "I am **Yahweh**; and I appeared to Abraham, Isaac, and Jacob, as God Almighty, but by My name, **Yahweh**, I was not known to them." (Exodus 6:2-3 LSB)

John MacArthur, a world-famous preacher and President of the Master's University and Seminary, announced the publication of the Legacy Standard Bible (LSB) by making particular note of the use of Yahweh in place of Jehovah. MacArthur states that it is of utmost importance that Christians know God's name. He states that calling God Yahweh is one of the principal reasons he considers the LSB "a priceless treasure—an amazing effort." But he obfuscates what he has actually done. He claims he is more reverent to God by stating his name, which he thinks is Yahweh, instead of the LORD. But he does not reveal that he is changing the name of the eternal God from Jehovah to Yahweh. To understand that, you would have to read Exodus 6:3, Psalms 83:18, Isaiah 12:2, and Isaiah 26:4 in the LSB.

> For about a year, linguistic scholars of the Master's University and the Master's Seminary have been working on a translation called the Legacy Standard Bible. It's come to completion. Now, the first printed form of it is the New Testament Psalms and Proverbs. It's the best English translation I have ever read. It's the most diligently prepared translation. **And one of the wonderful features of it is it calls God by the name he**

asked to be remembered by. When you say LORD, you're talking about his sovereignty. In all English Bibles, Yahweh is translated LORD in upper case letters. But that just repeats Adonai. It doesn't give you the name of God, which is the covenant name that expresses his eternal being. **He wants you to know his name. And you say it all the time. Every time you say hallelujah, you say praise, Yahweh. This translation, for that and a number of reasons, is a priceless treasure—an amazing effort.**[450]

The King James Bible usually translated Jehovah as "the LORD." That rendering is correct. The LSB changes the translation of the Hebrew (Jehovah) from "the LORD" to "Yahweh." Isaiah 40:3 is an example.

AV	LSB
The voice of him that crieth in the wilderness, Prepare ye the way of **the LORD**, make straight in the desert a highway for our God. (Isaiah 40:3 AV)	A voice is calling, "Prepare the way for **Yahweh** in the wilderness; Make smooth in the desert a highway for our God." (Isaiah 40:3 LSB)

God's inspired word in Mark 1:3 is evidence that "the LORD" is a correct rendering of the Hebrew (Jehovah). Mark 1:3 is a quote from the prophecy of Isaiah 40:3 regarding the coming of the Lord. "The voice of one crying in the wilderness, Prepare ye the way of **the Lord**, make his paths straight." (Mark 1:3 AV) It identifies Jesus Christ as "the Lord," the the eternal God, Jehovah. When the LSB renders the Mark 1:3 passage, is a quote from Isaiah 40:3, it follows the correct rendering of "the Lord." just as it is in the KJV.

THE VOICE OF ONE CRYING IN THE WILDERNESS,

'MAKE READY THE WAY OF **THE LORD**, MAKE HIS PATHS STRAIGHT.' (Mark 1:3 LSB)

If John MacArthur and the LSB were to be consistent, they would have rendered the quoted passage from Isaiah 4:3 in Mark 1:3 as "Yahweh." The fact that they rendered Mark 1:3 as "the Lord" impeaches their avowed fidelity to the original Hebrew and undermines their claim that Yahweh is the correct translation of the Hebrew tetragrammaton, YHVH. The LSB translators know it would be wrong to render "the Lord" in Mark 1:3 as "Yahweh." But they fail to understand that it is just as wrong to render "the LORD" in Isaiah 40:3 and Jehovah in Exodus 6:2-3 as "Yahweh."

The translators of the LSB have gone on record to say that the KJV is wrong. They claim that "Jehovah we do believe is an incorrect way of pronouncing it [the tetragrammaton, YHVH]. But what that is, it is a misreading of the vowels that appear on the letters YHWH on the word Yahweh."[451] The LSB translators criticize God's word in the KJV; they speak evil of the way of truth. That is a sign that they are among the pernicious false teachers who would privily sneak into the church bringing damnable heresies about whom Peter warned us in 2 Peter 2:1-2. Peter said, "many shall follow their pernicious ways; by reason of whom **the way of truth shall be evil spoken of.**" *Id.*

The rising popularity of the Hebrew Roots movement has spearheaded the recent upsurge in substituting Jehovah with Yahweh. The Hebrew Roots movement is a Zionist theology followed by Gentiles that emphasizes recovering Jewish legalism while claiming faith in Jesus. It is sometimes also called the Sacred Name movement. While those in the Hebrew Roots movement claim faith in Jesus, they have a different Jesus from the Biblical Jesus. There is no indication that James White or John MacArthur are part of the Hebrew Roots movement. But their adoption of Yahweh is an indication of how portions of the Hebrew Roots theology are wafting into the ersatz "Christian" churches.

Unsurprisingly, the Bible for the Hebrew roots movement, the Hebraic Roots Bible, substituted YAHWEH in every instance where the Hebrew word for JEHOVAH appears. Psalms 83:18 is one example.

AV	Hebraic Roots Bible
That men may know that thou, whose name alone is **JEHOVAH**, art the most high over all the earth. (Psalms 83:18 AV)	And let them know you; that Your name is **YAHWEH**, and all life comes from you, the Most High over all the earth. (Psalms 83:18 Hebraic Roots Bible)

The Hebrew consonant letters that have been translated Jehovah in English are often called the Tetragrammaton with the Hebrew letters *yod-hey-vav-hey* (י ה ו ה) (YHVH). The 'Y" in Hebrew takes on the "J" sound in English. There is no letter "J" in Hebrew. And the English alphabet did not have the letter "J" until the 16th century. But that does not mean that English did not have the "J" sound in their words. Prior to the 16th century the English letter "I" was used for both the "I" sound and the "J" sound. Indeed, in the 1611 King James Bible, you will find that Jesus was spelled "Iesus," but "Iesus" was pronounced as "Jesus."

It was during the 16th century that the letter "J" was introduced to distinguish the "I" sound from the "J" sound in English. The Tyndale Bible, published in 1525, used "J."[452] But that convention had not completely taken hold because the 1568 Bishops' Bible and the 1611 King James Bible used "I" for the "J" sound.

The English "J" sound in Hebrew is represented by the letter *yod* (י), which is written as "Y" in English. Indeed, check out the Old testament Hebrew for Jerusalem. It is "Yeruwshalaim," but no English speaker uses the soft "Y" sound to pronounce Jerusalem.

Psalms 119:73 in the KJV presents the Hebrew letter *yod* (׳), but lists it as *jod*. That indicates that the Hebrew letter *yod* (׳) takes on the "j" sound in English. By rendering the Hebrew letter *yod* (׳) as *Jod* in Englsih, God's inspired word in English instructs us that the Hebrew letter *yod* (׳) takes on the "j" sound when translated into English.

The King James translators knew how to translate the Hebrew into English. Forty-seven renowned experts in all languages translated the King James Bible. The translators' expertise in ancient and modern languages was unparalleled in history. For example, one of the KJV translators, Lancelot Andrews, was fluent in fifteen modern languages and six ancient languages. He had an encyclopedic knowledge of scripture and was gifted with a photographic memory. So esteemed was he as a linguist and scholar that Hugo Grotius, the great Dutch legal authority and historian, called meeting Andrews "one of the special attractions of a visit to England."[453]

Lancelot Andrews was joined by Dr. Miles Smith, an expert in rabbinical learning and well-versed in Hebrew, Chaldee, Syriac, and Arabic. He was often called a "walking library."[454] Another KJV translator, John Bois, could write Hebrew elegantly at six years old. They collaborated with other renowned Hebraists, including, but not limited to, Edward Lively, Laurence Chaderton, Francis Dillingham, Thomas Harrison, John Richardson, and Robert Spaulding. These men were divided among six different companies of translators. The members of each company reviewed each other's work. And the work of each company was also reviewed by every other company. Thus, every member of every company was a translator of the whole.[455] The learning and piety of the scholars who worked on the King James Bible puts to shame the sophomoric language skills of those who act as translators of the modern profane Bibles.

Dr. John Hinton, who is a Hebrew language expert, addresses the issue of those that erroneously insist that the Hebrew letter *yod* (a.k.a., *jod*) (Y) should always be pronounced in English as a soft "Y" rather than a hard "J." Dr. Hinton states:

> This is such an utterly silly and ignorant criticism that I find it embarrassing that there are actually Christians that present it as an argument. ... Y becomes a J in every name in English, French, and Spanish. In English the J is pronounced like J in Japan, while in French it is pronounced like S in pleasure, in Spanish it is pronounced like an H, in German it is pronounced like Y. This is a phonological and orthographical issue, not a theological one. There is no theological issue at stake in how one language interprets a certain phoneme. In every case of a name in Hebrew that begins with a *yod* (Y) it is pronounced with the appropriate phoneme for that language. This came about through phonological and orthographical changes in the developments of those languages. Even Hebrew itself went through huge phonological and orthographical changes in its long history. God's name is not a magic word to be chanted for power as the name cult seems to suggest for both the names of God and Jesus. My name [John] comes from a Hebrew word meaning given by God, which begins with a Y in Hebrew. It is Jean (zhan) in French, Juan (hwan) in Spanish, Giovanni in Italian, Hans in German, Yani in modern Greek, Ivan (eevan) in Russian, Yahya or Hanna (with a heavy H) in Arabic, and other variations exist in other languages. They all translate as John and I have no trouble adapting to

any of them within the respective cultures and there is no reason for me to be insulted by any of these names. On the other hand, being addressed by a made up name based on a pagan deity would insult me.

If these name cultists find the J so objectionable, why don't they refer to Elijah as Elaiyah, Jeramiah as Yeramaiyah, Jacob as Yakov, Jonathan as Yanatan, Jerusalem as Yerushaleem, and so forth. For that matter why don't they use the Hebrew pronunciation for all of the names in the Bible, such as Dahveed, Moshe (Moses), Shmu'el (Samuel), Sha'ul (Saul), Shlomo (Solomon), and so forth, if they consider the issue to be so important. Since those who call God by a name that is not even Hebrew at all, and since they do so without a scrap of evidence to override the very solid evidence to the contrary, why do they have any constraints at all about inventing whimsical pointings for other names in the Bible?

***

"The sound of the Hebrew letter jod came into English as the letter 'I,' used as a consonant and having the soft 'g' sound, like today's 'j.' In the past the letter 'I' was used as both a vowel (i) sound and as the consonant 'j' sound. The OED says that the sound of 'j,' though originally printed as 'I,' was pronounced as a soft 'g' (Oxford English Dictionary, Unabridged, 2nd Edition, Oxford: Clarendon Press, 1991, s.v. J). The 'JE' sound in JEHOVAH was spelled 'IE' and pronounced as 'JE.' To distinguish the consonant sound (soft 'g') of the letter 'I' from the vowel sound of 'I,' many scribes in the 1200s began putting a tail on the soft 'g' 'I,' making it look like our modern 'J.' The Spanish, in the 1500s, were the first to more consistently try to distinguish the consonant I (soft 'g') sound as the shape of a 'J.' At that same time English printers used 'J' and 'I' fonts interchangeably. ... During the 1600s, most languages began consistently using the extended 'I' form, now called a 'J,' to represent the 'j' (soft 'g') sound." [quoted in Riplinger, p. 418][456]

The Hebrew consonant letters for Jehovah are יהוה. Those Hebrew letters are read from right to left; their English representations are written from left to right (YHVH). The Hebrew letters י ה ו ה (YHVH) are only the consonant Hebrew letters without the vowel points. I will discuss the vowel points and their significance below. Hebrew words are read from right to left. And so *yod* (י) (Y or J), the tenth letter of the Hebrew alphabet is on the far right, followed by *hah* (ה) (H), the fifth letter of the Hebrew alphabet, followed by *vav* (ו) (V), which is the sixth letter of the Hebrew alphabet, and concluding with *hah* (ה) (H) again at the far left. It is commonly represented as YHVH; in Engish, it would be transliterated JHVH.

The Tetragrammaton (י ה ו ה) (YHVH or JHVH) is properly translated into English as JEHOVAH. And it would be properly pronounced as Jehovah in Englsih. The Hebrew letter *yod* (י), which is more correctly called *jod* in English (see Psalms 119:73 in the AV) takes on the "j" sound in English. And so words that begin with *yod* take on the constant "j" sound, like Jerusalem, Joseph, and Jehovah, which all start with *yod* (י) (a.ka., *jod*).

The next letter in the Tetragrammaton is *hah* (ה), which takes on the "h" sound in English. That is followed by the next letter in the Tetragrammatan, *vav* (ו), which takes on the consonant sound "v" in English. That is followed by *hah* (ה) as the last letter. When you look at Psalms 119 in the AV you will find the Hebrew alphabet listed in order. At Psalms 119:73 you will find *yod* listed as *jod* (י) in the AV. That means that *yod* takes on a hard consonant "j" sound (as in *jod*) in the inspired English word of God.

It is essential for English speakers reading an English Bible to understand the name of God in English correctly because when you read Exodus 6:2-3, you will realize that God was speaking to Moses. God was telling Moses his name in an audible voice. It is, therefore, important to accurately understand the truth of what God said. If God said his name is "Jehovah," which is how it is translated into English, then his name should be Jehovah in English.

E.W. Bullinger explains, "Jehovah means the Eternal, the Immutable One, He Who WAS, and IS, and IS TO COME. The Divine definition is given in Genesis 21:33."[457] (all capital letters in original) Nick Sayers explains: "In other words, God had appeared to Abraham, Isaac, and Jacob but not as 'the Eternal, Immutable One.' but as 'God Almighty.' But when God appeared to Moses, He made Himself known as Who He is, His very essence, i.e. Eternal."[458] Jesus is identified as Jehovah. The very name of Jesus means "Jehovah is salvation." Jesus stated: "I am Alpha and Omega, the beginning and the ending, saith the Lord, which is, and which was, and which is to come, the Almighty." Revelation 1:8. In that verse, we see that Jesus is thus revealing that he is Jehovah (i.e., the eternal God, who was, and is, and is to come). Is Yahweh, the Lord, which is, and which was, and which is to come, the Almighty? No! We will find out that Yahweh is the Midianite weather god.[459]

Later, when Moses penned Genesis, he used the word Jehovah to refer to the LORD. "These are the generations of the heavens and of the earth when they were created, in the day that the LORD [Jehovah] God made the earth and the heavens," (Genesis 2:4 AV)

But the heathen Schaff-Herzog Encyclopedia of Religious Knowledge undermines the eternal and sovereign deity of Jehovah and claims he is instead Yahweh, a heathen god worshiped by the nomadic Midianites:

> Yahweh appears as an old deity of Sinai, revered in untold antiquity as a weather god, and as such brought by Moses to Israel, to him revealed through his connection with the Midianite priestly family.[460]

Thus, the Schaff-Herzog Encyclopedia acknowledges that their rendition of YHVH as "Yahweh" is based on the encyclopedia writers' belief that the Jews worshipped a heathen weather god of Sinai called Yahweh. The encyclopedia writers have a preconceived idea that serves to undermine the divinity of Jehovah. The encyclopedia then claims that "the form was never pronounced as Yehovah (Jehovah)."[461] But the writers of the encyclopedia offer no evidence to support their claims. Indeed, the encyclopedia is full of conjecture and qualifying statements like "it is supposed" and "the hypothesis of the Yahweh cult" and "it is highly improbable" and "rich harvest of suggestion of Yahweh" and "indications suggest." The entire entry is full of suppositions and guesses. The writers were just making things up. It is not scholarship. It is false progpaganda. Indeed, their "the hypothesis of the Yahweh cult" is based on mere possibility. The encyclopedia entry says so.

> There remains the **possibility** that in the time before Moses a part of the people dwelt near Sinai and that by this part Yahweh was worshiped and that from it Moses learned of him.[462]

They have grafted the heathen god, Yahweh, in place of the Holy God, Jehovah. Historians state that Yahweh is one of the gods of the Syro-Palestinian pantheon, which included Baal. Heathen historians claim that Yahweh was adopted as a god by the Jews from the surrounding tribes and eventually emerged as the national god of Israel and Judah.

James Miller and John Hayes reveal that "Yahwehism and Baalism existed alongside each other with essentially the same cultic procedures and paraphernalia."[463] The mythology of heathen historians is that it was later that Israel worshiped Yahweh as a monotheistic god.[464] What becomes clear is that Yahweh is not an alternative pronunciation of YHVH. What is happening is that infidel historians in service of Satan are replacing eternal God Almighty, Jehovah, with the heathen weather god, Yahweh. There is no new thing under the sun. *See* Ecclesiates 1:9. This is what the lying prophets of old did. They replaced God's name with Baal. God explains in Jeremiah:

> I have heard what the prophets said, that prophesy lies in my name, saying, I have dreamed, I have dreamed. How long shall this be in the heart of the prophets that prophesy lies? yea, they are prophets of the deceit of their own heart; **Which think to cause my people to forget my name by their dreams which they tell every man to his neighbour, as their fathers have forgotten my name for Baal.** (Jeremiah 23:25-27)

John King, the translator and editor of John Calvin's Commentary, cites the elaborate investigation of the origin and import of the name Jehovah by Ernst Wilhelm Hengstenberg (1802-1869), Professor Extraordinarius of Theology at Berlin. King discovered that Hengstenberg refuted the folklore of impious historians. He concluded that "[...] (Jehovah) ... was not derived from any heathen source whatever. Consequently, it is to be traced to 'a Hebrew etymology.'"⁴⁶⁵

Dr. Nehemia Gordon is a renowned Hebraist. He is a Karaite Jew who recognizes the written Tanakh (Old Testament) as the sole religious authority. Dr. Gordon tried to track down the source of the Hebrew vowels for Yahweh. He researched extensively, trying to find the authority for Yahweh as the Tetragrammaton (YHVH) pronunciation. What he found surprised him. There was no ancient authority for pronouncing the Tetragrammaton (YHVH) as Yahweh.

> What do we have in Jewish sources, and what do we have in Hebrew Bible manuscripts? There isn't a single Hebrew Bible manuscript that has Yahveh or Yahweh, nothing, nowhere, anywhere. There isn't a single Jewish source that has Yahweh. Let's say an ancient or medieval Jewish source.⁴⁶⁶

Dr. Gordon was trying to find authority for pronouncing the Tetragrammaton (YHVH) as Yahweh. He contacted authorities from the Hebrew Roots movement to find out their source for Yahweh. Astoundingly, they admitted that the vowels for Yahweh have no Hebrew manuscript authority. They said that they constructed Yahweh from an unpointed Hebrew text. That is a text with no vowels.

That means that the Hebrew Roots movement is just making it up. They just inserted the vowels as they saw fit into the consonants of the Tetragrammaton (YHVH) to come up with the name Yahweh. The Hebrew roots people are doing the very same thing that the apostate Jews did when they created the unpointed Hebrew text so that they could make a passage mean whatever they wanted it to mean and not be restricted by the pesky vowels. An unpointed Hebew text is virtually meaningless. An unpointed text allows a mischievous rabbi to give his private interpretation of what vowels to insert to give a verse its meaning. Dr. Gordon states:

> I didn't have any manuscripts so I wrote to these Christian folks or maybe Hebrew Roots folks, who say Yahweh, and I say which vowels do I put in here? ... They said we don't use Hebrew vowels. Okay, but if it if you can't translate it into Hebrew, the Hebrew vowel system, then it has no meaning in Hebrew.[467]

Dr. Gordon cited 19 learned rabbis with eclectic backgrounds who, through history, all stated that Yehovah was the correct rendering of the Tetragrammaton (YHVH) in Hebrew. In Hebrew, it is pronounced Yehovah, whereas in English, it is pronounced Jehovah.

> Right now have 19 rabbis who explicitly say that the vowels of the name are Yehovah ... in Hebrew. ... You could say they're wrong. But what you can't say is this [Jehovah] is something that was invented by ignorant Christians because we have multiple rabbis, who, some of them were aware of what the Christians were saying others had no clue what the Christians were saying, and they all believed it was Jehovah. ... There is no Rabbi in historical sources who says it's Yahweh or Yahveh.[468]

Yehovah in Hebrew would be Jehovah in English. Dr. Gordon could not find any source for Yahweh as the pronunciation of the Tetragrammaton (י ה ו ה) (YHVH) before the German linguist Wilhelm Gesenius (1786-1842) in his Hebrew lexicon. Gesenius was the progenitor of pronouncing the Tetragrammaton (YHVH) as Yahweh.

Dr. Nehemia Gordon, Ph.D., researched the origins of

Yahweh and was shocked to find out that Yahweh is not the God of the Bible, but is a pagan god worshipped by the Samaritans.[469] The Romans worshipped Jupiter as the principal god in their henotheistic mythology. Josephus reveals that the Samaritans rededicated their temple to Jupiter (a.k.a., Zeus) in 168 B.C. The Samaritans called Jupiter Yoveh. In Latin, Yoveh was pronounced Yoweh, which ultimately became Yahweh.

Dr. Gordon quotes from Wilhelm Gesenius (1786-1842). Gesenius' Hebrew Lexicon is the foundation of Hebrew biblical studies at Hebrew University today. Gesenius championed the use of Yahweh as the name of God. Gesenius, in his Hebrew and Chaldee Lexicon of the Old Testament Scriptures, states: "I suppose this word [Yahweh] to be one of the most remote antiquity, perhaps of the same origin as Jovis, Jupiter, and transferred from the Egyptians to the Hebrews."[470]

Gesenius, the most authoritative advocate for YHVH being pronounced Yahweh instead of Jehovah, let the cat out of the bag. He confirmed that Yahweh, the name he championed as the name of the God who communed with Moses, was the name of a heathen god originating in Egypt. That was too much information. Some infidel scholars wanted to introduce Yahweh in place of Jehovah, and they did not like it to be known (at least at the outset) that Yahweh was a heathen god.

One infidel scholar realized that something had to be done to undermine Gesenius's statement. Enter Samuel Prideaux Tregelles (1813-1875). Tregelles was a member of the English revision committee for the abominable Revised Version of the Bible. After Gesenius' death, Tregelles became the editor of Gesenius' lexicon. In that capacity, Tregelles took the opportunity to put brackets in a later edition of Gesenius' lexicon alleging that Gesenius retracted his statement about the heathen origins of Yahweh.[471]

But the alleged statement of retraction sounds nothing like a retraction. In the alleged retraction, Gesenius referred to studies into derivations a "waste of time and labour." That is not the same as saying that what he found in his analysis of the derivation of Yahweh was incorrect. Of course, there are infidels like Tragelles who are interested in undermining Gesenius's statement and would desire that Gesenius would retract his finding of the heathen origins of Yahweh. Such a finding of the heathen origins of Yahweh by someone as esteemed as Gesenius, who championed the name, Yahweh, would be a damning indictment against using Yahweh to refer to God. And that is what Tregelles argued against. Tregelles said: "What an idea! God himself revealed this [Yahewh] as his own name; the Israelites could never have received it from the Egyptians."[472] Tregelles has an interest in undermining evidence of the heathen origins of Yahweh. He wants people to think that YHVH should be translated as Yahweh. After examining the evidence, Dr. Gordon concluded that Yahweh is NOT another way to pronounce Jehovah, the Tetragrammaton (YHVH), but is, in fact, a pagan deity, just as Gesenius revealed.[473]

Yahweh is not Jehovah. Modern scholars have confirmed what Gesenius revealed about the origins of Yahweh as a heathen god. They have taken up Gesenius's torch and argue, as he did, that YHVH is not the eternal God, Jehovah, but is instead a heathen god, Yahweh. For example, Daniel E. Fleming, Ph.D., researched the origin of Yahweh and determined it is the name of a heathen god. He has alleged that the heathen god, Yahweh, was absorbed and worshipped by the Jews. Dr. Fleming is the Ethel and Irvin A. Edelman Professor of Hebrew and Judaic Studies at New York University. Fleming is the author of many scholarly books.

In Fleming's book *Yahweh before Israel: Glimpses of History in a Divine Name,* he opines that Yahweh is not the name of the eternal God of heaven. Fleming researched the origins of Yahweh. He found reference to Yahweh in ancient Egyptian hieroglyphics. He states that the name, Yhw3, pronounced "Yahweh" originated as the name of of a nomadic people of Shasu-land that eventually became the name of a heathen god, Yahweh. He argues that the heathen god, Yahweh, was then adopted by the Jews during their sojourn in the desert after God rescued them from their Egyptian captivity.

Fleming opines that that Yhw3 of Shasu-land was a people, and that name became later the god Yahweh. He opined that "the people understood themselves to have as a divine patron a god so fully identified with them as to share their name."[474]

Prof. Israel Knohl. Ph.D., is the Yehezkel Kaufmann Professor of Bible at the Hebrew University of Jerusalem and a senior research fellow at the Shalom Hartman Institute. He holds a Ph.D. in Bible from Hebrew University. Knohl has written numerous highly aclaimed academic publications. Knohl mostly agrees with Dr. Fleming.

Dr. Fleming promotes a Shasu origin for Yahweh, which arguably excludes Midianites as the origin. But Dr. Knohl argues that while it was in the land of Shasu where the Jews adopted Yahweh, it was under the influence of the Midianites. Dr. Knohl states that "It thus appears that the Hebrews adopted the Midianite deity YHW or YHWH [Yahweh], whom they came to know in their stay in the area of Seir – Edom which is in "the land of Shasu YHW."[475] Dr. Knohl argues that YHWH is a heathen god, Yahweh, which was adopted by the Jews.

> But how did the deity YHW [Yahweh] become transformed into the God of Israel? ... It thus appears that the Hebrews adopted the Midianite deity YHW or YHWH, whom they came to know in their stay in the area of Seir – Edom which is in "the land of Shasu YHW."[476]

Unsurprisingly, the New International Version (NIV) Bible publishers have taken the position that "the majority opinion today is that 'Yahweh' is the original pronunciation"[477] of the tetragrammaton, YHWH. The NIV writes the tetragrammaton YHWH instead of YHVH because it more closely comports with its mythology that the tetragrammaton is pronounced, "Yahweh." The NIV wants to migrate people toward the worship of the heathen god, Yahweh.

One clue that Yahweh and Jehovah are not the same is that they carry two different meanings. Hebraist Dr. Nehemia Gordon, Ph.D., explains that Jehovah literally means He who was, He who is, and He who will be.[478] Dr. Israel Knohl explains that Yahweh has an entirely different meaning. He states:

> God reveals his name to Moses as "I am" from the Hebrew root, "being." The name YHWH, [Yahweh] however, originates in Midian, and derives from the Arabic term for "love, desire, or passion." ... [T]he name of Yahweh means Impassioned. It reflects Yahweh's passionate love for his worshipers.[479]

Yahweh and Jehovah carry two different meanings because Yahweh is NOT Jehovah. Jehovah is the eternal God of heaven, who was, who is, and who will be. In contrast, Yahweh is a heathen god of passion.

How did they change the *vav* (ו), which has a hard "v" sound to the soft w in Yahweh? It was started with the apostate Germans who wrote "w," for the hard "v" sound in the German language. The Schaff–Herzog Encyclopedia of Religious Knowledge was based on an earlier German encyclopedia, the *Realencyklopädie für protestantische Theologie und Kirche*. When transliterating from German to English, many English speakers often miss that the German "w" is pronounced as the English "v."

For example, the German Wagner would pronounced by a German as "Vagner," although it would still be spelled Wagner. What an English speaker would call wiener schnitzel with a soft "w"sound a German would call "veiner schnitzel" with a hard "v" sound. But the German spelling would remain as wiener schnitzel; the w would take on the "v" sound. When the German was transliterated into English, the English speakers read the "w" not as a hard "v" sound but as a soft "w" sound. That soft English "w" has given rise to the change causing the erroneous "weh" sound in Yahweh. Dr. John Hinton, Ph.D., states that "the Hebrew *vav* is pronounced as V not W. This error came about due to the misreading of German Hebrew grammars, which use W for the English V."[480] Gail Riplinger explains:

> Where did the phony 'weh' sound in Yahweh come from? As Green said, "German sources." In German "the "v" sound is rendered by the "double u" ("w"). Although the German critics spelled the name Yahweh, they pronounced it, Yahveh. ... Because Germans use the letter 'w' for the 'v' sound, those reading or translating German theological works have brought in the German letter 'w' for 'v.' It is not to be pronounced like an English 'w,' but like a 'v.'[481]

Changing what God said his name is (Jehovah) to Yahweh is changing what God said. Yahweh is not at all Jehovah. Yahweh is a heathen god. And the original promoters of Yahweh say so. God has commanded us not to even mention the names of other gods. Imagine his dipleasure against those who would change his scriptures to replace his name "Jehovah" with a heathen god, "Yahweh."

> And in all things that I have said unto you be circumspect: and make no mention of the name of other gods, neither let it be heard out of thy mouth.

(Exodus 23:13 AV)

This modern trend of pronouncing the Tetragrammaton as Yahweh began in Germany. Gail Riplinger explains:

> In the 19th century, as unbelieving German critics of the Bible were hammering away at the word of God, they tried to refashion God's name, JEHOVAH. They asserted that the God of Israel's name should be pronounced Yahweh because, to them, he was nothing more than an offshoot of the pagan deity "Yaho."[482]

That corruption by the German liberals was a deviation from the traditional translation of YHVH as Jehovah. Gail Riplinger reveals:

> In his scholarly book, *A Dissertation Concerning the Antiquity of the Hebrew Language, Letters, Vowel-Points and Accents*, John Gill (1697-1771), eminent theologian and writer, documents the use of the very name JEHOVAH from before 200 B.C. and throughout the centuries of the early church and the following millennium. ... Even commentators such as Nicholas of Lyra, Tostatus, Cajetan, and Bonfrere defended the pronunciation 'JEHOVAH' as received by Moses on Mt. Horeb. The name is found in the writings of Raymund Martin in the 1200s and Porchetus in the 1300s. Theodore Beza, Galatinus, and Cajetan, among many others, use it in the 1500s. Scholars such as Michaelis, Drach and Stier proved the name as the original. The 1602 Spanish Bible uses the name Iehova and gave a lengthy defense of the pronunciation Jehovah in its preface. In "the 17th century the pronunciation JEHOVAH was

zealously defended by Fuller, Gataker, Leusden and others.[483]

But the heathen servants of Satan got to it and sought to undermine Jehovah and replace him with their heathen god, Yahweh. Gail Riplinger elaborates:

> Genebrardus seems to have been the first to suggest the pronunciation Iahue [pronounced Yahweh], but it was not until the 19th century that it became generally accepted" (EB, pp. 311-314). Anti-Semitic German liberals, like Driver and Delitzsch, eagerly grasped the new pronunciation, Yahweh. They and other unsaved 'higher critics,' denied that the Old Testament was actually given by God. They grasped at any straw to shelter their unbelief, asserting that the Old Testament was the creation of men who adopted and adapted stories, words, and names from neighboring pagan religions and languages. The higher critics used the new pronunciation, Yahweh, as so-called proof that the God of Israel was nothing more than a tribal god, whose name had evolved from pagan gods like Yaho or Ya-ve, worshipped by the Babylonians and Canaanites, the Hebrews' captors and neighbors. They said, Yahweh "meant Destroyer."[484]

Dr. Hinton explains that the Hebrew text does not support the soft English "W". It is wrong to translate the Hebrew *vav* (ו) in English as "W."

> Those who are opposed to the KJV and call God by name Yahweh are not only giving an erroneous pronunciation of his name according to the pointing of the text, but according to the

pronunciation of the Hebrew itself. As Gail Riplinger astutely points out in her *Awe of Thy Word*, the Hebrew *vav* is pronounced as V not W. This error came about due to the misreading of German Hebrew grammars, which use W for the English V (note: the German V is pronounced like the English F). If these Bible "correctors" want to ignore the Hebrew text and pronounce his name as suggested by 19th century atheistic mythologists, they should use the name Yahveh so that at least they would appear less ignorant. It always puzzled me to hear atheistic scholars at Harvard pronounce the name as Yahweh when the same scholars would always pronounce the *vav* as a V every other place that they use it. Apparently this perversion of his name has become so well established within the Bible-scoffing and Bible-correcting communities that even those who know better mispronounce even the perverted variation of his name. It confused me that they would pronounce it as if it were an Arabic word instead of Hebrew word until I understood the purpose of the corruption.[485]

Dr. Nehemia Gordon, Ph.D., is a Hebraist who has worked as a translator on the Dead Sea Scrolls and a researcher deciphering ancient Hebrew manuscripts.[486] He confirms the opinion of Dr. Hinton. Dr. Gordon states that the proper pronunciation of the Hebrew *vav* (ו) is with the hard "v" sound. He states that Arabic also has a *vav* (ו), and it is pronounced as "wow" in Arabic because Arabic does not have a "va" sound. But Arabic is not Hebrew, and the Hebrew *vav* (ו) is pronounced with a hard "v." Dr. Gordon states that the only Jews who pronounce the *vav* (ו) with a soft "w" sound are Jews in Arabic lands who are speaking Arabic.[487] The soft "w" sound is an Arabic pronunciation of *vav* (ו); it is not Hebrew. Thus, Yahweh is an incorrect pronunciation of YHVH (יהוה).

Satan's minions have created a little deception. He has his own set of lying alleged Hebraists who claim that the historical pronunciation of *vav* (ו) is with a "w." Jeff A. Benner is an example. Benner is an adherent to the Hebrew Roots theology.[488] He claims first that the King James Bible is not the inspired word of God. He also claims that the Old Testament was written in an "Old Hebrew" that is different from the Hebrew we see today. Armed with his new, made-up Hebrew, Benner can argue that the original sound for *vav* in ancient Hebrew was a soft "w" and not the hard "v," as in modern Hebrew.

Jeff A. Benner has used his new reconstructed Hebrew phonics to claim that YHVH should be read as Yahweh and not JEHOVAH.[489] Dr. Nehehmia Gordon has completely impeached Benner and has proven that Benner's claim is wrong.[490] Regarding the letter *vav* (ו), Dr. Gordon explains that the proper pronunciation of the Hebrew *vav* (ו) is with the hard "v" sound. Dr. Gordon states that the claim that *vav* (ו) has ever been pronounced as "wow" is simply wrong. It is only in Arabic that *vav* (ו) is pronounced as "wow." Dr. Gordon proved that *vav* (ו) has always been pronounced as "v" in ancient and modern Hebrew. He demonstrated that fact with two words from the ancient Hebrew in Ezekiel.[491]

In the book of Ezekiel at 10:12, we find the Hebrew word *gav* (גב), meaning back(s). Reading the Hebrew word right to left, the second letter in that word is a *beyt* (ב). When *beyt* (ב) appears at the end of the word it takes on the "v" sound, hence *gav*. In Ezekiel 23:35 we also find the Hebrew word *gav* (גו). But this time, the second letter is a *vav* (ו) which takes on the "v" sound because, again, the Hebrew word is *gav* (meaning back). These are two Hebrew words, both meaning "back." They are actually the same word, with the same pronunciation, "*gav*," meaning back.

They are just spelled differently. But in Ezekiel 23:35, *gav* (back) is spelled using a *vav* (ו) as the second letter, which necessarily must take on the "v" sound to get "*gav*." The only way this would be possible is if the letter *vav* (ו) in the word *gav* (ו ג) is pronounced with a "v." Ezekiel was written circa 592 to 570 B.C. and would be ancient Hebrew. The Ezekiel passages containing *gav* with two different spellings with one containing a *vav* (ו) are proof that that *vav* (ו) has always taken on the "v" sound in Hebrew.

Put another way, the Hebrew word for "back" is *gav*. The second consonant sound at the end of *gav* is *beyt* (ב) in Ezekiel 10:12. *Beyt* takes on the "v" sound at the end of a Hebrew word. *Gav* (back) is always pronounced with a "v" sound. That fact is established beyond any doubt. When we read *gav*, meaning back, again in Ezekiel 23:35, this time spelled differently in Hebrew, with the second consonant letter *vav* (ו), it can only mean one thing. *Vav* (ו) takes on the "v" sound in Ezekiel 25:35. Ezekiel 10:12 rendering of *gav* confirms the Ezekiel rendering of *gav* in Ezekiel 23:35. That means that *vav* (ו) takes on the "v" sound in ancient Hebrew, just as in modern Hebrew.

Jeff A. Benner was unwilling to budge from his erroneous position when Dr. Gordon proved that *vav* (ו) has always taken on the "v" sound in ancient and modern Hebrew.[492] He realized that if he yielded that point his Hebrew Roots' house of cards would collapse. Benner's opinion is corrupted by his belief that the English AV Bible is not the inspired word of God and that God's name is Yahweh.[493] Benner has an agenda to maintain the myth that the original pronunciation for vav is "w" which is one of the keystones for the claim that God's name is Yahweh and not Jehovah.[494] Benner cares not for the truth.

Satan figured out a way to change Jehovah into Yahweh by removing the vowel points that locked in Jehovah as the name of God. Satan and his minions had to reduce the Hebrew scripture to only the consonants before they could fill in their own vowels. They started with YHVH. With the vowels gone, they could argue that YHVH means YAHWEH.

In order for that scheme to work, they needed to float a lie that the original Hebrew scriptures did not have vowel points. They claimed that the vowel points were added much later and were not part of the inspired scriptures. Hebrew script uses vowel points, which are small marks indicating vowels. On or about 1538 Elias Levita, a famous Jewish grammarian, floated a theory that the original Hebrew text did not have vowel points.[495] He theorized that the original Hebrew text was made up of only consonants. He claimed that the Masorites added vowel points based on the Jewish oral traditions to create the Hebrew Old Testament we know today. Levita's mythology, if true, would mean that the Hebrew Old Testament is uninspired because the words would only have meaning through the vowels supplied by the oral traditions of men rather than from prophets as they were moved by God. Invoking oral traditions is the very thing that Jesus criticized the Jews for doing.

> Howbeit in vain do they worship me, teaching for doctrines the commandments of men. **For laying aside the commandment of God, ye hold the tradition of men,** as the washing of pots and cups: and many other such like things ye do. And he said unto them, Full well **ye reject the commandment of God, that ye may keep your own tradition.** (Mark 7:7-9 AV)

In contrast, God states that the holy scriptures are not subject to the will of man or the private interpretation of the Masoretes or anyone else. All scripture was given to men as the Holy Ghost moved them.

> Knowing this first, that no prophecy of the

scripture is of any private interpretation. For the prophecy came not in old time by the will of man: but holy men of God spake as they were moved by the Holy Ghost." (2 Peter 1:20-21 AV)

Did the Hebrew original scripture have vowels? Yes they did. The modern popular deception that the original Hebrew scriptures had no vowels is a lie constructed by Jews and their fellow travelers who want to conceal the prophecies about Jesus Christ and undermine the authority of God. The Jews removed the points that indicated vowel sounds in the scripture they used in their synagogues so that they could then reconstruct a phony scripture to conceal the deity of Jesus Christ.

Vowels in Hebrew are represented by marks called points. Hebraist Dr. Nehemia Gordon did extensive research into ancient Hebrew texts and found that the vowel points for the Tetragrammaton (יהוה) (YHVH) always have been *sheva, holem,* and *kamatz*.[496] Thus, the English pronunciation of the pointed Tetragrammaton (YHVH) can only be Jehovah. He concluded that the Tetragrammaton (YHVH) pronunciation cannot be Yahweh. Indeed, Dr. Gordon determined that the Tetragrammaton (YHVH) pronunciation in Hebrew has always been Yehovah (in English, it would be pronounced Jehovah). Dr. Gordon uncovered more than 1.000 ancient Hebrew Bible manuscripts containing the vowel points that render the Tetragrammaton (YHVH) in Hebrew as Yehovah; in English it would be pronounced Jehovah.[497]

Below are two representations of the Tetragrammaton (YHVH or JHVH) (יהוה). The one on the left is without any vowel points and the one on the right is pointed with vowels. The pointed version of the Tetragrammaton was the Hebrew text from which the AV English was translated.

YHVH Without Vowel Points   **JEHOVAH With Vowel Points**

In the graphic below, you can see how the different vowel points lock in the word Jehovah. Recall that you must read Hebrew from right to left. The consonant are *yod* (י), on the far right, followed by *hah* (ה), followed by *vav* (ו), and concluding with *hah* (ה) again at the far left. When translated into English with the vowel points the word is Jehovah. With the vowel points, it is impossible to translate YHVH as Yahweh.

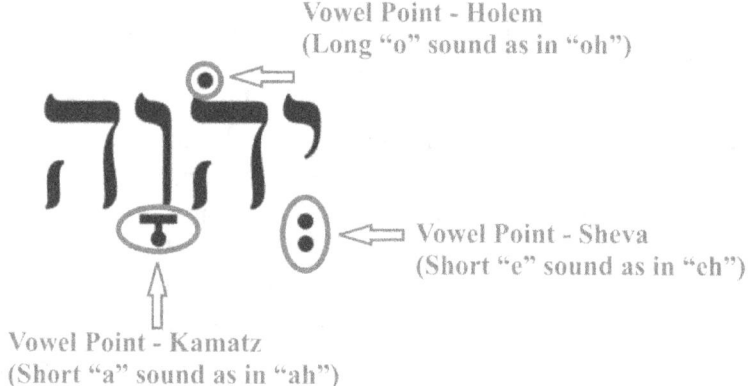

Above is the Hebrew word for JEHOVAH reading right to left. The vowels are indicated by the circled points. The consonants are, from right to left, *yod* (י) (J), *hah* (ה) (H), *vav* (ו) (V), and *hah* (ה) (H).

John Gill (1697-1771) traced the authenticity of the Hebrew Bible's vowel points back through the centuries to Moses.[498] His extensive research proves that the Hebrew Bible was written with vowel points. Gill found that the claim that vowel points were added by the Masoretes around 1000 A.D. is a myth that does not stand up to the historical evidence.

Not only that, but God himself informs us that the Hebrew scriptures were written with vowel points. Jesus stated: "For verily I say unto you, Till heaven and earth pass, **one jot or one tittle** shall in no wise pass from the law, till all be fulfilled." (Matthew 5:18 AV) A jot is "the least part of anything."[499] A tittle is a "small stroke or point in writing."[500] It is "[a] dot or other small mark used as a diacritic."[501] A diacritic is "a sign placed above or below a character or letter to indicate that it has a different phonetic value, is stressed, or for some other reason."[502] That is precisely what is done in Hebrew with the vowel points.

The jots and titles to which Jesus referred are an allusion to the diacritical marks used in Hebrew to designate the vowel sounds. Jesus was speaking about "the law," which is a reference to the law as it appeared in the Hebrew scriptures. That indicates that the original Hebrew scriptures had vowel points. That passage in Matthew 5:18 impeaches the claim that the vowel points were a later emendation made by men to the inspired Hebrew scriptures. The vowel points were, in fact, there from the beginning. And that is precisely what John Gill found in his extensive research.

Unpointed Hebrew Old Testament texts (Jews call it the Tanakh) have been constructed by Jews in order to have text that allows for wider interpretation and manipulation. Gill stated that without any points (vowels) a combination of consonants could be used to create up to ten different words. John Gill explains:

> There are other reasons why unpointed copies are kept and used in the synagogues of the Jews. They may help us to ascertain the origin of this custom and the reason for its continuance. One reason that the Cabalists, and those who interpreted the scriptures allegorically, might have the opportunity of establishing their own various senses of them.

An unpointed Bible will do this, but a pointed Bible will not. ... This is what R. Bechai plainly suggested was the original cause and reason for using unpointed copies: "Letters which are not pointed give various senses. They are divided into various meanings. Because of this we are commanded not to point the book of the law because the literal sense of every word is according to the punctuation. There is only one literal sense in a pointed word, but an unpointed word a man may understand many ways and find out many wonderful and excellent things."[503]

Armed with the unpointed text, the Jews could rewrite the scriptures to their liking. Of course, that is not new for the Jews. They are repeat offenders. In Mark 7:7-9, Jesus explained how the Jews laid aside the commandments of God so that they could hold the traditions of men. They rejected the commandments of God to follow their own traditions.

Gill concluded that a particular motivation for the Jews to remove the vowel points was to change the meaning of passages in the Bible. For example, we find in the Chabad: The Complete Jewish Bible that in Isaiah 9:6, they removed the prophecy regarding the birth of Jesus Christ, who is to be called the "Wonderful, Counsellor, The mighty God, The everlasting Father, The Prince of Peace." They replace it with a passage where God calls a child "the prince of peace." That corrupted passage in the Jewish Bible removes the eternal deity of Christ as the "Wonderful, Counsellor, The mighty God, The everlasting Father." Note that the Chabad Complete Jewish Bible is missing the verse at Isaiah 9:1 and so Isaiah 9:6 is numbered Isaiah 9:5 in the Chabad Complete Jewish Bible.

AV	Chabad Jewish Bible
For unto us a child is born, unto us a son is given: and the government shall be upon his shoulder: and **his name shall be called Wonderful, Counsellor, The mighty God, The everlasting Father, The Prince of Peace.** (Isaiah 9:6 AV)	For a child has been born to us, a son given to us, and the authority is upon his shoulder, and **the wondrous adviser, the mighty God, the everlasting Father, called his name, "the prince of peace."** Isaiah 9:5 (Isaiah 9:6 in Englsih Bibles) Chabad: The Complete Jewish Bible.

All one need do is read the Bible and it becomes clear that the Hebrew scriptures were written with vowel points. For instance, in Deuteronomy 27:8, God commands: "And thou shalt write upon the stones all the **words** of this law very **plainly**." How were the Jews to write plainly all the words of God's law without using vowel points. There is no way to be faithful to God's commands by only using consonants and no vowels. Such initialisms would not even be "words." And they would not be written "very plainly." Such a text would be obfuscation.

Indeed, a text made up only of consonants contains no words. Each series of consonants would be an initialism. Words require vowels. Indeed, you cannot even say the consonant letters without adding a vowel. For example, the English letter "b" is pronounced "be" and the English letter "v" is pronounced "ve." A series of consonants without vowels becomes a meaningless initialism. The string of consonants can only be given meaning by adding vowels.

We know the Old Testament had vowel points because God states that the "**words** of the LORD are pure words." Psalm 12:6. He has promised to keep and preserve his "**words**" from "this generation for ever." Psalms 12:7. Jesus promised that

"Heaven and earth shall pass away, but my **words** shall not pass away." Matthew 24:35. Consonants without vowels are initialisms. Initialisms are not words. God did not give us initialisms in the Old Testament. He gave us his **words**. It is a lie that the original Hebrew Old Testament did not have vowel pointings. Notice that throughout scripture, God identifies his **words** being spoken. Consonants with no vowels are not **words** that can be spoken.

> As for me, this is my covenant with them, saith the LORD; My spirit that is upon thee, and my **words** which I have **put in thy mouth**, shall not depart **out of thy mouth**, nor **out of the mouth of thy seed**, nor **out of the mouth of thy seed's seed**, saith the LORD, from henceforth and for ever. (Isaiah 59:21 AV)

The Roman Catholic Church could not be happier with Levita's new theory of an unpointed Hebrew Old Testament. Thoms Ross explains:

> The idea of the recent addition of the points was popular among the Catholics, for it lent support to their idea of the superiority of the Latin Vulgate to the Hebrew (and Greek) original, formally canonized in the Council of Trent, and became a tool in anti-Protestant polemic, for the ambiguity which resulted from the removal of the points mitigated the Reformers' doctrine of the perspicuity of Scripture and supported the Romanist contention for the necessity of infallible interpretation by their organization.[504]

John Morinus (1591-1659), a Catholic convert from Protestantism, represents a typical counter-reformation apologetic that the resulting ambiguities in the unpointed Hebrew scriptures elevated the Roman Catholic priesthood to prominence in interpreting the meaning of the Bible.

> The reason why God ordained the Scriptures to be written in this ambiguous manner [without points] is because it was His will that every man should be subject to the Judgment of the Church, and not interpret the Bible in his own way. For seeing that the reading of the Bible is so difficult, and so liable to various ambiguities, from the very nature of the thing, it is plan that it is not the will of God that every one should rashly and irreverently take upon himself to explain it; nor to suffer the common people to expound it at their pleasure; but that in those things, as in other matters respecting religion, it is His will that the people should depend upon the priests.[505]

In 1748, Hebraist Peter Whitfield soundly debunked the myth constructed by Elias Levita that the vowel points were later emendations by the Masoretes.[506] Whitfield proved, through historical evidence and scripture itself, that Levita's claim was impossible. He gives many examples where the same consonants with different points create different words and, thus, entirely different meanings. Dr. Thomas Strouse of Emanual Baptist Seminary reviewed Whitfield's work and concluded that Whitfield was correct. He agrees with Whitfield that "Scripture is based on words and words are based on consonants and vowels. If there are no vowels in the Hebrew OT originals, then there is no Divine authority of the Hebrew OT Scriptures."[507] Dr. Strouse added his own analysis of why it is impossible for the inspired Hebrew Old Testament to have been written without Hebrew vowel points.

> When the Lord renewed His covenant with Israel, He used Moses to write the very same words that were on the initial tablets (Ex. 34:1 ff.). The Lord said to Moses, "Write thou these words: for after

the tenor of these words I have made a covenant with thee and with Israel" (v. 27). The expression "after the tenor of these words" (`*al piy hadevariym ha'elleh*) could be translated literally "on [the basis of] the mouth of these words." The only way Moses could have written the Lord's spoken words was to hear the vowels in the consonants and then to write the words with the vowels intact. The Mosaic Law, then, constituted the very written words of Jehovah, including the consonants and vowels. Furthermore, the Jews were to obey the Mosaic Law in minute detail, not adding to nor diminishing from it (Dt. 4:2). They were to keep or preserve (*shamar*) the Law and not forget the things they had seen and were written down in it, and then to teach their children the Mosaic Law (vv. 6, 9, 10; cf. 6:7; 32:46). These verses conclusively argue against any notion that the vowel sounds were merely given to Moses who passed on the oral tradition of the pronunciation until the Masoretes invented a system to approximate the vowels. Levitas' speculation that the Masoretes invented the points has nothing to commend it but has all Scriptural authority to condemn it.[508]

Dr. Strouse states that God's commending one who meditates on his law would be meaningless without vowel points.

The initial Psalm addresses the blessed man and his responsibility to delight in and meditate on the law of the Lord, stating: "But his delight is in the law of the LORD; and in his law doth he meditate day and night"(Ps. 1:2). The word "meditate" comes from hagah that means "to mutter" and suggests the deliberate pronunciation of the words of Scripture. It is impossible to recite consonants without vowels and it is impossible to delight (*chaphatz*) in consonants with non-authoritative vowels. Again, the fallacious view that man invented the Hebrew vowel points has nothing to commend it. Is there any reason that Bible believers must countenance the view that the Lord God, the Creator of language, disdains vowels, at least to the extent that He would preserve them in written form? After all, has not the Lord Jesus Christ referred to Himself as the *Alpha* and *Omega* (Rev. 1:8; 21:6), the first and last vowels of the Greek language?[509]

The brilliant linguist John Owen (1616-1683), whom many view as the greatest British theologian of the 17th century,[510] disproved Levita's claim. Owen was fluent in Greek, Latin, and Hebrew. His mastery of those languages is apparent in his writings. For example, in his book *The Devine Origin of Scripture*,[511] Owen segued from English to Greek to Latin to Hebrew with aplomb and adroitness. Owen concluded that the scriptural and historical evidence proves that the original Hebrew scriptures were pointed.

Owen averred that the Hebrew points in the holy scriptures were of utmost importance because "[v]owels are the life of words; consonants without them are dead and immovable."[512] Owen favorably quoted Hebraist Radulphus Cevallerius who opined that having an unpointed Hebrew text of scripture is to pluck up the scripture by the roots "for without the vowels and notes of distinction it hath nothing firm and certain."[513] Owen also favorably quoted Professor of Hebrew Johannes Isaac (1515-1557): "He that reads the Scriptures without points is like a man that rides a horse without a bridle; he may be carried he knows not whither."[514] An unpointed Hebrew Old Testament would make God the author of confusion, which he is certainly not. *See* 1

Corinthians 14:33.

The issue was of utmost importance in the 17th and 18th centuries. The 17th century Helvetic (Swiss) Consensus Formula of 1675 noted the particular vowel points of the Hebrew Old Testament as being inspired by God.

> But, in particular, The Hebrew original of the OT which we have received and to this day do retain as handed down by the Hebrew Church, "who had been given the oracles of God" (Rom 3:2), is, **not only in its consonants, but in its vowels either the vowel points themselves, or at least the power of the points not only in its matter, but in its words, inspired by God.** It thus forms, together with the Original of the NT the sole and complete rule of our faith and practice; and to its standard, as to a Lydian stone, all extant versions, eastern or western, ought to be applied, and wherever they differ, be conformed.[515]

In a video titled, *The Legacy Standard Bible Exposed*, the narrator explained:

> If the integrity of verbal plenary inspiration could be undermined by the denial of the originality of the Hebrew vowel points and the universalist view of Semitic religions could be granted and the obnoxious traditions of the Jews and their fables could be venerated then the stage was set for the stripping of the very name of God himself out of his people's mouths.[516]

He explained Satan's strategy to get people to forget God's true name and substitute the title of heathen god in his place. His strategy will fail because God examines the heart of his worshippers and understands that his sheep can be led astray. God states:

> **If we have forgotten the name of our God, or stretched out our hands to a strange god; Shall not God search this out? for he knoweth the secrets of the heart.** (Psalms 44:20-21 AV)

That does not mean that God's name is unimportant to him. Indeed, from his name flows great blessings.

> Because he hath set his love upon me, therefore will I deliver him: I will set him on high, **because he hath known my name. He shall call upon me, and I will answer him:** I will be with him in trouble; I will deliver him, and honour him. With long life will I satisfy him, and shew him my salvation. (Psalms 91:14-16 AV)

It is for this reason that God is against the publishers of the modern Bibles who conceal his name from people and substitute heathen gods like Baal and Yahweh. The Bible publishers "steal' God's words from his Holy Bible.

> How long shall this be in the heart of the prophets that prophesy lies? yea, they are prophets of the deceit of their own heart; **Which think to cause my people to forget my name** by their dreams which they tell every man to his neighbour, **as their fathers have forgotten my name for Baal**. The prophet that hath a dream, let him tell a dream; and he that hath my word, **let him speak my word faithfully**. What is the chaff to the wheat? saith the LORD. Is not my word like as a fire? saith the LORD; and like a hammer that breaketh the rock in pieces? Therefore, behold, **I am against the**

prophets, saith the LORD, that steal my words every one from his neighbour. Behold, **I am against the prophets, saith the LORD, that use their tongues, and say, He saith.** (Jeremiah 23:26-31 AV)

Sadly, the myth started by Elias Levita that the original Hebrew text was unpointed is the orthodox view today. Nowadays, the pointings in the Hebrew text are widely rejected as modern emendations made by the Masorites. Through that one myth, the apostate "Christians" have joined with the Jews and Catholics to remove the pesky vowels from the Hebrew Old Testament. The minions of Satan are now able to reconstruct YHVH and change it from Jehovah to Yahweh.

Dr. John Hinton, Ph.D., deconstructs the myth that the original Hebrew scriptures did not have vowel points.

> First we must deal with the common myth and that is that there are no vowels expressed in the Hebrew text. This is a convenient line of nonsense for those who want to change the text to fit their own views, but it is a dishonest line. Elaborate diacritic marks, called pointing by English-speaking Hebrew scholars, provide extensive information for vowels, doubled letters, stops, and other phonological features. Bible "correctors" are either ignorant of this fact or they pretend that they do not exist. Those who are aware of them and argue that they may be ignored because they were introduced into the text by the Massoretes at a later date are giving themselves free rein to alter virtually every word in the entire Hebrew Old Testament. Not only do these biblical detractors deny God's promise to forever preserve his word, every jot and tittle, but they open the door for Bible manipulation that has

no other criteria than personal judgment or fancy. If we are to deny the Masoretic reading we can do no end of mischief to the text by inserting our own vowels, doubled letters, and stops. This allows us to change positives into negatives, passives into actives and vice versa, statement verbs into causative verbs and vice versa, to convert verbs into nouns and vice versa, and to even change the entire meaning of the verb itself. Many words could have several or even a dozen different varied meanings by toying with the pointing. Furthermore, some diacritics indicate different letters entirely. A dot over the right side of a shin indicates an SH, while a dot over the left side of it indicates an S. A dot inside of a *vav* is pronounce like a long U while a dot over the *vav* turns it into an O, so the removal or addition of such a dot is fair game to the Yahweh crowd. A dot inside a Pe is pronounced like P, while if it lacks a dot it become an F. Similarly a Bet with a dot is a B and a V without one. A number of other letters have similar features of changing their sounds according to the presence or position of a dot. If we are to ignore the vowel pointings, we are equally justified in changing S to SH and vice versa, or many other consonant changes, since the Massoretes were responsible for the consonant identifying diacritics as well. Suggestions to alter the text is a common method of attacking the Bible that has been employed by Bible-scoffing scholars in academia for over 100 years, it is a common practice that I encountered frequently among fellow students in Hebrew classes. The practice is taught and encouraged by those who consider the Bible to be mythology.

It is amazing to see this being done by people who

claim to honor the Bible. Dr. G.A. Riplinger, in her tome, In Awe of His Word, points out that ignoring the vowel marks in the Hebrew allow Jews and atheists to remove future references to our Saviour from the Old Testament by toying with these vowels. [Riplinger, pp. 433-434]. For this reason vowelless Tanakhs (Hebrew name for Old Testament) are sometimes used. In fact, if the Masoretic diacritics are ignored, there is scarcely a word in the entire Bible, if there is any at all, that cannot be altered or changed completely. Why is it that alleged Bible-believers think that it is wrong to change words in the Bible into entirely different words, but it is alright to ignore the reading of the Hebrew text and alter the name of God without any evidence to support their altered reading other than the opinion of 19th century atheists? In fact, they are changing it when linguistic evidence shows that the pronunciation that they are using is wrong.[517]

The vowel points for YHVH prove that the Hebrew YHVH cannot be translated into Yahweh. Yahweh is missing a vowel. There are three vowel points. Yahweh only has two vowels. *Vav* (ו) can only be pronounced as a hard "v" sound in this context. Yahweh argues for a soft "w" sound. The soft "w" sound is an Arabic pronunciation of *vav* (ו); it is not Hebrew.[518] The soft vowel sound required for Yahweh makes no sense; since, in this context, the *vav* (ו) would be preceded by the vowel point *holem* having a long "o" sound and followed by another vowel point *kamatz* with a short "a" sound. That would be three vowel sounds in a row. If we stick with the three vowel points and go with the soft consonants preferred by the Yahweh camp, the actual pronunciation for Yahweh ends up being Yahowah (Y-eh-h-oh-ow-ah-h). That sounds nothing like Yahweh. The proper construction should be Jehovah (J-eh-h-oh-v-ah-h). Finally, the correct English translation for *yod* (׳) require a hard "J" sound. Indeed, all the Hebrew words starting with *yod* (׳) like Joseph, Jerusalem, Jericho, etc. are translated with a hard "J" sound in English. *See* Psalms 119:73 in the KJV where *yod* (׳) is rendered *jod* in English. But Yahweh needs a soft "Y" sound.

The vowel points in the original Hebrew Old Testament scriptures impeach the claim that the Tetragrammaton YHVH is Yahweh. The clear evidence establishes that the AV translation of Jehovah is correct. Dr. John Hinton explains how the duped "Christians" are being led astray by ignorantly following the superstitious beliefs of heathen scholars and their god, Yahweh.

> What is amusing is that those who make a big deal out of the conversion to J, and who contradict the Bible by calling God Yahweh while still calling themselves Bible-believers generally know about as much about Hebrew as the average Australian aborigine knows about Lithuanian. It troubles me how very few people realize that the god that they now worship, named Yahweh, is derived from a storm god created by atheist scholars following in the steps of the late 19th century skeptics, and that these atheists are feeding them much of their theology.[519]

God has locked in Jehovah as his name in his inspired Old Testament. In Psalms 68:4 we find that God identifies himself as **JAH**, a contraction of ***JEHOVAH***.

> Sing unto God, sing praises to his name: extol him that rideth upon the heavens by his name **JAH**, and rejoice before him. (Psalms 68:4 AV)

In Exodus 15:2, the AV translators translated **JAH** as LORD.

> **The LORD [JAH]** is my strength and song, and he is become my salvation: he is my God, and I will prepare him an habitation; my father's God, and I will exalt him. **The LORD [JEHOVAH]** is a man of war: **the LORD [JEHOVAH]** is his name." (Exodus 15:2-3 AV)

JAH (י ה) is a contraction of *JEHOV*AH. The AV translators correctly rendered JAH as LORD in the AV. Indeed at Exodus 15:2. Jehovah was commonly translated as the LORD with all capital letters in the AV. For example, in the very next verse, after we find the AV translators rendered JAH as the LORD in Exodus 15:2, the AV translators translated Jehovah as the LORD in Exodus 15:3. The translators understood that **JAH** was a contraction of *JEHOV*AH.

God himself said his name is JAH in Psalms 68:4; he also said his hame is JEHOVAH in Exodus 6:3. Thus equating the two names, and confirming that JAH is a contraction of JEHOVAH. Indeed, God states in Psalms 83:10 "That men may know that thou, **whose name alone is JEHOVAH**, art the most high over all the earth."

A theophoric name embeds the name of God in a person's name and indicates something about God or a person's relationship with God. God has locked in his name as Jehovah by using of two sets of theophoric names.[520] JAH is seen as part of the theophoric names in the Bible.[521] JAH = IAH as a suffix in theophoric names. Below are some examples.

Ama**zi**ah (1 Kings 12:21) means Jehovah is

mighty.

Athal**iah** (2 Kings 11:3) means afflicted of Jehovah.

Hezek**iah** (2 Kings 18:1) means Jehovah is my strength.

Jedid**iah** (2 Samuel 12:25) means beloved of Jehovah.

Jerem**iah** (Jeremiah 27:1) means Jehovah has founded.

Jos**iah** (1 Kings 13:2), means whom Jehovah heals.

Obad**iah** (1 Chronicles 3:21) means servant of Jehovah.

Ur**iah** (2 Samuel 11:3), means Jehovah is my light.

Zachar**iah** (2 Kings 14:29) means Jehovah remembers.

Zedek**iah** (1 Kings 22:11) means Jehovah is righteous.

The Yahweh worshipers claim that JAH is not a contraction of Jehovah but rather an abbreviation of Yahweh that should be rendered YAH. Indeed, the LSB changes JAH to YAH in Psalms 68:4, with a footnote claiming that YAH is a "shortened form of Yahweh." There is a problem with that argument. The theophoric name Elijah is a fly in their ointment. Eli**jah** means my God is **JAH (JEHOVAH)**. The LSB translators did not change Elijah's name. The LSB repeatedly refers to him as Elijah, not Eliyah, as their allegiance to Yahweh requires. *See, e.g.*, 1 Kings 18 LSB. Indeed, all English Bible Versions, including the Hebraic Roots Bible, render the Hebrew as Elijah in English.

The theophoric name Eli**jah** stands as testimony that God's name in English is **JAH**, which is a contraction of **JEHOVAH**. The very text of the LSB containing Eli**jah**'s name impeaches the LSB claim that the LORD's name is Yahweh.

Another problem with the Yahweh worshipers' argument

is that there is another set of theophoric names based on an abreviation of God's name. Those theophoric words make Yahweh an impossibility. Those thosphoric names start with **JEHO**, which is an abbreviation of **JEHO***VAH*. **JEHO** uses the first two consonants of **JEHO***VAH* to form the prefix in theophoric names. Below are some examples.

> **Jeho**adah (1 Chronicles 8:36) means Jehovah has adorned.
> **Jeho**addan (2 Chronicles 25:1) means Jehovah delights.
> **Jeho**ahaz (2 Kings 10:35) means Jehovah has grasped.
> **Jeho**ash (2 Kings 11:21) means Jehovah is strong.
> **Jeho**hanan (1 Chronicles 26:3) means Jehovah has been gracious.
> **Jeho**iachin (2 Kings 24:6) means Jehovah appoints.
> **Jeho**iada (2 Samual 8:18) means Jehovah knows.
> **Jeho**iakim (2 Kings 23:34) means Jehovah raises up.
> **Jeho**iarib (1 Chronicles 9:10) means Jehovah contends..
> **Jeho**nadab (2 Kings 10:15) means Jehovah is noble.

Notice that JEHO has two syllables. That fact excludes Yahweh as the root because Yahweh has two syllables in total, and the vowel sounds are not the same. JEHO has a short "e" sound followed by a long "o" sound. There is no long "o" sound in Yahweh. Yahweh has a short "a" sound followed by a short "e" sound. The vowels in the theophoric names beginning with JEHO do not match the vowel sounds in Yahweh. God is revealing through the theophoric names that his name in English can only be Jehovah; it is impossible that God's name is Yahweh.

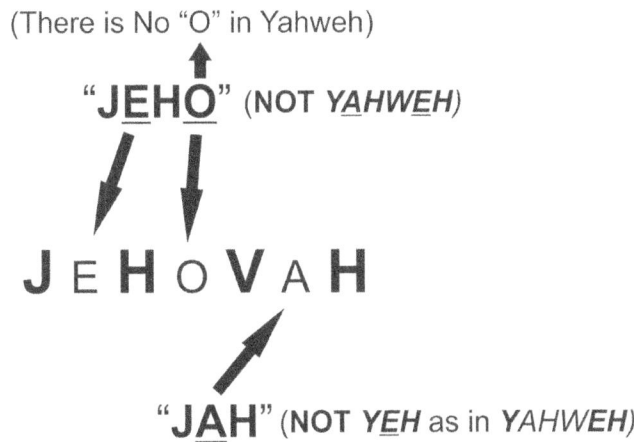

Elijah means my God is **JAH** (**JEHOVAH**)

JAH is a contraction of **JEHOVAH**. See Psalms 68:4. It is used in the suffix of theophoric names in the Bible in the form of IAH, as in Jos**iah**. **JEHO** is an abbreviation of **JEHO**VAH. It is used in the prefix of theophoric names such as **Jeho**adah. The "o" poses a serious problem for the Yahweh promoters. There is no "o" in Yahweh. There is no way to fit Yahweh into both sets of theophoric names. The vowels must be as in Jehovah and cannot be as in Yahweh. God has locked in his divine name as Jehovah in English by these two sets of theophoric names. Confirmation that God's name in English is Jehovah is found in the theophoric name Elijah. Eli**jah** means my God (אל) is **JAH** (יה) (**JEHOVAH**). The theophoric name Elijah makes Yahweh an impossibility. All English Bible versions, including the LSB and the Hebraic Roots Bible, render the Hebrew אליה as Eli**jah** in English. The theophoric name Elijah impeaches rendering the Tetragrammaton (YHVH) as Yahweh in the modern English Bible versions.

44 Jesus is Lord

English-speaking devotees in the Hebrew Roots movement eschew the name of Jesus. They replace the name of Jesus with Yahoosha, Yehoshua, Yahshua, Yeshu, and many other variations. For example, a Hebrew Roots movement Bible, the Hebraic Roots Bible, substituted Yahshua in place of Jesus. Those in the Hebrew Roots movement claim faith in Christ, but they reject the name Jesus because their Christ is not the biblical Jesus Christ.

AV	Hebraic Roots Bible
The book of the generation of **Jesus** Christ, the son of David, the son of Abraham. (Matthew 1:1 AV)	The Book of the genealogy of **Yahshua** Messiah the Son of David, the son of Abraham. (Matthew 1:1 Hebraic Roots Bible)

The Sacred Name movement (a.k.a. Hebrew Roots movement) is founded on the mystical philosophy of the Jewish Kabbalah.[522] Practitioners of the Kabbalah use the names of God as magical incantations to cast "spells" and invoke the power of devils to serve them.[523]

Michael Hoffman explains that "[l]ike the Talmud, the Kabbalah supersedes, nullifies and ultimately replaces the Bible."[524] Lawrence Fine, Professor of Jewish Studies and prominent scholar of medieval Judaism and Jewish mysticism, reveals that the Kabbalah contains the "true" meaning of the Old Testament. The "simple" meaning of the biblical language recedes into the background as the symbolic meaning contained in the Kabbalah supersedes the Bible and takes control. There is a code to the true meaning in the bible that can only be unlocked through the Kabbalah.

> [T]he reader must become accustomed to regarding biblical language in a kabbalistically symbolic way. The Kabbalists taught that the Torah is not only the speech or word of God, but is also the many names of God or expression of God's being. It is a vast body of symbols, which refers to the various aspects of divine life, the sefirot, and their complex interaction. **The simple meaning of biblical language recedes into the background as symbolic discourse assumes control**. The true meaning of Scripture becomes manifest only when it is read with the proper (sefirotic) code. **Thus the Torah must not be read on the simple or obvious level of meaning; it must be read with the knowledge of a kabbalist who possesses the hermeneutical keys with which to unlock its *inner* truths.**[525]

The Kabbalah at Zohar III, 152a states: "Thus the tales related to the Torah are simply her outer garments, and woe to the person who regards that outer garb as the Torah itself! For such a person will be deprived of a portion in the world to come."[526] That passage in the Kabbalah puts a curse on anyone who tries to read the bible for what it actually says, instead of with the mystical gloss put on it by the Kabbalah.

The Kabbalah is Judaic mystical practices that were adopted by the Jews from Babylon. Mystic and founder of the pantheistic Theosophical Society, H.P. Blavatsky, described the Kabbalah as: "The hidden wisdom of the Hebrew Rabbis of the middle ages derived from the older secret doctrines concerning divine things and cosmogony, which were combined into a theology after the time of the captivity of the Jews in Babylon. All the works that fall under the esoteric category are termed Kabalistic."[527]

The Jewish Encyclopedia acknowledges the Babylonian (a/k/a Chaldean) origins of the Kabbalah (a/k/a Cabala). In addition, the Jewish Encyclopedia explains that Gnosticism flowed from the Jews to the ersatz "Christians." That is yet more authority that Gnosticism flowed from Babylon via the Jewish Gnostics to lay the foundation for the Roman Catholic theology. The esoteric Gnosticism imbued in the Catholic theology was based upon the Jewish Kabbalah.

> The Pythagorean idea of the creative powers of numbers and letters, upon which the "Sefer Yez.irah" is founded, and which was known in tannaitic times . . . is here proved to be an old cabalistic conception. In fact, the belief in the magic power of the letters of the Tetragrammaton and other names of the Deity . . . seems to have originated in Chaldea . . . Whatever, then, the theurgic Cabala was, which, under the name of "Sefer (or "Hilkot" Yez.irah,") induced Babylonian rabbis of the fourth century to "create a calf by magic."

* * *

> But especially does Gnosticism testify to the antiquity of the Cabala. Of Chaldean origin, as

suggested by Kessler . . . and definitively shown by Anz . . . Gnosticism was Jewish in character long before it became Christian.[528]

Magic and occult mysticism runs throughout the Kabbalah. Judith Weill, a professor of Jewish mysticism stated that magic is deeply rooted in Jewish tradition, but the Jews are reticent to acknowledge it and don't even refer to it as magic.[529] Gershom Scholem (1897-1982), Professor of Kabbalah at Hebrew University in Jerusalem, admitted that the Kabbalah contains a great deal of black magic and sorcery, which he explained involves invoking the powers of devils to disrupt the natural order of things.[530] Professor Scholem also stated that there are devils who are in submission to the Talmud; in the Kabbalah these devils are called *shedim Yehuda'im*.[531]

The *Jewish Chronicle* revealed that occult practices such as making amulets, charms, and talismans are taught in Jerusalem at the rabbinic seminary Yeshivat Hamekubalim.[532] That is why Jesus said to the Jews: **"Ye are of your father the devil, and the lusts of your father ye will do."** John 8:44. The bible states clearly that the magic arts are an abomination to the Lord.

> There shall not be found among you any one that maketh his son or his daughter to pass through the fire, or that useth divination, or an observer of times, or an enchanter, or a witch, Or a charmer, or a consulter with familiar spirits, or a wizard, or a necromancer. For all that do these things *are* an abomination unto the LORD: and because of these abominations the LORD thy God doth drive them out from before thee. (Deuteronomy 18:10-12)

The Kabbalah, like the Talmud, graphically blasphemes Jesus. For example, in Zohar III, 282a, the Kabbalah refers to Jesus as a dog who resides among filth and vermin.[533]

The Hebrew Roots movement has a particular animus toward Jesus. Many in the Hebrew Roots movement (a.k.a., Sacred Name movement) claim that Roman Church officials changed Christ's name from YAHSHUA to JESUS. Dr. James A. Robinson of End Times Issue Ministries is one of many persons, who claims that Jesus' name is a "demonic name" that means "hail Zeus." The "hail Zeus" theory for the name Jesus is endemic in the Sacred Name movement.[534] Robinson claims that Christ's name should be "Yahoosha."[535] It is kind of a free-for-all regarding what Christ's true name should be, whether Yahshua or Yahoosha or any number of similar variants. But one thing they agree on is that "Jesus" is some kind of hybrid Greek/Latin that some of them allege means "Hail Zeus." They claim "this change was made to make [the Roman Catholic] religion more acceptable to the pagan culture. Zeus was chief of the Greco-Roman pantheon of gods, so, according to this theory, the supposed new demigod was easily accepted and Christianity was melded with paganism."[536]

One sect in the Sacred Name free-for-all is the Assembly of the Kingdom of Heaven (AKH). AKH has a variant Hebrew construction for Christ, YaHVaHShooa Ha MASHIACH. AKH explains:

> YaHVaHShooa Ha MASHIACH was born a Jew of the tribe of Yudah. He said, "Salvation is of the Jew." He should therefore have the Jewish name. Jesus on the other hand is a combination of Medo-Grecian name; a combination of IEU and Zeus; a marriage between paganism and christianity--Jesus did not exist till the 1700 AD. YaHVaHShooa is the Truth, the true name of the Son of YaHVaH, ELOHIM. Jesus, on the other hand, is a fake, false and strange name popularised and propagated by religion, a counterfeit--a combination of IEU+ZEUS=IESUS, in AD1700 became Jesus.[537]

Please understand that YaHVaHShooa is not a renaming of Jesus; it is a replacement of Jesus. AKH states that "YaHVaHShua and Jesus are not one, nor the same. ... YaHVaHShooa is the Truth, Jesus is the counterfeit, the false or a lie sown by Satan. ... JESUS CHRIST IS AN OUTRIGHT LIE."[538] (uncials in original)

The House of Yahweh® (HOY) is another Sacred Name organization that denies that Jesus is the Christ.[539] Neither HOY nor any Sacred Name sect is a Christian organization because "[w]hosoever denieth the Son, the same hath not the Father: but he that acknowledgeth the Son hath the Father also." 1 John 2:23.

HOY claims that Christ is Yahshua. HOY claims that Jesus Christ is an amalgam of the Greek god Zeus and the Hindu god Krishna. HOY claims that those two gods were joined into one deity, Jesus Christ, by a political decree of the Emporer Constantine.

According to HOY, **"Zeus+Krishna=Jesus Christ."**[540] Thus, HOY claims that Jesus Christ is a heathen composite god who must be rejected. Indeed, HOY calls Jesus a "detestable pagan God."[541] Below is a graphic posted on HOY's website depicting HOY's claimed composition of Jesus Christ.

The chosen Christ of the House of Yahweh (HOY) is "Yahshua." Yahshua is not a another name for Jesus, he is a replacement. HOY has stripped Yahshua of his eternal godhood. HOY states that "Yahshua died; Yahshua suffered death, proving by His dying that He was not an immortal, pre-existent Being."[542] HOY's god Yahshua is clearly a different Jesus Christ from the Jesus Christ of the Bible. Jesus is the eternal God Almighty, creator of heaven and earth. "All things were made by him; and without him was not any thing made that was made." John 1:3. "For by him were all things created, that are in heaven, and that are in earth, visible and invisible,." Colossians 1:16. "Behold, a virgin shall be with child, and shall bring forth a son, and they shall call his name Emmanuel, which being interpreted is, **God with us**." (Matthew 1:23 AV) "I and my Father are one." John 10:30.

> For unto us a child is born, unto us a son is given: and the government shall be upon his shoulder: and his name shall be called Wonderful, Counsellor, The **mighty God, The everlasting Father**, The Prince of Peace. Isaiah 9:6.

We read in Revelation 1:12-13 that Pergamos is the location of "Satan's seat." And what was found in Pergamos? There was a massive temple built to none other than Zeus.[543] So we have it on the authority of God Almighty that Zeus is Satan.

> And to the angel of the church in **Pergamos** write; These things saith he which hath the sharp sword with two edges; I know thy works, and where thou dwellest, even where **Satan's seat** is: and thou holdest fast my name, and hast not denied my faith, even in those days wherein Antipas was my faithful martyr, who was slain among you, where **Satan dwelleth**. (Revelation 2:12-13)

The Hebrew Roots movement is not another kind of

Christianity. It is anti-Christian. Those who hold to the mythology that Jesus is Zeus or any other heathen god have committed the unpardonable sin of ascribing to God the characteristics of the devil. Matthew 12:24-32. They are calling Jesus Satan. Their claim that Jesus Christ instead should be replaced with Yahshua is a rejection of Jesus Christ.

Dr. Michael Brown, who has a Ph.D. in Semitic Languages, states that one could argue for the Hebrew Yeshua for Jesus, but there is no authority for "Yahshua." It is a made-up name not supported by any Biblical authority.

> Why then do some people refer to Jesus as Yahshua? There is absolutely no support for this pronunciation—none at all—and I say this as someone holding a Ph.D. in Semitic languages.[544]

Dr. Brown is mystified by those who would substitute "Yahshua" for Jesus. He addresses the weird and blasphemous claim by some in the Hebrew roots movement that Jesus is a hidden reference to the heathen god Zeus.

> What about the alleged connection between the name Jesus (Greek I--esous) and Zeus?
>
> This is one of the most ridiculous claims that has ever been made, but it has received more circulation in recent years (the Internet is an amazing tool of misinformation), and there are some believers who feel that it is not only preferable to use the original Hebrew/Aramaic name, Yeshua, but that it is wrong to use the name Jesus. Because of this, we will briefly examine this claim and expose the fallacies that underlie it.
>
> According to the late A. B. Traina in his Holy

Name Bible, "The name of the Son, Yahshua, has been substituted by Jesus, Iesus, and Ea-Zeus (Healing Zeus)."

In this one short sentence, two complete myths are stated as fact: First, there is no such name as Yahshua (as we have just explained), and second, there is no connection of any kind between the Greek name I--esous (or the English name Jesus) and the name Zeus. Absolutely none! You might as well argue that Tiger Woods is the name of a tiger-infested jungle in India as try to connect the name Jesus to the pagan god Zeus. It is that absurd, and it is based on serious linguistic ignorance.[545]

***

Although it is claimed that the Encyclopedia Britannica says that "the name Ieusus (Jesus) is a combination of 2 mythical deities, IEU and SUS (ZEUS, a Greek god)" it actually says no such thing. This is a complete fabrication, intentional or not.

In short, as one Jewish believer once stated, "Jesus is as much related to Zeus as Moses is to mice."

Unfortunately, some popular teachers continue to espouse the Jesus-Zeus connection, and many believers follow the pseudo-scholarship in these fringe, "new revelation" teachings. Not only are these teachings and practices filled with error, but they do not profit in the least.

So, to every English-speaking believer I say: Do not be ashamed to use the name JESUS! That is the proper way to say his name in English—just as Michael is the correct English way to say the Hebrew name mi-kha-el and Moses is the correct English way to say the Hebrew name mo-sheh.[546]

There is no good reason for an English speaker to adopt a different language when preaching the gospel to other English speakers. Such conduct only serves to confuse. And "God is not the author of confusion." 1 Corinthians 14:33. The contrivance of English speakers calling Jesus by a purported Hebrew name is a satanic stratagem to beguile the unlearned and unwary to turn away from the true gospel and true Jesus and follow a different gospel and a different Jesus. See 2 Corinthians 11:4.

Calling our Lord "Jesus" in English is important in light of the passage in the inspired English Holy Bible (KJV) that states emphatically that there is no other name under heaven whereby we must be saved.

> Be it known unto you all, and to all the people of Israel, that **by the name of Jesus Christ of Nazareth**, whom ye crucified, whom God raised from the dead, even by him doth this man stand here before you whole. This is the stone which was set at nought of you builders, which is become the head of the corner. **Neither is there salvation in any other: for there is none other name under heaven given among men, whereby we must be saved.** Acts 410-12.

Yahshua is a different Jesus based on a different gospel warned about in the Bible.

> For if he that cometh preacheth **another Jesus**, whom we have not preached, or if ye receive another spirit, which ye have not received, or

another gospel, which ye have not accepted, ye might well bear with him. 2 Corinthians 11:4.

God makes it clear that Jesus Christ is Lord. And God has given Jesus a name that is above all names. In the name of Jesus, every knee shall bow, and every tongue will confess that Jesus Christ is Lord.

Wherefore God also hath highly exalted him, and given him a **name** which is above every name: **That at the name of Jesus every knee should bow**, of things in heaven, and things in earth, and things under the earth; And that **every tongue should confess that Jesus Christ is Lord**, to the glory of God the Father. Philippians 2:9-11.

A little known fact is that one of the names used for Jesus by the Hebrew roots movement, Yeshu, is used by Jews as a curse against Jesus.[547] Tuvia Pollack, writing for *Kehila Times*, reveals that "the name Yeshu can be seen as an abbreviation of *'Yimach Shmo Uzichro,'* may his name and memory be blotted out."[548] Jesus is regularly cursed in the Jewish Talmud by the name of Yeshu.[549] Indeed, there is an ancient Jewish text that is called the *Sefer Toledot Yeshu,* which presents a blasphemous attack on Jesus by rabbinical Jewish authorities.[550] The *Sefer Toledot Yeshu* alleges that Jesus was an illegitimate child, whose miracles were by means of sorcery, who taught a heretical form of Judaism, seduced women, and died a shameful death.[551]

The Talmud, which calls Jesus Yeshu, as an epithet, is the authoritative religious book in Judaism. The Talmud memorializes the traditions of the Jews. Jesus upbraided the Jews for replacing his laws with their man-made traditions.

And he said unto them, Full well ye reject the commandment of God, that ye may keep your own tradition. ... Making the word of God of none effect through your tradition, which ye have delivered: and many such like things do ye. (Mark 7:9, 13 AV)

To what traditions was Jesus referring when he upbraided the Pharisees for using them to transgress and replace the laws of God? Can we find out about those traditions today? Yes; the Talmud is a codification of the traditions of the scribes and Pharisees to which Jesus spoke. Michael Rodkinson (M. Levi Frumkin), who wrote the first English translation of the Babylonian Talmud, states the following in his book *The History of the Talmud*:

> Is the literature that Jesus was familiar with in his early years yet in existence in the world? Is it possible for us to get at it? To such inquiries the learned class of Jewish rabbis answer by holding up the Talmud. **The Talmud then, is the written form of that which, in the time of Jesus, was called the Traditions of the Elders**, and to which he makes frequent allusions.[552] (emphasis added)

So we see that the traditions of the Jews are memorialized in the Talmud. During the time of Christ, the Talmud existed only in oral form, which Jesus referred to as the traditions of the scribes and Pharisees. This early oral tradition is called the Mishnah. It was only after Christ's crucifixion that the Mishnah was reduced to writing. The rabbis later added rabbinical commentaries to the Mishnah, which are called the Gemara.[553] Together these comprise the Talmud, which is now a collection of books.

There are today two basic Talmudic texts, the Babylonian Talmud and the Jerusalem Talmud. The Babylonian Talmud is regarded as the authoritative version and takes precedence over the Jerusalem Talmud.[554] The Babylonian Talmud is based on the mystical religious practices of the Babylonians, which the Jewish Rabbis assimilated during their Babylonian captivity around 600 B.C. The Rabbis then used these occult traditions in place of the word of God. In rabbinic Judaism, the Talmud has primacy and authority over God's word in the Old Testament.[555]

According to the Babylonian Talmud, Tractate 'Abodah Zarah, Folio 17a, Christians are allied with hell. Tractate Sanhedrin, Folio 106a curses Jesus. In Tractate Gittin, Folio 57a, Jesus is described as being tormented in boiling hot semen. In Tractate Gittin, Folio 57b, Jesus has been sent to hell, where he is being punished by boiling excrement for mocking the Rabbis. In Tractate Sanhedrin, Folios 90a and 100b, it states that those who read the gospels are doomed to hell. In Tractate Shabbath, Folio 116a, it states that the New Testament is blank paper and is to be burned. The hatred by Jews against Christ, Christians, and the gospel is so intense that Jews are taught to utter a curse when passing a Christian Church, calling on their heathen god (Hashem) to "destroy this house of the proud."[556]

Rabbi ben Yohai, who believed he was beyond the jurisdiction of God, did not think gentiles were even worthy to live. His views regarding gentiles were that "even the best of gentiles should all be killed."[557] Rabbi ben Yohai is not a rabbi on the fringes of Judaism; he is in fact one of the most revered of rabbis in Judaism; his grave is a shrine in Israel. He authored the Zohar, which is the principle work of the Kabbalah.

The Jews recite *Amidah*, which is a set of eighteen (by some accounts nineteen) weekly Jewish prayers. The twelfth prayer is called *Birkat ha-minim*. The *Birkat ha-minim* is actually a hateful curse against heretics and enemies of the Jews, particularly Christians. The curse was first introduced in the *Amidah* in the first century at Jabneh by Samuel ha Katan, at the request of Rabban Gamaliel II in order to drive followers of Jesus Christ from the synagogues.

The common Jews are as much victims of the Jewish hierarchy as are the Gentiles and Christians. The common Jews are being spiritually brainwashed to the bidding of their rabbis. Jesus explained the process: "Woe unto you, scribes and Pharisees, hypocrites! for ye compass sea and land to make one proselyte, and when he is made, ye make him twofold more the child of hell than yourselves." (Matthew 23:15)

Jews view "Christian" Zionists in the Hebrew Roots movement as "useful idiots," which is a pejorative phrase used by communists to describe Gentile communist propagandists who do not understand the Jewish goals behind communism. Jews have a secret that they keep from the "Christian" Zionists. According to the previously mentioned tractate in the Talmud (*Sanhedrin Folio* 90a), Christians, who are described as those who read the New Testament ("uncanonical books"), have no portion in the world to come.[558] In fact, Jews have a particular hatred for Christians. The hatred by Jews against Christians is so intense that Jews are taught to utter a curse when passing a Christian Church, calling on their heathen god (Hashem) to "destroy this house of the proud."[559] For more information about "Christian" Zionists, read this author's book, *Bloody Zion*.

God warned about just such Jewish machinations, giving rise to Jewish fables and commandments of men that have taken hold in the Hebrew Roots movement.

> For there are many unruly and vain talkers and deceivers, **specially they of the circumcision**: Whose mouths must be stopped, who subvert whole houses, teaching things which they ought not, for filthy lucre's sake. One of themselves, even a prophet of their own, said, The Cretians are alway liars, evil beasts, slow bellies. This witness is true. Wherefore rebuke them sharply, that they may be sound in the faith; **Not giving heed to**

> **Jewish fables, and commandments of men, that turn from the truth.**" (Titus 1:10-14)

Paul speaks to the Galatians about the very Titus, whom he warned in Titus 1:10-14 about not following Jewish fables. Paul reveals in Galatians 2:2-4 that as a Gentile Christian, Titus was not required to be circumcised according to the custom under the Jewish law. Jesus Christ, as the fulfillment of the promise sealed by circumcision, has freed all who believe in him from the circumcision commandment given to Abraham in Genesis 17:11-12. *See* Romans 4:10-14, Galatians 5:2-11. "Behold, I Paul say unto you, that if ye be circumcised, Christ shall profit you nothing." Galatians 5:12. The false brethren, that is, false Christians, were trying to bring Christians into bondage under the Jewish customs. That is what the Hebrew Roots movement today seeks to do.

> And I went up by revelation, and communicated unto them that gospel which I preach among the Gentiles, but privately to them which were of reputation, lest by any means I should run, or had run, in vain. But **neither Titus, who was with me**, being a Greek, was compelled to be circumcised: **And that because of false brethren unawares brought in, who came in privily to spy out our liberty which we have in Christ Jesus, that they might bring us into bondage:** (Galatians 2:2-4)

Paul upbraided Peter for doing some of the same things the Hebrew Roots movement promote. Jesus fulfilled the law. We are saved by God's Grace through faith in Jesus Christ, not by obedience to the ceremonial laws of the Old Testament.

> But when Peter was come to Antioch, I withstood him to the face, because he was to be blamed. For before that certain came from James, he did eat

> with the Gentiles: but when they were come, he withdrew and separated himself, **fearing them which were of the circumcision**. And the other **Jews dissembled likewise with him**; insomuch that **Barnabas also was carried away with their dissimulation**. But when I saw that **they walked not uprightly according to the truth of the gospel**, I said unto Peter before them all, If thou, being a Jew, livest after the manner of Gentiles, and not as do the Jews, **why compellest thou the Gentiles to live as do the Jews?** We who are Jews by nature, and not sinners of the Gentiles, Knowing that **a man is not justified by the works of the law, but by the faith of Jesus Christ**, even we have believed in Jesus Christ, that we might be justified by the faith of Christ, and not by the works of the law: for **by the works of the law shall no flesh be justified.** (Galatians 2:11-16)

Paul made it clear in Galatians 5:2-4 that we are to stand in the liberty God has given us. Once one is born again, there is no need for circumcision. Paul states, by the inspiration of God, that if one gets circumcised, that is evidence that they are seeking to be justified by the law. That person has "fallen from grace."

> Stand fast therefore in the liberty wherewith Christ hath made us free, and be not entangled again with the yoke of bondage. **Behold, I Paul say unto you, that if ye be circumcised, Christ shall profit you nothing.** For I testify again to every man that is circumcised, that he is a debtor to do the whole law. **Christ is become of no effect unto you,** whosoever of you are justified by the law; ye are fallen from grace. (Galatians 5:1-4)

Lo and behold, what does the Hebrew Roots movement

advocate? Circumcision! Tim Kelley, writing for *Al Yisrael*, which is "a Hebrew Roots Fellowship," argues that for Christians, "physical circumcision is still a very important part of God's law."[560] *119 Ministries* is yet another Hebrew Roots organization. It states: "We believe that we are to teach all nations to obey the Torah (Law of God)."[561] *119 Ministries* argues that while circumcision is not required for salvation, Christians should be circumcised in obedience to the law.[562]

This movement calling for circumcision is not new. The Book of Acts reveals:

> Forasmuch as we have heard, that certain which went out from us have troubled you with words, subverting your souls, saying, Ye must be circumcised, and keep the law: to whom we gave no such commandment: (Acts 15:24)

Why are Christians allowed not to get circumcised? The answer is that once one believes in Jesus Christ, he is circumcised inwardly. There is no need for an outward circumcision.

> For he is not a Jew, which is one outwardly; neither is that circumcision, which is outward in the flesh: But he is a Jew, which is one inwardly; and circumcision is that of the heart, in the spirit, and not in the letter; whose praise is not of men, but of God. Romans 2:28-29.

The purpose of the law was to bring us to Christ. Once Christ redeems us by his grace through faith in Jesus Christ, we are no longer under the law. The law is then written in our inward parts. We obey because Christ works through us.

> But before faith came, we were kept under the law, shut up unto the faith which should afterwards be

revealed. Wherefore the law was our schoolmaster to bring us unto Christ, that we might be justified by faith. But after that faith is come, we are no longer under a schoolmaster. For ye are all the children of God by faith in Christ Jesus. (Galatians 3:23-26)

Another name variant for Jesus' name used by many Hebrew Roots movement adherents is Yeshua. They have been taught that, as a Jew, Jesus' actual name in Hebrew should be Yeshua. Jews indeed render Jesus' name in Hebrew as Yeshua.

The Tree of Life Version (TLV) of the Bible is marketed as "a translation created to highlight the Jewish roots of the Christian faith."[563] It replaces Jesus with *Yeshua*. Where in English it states that at the name of Jesus every knee shall bow, the TLV changes it to say that in the name of *Yeshua* every knee shall bow. The average English speaker hearing the name of *Yeshua* would not know who *Yeshua* is. And that is the idea behind the TLV and the Hebrew Roots movement.

KJV	TLV
Wherefore God also hath highly exalted him, and given him a name which is above every name: That at the name of **Jesus** every knee should bow, of things in heaven, and things in earth, and things under the earth; And that every tongue should confess that **Jesus Christ is Lord**, to the glory of God the Father. (Philippians 2:9-11 KJV)	For this reason God highly exalted Him and gave Him the name that is above every name, that at the name of ***Yeshua*** every knee should bow, in heaven and on the earth and under the earth, and every tongue profess that ***Yeshua* the Messiah is Lord**—to the glory of God the Father. (Philippians 2:9-11 TLV) (italics in original)

Notice that the KJV passage says that **"every tongue should confess that Jesus Christ is Lord."** Tongue, in that context, is a word pregnant with meaning. Tongue not only means "[s]peech; words or declarations,"[564] it also means "[a] language; the whole sum of words used by a particular nation. The English tongue...."[565] The Bible distinguishes people by their different tongues (i.e., languages). "I will gather all nations and tongues." Isaiah 66:18.

The TLV has an agenda. It selectively chose to only change the English name for **Jesus** to the Hebrew *Yeshua*. Notably, when it comes to other Jewish names, the TLV sticks with the English rendering and does not change them to the Hebrew tongue. For example, the TLV of Acts 7:14 states: "So **Joseph** sent and called for **Jacob** and all his relatives—seventy-five persons. (Acts 7:14 TLV) The Hebrew name for Joseph is *Yosef*,[566] and the Hebrew name for Jacob is *Yaakov*.[567] However, the TLV does not render their names in Acts 7:14 in Hebrew; instead, it renders them as the English names Joseph and Jacob. But the TLV uses a different rule when it comes to Jesus. The TLV, which purports to be an English translation of the Bible, changed the Lord's name in English (Jesus) to the Hebrew *Yeshua*.

Philippians 2:9-11 informs us that every person will confess that Jesus Christ is Lord in his native tongue. The TLV of Philippians of 2:11 is a strange amalgam of Hebrew (*Yeshua*), Anglicized Hebrew (the Messiah), and English (Lord). Neither a Hebrew speaker nor an English speaker would say *"Yeshua* the Messiah is Lord" as rendered in the TLV of Philippians 2:11. A Hebrew speaker would confess that *Yeshua HaMashiach hoveh Adonai*, and an English speaker would confess that Jesus Christ is Lord.

An English speaker will not confess in the foreign language of Hebrew *Yeshua HaMashiach hoveh Adonai*. But the TLV suggests that an English speaker will confess partly in Hebrew by calling Jesus *Yeshua*. Indeed, the TLV of Philippians 2:11 uses the English Lord instead of the Hebrew Adonai, thus revealing that it is arbitrary and capricious in its use of Hebrew names and titles for God. An English speaker's tongue is English, not Hebrew. It is a contrived affectation for an English speaker to adopt a Hebrew name (*Yeshua*) for Jesus. Hebrew is a foreign tongue not understood by an English speaker. The King James Bible passage in Philippians 2:9-11 impeaches the Hebrew Roots movement's adoption of the Hebrew *Yeshua* in place of the English Jesus. English speakers adopting a Hebrew title for Jesus is part of a nefarious plan to Judaize the gospel.

The TLV is an English Bible, yet it tells English speakers to speak Hebrew when confessing that Jesus Christ is Lord in Philippians 1:9 11. The TLV instructs English speakers that they must confess not that Jesus Christ is Lord but that "*Yeshua* the Messiah is Lord." In Philippians 1:9-11 the TLV uses the anglicized Hebrew "the Messiah" instead of the English "Christ." But in Acts 4:10-12, the TLV uses the Hebrew *ha-Mashiach* instead of the anglicized Hebrew "the Messiah" or English

"Christ." According to the TLV, English speakers must understand that there is no other name under heaven by which we must be saved but *Yeshua ha-Mashiach ha-Natzrati*. The problem is that most English speakers do not know what that means. That English Bible passage in the TLV is not English but Hebrew. It is a foreign language to an English speaker. It is not understandable; it is confusing. "God is not the author of confusion." 1 Corinthians 14:33. Indeed, The TLV tries to reverse what God did at Pentecost, where God ensured that "every man heard them speak in his own language." *See* Acts 2:1-5. God intends for people to get his inspired gospel in their language. A person must receive the gospel in his tongue for him to understand the gospel. The gospel presented in a foreign tongue leaves the recipient without understanding, i.e., without inspiration.

KJV	TLV
Be it known unto you all, and to all the people of Israel, that **by the name of Jesus Christ of Nazareth**, whom ye crucified, whom God raised from the dead, even by him doth this man stand here before you whole. This is the stone which was set at nought of you builders, which is become the head of the corner. **Neither is there salvation in any other: for there is none other name under heaven given among men, whereby we must be saved.** (Acts 410-12 KJV)	[L]et it be known to all of you and to all the people of Israel, that by the name of *Yeshua ha-Mashiach ha-Natzrati*—whom you had crucified, whom God raised from the dead—this one stands before you whole. This *Yeshua* is 'the stone—rejected by you, the builders—that has become the chief cornerstone.' **There is salvation in no one else, for there is no other name under heaven given to mankind by which we must be saved!** (Acts 4:10-12 TLV) (italics in original)

As previously explained, Jews often drop the "a" and call

him Yeshu, which is an epithet against him. The practice of English speakers to call Jesus Yeshua is part of a sinister scheme. It is a devilish stratagem by Judaizers to corrupt the gospel of grace.

The religion of the Jews is a mixture that, on the surface, appears godly but is, in fact, a wholly leavened loaf of heathenism. "Then Jesus said unto them, Take heed and beware of the leaven of the Pharisees and of the Sadducees. . . . Then understood they how that he bade them not beware of the leaven of bread, but of the doctrine of the Pharisees and of the Sadducees." (Matthew 16:6, 12) Paul also warned about the Judaizers who were trying to inject their Judaic doctrine into the church. He warned: "A little leaven leaveneth the whole lump." (Galatians 5:9)

Changing Jesus' name to Yeshua is a subtle way to change the doctrines of the gospel. Rabbi Mordecai Griffin founded Lapid Judaism, which is part of the Hebrew Roots movement. Rabbi Griffin reveals that changing the English Jesus into the Hebrew Yeshua is to change who the Messiah is. Changing Christ's name in English from the English Jesus to the Hebrew Yeshua is a trick by the subtle serpent (see Genesis 3:1) to substitute a false Jesus (called Yeshua) for the true Jesus of the gospel, just as Paul warned would happen in 2 Corinthians 11:4. Rabbi Griffin let the cat out of the bag and disclosed that Yeshua of the Hebrew Roots movement is NOT Jesus. He states that Jesus means nothing.

> When we say that we beleive in Yeshua as the Messiah is THAT the same thing as saying that we believe in "Jesus"?? Yeshua means "salvation". Ychoshua (the longer form of the Messiah's Name) means "HaShem Saves." The name Jesus literally means nothing. It has no meaning what-so-ever.[568]

Rabbi Griffin reveals that calling the Messiah (Christ) Yeshua is for the purpose of bringing Christians back under the yoke of the Jewish law. Rabbi Griffin states:

> Lapid Judaism exists to restore the original faith of Yeshua, the Messiah of Israel. Our mission and vision is to restore Yeshua-centered Judaism to the world. To accomplish this mission, we intend to bring complete and lasting transformation by making true disciples, strengthen families, building communities and proclaiming Yeshua as Messiah expressed in an authentically Jewish Torah observant lifestyle.[569]

When Rabbi Griffin uses the word Torah he is including also the traditions of the Jews memorialized in the Talmud.

> Lapid Judaism is referred to as an "Orthodox" Jewish movement because it adheres to Jewish practice and observance within the guidelines of Talmudic law and its codifiers.[570]

Lapid Judaism is a way to corrupt the gospel of grace and change it into subjugation under Orthodox Hassidic (a.k.a., Chassidic) Judaism.

> Lapid Judaism, as a movement, is defined as Yeshua-Centered Judaism. It is a return, restoration and revival of the original faith of Moshiach and His Talmidim (disciples). Lapid is a tradition with its roots in the Orthodox tradition and its soul linked to the Chassidic movement.[571]

Hassidic Judaism is Phariseeism. Indeed, Rabbi Griffin reveals that the Yeshua of Lapid Judaism is a Pharisee.

> Jesus the Pharisee? Was Jesus (actually It's Yeshua) from the Pharisees? Yeshua the Messiah

was a Pharisee. He taught as a Pharisee, lived as a Pharisee, affirmed the religious practice of the Pharisees, and supported both the Written and Oral Torah as a Pharisee.[572]

What more proof does one need to understand that Yeshua of the Hebrew Roots movement is NOT the Jesus of the Bible? Changing Jesus' name to Yeshua is a change in who Jesus is. Yeshua of the Hebrew Roots movement is a devilish Pharisee. Jesus Christ of the gospel states his unequivocal opinion about the Pharisees that they are vipers and children of hell.

> But woe unto you, scribes and Pharisees, hypocrites! for ye shut up the kingdom of heaven against men: for ye neither go in yourselves, neither suffer ye them that are entering to go in. Woe unto you, scribes and Pharisees, hypocrites! for ye devour widows' houses, and for a pretence make long prayer: therefore ye shall receive the greater damnation. Woe unto you, scribes and Pharisees, hypocrites! for ye compass sea and land to make one proselyte, and when he is made, ye make him twofold more the child of hell than yourselves. Woe unto you, ye blind guides, ... Ye fools and blind: ... Ye fools and blind: ... Woe unto you, scribes and Pharisees, hypocrites! ... Woe unto you, scribes and Pharisees, hypocrites! ... Thou blind Pharisee, ... Woe unto you, scribes and Pharisees, hypocrites! for ye are like unto whited sepulchres, which indeed appear beautiful outward, but are within full of dead men's bones, and of all uncleanness. Even so ye also outwardly appear righteous unto men, but within ye are full of hypocrisy and iniquity. Woe unto you, scribes and Pharisees, hypocrites!... Ye serpents, ye generation of vipers, how can ye escape the damnation of

hell? (Matthew 23:13-33 AV)

The Hebrew Roots movement is a satanic attack on Jesus Christ. This author was sharing Christian tracts that I had prepared with someone who had contacted me. He was passing out the tracts. But in an email, he suddenly asked for the tracts to be in an editable format so that he could change Jesus to "Yahusha."

I responded, in pertinent part:

> Absolutely NOT! You want to replace Jesus with Yahusha because you reject Jesus. [... You] stated, "Jesus has no meaning in Hebrew nor in English." Thus, Yahusha is not a different name for Jesus Christ; Yahusha is a replacement for Jesus Christ. That means that Yahusha is NOT Jesus Christ. You have rejected Jesus Christ. ... You are a devotee of the Hebrew Roots Movement, which is Jewish heathenism. Changing Jesus' name to Yahusha or Yeshua is a subtle way to change the doctrines of the gospel.[573]

That person responded by sending me an email with the following message: "jesus is satan 666 gee zi sigma."[574] That statement reveals the underlying theology of the Hebrew Roots movement. I responded to that email by explaining to him:

> Did you just say "Jesus is Satan"? That is the unforgivable sin! Jesus explains in Matthew 12:24-32 that to attribute to God the characteristics of the devil is the unpardonable sin of blaspheming the Holy Spirit.[575]

He replied with an email containing a series of graphics prepared by one of the many Hebrew Roots movement websites that distinguished Jesus Christ from "Yahusha Messiah."[576] One of the graphics stated: "Yahusha Messiah came from heaven, became flesh was born of a virgin and came from the tribe of Judah and spoke Hebrew." The tract also stated: "Jesus Christ did not come from heaven, was not the Son of Yahuwah and did not die for our sins on a tree." Thus, according to the Hebrew Roots movement "Yahusha Messiah" is not another name for Jesus Christ; "Yahusha Messiah" is another god. It gets worse; the graphics equated Jesus Christ with Baphomet.

The statements by the email writer reveal that Yahusha and the other variants of Jesus in the Hebrew Roots movement are not different Hebrew renderings of Jesus. Those words are replacements of Jesus. They blaspheme Jesus. The Hebrew Roots movement preaches the different Jesus about whom the Apostle Paul warned in 2 Corinthians 114. Calling Jesus Satan is the unforgivable sin. Jesus explains in Matthew 12:24-32 that to attribute to God the characteristics of the devil is the unpardonable sin of blaspheming the Holy Spirit. Those who remain in the Hebrew Roots movement are accursed, just as Paul warned in Galatians 1:8: "But though we, or an angel from heaven, preach any other gospel unto you than that which we have preached unto you, let him be accursed." The logical conclusion of the graphics cited by the email correspondent is that the Hebrew Roots movement considers Jesus Christ to be Baphomet (i.e., Satan). Indeed, that is the conclusion to which the email correspondent came.

The Hebrew Roots movement is based on the principles in the blasphemous Jewish Kabbalah, which is the foundation of Phariseeism. The Pharisees were principally behind the crucifixion of Jesus Christ. Recall, in Matthew 12:24 it was the Pharisees who claimed that Jesus Christ was using the power of Beelzebub to cast out devils.

> But when the Pharisees heard it, they said, This fellow doth not cast out devils, but by Beelzebub

the prince of the devils. ... Wherefore I say unto you, All manner of sin and blasphemy shall be forgiven unto men: but the **blasphemy against the Holy Ghost shall not be forgiven unto men.** And whosoever speaketh a word against the Son of man, it shall be forgiven him: but **whosoever speaketh against the Holy Ghost, it shall not be forgiven him, neither in this world, neither in the world to come.** Matthew 12:24, 31-32.

The Pharisees were the first to be recorded in the Scriptures as committing the unforgivable sin. The Pharisees have not changed; they continue to blaspheme the Holy Spirit through the Kabbalistic Hebrew Roots movement.

Please understand that not all those in the Hebrew Roots movement have committed the unforgivable sin. It is only those who have sunk to such a degree of spiritual depravity to attribute to Jesus Christ the characteristics of the devil who have committed the unforgivable sin. English speakers hoodwinked into calling Jesus Christ Yahoosha, Yahusha, Yahshua, YaHVaHShooa, Yeshua, or Yeshu have not committed an unpardonable sin. But to call Jesus Christ Satan is an unforgivable sin. Why would anyone take part in a movement that portrays itself as "Christian" yet whose leadership rejects and blasphemes Jesus Christ and even calls him Satan?

45   The Dark Secret of the TNIV

According to *The Catholic Encyclopedia*, the Jewish liturgy is the source for the Eucharistic liturgy of the Catholic Church.[577] Athol Bloomer offers a more detailed explanation. Bloomer explains that the Cabalistic mystical concept of the Shekinah presence of God is the source for the Catholic mystical concept of the presence of God in the Eucharist. One scheme used by Jews to alter church doctrines to align with their own is to get the church to buy into the unbiblical terms used in Jewish tradition. Shekinah is an example of that scheme. The word Shekinah appears nowhere in either the Old or New Testaments. Shekinah is a wholly Jewish concept born of their Kabbalah; it is also found in the Jewish Talmud and Targums.

The *Missionary Priests of the Blessed Sacrament* describe the Catholic theology of Christ being really and actually present in the Eucharistic host. The Eucharist is not symbolic; Catholic theology is that the Eucharist is the actual body, blood, soul, and divinity of Christ; it is the visible manifestation of God; it is Shekinah.[578]

The Catholic theology is that the Eucharist is God actually present as Shekinah in the form of bread, and is to be worshiped as God. Pope Benedict XVI, when he held the previous title of

Joseph Cardinal Ratzinger and was formerly the Prefect for the Vatican Office of the Congregation for the Doctrine of the Faith, was viewed as being the preeminent Catholic theologian of his time. Before becoming Pope Benedict XVI, Cardinal Ratzinger explained how the attendant worship of the host during the Catholic liturgy is based upon the Eucharist being Shekinah.[579]

Shekinah was inculcated into the Catholic theology from Judaism. There is an esoteric meaning to Shekinah that is only understood by those initiated into the occult theology of Judaism and Catholicism. Michael Hoffman in his book *Judaism Discovered* reveals that **Shekinah is a Babylonian female goddess**. Shekinah is supposed to represent the benevolent spirit to balance out the malevolent spirit of Lilith. Michael Hoffman explains the secret doctrine of the dual spirits is that they are actually one and the same spirit.[580] "The bogus claim that Lilith and Shekhinah are two distinct entities representing separate forces of black magic and white magic is strictly for the *peti yaamin lekhol davar* ['The fool who will believe anything.']"[581]

Michael Hoffman further explains: "The nucleus of Orthodox Judaism at its deepest, most esoteric level is the sexual propitiation of the myrionymous ['many named'] goddess, Isis-Hecate-Demeter-Ishtar-Shekhinah-Lilith. The consummation of the spiritual and sexual union of the female goddess *Shekhinah* with her male consort (Sefirah Tiferet), the 'Holy One,' into one androgynous being (the *mysterium coniunctionis* of alchemy), is one of the charter objectives of Kabbalistic Judaism, and this mirrors uncannily the theology of the sorcerers of ancient Egypt and Babylon, whose ritual working was dedicated to the magical union of the goddess and the god."

The Catholic/Judaic/Babylonian androgynous god/goddess needs a Bible to support its androgyny. The agents of the Catholic/Judaic/Babylonian religion have done that with an androgynous Bible version. The book publisher Zondervan decided to add insult to injury and further muddy the pure water of God's word with a variation of the New International Version (NIV), it calls Today's New International Version (TNIV). Zondervan is owned by Rupert Murdoch, who is a front man for powerful Jewish interests. Terry Watkins explains:

> In Hebrews 2:17, the TNIV starts wading in some very treacherous water. Some very treacherous and very polluted water.
>
> Hebrews 2:16-17, describes how the Lord Jesus physically came through the seed of Abraham. Verse 17 says that the Lord Jesus, was physically ". . . made like his brethren [Jews]. . ." The TNIV translators, without any Greek evidence, in any manuscript, inserts the female gender "sisters" into the verse. This is a flagrant disregard for the Greek text and adding to God's Word. And it opens the door for some serious satanic feminist and new age teaching. Namely, that Jesus Christ was androgynous – both male and female.
>
> Hebrews 2:16-17, KJB
>
> For verily he took not on him the nature of angels; but he took on him the seed of Abraham. Wherefore in all things it behoved him to be made like unto his brethren, that he might be a merciful and faithful high priest in things pertaining to God, to make reconciliation for the sins of the people.
>
> Hebrews 2:16-17, TNIV
>
> For surely it is not angels he helps, but Abraham's descendants. "For this reason he had to be made like his brothers and sisters in every way, in order

that he might become a merciful and faithful high priest in service to God, and that he might make atonement for the sins of the people"

". . . made like his brothers and sisters IN EVERY WAY. . ."

Notice the TNIV translators addition of "IN EVERY WAY". Why in the world did they "add" the words "in EVERY way"? What in the world do they mean "in EVERY way"?

That's opening the door for some serious false doctrine. Serious. . . Wicked. . . Blasphemous. . . Errors.

In the popular new-age book, The Coming of the Cosmic Christ, author Matthew Fox, writes of this, "made like his brothers and sisters in every way", Christ the TNIV translators have tapped into.

"The Cosmic Christ can be both female and male, . . ." (Matthew Fox, The Coming of the Cosmic Christ)

Feminist Rosemary Radford Ruether, in Sexism and God-Talk, also describes this "made like his brothers and sisters in every way" Christ. Ruether, says ". . .we can encounter Christ in the form of our sister". That's almost identical to the perverted claims of the TNIV translators in Hebrews 2:17 – ". . . made like his brothers and sisters in every way. . ."

"Christ is not necessarily male, nor is the redeemed community only women, but a new humanity, female and male. . . In the language of early Christian prophetism, we can encounter Christ in the form of our sister" (Rosemary Radford Ruether, Sexism and God-Talk)

Radical feminist and lesbian author, Virginia Ramey Mollenkott, was stylistic consultant for the "original" New International Version (NIV). Mollenkott is also a major player in the push for gender-inclusive Bibles [such as the TNIV]. In fact, Mollenkott was a team member of the very first gender inclusive scriptures ever published, An Inclusive Language Lectionary. Not surprising, Mollenkott, also promotes the "male-female" Christ [". . .made like his brothers and sisters in every way. . ."]

"[T]he combination of Wisdom/Christ leads to a healthy blend of male and female imagery that empowers everyone and works beautifully to symbolize the One God who is neither male nor female yet both male and female". (Mollenkott, Virginia Ramey. The Divine Feminine. P. 104).

"The creation story begins by affirming that God is neither male nor female, but both. The first chapter of Genesis emphasizes that both male and female are made in the image of the creator God." (Virginia Ramey Mollenkott, Gender Diversity and the Christian Community, www.theotherside.org/archive/may jun01/mollenkott.html)

NIV member and homosexual activist, Mollenkott, seems to have no respect for the Lord Jesus. As she even perverts the Lord Jesus Christ into an effeminate, "gender-bender", "fairy":

"Jesus, whom Paul refers to as the second adam (sic), also defied gender norms. He didn't marry, although he had the religious obligation to do so at eighteen. He performed acts like cooking or washing the feet of his disciples – acts culturally assigned to wives or slaves, not to a free male, . . ." (Virginia Ramey Mollenkott, Gender Diversity and the Christian Community, www.theotherside.org/archive/may-jun01/mollenkott.html)

NIV consultant Mollenkott also stated in a news conference, that Jesus Christ was "chromosomally female":

"You might be interested to know that. . . Jesus remained chromosomally female throughout life." (Virginia Mollenkott, National Council of Churches news conference, cited in The Language of the King James Bible, Gail Riplinger, p. 114)

Researching the TNIV, I kept asking myself, "What happened to the fear of the Lord?" How can the TNIV translators (CBT), publisher (Zondervan) and copyright holder (IBS) intentionally add, delete, change and distort the words of God? How can they intentionally add words that clearly pervert the Lord Jesus Christ?[582]

Throughout the TNIV can be found subtle changes aimed at de-masculinizing Jesus Christ. Typically, this is done by replacing the masculine pronoun or noun with a neuter pronoun or noun.

AV (KJV)	TNIV
For since by man came death, by **man** came also the resurrection of the dead For as in Adam all die, even so in Christ shall all be made alive. 1 Corinthians 15:21-22 AV (KJV).	For since death came through a human being, the resurrection of the dead comes also through a **human being**. For as in Adam all die, so in Christ all will be made alive. 1 Corinthians 15:21-22 (TNIV).

The passage in 1 Timothy 2:5 has been changed in the TNIV from describing Jesus as a man to describing him as the neuter "human."

AV (KJV)	TNIV
For there is one God, and one mediator between God and men, **the man Christ Jesus**. 1 Timothy 2:5. AV (KJV)	For there is one God and one mediator between God and human beings, **Christ Jesus, himself human**. 1 Timothy 2:5 (TNIV)

Jesus goes from "he" who came down as the bread of life to "that" bread of life in the TNIV John 6:33.

AV (KJV)	TNIV
For the bread of God is **he** which cometh down from heaven, and giveth life unto the world. John 6:33 AV (KJV)	For the bread of God is **that** which comes down from heaven and gives life to the world. John 6:33 (TNIV)

In John 15:13, Jesus is a "man" who laid down "his" life for "his" friends. In the TNIV they went through the odd phraseology in describing Jesus in the neuter as "one" who laid down "one's" life for "one's" friends.

AV (KJV)	TNIV
Greater love hath no **man** than this, that a **man** lay down **his** life for **his** friends. John 15:13 AV (KJV)	Greater love has no **one** than this: to lay down **one's** life for **one's** friends. John 15:13 (TNIV)

There are clues to the Jewish influence in the new Bible versions. Babylonian Judaism is a religion of devils. In the New Revised Standard Version (NSRV) of Isaiah 34:14, it mentions a night devil, Lilith, that is unique to the traditions of Babylonian Judaism (e.g., Baba Bathra 73a), but is not supported by the original tongue of the Isaiah passage, Hebrew. "Wildcats shall meet with hyenas, goat-demons shall call to each other; there too **Lilith** shall repose, and find a place to rest." (Isaiah 34:14 NRSV) The correct translation of Isaiah 34:14 makes no mention of Lilith: "The wild beasts of the desert shall also meet with the wild beasts of the island, and the satyr shall cry to his fellow; the screech owl also shall rest there, and find for herself a place of rest." (Isaiah 34:14 AV)

Lilith is known in demonology as a succubus. Talmud, tractate Shabbath, folio 151b states: "One may not sleep in a house alone, and whoever sleeps in a house alone is seized by Lilith." A footnote in Niddah, folio 24b describes Lilith as "[a] female demon of the night, reputed to have wings and a human face." One researcher stated: "Lilith is equated with a 'first Eve', the feminine dark side of the divine and goddesses such as Isis, Astarte, the Black Madonna or Queen of Demons and other false gods. The myth of Lilith is a gnostic perversion of the Biblical account of Creation and Adam and Eve."[583]

Someone with an intimate knowledge of the Babylonian traditions of Judaism inserted the night devil Lilith into the NRSV Isaiah 34:14 passage. God speaks of days like today, with the new corrupted Bible versions. "Behold, the days come, saith the Lord GOD, that I will send a famine in the land, not a famine of bread, nor a thirst for water, but of hearing the words of the LORD. Amos 8:11.

The TNIV is using gender-neutral language to describe Jesus as an esoteric means of subliminally conditioning the *goyim* to accept the androgynous god/goddess that is part and parcel of the Judaic/Catholic/Babylonian theosophy. Prominent scholar and professor of Jewish studies Lawrence Fine states that the true meaning of the Old Testament can only be unlocked through the "sefirotic code" in the Kabbalah.[584] Fine states that the covert symbolic language of the Kabbalah supersedes the simple overt meaning of biblical language.[585] Fine explains that the Kabbalah reveals "the many names of God or expression of God's being."[586] There is a vast body of hidden symbols and codes in the Kabbalah which reveal the various ways in which the gods (sefirot) of the Kabbalah interact with one another.

Athol Bloomer explains that this secret "sefirotic code" in the Kabbalah is the foundation for the true, but hidden, meaning behind the Catholic Eucharist. Bloomer explains that the god of the Kabbalah, who is called Ein Sof is made up of ten attributes (sefirot). Each sefirah (singular of sefirot) is not only designated as a particular trait of Ein Sof but is also an anthropomorphic part of that one god. In addition, each sefirah is either a god or a goddess in its own right.

The first nine sefirot (plural of sefirah) are, in turn, divided evenly into three triads, containing three sefirot each and representing three major sections of the anthropomorphic parts of the mystical body of Ein Sof. The tenth sefirah is the Shekinah (a/k/a Malkuth), which is not part of the three triads.[587] When Jewish Catholics speak of the Trinity they are not referring to the Father, Son, and Holy Spirit as revealed in the Bible, but rather to the three triads set forth in the Kabbalah.

The Kabbalah describes the lower third triad of its heathen

god (Ein Sof) as made up of three sefirot: 1) Netzach (Endurance/Victory), 2) Hod (Majesty/Glory), and 3) Yesod (Foundation).[588] Athol Bloomer reveals that Netzach and Hod are the right and left legs of Ein Sof, and Yesod is Ein Sof's phallus. Bloomer explains that the light and power of the sefirot are channeled through the phallic god Yesod to the last Sefirah, which is the Shekinah (a/k/a Malkuth).[589] This phallic god is part of the blatantly erotic interpretation of the Jewish god found in the Kabbalah.[590] Rabbi Geoffrey W. Dennis in *The Encyclopedia of Jewish Myth, Magic, and Mysticism* explains: "The *Zohar* includes multiple interpretations built around the concept of God's genitals."[591]

The Kabbalah infuses orthodox Judaism with a powerful undercurrent of phallic worship and practice, including sex magic.[592] The sex magic is an offshoot of the secret doctrine in Judaism, which is a common doctrine found in secret societies, that the mystic can find redemption through an "heroic" willingness to do evil.[593] The secret rabbinic doctrine is that evil can be redeemed by embracing it; there is a spiritual good in doing evil.[594] That explains why Jesus said to the Jews: "Ye are of your father the devil, and the lusts of your father ye will do."John 8:44.

Moshe Idel, in *Hasidism Between Ecstasy and Magic*, explains that "the concept of the descent of the *Zaddiq* [Jewish mystic or saint], which is better known by the Hebrew phrase, *Yeridah zorekh Aliyah*, namely the descent for the sake of the ascent, the transgression for the sake of repentance. . . . Much attention has been paid to this model because of its essential affinities with Zoharic and Lurianic Kabbalah . . . this model was a very important one in Hasidic thought."[595] That concept is the core belief in the system of "black magic." The source of this secret doctrine of "black magic" is Babylon.[596] The oldest texts for this Babylonian black magic in Judaism are the texts *Sifrei h-Iyyun*, *Sefer ha-Bahair*, and the *Hikoth Yesirah*, which is also known as the *Sefer Yetzirah*.[597]

Athol Bloomer explains that the Yesod (Jesod) unites the Shekinah and the Tif'eret. Tif'eret is the offspring of Hokhmah and Binah.⁵⁹⁸ The Hokmah and Binah are two of the three sefirot of the divine head of the mystical body of the Ein Sof (Kether is the third sefirah). Tif'eret is not only a god himself, but he also represents the heart and torso of the body of the Kabbalah god, Ein Sof.

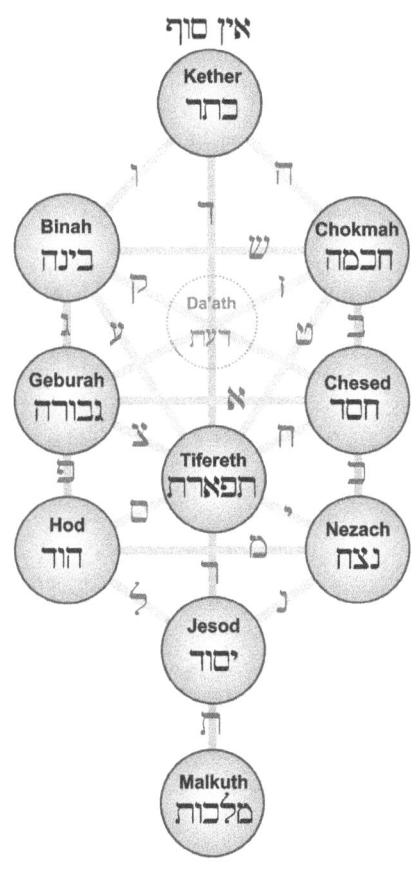

The "tree of life" diagram⁵⁹⁹ depicts the 10 siefrots as they are presented in the Sefer Yetzirah (Book of Formation) and gives a visual representation of the relationship between the different sefirot within the Ein Sof. Note that Malkuth and Shekinah are the same sefirah. In the diagram, only Malkuth is depicted. Note also that the spelling varies somewhat from source to source. For example, Chokmah in the diagram is the same as Hokmah and Jesod is the same as Yesod to which Bloomer referred. Jewish scholars readily acknowledge that are many parallels between the Cabalistic concept of god and that found in Buddhism, Hinduism, and so-called Gnosticism.⁶⁰⁰ That is unsurprising since they all flow from the same mystical waters of Babylon. For more information about the Jewish influence in the Roman Catholic Chruch read this author's book, *Solving the Mystery of Babylon the Great*.

From the beginning, it was the Jewish leaders who tried to stop the spread of the gospel. "And they called them, and commanded them not to speak at all nor teach in the name of Jesus." (Acts 4:18 AV) Having failed to stop the gospel, the Jews came up with a plan to plant a false gospel using profane Bibles. This plan was hatched by their god, Satan. Jesus was not using hyperbole when he said to the Jews:

> **Ye are of your father the devil, and the lusts of your father ye will do.** He was a murderer from the beginning, and abode not in the truth, because there is no truth in him. When he speaketh a lie, he speaketh of his own: for he is a liar, and the father of it. John 8:44.

Satan is the kingpin of the heathen religion of the Jews and the apostate religion of their fellow travelers, the Roman Catholics.

> For we wrestle not against flesh and blood, but against principalities, against powers, against the rulers of the darkness of this world, against spiritual wickedness in high places. Ephesians 6:12.

Endnotes

1. What We Believe, Congregational Methodist Church, https://cm-church.org/about-us/what-we-believe/ (last visited on November 3, 2023).

2. Chelsen Vicari, What are America's largest seminaries in 2019?, Christian Post, October 1, 2019, https://www.christianpost.com/voices/what-are-americas-largest-seminaries-in-2019.html.

3. Doctrinal Statement, Dallas Theological Seminary, https://www.dts.edu/about/doctrinal-statement/ (last visited on November 3, 2023).

4. Moody Bible Institute Doctrinal Statement, https://www.moodybible.org/beliefs/ (last visited on November 11, 2023).

5. Wheaton College, Statement of Faith and Educational Purpose.

6. What We Believe, Creation Ministries International, http://creation.com/about-us#what_we_believe.

7. Creation Research Society, Statement of Belief, https://www.creationresearch.org/index.php/about-crs/statement-of-belief (last visited on March 21, 1956).

8. Creation Research Society, Statement of Faith, supra.

9. Bruce M. Metzger and Bart D. Ehrman, the Text of the New Testament: Its Transmission, Corruption, and Restoration, Fourth Edition, Oxford University Press, at 273 (2005).

10. Bruce M. Metzger and Bart D. Ehrman, the Text of the New Testament: Its Transmission, Corruption, and Restoration, Fourth Edition, Oxford University Press, at 274, n.5 (2005).

11. Bruce M. Metzger and Bart D. Ehrman, the Text of the New Testament: Its Transmission, Corruption, and Restoration, Fourth Edition, Oxford University Press, at 322 (2005).

12. Bruce M. Metzger and Bart D. Ehrman, the Text of the New Testament: Its Transmission, Corruption, and Restoration, Fourth Edition, Oxford University Press, at 275 (2005).

13. Bruce M. Metzger and Bart D. Ehrman, the Text of the New Testament: Its Transmission, Corruption, and Restoration, Fourth Edition, Oxford University Press, at 340 (2005).

14. Aaron Brake, Does the Lack of Original Autographs Make Biblical Inerrancy Irrelevant?, March 2, 2018, https://www.str.org/w/does-the-lack-of-original-autographs-make-biblical-inerrancy-irrelevant-#fn:1, quoting Bart D. Ehrman, Misquoting Jesus: The Story Behind Who Changed the Bible and Why (New York: HarperOne, 2007), 7.

15. Bart D. Ehrman, Biography, https://www.bartehrman.com/barts-biography/ (last visited on November 3, 2023).

16. Bart D. Ehrman, Biography, https://www.bartehrman.com/barts-biography/ (last visited on November 3, 2023).

17. Bruce Metzger, Society of Biblical Literature, https://www.sbl-site.org/publications/article.aspx?articleId=638 (last visited on November 3, 2023).

18. See Edward Hendrie, Antichrist:The Beast Reveaed, Great Mountain Publishing, ISBN: 978-0983262787.

19. The Bart Ehrman Blog, Dr. Bruce Metzger – The Greatest New Testament Scholar in North America, September 19, 2015, https://ehrmanblog.org/do-i-have-a-grudge-against-bruce-metzger/.

20. LES GARETT, WHICH Bible CAN WE TRUST?, p. 16 (1982); *See also,* COLLIER'S ENCYCLOPEDIA, volume 22, p. 563.

21. *Id.*

22. Maria Monk, Maria Monk, Awful Disclosures (with supplemental appendix), at 18 (1836) (French language recitation deleted).

23. Paul Serup, Who Killed Abraham Lincoln?, at 228 (2008).

24. Paul Serup, Who Killed Abraham Lincoln?, at 228-29 (2008), quoting The Life and Labours Of the Reverend Father Chiniquy, at 5 (1861).

25. Rebecca Theresa Reed, Six Months in a Convent, at 133 (1835).

26. 1611 King James Bible Introduction, https://www.kingjamesbibleonline.org/1611-Bible/1611-King-James-Bible-Introduction.php (last visited on December 19, 2023).

27. 1611 King James Bible Introduction, https://www.kingjamesbibleonline.org/1611-Bible/1611-King-James-Bible-Introduction.php (last visited on December 19, 2023).

28. 1611 King James Bible Introduction, https://www.kingjamesbibleonline.org/1611-Bible/1611-King-James-Bible-Introduction.php (last visited on December 19, 2023).

29. 1611 King James Bible Introduction, https://www.kingjamesbibleonline.org/1611-Bible/1611-King-James-Bible-Introduction.php (last visited on December 19, 2023).

30. 1611 King James Bible Introduction, https://www.kingjamesbibleonline.org/1611-Bible/1611-King-James-Bible-Introduction.php (last visited on December 19, 2023).

31. DR. LAWRENCE DUNEGAN, NEW ORDER OF BARBARIANS (1990), http://www.thewinds.org/library/order1.html (current as of March 24, 2002).

32. G. A. RIPLINGER, NEW AGE Bible VERSIONS, p. 141-148 (1993).

33. White, James R. The King James Only Controversy: Can You Trust the Modern Translations? (1995), quoted in pertinent part by Peter S. Ruckman, The Scholarship Only Controversy, at 111 (1996).

34. Peter S. Ruckman, The Scholarship Only Controversy, at 111 (1996), quoting Edward F. Hills, Introduction to Unholy Hands on the Bible, Vol. 1, at 25-26.

35. GERARDUS D. BOUW, GEOCENTRICITY, p. 120 (1992).

36. *Id.*

37. You Call *This* a Heresy? The Views of Arius, In His Own Words, The Bart Ehrman Blog, April 25, 2021, https://ehrmanblog.org/the-actual-heretical-views-of-arius-in-his-own-words/.

38. You Call *This* a Heresy? The Views of Arius, In His Own Words, The Bart Ehrman Blog, April 25, 2021, https://ehrmanblog.org/the-actual-heretical-views-of-arius-in-his-own-words/.

39. LES GARRETT, WHICH Bible CAN WE TRUST?, p. 82 (1982).

40. *Id.*

41. SAMUEL C. GIPP, AN UNDERSTANDABLE HISTORY OF THE Bible, p. 70 (1987).

42. *Id.*

43. *Id.* at p. 71.

44. *Id.* at p. 70.

45. *Id.* at p. 71.

46. Samuel KJBB, Tares Among The Wheat (Sequel to "A Lamp in the Dark"), Published on April 29, 2014, https://www.youtube.com/watch?v=-aiHcghIdjM&spfreload=5.

47.Samuel KJBB, Tares Among The Wheat (Sequel to "A Lamp in the Dark"), Published on April 29, 2014, https://www.youtube.com/watch?v=-aiHcghIdjM&spfreload=5.

48.Samuel KJBB, Tares Among The Wheat (Sequel to "A Lamp in the Dark"), Published on April 29, 2014, https://www.youtube.com/watch?v=-aiHcghIdjM&spfreload=5.

49.Samuel KJBB, Tares Among The Wheat (Sequel to "A Lamp in the Dark"), Published on April 29, 2014, https://www.youtube.com/watch?v=-aiHcghIdjM&spfreload=5.

50.*Id.* at p. 71.

51.*Id.*

52.*Id.* at p. 72.

53.LES GARRETT, WHICH Bible CAN WE TRUST?, p. 151 (1982).

54.John William Burgon, The Revision Revised, at 58 (1871).

55.John William Burgon, The Traditional Text of the Holy Gospels, at 85 (1896).

56.LES GARRETT, WHICH Bible CAN WE TRUST?, p. 151 (1982).

57.LES GARRETT, WHICH Bible CAN WE TRUST?, p. 151 (1982).

58.G.A. RIPLINGER, NEW AGE Bible VERSIONS, p. 433 (1993), quoting DEAN BURGON, THE

REVISION REVISED.

59. SAMUEL C. GIPP, AN UNDERSTANDABLE HISTORY OF THE Bible, p. 82 (1987).

60. SAMUEL C. GIPP, AN UNDERSTANDABLE HISTORY OF THE Bible, p. 116-130 (1987).

61. *Id.*

62. *Id.* at 126-29.

63. *Id.* at 131-68.

64. *Id.*

65. *Id.*

66. *Id.*

67. *Id.*

68. *Id.*

69. *Id.* at p. 405.

70. *Id.* at p. 400.

71. *Id.*

72. *Id.* at p. 406.

73. G.A. RIPLINGER, NEW AGE Bible VERSIONS, p. 435 (1993).

74. *Id.* at p. 432.

75. G. A. RIPLINGER, THE LANGUAGE OF THE KING JAMES Bible, p. 66 (1998).

76.*Id.* at p. 132 (quoting *Carlo Martini, In the Thick of the Ministry,* p. 42, the Liturgical Press, Collegeville, Minn., 1990).

77.Arthur Fenton Hort, Life and Letters of Fenton John Anthony Hort, Vol. I, at 111 (1896).

78.G. A. RIPLINGER, THE LANGUAGE OF THE KING JAMES BIBLE, p. xv (1998).

79.*Id.* at p. xv.

80.G.A. RIPLINGER, BLIND GUIDES, p. 19.

81.G.A. RIPLINGER, BLIND GUIDES, p. 19.

82.G.A. RIPLINGER, BLIND GUIDES, p. 19.

83.Gail Riplinger, In Awe of Thy Word, at 441 (2003).

84.Gail Riplinger, In Awe of Thy Word, at 441 (2003), quoting Gerald Hammond, qtd. in Ward S. Allen, The Coming of the King James Gospels, Fayetteville: University of Arkansas Press, 1995, p. 48.

85.Gail Riplinger, In Awe of Thy Word, at 443-445 (2003).

86.DONALD WAITE, DEFENDING THE KING JAMES BIBLE, pp. 241-242.

87.*Id.* at p. 159.

88.JAMES H. SON, THE NEW ATHENIANS, p. 96 (1992).

89.G. A. RIPLINGER, THE LANGUAGE OF THE KING JAMES BIBLE, p. 114 (1998).

90. G.A. RIPLINGER, NEW AGE BIBLE VERSIONS, p. 2 (1993).

91. G. A. RIPLINGER, THE LANGUAGE OF THE KING JAMES BIBLE, p. 128 (1998).

92. Company History: Zondervan Corporation, http://www.answers.com/topic/zondervan (last visited on April 5, 2010).

93. Anton La Vey, Satanic Bible, Harper Collins, *available at* http://www.harpercollins.com/book/index.aspx?isbn=9780380015399 (on sale 12/1/1976); NIV Bible, Harper Collins *available at* http://www.harpercollins.com/books/9780310949862/NIV_Bible/index.aspx.

94. G. A. RIPLINGER, THE LANGUAGE OF THE KING JAMES BIBLE, p. 128 (1998).

95. G. A. RIPLINGER, THE LANGUAGE OF THE KING JAMES BIBLE, p. 128 (1998).

96. Rupert Murdoch's Jewish Origins: a Matter of Controversy, *at* http://www.fpp.co.uk/online/02/05/Murdoch2.html (May 25, 2002).

97. G. A. RIPLINGER, THE LANGUAGE OF THE KING JAMES BIBLE, p. 128 (1998).

98. Copyright in Derivative Works and Compilations, U.S. Copyright Office, https://www.copyright.gov/circs/circ14.pdf (last visited on January 1, 2023).

99. Copyright in Derivative Works and Compilations, U.S. Copyright Office, https://www.copyright.gov/circs/circ14.pdf (last visited on January 1, 2023).

100. Moody Monthly, June 1982, back cover.

101. http://www.kj21.com/.

102. http://www.whidbey.net/~dcloud/fbns/21st.htm.

103. http://www.kj21.com/.

104. Allen Parr, Is the NIV a Corrupt Bible Translation and the KJV the only "Inspired" Translation?, https://www.youtube.com/watch?v=ns-SWo0d77k&t=305s (last visited on January 1, 2023).

105. Of, Webster's American Dictionary of the English Language, https://webstersdictionary1828.com/Dictionary/of (last visited on November 28, 2023).

106. Will Kinney, Calvinism and the King James Bible, http://www.scionofzion.com/calvinism_kjb.htm (web address current as of October 9, 2005).

107. Will Kinney, Calvinism and the King James Bible, http://www.scionofzion.com/calvinism_kjb.htm (web address current as of October 9, 2005).

108. Brooke Foss Westcott, Some Lessons of the Revised Version of the New Testament, at 204-05 (1897).

109. Brooke Foss Westcott, Some Lessons of the Revised Version of the New Testament, at 184-85 (1897).

110. Arthur Fenton Hort, Life and Letters of Fenton John Anthony Hort, Vol. II, at 138-39 (1896).

111. Arthur Fenton Hort, Life and Letters of Fenton John Anthony Hort, Vol. I, at. 250 (1896).

112. Mike Leake, On Those Missing Verses In Your ESV and NIV Bible, July 14, 2015, https://www.mikeleake.net/2015/07/on-those-missing-verses-in-your-esv-and-niv-bible.html.

113. The New Athenians.

114. F. J. A. Hort, The Apocalypse of St. John 1-3, with Introduction, Commentary, and Additional Notes, http://www.westcotthort.com/bookshelf.html (last visited on December 12, 2023).

115. You Call *This* a Heresy? The Views of Arius, In His Own Words, The Bart Ehrman Blog, April 25, 2021, https://ehrmanblog.org/the-actual-heretical-views-of-arius-in-his-own-words/.

116. You Call *This* a Heresy? The Views of Arius, In His Own Words, The Bart Ehrman Blog, April 25, 2021, https://ehrmanblog.org/the-actual-heretical-views-of-arius-in-his-own-words/.

117. White, James R. The King James Only Controversy: Can You Trust the Modern Translations? (1995), quoted in pertinent part by Peter S. Ruckman, The Scholarship Only Controversy, at 111 (1996).

118. Everlasing, American Dictionary of the English Language, https://webstersdictionary1828.com/Dictionary/everlast

ing (last visted on December 12, 2023).

119. D. A. Waite, The Theological Heresies of Westcott and Hort, As Seen in Their Own Writings, The Bible for Today, 1979, https://faithsaves.net/heresies-westcott-hort/.

120. F. J. A. Hort, The Apocalypse of St. John 1-3, with Introduction, Commentary, and Additional Notes, http://www.westcotthort.com/bookshelf.html (last visited on December 12, 2023).

121. Brooke Foss Westcott, Some Lessons of the Revised Version of the New Testament, at 201 (1897).

122. Arthur Fenton Hort, Life and Letters of Fenton John Anthony Hort, Vol. I, at. 414 (1896).

123. Arthur Fenton Hort, Life and Letters of Fenton John Anthony Hort, Vol. I, at. 416 (1896).

124. LES GARRETT, WHICH BIBLE CAN WE TRUST?, p. 49 (1982).

125. Irenaeus, Against Heresies, Book I, Ch. XXIV.

126. Irenaeus, *Against Heresies*, Book III, Chapter XXI, *available at* http://www.ccel.org/ccel/schaff/anf01.ix.iv.xxii.html (last visited March 24, 2010).

127. Rabbi Tovia Singer, Does the Hebrew Word Alma Really Mean "Virgin"?, *available at* http://www.outreachjudaism.org/alma.htm (last visited on April 17, 2010). See also Rabbi Shraga Simmons, Ask Rabbi Simmons, Jesus as the Messiah, *at* http://judaism.about.com/library/3_askrabbi_o/bl_simmons_messiah3.htm (last visited on April 17, 2010).

128. The Word Made Flesh, The Ligonier Statement on Christology, https://store.ligonier.org/the-word-made-flesh-paperback (last visited on November 21, 2023).

129. Ligonier Ministries, https://www.ligonier.org/about (last visited on January 1, 2023).

130. Email from Ask Ligonier to Edward Hendrie, January 4, 2023.

131. Email from Ask Ligonier to Edward Hendrie, January 5, 2023.

132. Email from Ask Ligonier to Edward Hendrie, January 4, 2023.

133. Email from Edward Hendrie to Ask Ligonier, January 5, 2023.

134. Email from Ask Ligonier to Edward Hendrie, January 5, 2023.

135. Email from Edward Hendrie to Ask Ligonier, December 9, 2022.

136. Air Masses, National Oceanic and Atmospheric Administration, https://www.noaa.gov/jetstream/synoptic/air-masses (last visited on January 22, 2024). See also Air Masses and Fronts, National Wildfire Coordinating Group, https://www.nwcg.gov/publications/pms425-1/air-masses-and-fronts#:~:text=Continental%20polar%20air%20masses%20originate,condensed%20onto%20the%20snow%20surface. (last visited on January 22, 2024).

137. Atmospheric Moisture, National Wildfire Coordinating Group, https://www.nwcg.gov/publications/pms425-1/atmospheric-moisture (last visited on Janaury 22, 2024).

138. Air Masses, National Oceanic and Atmospheric Administration, https://www.noaa.gov/jetstream/synoptic/air-masses (last visited on January 22, 2024).

139. Absolute vs. Relative Humidity – What's the Difference?, September 25, 2014, https://www.zehnderamerica.com/absolute-vs-relative-humidity-whats-the-difference/.

140. ALBERTO RIVERA, THE GODFATHERS, Chick Publications, p. 32, 1982 (quoting The Registers of Boniface VIII, The Vatican Archives, L. Fol. 387 and THE CATHOLIC ENCYCLOPEDIA, Encyclopedia Press (1913)).

141. *Id.* at § 881-882.

142. J. A. Wylie, The Papacy is the Antichrist, at 36-37.

143. JOHN PAUL II, CROSSING THE THRESHOLD OF HOPE, p. 11, 1994.

144. ALBERTO RIVERA, DOUBLE CROSS, Chick publications, p. 27, 1981(quoting THE GREAT ENCYCLICAL LETTERS OF POPE LEO XIII, p. 304, Benziger Brothers (1903).

145. Las Angeles Times, December 12, 1984 (quoted by Arthur Noble, The Pope's 'Apology' the First Great Laugh of the New Millennium, http://www.ianpaisley.org/article.asp?ArtKey=apology).

146. ORDERED BY THE COUNCIL OF TRENT, EDITED UNDER ST. CHARLES BORROMEO, PUBLISHED BY DECREE OF POPE ST. PIUS V, 1566, TAN Books, p. 331, 1982.

147. AVRO MANAHATTAN, THE VATICAN BILLIONS, Chick Publications, p.183 (1983).

148. AVRO MANAHATTAN, THE VATICAN BILLIONS, Chick Publications, p.41 (1983).

149. RALPH E. WOODROW, BABYLON MYSTERY RELIGION, p. 72, 1966.

150. COLLIER'S ENCYCLOPEDIA, volume 19, p. 239 (1991).

151. Medieval Sourcebook: Boniface VIII, Unam Sanctam, 1302, http://www.fordham.edu/halsall/source/b8-unam.asp. See also, ALBERTO RIVERA, THE GODFATHERS, Chick Publications, p. 32, 1982 (quoting The Registers of Boniface VIII, The Vatican Archives, L. Fol. 387 and THE CATHOLIC ENCYCLOPEDIA, Encyclopedia Press (1913)).

152. A letter from Cardinal Giuseppe Sarto (who became Pope Pius X in 1903) as quoted in Publications of the Catholic Truth Society Volume 29 (Catholic Truth Society: 1896): 11.

153. The Pontifical Biblical Commission, *The Jewish People and Their Sacred Scriptures in the Christian Bible*, section II A 7, 2002, http://www.vatican.va/roman_curia/congregations/cfaith/pcb_documents/rc_con_cfaith_doc_20020212_popolo-ebraico_en.html#5.%20The%20Unity%20of%20Go

d%27s%20Plan%20and%20the%20Idea%20of%20Fulfilment

154. CATECHISM OF THE CATHOLIC CHURCH, § 882, 1994.

155. *See* CHINIQUY, THE PRIEST, THE WOMAN, AND THE CONFESSIONAL, Chick Publications.

156. Rosamond Culbertson, A Narrative of the Captivity and Sufferings of an American Female Under the Popish Priests, in the Island of Cuba; With a Full Disclosure of Their Manners and Customs, at 48 (1837).

157. Margaret Shepherd, My Life in the Convent: or The Marvelous Personal Experiences of Margaret Shepherd, 216 (1892), https://archive.org/details/mylifeinconvento00shepuoft.

158. Amazing Statements Regarding the Roman Catholic Church, Let There Be Light Ministries, http://www.lightministries.com/id524.htm (last visited on June 19, 2014), quoting Pope Paul VI, as in turn quoted in The Apostolic Digest, by Michael Malone, Book 6: "The Book of Sentimental Excuses", Chapter 4: "The Dogmas of Faith Admit No Alteration Whatsoever," quoting St. Alphonsus De Liguori, True Spouse of Christ, p 352, Benziger Brothers, NY.

159. A. Wylie, The Papacy is the Antichrist, at 36-38.

160. A. Wylie, The Papacy is the Antichrist, at 36-38.

161. A. Wylie, The Papacy is the Antichrist, at 36-38.

162. Webster's American Dictionary of the English Language,

https://webstersdictionary1828.com/Dictionary/immoral (last visited on November 29, 2023).

163. Sam Allberry, Andy Stanley's 'Unconditional' Contradiction, Christianity Today, October 4, 2023, https://www.christianitytoday.com/ct/2023/october-web-only/andy-stanley-unconditional-conference-theology-lgbt.html.

164. Sam Allberry, Andy Stanley's 'Unconditional' Contradiction, Christianity Today, October 4, 2023, https://www.christianitytoday.com/ct/2023/october-web-only/andy-stanley-unconditional-conference-theology-lgbt.html.

165. Sam Allberry, Andy Stanley's 'Unconditional' Contradiction, Christianity Today, October 4, 2023, https://www.christianitytoday.com/ct/2023/october-web-only/andy-stanley-unconditional-conference-theology-lgbt.html.

166. Sam Allberry, Andy Stanley's 'Unconditional' Contradiction, Christianity Today, October 4, 2023, https://www.christianitytoday.com/ct/2023/october-web-only/andy-stanley-unconditional-conference-theology-lgbt.html.

167. The Shocking Question Stanley Asked || Damage control week at Stanley's North Point Community Church, October 6, 2023, https://www.youtube.com/watch?v=JQtGOF-IUYQ.

168. Thanks and Praise from Pastors, NIV, https://www.thenivbible.com/pastor-endorsements/ (last visited on November 11, 2023).

169. Michael Gryboski,, Latest NIV Bible Translation Clearer on Homosexual Sins, Says Theologian, The Christian Post, January 4, 2012, https://www.christianpost.com/news/latest-niv-bible-translation-clearer-on-homosexual-sins-says-theologian.html.

170. Peter Tiersma, Did Clinton Lie?: Defining "Sexual Relations", Chicago-Kent Law Review, Volume 79, Issue3, Articel 24, October 2004, https://scholarship.kentlaw.iit.edu/cgi/viewcontent.cgi?article=3457&context=cklawreview.

171. Did President Clinton's oral sex change US attitudes towards oral sex?, https://www.reddit.com/r/AskHistorians/comments/7ncz6b/did_president_clintons_oral_sex_change_us/ (last visited on November 11, 2023).

172. Did President Clinton's oral sex change US attitudes towards oral sex?, https://www.reddit.com/r/AskHistorians/comments/7ncz6b/did_president_clintons_oral_sex_change_us/ (last visited on November 11, 2023).

173. Stephanie A. Sanders & June Machover Reinisch. Would You Say You "Had Sex" If...?, 281 JAMA 275, 276 (1999), cited by Peter Tiersma, Did Clinton Lie?: Defining "Sexual Relations", Chicago-Kent Law Review, Volume 79, Issue3, Articel 24, at 943, October 2004, https://scholarship.kentlaw.iit.edu/cgi/viewcontent.cgi?article=3457&context=cklawreview.

174. Peter Tiersma, Did Clinton Lie?: Defining "Sexual Relations", Chicago-Kent Law Review, Volume 79, Issue3, Articel 24, October 2004,

https://scholarship.kentlaw.iit.edu/cgi/viewcontent.cgi?article=3457&context=cklawreview.

175. Why Arab Men Hold Hands, The New York Times, May 1, 2005, http://www.nytimes.com/2005/05/01/weekinreview/01basics.html?_r=0.

176. Why Arab Men Hold Hands, The New York Times, May 1, 2005, http://www.nytimes.com/2005/05/01/weekinreview/01basics.html?_r=0.

177. Nadya Labi, The Kingdom in the Closet, The Atlantic, May 1, 2007, http://www.theatlantic.com/magazine/archive/2007/05/the-kingdom-in-the-closet/305774/.

178. Vlad Tepes, Western Complicity in the Rape of Boys in the Islamic World, August 12, 2011, http://vladtepesblog.com/2011/08/12/western-complicity-in-the-rape-of-boys-in-the-islamic-world/.

179. Nadya Labi, The Kingdom in the Closet, The Atlantic, May 1, 2007, http://www.theatlantic.com/magazine/archive/2007/05/the-kingdom-in-the-closet/305774/.

180. Nadya Labi, The Kingdom in the Closet, The Atlantic, May 1, 2007, http://www.theatlantic.com/magazine/archive/2007/05/the-kingdom-in-the-closet/305774/.

181. Effeminate, Webster's American Dictionary of the English Language, https://webstersdictionary1828.com/Dictionary/effeminate (last visited on November 29, 2023).

182. Steve Warren, 'This Is Blasphemy': Dallas Church Pledges Allegiance to Drag Queens and LGBT Agenda, CBN, September 20, 2023, https://www2.cbn.com/news/us/blasphemy-dallas-church-pledges-allegiance-drag-queens-and-lgbt-agenda.

183. Steve Warren, 'This Is Blasphemy': Dallas Church Pledges Allegiance to Drag Queens and LGBT Agenda, CBN, September 20, 2023, https://www2.cbn.com/news/us/blasphemy-dallas-church-pledges-allegiance-drag-queens-and-lgbt-agenda.

184. Krishnadev Calamur, 'Call Me Caitlyn': Bruce Jenner Reveals New Name, June 1, 2015, NPR.

185. Emily Blake, 'I Am Cait': Is Caitlyn Jenner attracted to men?, Entertainment, August 6, 2015, https://ew.com/article/2015/08/06/caitlyn-jenner-sexuality/#:~:text=%22No%2C%20I'm%20not,and%20it's%20apples%20and%20oranges.

186. Caitlyn Jenner vows to 'reshape the landscape' in ESPYS speech, ESPN, July 15, 2015, https://www.espn.com/espys/2015/story/_/id/13264599/caitlyn-jenner-accepts-arthur-ashe-courage-award-espys-ashe2015.

187. Caitlyn Jenner vows to 'reshape the landscape' in ESPYS speech, ESPN, July 15, 2015, https://www.espn.com/espys/2015/story/_/id/13264599/caitlyn-jenner-accepts-arthur-ashe-courage-award-espys-ashe2015.

188. Anugrah Kumar, Christian Post, Christian Bakery Closed for Refusing Lesbian Wedding Cake Breaks Record on Crowdfunding Site With $352,000, July 18, 2015.

189. Anugrah Kumar, Christian Post, Christian Bakery Closed for Refusing Lesbian Wedding Cake Breaks Record on Crowdfunding Site With $352,000, July 18, 2015, http://www.christianpost.com/news/christian-bakery-closed-for-refusing-lesbian-wedding-cake-breaks-record-on-crowdfunding-site-with-352000-141657/#aORrHCwjI0oKMXVS.99.

190. Todd Starnes, Fox News, Oregon Ruling Really Takes the Cake -- Christian Bakery Guilty of Violating Civil Rights of Lesbian Couple, January 21, 2014, http://www.foxnews.com/opinion/2014/01/21/christian-bakery-guilty-violating-civil-rights-lesbian-couple.html.

191. Anugrah Kumar, Christian Post, Christian Bakery Closed for Refusing Lesbian Wedding Cake Breaks Record on Crowdfunding Site With $352,000, July 18, 2015.

192. Todd Starnes, Fox News, Christian Bakers Face Government Wrath for Refusing to Make Cake for Gay Wedding, February 3, 2015, http://www.foxnews.com/opinion/2015/02/03/christian-bakers-face-government-wrath-for-refusing-to-make-cake-for-gay.html.

193. Todd Starnes, Fox News, Christian Bakers Face Government Wrath for Refusing to Make Cake for Gay Wedding, February 3, 2015, http://www.foxnews.com/opinion/2015/02/03/christian-bakers-face-government-wrath-for-refusing-to-make-cake-for-gay.html.

194. Todd Starnes, Fox News, Christian Bakers Face Government Wrath for Refusing to Make Cake for Gay

Wedding, February 3, 2015, http://www.foxnews.com/opinion/2015/02/03/christian-bakers-face-government-wrath-for-refusing-to-make-cake-for-gay.html.

195. Todd Starnes, Fox News, Christian Bakers Face Government Wrath for Refusing to Make Cake for Gay Wedding, February 3, 2015, http://www.foxnews.com/opinion/2015/02/03/christian-bakers-face-government-wrath-for-refusing-to-make-cake-for-gay.html.

196. Masterpiece Cakeshop v. Colorado Civil Rights Commission, 584 U.S. ___ (2018).

197. 135 S. Ct. 2584 (2015).

198. Masterpiece Cakeshop v. Colorado Civil Rights Commission, 584 U.S. ___ (2018) (Thomas, J., concurring).

199. Rod Dreher, The Persecution Of Jack Phillips, August 15, 2018, https://www.theamericanconservative.com/dreher/the-persecution-of-jack-phillips/.

200. Pentagon Manual Details Rules for Transgender Military Personnel, Fox News, July 19, 2016, http://www.foxnews.com/politics/2016/07/19/pentagon-manual-details-rules-for-transgender-military-personnel.html.

201. Howard Slugh Aylana Meisel, Anti-discrimination Laws Are Wielded Against a Shelter for Battered Women, August 16, 2018, https://www.nationalreview.com/2018/08/anti-discrimination-laws-used-against-battered-women-shelter/.

202. Howard Slugh Aylana Meisel, Anti-discrimination Laws Are Wielded Against a Shelter for Battered Women, August 16, 2018, https://www.nationalreview.com/2018/08/anti-discrimination-laws-used-against-battered-women-shelter/.

203. Michael Swift's 1987 Gay Manifesto, http://www.blessedcause.org/protest/Gay%20Manifesto.htm.

204. Steve Baldwin, Child Molestation and the Homosexual Movement, 14 REGENT L. REV. 267, 278 (2002), http://www.mega.nu/ampp/baldwin_pedophilia_homosexuality.pdf.

205. Baldwin, supra, at 271, 278 citing W.D. Erickson et al., *Behavior Patterns of Child Molesters*, 17 ARCHIVES SEXUAL BEHAV., at 83 (1988).

206. Baldwin, supra, at 278.

207. Baldwin, supra, at 274.

208. Baldwin, supra, at 268.

209. Baldwin, supra, at 272-73, 277.

210. Baldwin at 272.

211. Reptilian Pets - Viewer Discretion Advised, Mar 8, 2016, at 8:15, https://www.youtube.com/watch?v=lYRuQ56Mie8.

212. Antonio Subirats, Flat Earth: Globe Earthers Endorse Paedophiles, August 11, 2018, https://www.youtube.com/watch?v=0ihL7lAsEto.

213. TEDx tries to Normalise Pedophilia, July 22, 2018, https://www.youtube.com/watch?v=Wn4ok_W-7d4. TEDx Talk under Review, June 19, 2018, https://blog.ted.com/tedx-talk-under-review/.

214. U.S. House of Representatives, 8th District of Wisconsin, Press Release, U.S. House Passes Rep. Green "Two Strikes Bill," http://www.house.gov/markgreen/PRESS/2000/July00News/NR072500TwoStrikesPassage.htm (website address current as of August 16, 2003). See also http://www.geocities.com/Wellesley/2726/Molester.html (website address current as of August 16, 2003); Jon Donenberg, Keller Attacks Johnson's Vote On 1987 Bill, The Daily Illini Online, October 3, 2000, http://www.dailyillini.com/oct00/oct03/news/printer/news01.shtml (website address current as of August 16, 2003).

215. TEDx tries to Normalise Pedophilia, July 22, 2018, https://www.youtube.com/watch?v=Wn4ok_W-7d4. TEDx Talk under Review, June 19, 2018, https://blog.ted.com/tedx-talk-under-review/.

216. Bill Hoffmann, Tom DeLay: Justice Dept. Wants to Legalize 12 'Perversions', 30 June 2015, NEWSMAX, http://www.newsmax.com/Newsmax-Tv/Tom-DeLay-Justice-Department-perversions/2015/06/30/id/652929/.

217. PAUL ENNS, THE MOODY HANDBOOK OF THEOLOGY, p. 113, 333-34, 391-92 (1989).

218. Paul Enns, The Moody Handbook of Theology, p. 113, 333-34, 391-92, 389-94 (1989).

219. THE COMPACT EDITION OF THE OXFORD ENGLISH DICTIONARY, COMPLETE TEXT REDUCED MICROGRAPHICALLY, OXFORD UNIVERSITY PRESS (1979). *See also,* NOAH WEBSTER, AMERICAN DICTIONARY OF THE ENGLISH LANGUAGE (1828).

220. THE COMPACT EDITION OF THE OXFORD ENGLISH DICTIONARY, COMPLETE TEXT REDUCED MICROGRAPHICALLY, OXFORD UNIVERSITY PRESS (1979).

221. NOAH WEBSTER, AMERICAN DICTIONARY OF THE ENGLISH LANGUAGE (1828).

222. NOAH WEBSTER, AMERICAN DICTIONARY OF THE ENGLISH LANGUAGE (1828). *See also,* D.P. SIMPSON, CASSELL'S LATIN DICTIONARY p. 500-01 (1982).

223. D.P. SIMPSON, CASSELL'S LATIN DICTIONARY p. 501 (1982).

224. *Id.* at 392.

225. *Id.* at 392.

226. C.E. Carlson, The Zionist Created Scofield "bible," http://christianparty.net/scofield.htm (website address current as of August 9, 2003).

227. C.E. Carlson, The Zionist Created Scofield "bible," http://christianparty.net/scofield.htm (website address current as of August 9, 2003).

228. C.E. Carlson, The Zionist Created Scofield "bible," http://christianparty.net/scofield.htm (website address current as of August 9, 2003).

229. C.E. Carlson, The Zionist Created Scofield "bible," http://christianparty.net/scofield.htm (website address current as of August 9, 2003).

230. CYRUS SCOFIELD -- WHO WAS HE? Excerpt from "The Unified Conspiracy Theory," http://www.sweetliberty.org/issues/hoax/scofield.htm (website address current as of August 9, 2003).

231. CYRUS SCOFIELD -- WHO WAS HE? Excerpt from "The Unified Conspiracy Theory," http://www.sweetliberty.org/issues/hoax/scofield.htm (website address current as of August 9, 2003).

232. CYRUS SCOFIELD -- WHO WAS HE? Excerpt from "The Unified Conspiracy Theory," http://www.sweetliberty.org/issues/hoax/scofield.htm (website address current as of August 9, 2003).

233. C.E. Carlson, The Zionist Created Scofield "bible," http://christianparty.net/scofield.htm (website address current as of August 9, 2003).

234. CYRUS SCOFIELD -- WHO WAS HE? Excerpt from "The Unified Conspiracy Theory," http://www.sweetliberty.org/issues/hoax/scofield.htm (website address current as of August 9, 2003).

235. CYRUS SCOFIELD -- WHO WAS HE? Excerpt from "The Unified Conspiracy Theory," http://www.sweetliberty.org/issues/hoax/scofield.htm (website address current as of August 9, 2003).

236. CYRUS SCOFIELD -- WHO WAS HE? Excerpt from "The Unified Conspiracy Theory," http://www.sweetliberty.org/issues/hoax/scofield.htm (website address current as of August 9, 2003).

Scofield: The Christian Leader With Feet of Clay, http://www.virginiawater.co.uk/christchurch/articles/scofield1.html (website address current as of August 9, 2003).

237. CYRUS SCOFIELD -- WHO WAS HE? Excerpt from "The Unified Conspiracy Theory," http://www.sweetliberty.org/issues/hoax/scofield.htm (website address current as of August 9, 2003).

238. CYRUS SCOFIELD -- WHO WAS HE? Excerpt from "The Unified Conspiracy Theory," http://www.sweetliberty.org/issues/hoax/scofield.htm (website address current as of August 9, 2003).

239. Scofield: The Christian Leader With Feet of Clay, http://www.virginiawater.co.uk/christchurch/articles/scofield1.html (website address current as of August 9, 2003).

240. Scofield: The Christian Leader With Feet of Clay, http://www.virginiawater.co.uk/christchurch/articles/scofield1.html (website address current as of August 9, 2003).

241. G.A. RIPLINGER, NEW AGE BIBLE VERSIONS, p. 405 (1993).

242. Luisa Kroll, Megachurches, Megabusinesses, Forbes, September 17, 2003.

243. Luisa Kroll, Megachurches, Megabusinesses, Forbes, September 17, 2003.

244. Rick Meisel, Chuck Smith, General Teachings/Activities, *Biblical Discernment Ministries*, January 2002, http://www.rapidnet.com/~jbeard/bdm/exposes/smith/g

eneral.htm (web address current as of September 24, 2005), quoting Chuck Smith, Answers for Today, p. 157 (1993).

245. Luisa Kroll, Megachurches, Megabusinesses, Forbes, September 17, 2003.

246. NKJV The Scofield Study Bible III, Black Genuine Leather, Thumb Index, Calvary Chapel, Pasadena, https://store.calvarychapelpasadena.com/products/nkjv-the-scofield-study-bible-iii-black-genuine-leather.

247. 'Largest' Christian Publisher Zondervan, is a Division of Harper Collins, which Publishes the Satanic Bible, http://truthinheart.com/Zondervan.htm (web address current as of October 8, 2005).

248. Edward Hendrie, *The Anti-Gospel, Perverting Christ's Gospel of Grace*, at 63-68 (2010), available at http://www.antichristconspiracy.com/PDFDocs/Antigospel.pdf.

249. Temple Mount Fanatics Foment a New Thirty Years' War, *Executive Intelligence Review,* November 3, 2000, http://www.larouchepub.com/other/2000/temple_mount_2743.html (web address current as of November 11, 2005).

250. Temple Mount Fanatics Foment a New Thirty Years' War, *Executive Intelligence Review,* November 3, 2000, http://www.larouchepub.com/other/2000/temple_mount_2743.html (web address current as of November 11, 2005).

251. Temple Mount Fanatics Foment a New Thirty Years' War, *Executive Intelligence Review,* November 3, 2000, http://www.larouchepub.com/other/2000/temple_mount_2743.html (web address current as of November 11, 2005).

252. Temple Mount Fanatics Foment a New Thirty Years' War, *Executive Intelligence Review,* November 3, 2000, http://www.larouchepub.com/other/2000/temple_mount_2743.html (web address current as of November 11, 2005).

253. Arno Weinstein, In the Shadow of Stern: The Inside Story of a LEHI Intelligence Officer, B'tzedek, http://www.btzedek.com/focus/focus01.html (web address current as of November 11, 2005).

254. Arno Weinstein, In the Shadow of Stern: The Inside Story of a LEHI Intelligence Officer, B'tzedek, http://www.btzedek.com/focus/focus01.html (web address current as of November 11, 2005).

255. Evangelical Christians and the Building of the Temple, The Hebrew University of Jerusalem, http://sicsa.huji.ac.il/20Ariel.html (web address current as of November 11, 2005).

256. Evangelical Christians and the Building of the Temple, The Hebrew University of Jerusalem, http://sicsa.huji.ac.il/20Ariel.html (web address current as of November 11, 2005).

257. Evangelical Christians and the Building of the Temple, The Hebrew University of Jerusalem, http://sicsa.huji.ac.il/20Ariel.html (web address current

as of November 11, 2005).

258. M. H. Reynolds, The New King James Bible Examined, https://av1611.com/kjbp/articles/_reynolds-nkjv.html (last visited on November 11, 2023).

259. Christian Zionism, http://www.theocracywatch.org/christian_zionism.htm (last visited on January 2, 2011).

260. Christian Zionism, http://www.theocracywatch.org/christian_zionism.htm (last visited on January 2, 2011).

261. Sean McBride, *On a Learjet to Hell*, 16 May 2007, http://www.mail-archive.com/political-research@yahoogroups.com/msg07361.html.

262. Thomas L. McFadden, *PASTOR JOHN HAGEE: Is the Devil in Him?*, American Free Press May 7, 2010, http://www.americanfreepress.net/html/john_hagee_devil_221.html.

263. Thousand, American Dictionary of the English Language, https://webstersdictionary1828.com/Dictionary/thousand (last visited on November 25, 2023).

264. Thousand, Webster's New World College Dictionary, Fifth Edition Copyright © 2014 by Houghton Mifflin Harcourt Publishing Company. All rights reserved,

265. Thousand, Webster's 1913 Dictionary, http://www.webster-dictionary.org/definition/thousand (last visited on November 25, 2023).

266. The Left Behind Series, *at* http://www.rapidnet.com/~jbeard/bdm/BookReviews/left.htm (last visited on March 14, 2010).

267. WILLIAM R. KIMBALL, THE RAPTURE, A Question of Timing, p. 31 (1985) (quoting LEROY E. FROOM, THE PROPHETIC FAITH OF OUR FATHERS, vol. 2, pp. 243-44).

268. JOHN L. BRAY, THE MAN OF SIN OF II THESSALONIANS 2, p. 8 (1997) (Incidentally, Bray does not believe that the Pope of Rome is the man of sin mentioned in II Thessalonians 2. He quotes from some of the traditional Protestant confessions of faith only to explain the historical Protestant view. While his survey of the historical confessions of faith is accurate, he is wrong regarding his conclusion about the Pope.).

269. JOHN L. BRAY, MILLENNIUM - THE BIG QUESTION, P. 59 (1984) (quoting ERNEST R. SANDEEN, THE ROOTS OF FUNDAMENTALISM, p. 37 (1970)).

270. JOHN L. BRAY, MILLENNIUM - THE BIG QUESTION, P. 59 (1984) (quoting ERNEST R. SANDEEN, THE ROOTS OF FUNDAMENTALISM, p. 37 (1970)); WILLIAM R. KIMBALL, THE RAPTURE, A Question of Timing, p. 31 (1985) (OSWALD T. ALLIS, PROPHECY AND THE CHURCH, p. 297).

271. WILLIAM R. KIMBALL, THE RAPTURE, A Question of Timing, p. 31 (1985).

272. *Id.*

273. WILLIAM R. KIMBALL, THE RAPTURE, A Question of Timing, p. 31 (1985) (quoting LEROY E. FROOM, THE PROPHETIC FAITH OF OUR FATHERS, vol. 2, p. 495).

274. WILLIAM R. KIMBALL, THE RAPTURE, A Question of Timing, p. 32 (1985).

275. *Id.*

276. *Id.*

277. Anti-Zion, Jews on the Jewish Question, http://www.diac.com/~bkennedy/az/A-E.html (current as of September 10, 2001).

278. Ivan Fraser, Protocols of the Learned Elders of Zion, Proofs of an Ancient Conspiracy, http://www.vegan.swinternet.co.uk/articles/conspiracies/protocols_proof.html (current as of September 10, 2001).

279. Robert Maryks, *Jesuits of Jewish Ancestry. A Biographical Dictionary* (2008), at http://sites.google.com/a/jewishjesuits.com/www/.

280. JOHN L. BRAY, MILLENNIUM - THE BIG QUESTION, P. 34 (1984).

281. The Temple Mount and Fort Antonia, http://askelm.com/temple/t980504.htm (web address current as of October 30, 2003).

282. The Secret Key to the Dome of the Rock, http://askelm.com/temple/t991001.htm (web address current as of October 30, 2003).

283. ALBERTO RIVERA, THE GODFATHERS, Chick Publications, p. 32, 1982 (quoting The Registers of Boniface VIII, The Vatican Archives, L. Fol. 387 and THE CATHOLIC ENCYCLOPEDIA, Encyclopedia Press (1913)).

284. ALBERTO RIVERA, DOUBLE CROSS, Chick publications, p. 27, 1981(quoting THE GREAT ENCYCLICAL LETTERS OF Pope LEO XIII, p. 304, Benziger Brothers (1903).

285. WILLIAM R. KIMBALL, THE RAPTURE, A Question of Timing, p. 35 (1985); JOHN L. BRAY, MILLENNIUM - THE BIG QUESTION, P. 34 (1984).

286. JOHN L. BRAY, THE ORIGIN OF THE PRETRIBULATION RAPTURE TEACHING, p. 17, 24 (1982); JOHN L. BRAY, MILLENNIUM - THE BIG QUESTION, P. 34 (1984).

287. TIM WARNER, HISTORY OF THE PRE-TRIB DEVELOPMENT (2000), http://www.geocities.com/lasttrumpet_2000/timeline/ (current as of April 5, 2002).

288. WILLIAM R. KIMBALL, THE RAPTURE, A Question of Timing, p. 38 (1985).

289. *Id.* at 38.

290. *Id.* at 38.

291. *Id.* at 38.

292. JOHN L. BRAY, ROBERT BAXTER AND THE MID-TRIBULATION RAPTURE TEACHING (1994) (citing ROBERT BAXTER, NARRATIVE FACTS CONCERNING THE UNKNOWN TONGUES AND

SPIRITUAL MANIFESTATIONS IN MEMBERS OF THE REV. EDWARD IRVING'S CONGREGATION, AND OTHER INDIVIDUALS, AND FORMERLY IN THE WRITER HIMSELF (1833)).

293.JOHN L. BRAY, ROBERT BAXTER AND THE MID-TRIBULATION RAPTURE TEACHING, p. 3 (1994)

294.*Id.* at p. 1, 3, 4.

295.*Id.* at 36.

296.PAUL ENNS, THE MOODY HANDBOOK OF THEOLOGY, p. 389-94 (1989).

297.Clifton A. Emahiser, *Old Jerusalem Shall Never Rise Again*, at 3, at http://www.israelect.com/reference/CliftonAEmahiser/studies/Old%20Jerusalem%20Shall%20Never%20Rise%20Again.pdf (last visited on March 15, 2010) (quoting John Bray, *Israel in Bible Prophecy*, at 30).

298.Michael Hoffman II, Secret Societies and Psychological Warfare, at p. 75 (2001).

299.Michael Hoffman II, Secret Societies and Psychological Warfare, at p. 75 (2001).

300.Ted Pike, ADL's Foxman: New Testament Is Anti-Semitic, February 15, 2006, http://truthtellers.org/alerts/ntantisemitic.html, quoting Abraham Foxman, Never Again? The Threat of the New Anti-Semitism, at 47-48.

301.*Israeli Youths Burn New Testaments*, USA Today, May 21, 2008, *at* http://www.usatoday.com/news/religion/2008-05-21-je

wish-new-testament_N.htm.

302. *Israeli Youths Burn New Testaments*, USA Today, May 21, 2008, *at* http://www.usatoday.com/news/religion/2008-05-21-jewish-new-testament_N.htm.

303. Contemporary Global Anti-Semitism: A Report Provided to the United States Congress, Released by the Special Envoy to Monitor and Combat Anti-Semitism, Gregg J. Rickman, United States Department of State, March 13, 2008, http://www.state.gov/j/drl/rls/102406.htm.

304. Report on Global Anti-Semitism, U.S. Department of State, Released by the Bureau of Democracy, Human Rights, and Labor, January 5, 2005, http://www.state.gov/j/drl/rls/40258.htm.

305. Report on Global Anti-Semitism, U.S. Department of State, Released by the Bureau of Democracy, Human Rights, and Labor, January 5, 2005, http://www.state.gov/j/drl/rls/40258.htm.

306. Ted Pike, ADL's Foxman: New Testament Is Anti-Semitic, February 15, 2006, http://truthtellers.org/alerts/ntantisemitic.html, quoting Abraham Foxman, Never Again? The Threat of the New Anti-Semitism, at 47.

307. Ted Pike, ADL's Foxman: New Testament Is Anti-Semitic, February 15, 2006, http://truthtellers.org/alerts/ntantisemitic.html.

308. Ted Pike, ADL's Foxman: New Testament Is Anti-Semitic, February 15, 2006, http://truthtellers.org/alerts/ntantisemitic.html, quoting

Abraham Foxman, Never Again? The Threat of the New Anti-Semitism, at 47-48.

309.*See* Noah Webster, THE AMERICAN DICTIONARY OF THE ENGLISH LANGUAGE (1828); THE COMPACT EDITION OF THE OXFORD ENGLISH DICTIONARY, Oxford University Press, at 2400 (1979). *See also,* THE AMERICAN HERITAGE ILLUSTRATED ENCYCLOPEDIC DICTIONARY (1987).

310.CREATION, June-Aug. 1999, Vol. 21, No. 3, at 22.

311.Bobby O'Connor, *The Racism of Evolution Theory,* CHARLESTON GAZETTE, June 25, 1998 at P18. (Quoting CHARLES DARWIN, THE DESCENT OF MAN (1874)). *See also* Benno C. Schmidt, *Principle and Prejudice: The Supreme Court and Race in the Progressive Era. Part 1: The Heyday of Jim Crow,* 82 COLUM. L. REV. 444, 453 (1982).

312.*Id.*

313.Raj Bhopal, *Is Research Into Ethnicity and Health Racist, Unsound, or Important to Science?,* BRITISH MEDICAL JOURNAL, June 14, 1997.

314.Jim Dawson, *'Race' is Social Notion With No Base in Biology, Genetics, Scientists Say,* STAR TRIBUNE (Minneapolis, MN), February 20, 1995, at 6A.

315. 481 U.S. 604 (1987).

316.*Id.* at 610 n. 4.

317. Norman Hammond, Archaeology Correspondent, Expert Views Differ on Jesuit's Role in the Piltdown Man forgery, *London Times*, July 15, 1980, http://www.clarku.edu/~piltdown/map_prim_suspects/Teilhard_de_Chardin/Chardin_Prosecution/expertsdiffer.html (website address current as of February 28, 2005).

318. MARSHAL HALL, THE EARTH IS NOT MOVING, p. 97 (1991)

319. GERARDUS BOUW, GEOCENTRICITY, p. 254-56 (1992).

320. GERARDUS BOUW, GEOCENTRICITY, p. 303 (1992).

321. Circle, https://www.merriam-webster.com/dictionary/circle.

322. GAIL RIPLINGER, THE LANGUAGE OF THE KING JAMES, pp. 47-50 (1998).

323. Wyatt Houtz, John Calvin on Nicolaus Copernicus and Heliocentrism, October 28, 2014, https://biologos.org/articles/john-calvin-on-nicolaus-copernicus-and-heliocentrism/, quoting John Calvin, "Sermon on 1 Corinthians 10:19-24", Calvini Opera Selecta, Corpus Refomatorum, Vol 49, 677, trans. by Robert White in "Calvin and Copernicus: the Problem Reconsidered", Calvin Theological Journal 15 (1980), p233-243, at 236-237.

324. Gospel, Webster's Revised Unabridged Dictionary, 1913 Edition, https://www.webster-dictionary.org/definition/gospel (last visited on June 14, 2019).

325. Gospel, Oxford English Dictionary (Unabridged).

326. Harper's Bible Dictionary, at 354 (1985).

327. Harper's Bible Dictionary, at 354 (1985).

328. The New International Dictionary of the Bible, at 398 (1984).

329. Gospel, Oxford English Dictionary (Unabridged).

330. Gospel, Oxford English Dictionary (Unabridged).

331. Spell, American Dictionary of the English Language (1828), http://webstersdictionary1828.com/Dictionary/spell.

332. The New International Dictionary of the Bible, at 398 (1984).

333. Gospel, Oxford English Dictionary (Unabridged).

334. Gospel, Oxford English Dictionary (Unabridged).

335. Gail Riplinger, The Language of the King James Bible, at 49-50 (1998), http://nashpublications.com/wp-content/uploads/2013/10/King_James_Bible/Riplinger_Books/Language-of-the-KJB.pdf, quoting Kittel, The Theological Dictionary of the New Testament (p. 660, Vol. 10).

336. Gail Riplinger, The Language of the King James Bible, at 49-50 (1998), http://nashpublications.com/wp-content/uploads/2013/10/King_James_Bible/Riplinger_Books/Language-of-the-KJB.pdf.

337. Gospel, Oxford English Dictionary (Unabridged).

338. Gospel, Oxford English Dictionary (Unabridged).

339. Gospel, Oxford English Dictionary (Unabridged).

340. E.g., Gospel, Online Etymology Dictionary, https://www.etymonline.com/word/gospel (last visited on June 19, 2019).

341. Gail Riplinger, Hazardous Materials, at 1140-41.

342. FlatEarthDoctrine, Kent Hovind FINALLY Admits that the Bible... (FLAT EARTH), June 4, 2018, https://www.youtube.com/watch?v=n5bRSp-kueM. Don Fortner, In Christ (Romans 16:7), September 23, 2018, at 20:00, https://www.youtube.com/watch?v=RKDB26EN64w&feature=youtu.be.

343. Dr. Neelak S. Tjernagel, Holy Scripture Is the Word of God (1984).

344. Gospel, Oxford English Dictionary (Unabridged).

345. Gospel, Oxford English Dictionary (Unabridged).

346. Gail Riplinger, The Language of the King James Bible, at 50 (1998),
http://nashpublications.com/wp-content/uploads/2013/10/King_James_Bible/Riplinger_Books/Language-of-the-KJB.pdf.

347. Gail Riplinger, The Language of the King James Bible, at 49-50 (1998),
http://nashpublications.com/wp-content/uploads/2013/10/King_James_Bible/Riplinger_Books/Language-of-the-KJB.pdf.

348. Gospel, Oxford English Dictionary (Unabridged).

349. Gail Riplinger, The Language of the King James Bible, at 49-50 (1998), http://nashpublications.com/wp-content/uploads/2013/10/King_James_Bible/Riplinger_Books/Language-of-the-KJB.pdf, citing Webster's Encyclopedic Dictionary.

350. Gospel, Webster's Dictionary of the English Language, 1828, http://webstersdictionary1828.com/Dictionary/gospel.

351. Euaggelion, https://biblehub.com/str/greek/2098.htm (last visited on June 16, 2019).

352. Tidings, American Dictionary of the English Language (1828), http://webstersdictionary1828.com/Dictionary/tidings; Tidings, Webster's 1913 Dictionary, https://www.webster-dictionary.org/definition/tidings.

353. Tidings, American Dictionary of the English Language (1828), http://webstersdictionary1828.com/Dictionary/tidings.

354. Intelligence, American Dictionary of the English Language (1828), http://webstersdictionary1828.com/Dictionary/intelligence.

355. Intelligence, American Dictionary of the English Language (1828), http://webstersdictionary1828.com/Dictionary/intelligence.

356. Good, American Dictionary of the English Language (1828), http://webstersdictionary1828.com/Dictionary/good.

357. Tidings, American Dictionary of the English Language (1828), http://webstersdictionary1828.com/Dictionary/tidings; Tidings, Webster's 1913 Dictionary, https://www.webster-dictionary.org/definition/tidings.

358. Intelligence, American Dictionary of the English Language (1828), http://webstersdictionary1828.com/Dictionary/intelligence.

359. Big Think, 3 Proofs That Debunk Flat-earth Theory | NASA's Michelle Thaller, May 23, 2018, https://www.youtube.com/watch?v=CGjFAe018oA.

360. Big Think, 3 Proofs That Debunk Flat-earth Theory | NASA's Michelle Thaller, May 23, 2018, https://www.youtube.com/watch?v=CGjFAe018oA.

361. Big Think, 3 Proofs That Debunk Flat-earth Theory | NASA's Michelle Thaller, May 23, 2018, https://www.youtube.com/watch?v=CGjFAe018oA.

362. Michael StGeorge, The Survival Of A Fitting Quotation, http://anonpress.org/spencer/ (last visited on December 26, 2017).

363. Email from Frank Hall to Edward Hendrie, January 13, 2019.

364. Alan James O'Reilly, Dr D. A. Waite and The DBS, Dead Bible Society, Translation Without Inspiration is Extinction, https://d3hgrlq6yacptf.cloudfront.net/5f4766d57c3ad/content/pages/documents/1446501024.pdf (last visited on November 9, 2023).

365. Dean Burgon Society, Statement of Faith, https://deanburgonsociety.blog/statement-of-faith/ (last visited on November 11, 2023).

366. Alan James O'Reilly, supra.

367. Alan James O'Reilly, supra.

368. Alan James O'Reilly, supra, quoting D. A. Waite, A Warning!! On Gail Riplinger's KJB & Multiple Inspiration HERESY, https://biblefortoday.org/PDF/heresy.pdf (last visited on November 11, 2023).

369. Alan James O'Reilly, supra.

370. Position Statements, Bible Translations, Bob Jones University, https://www.bju.edu/about/positions.php (last visited on November 11, 2023).

371. Position Statements, Bible Translations, Bob Jones University, https://www.bju.edu/about/positions.php (last visited on November 11, 2023).

372. Jones, Bob Jr., Cornbread and Caviar. 1985, Greenville: SC, Bob Jones University Press, pp. 179-181, https://dbts.edu/2012/05/16/is-the-preface-to-the-king-james-version-really-an-embarrassment-to-the-kjv-only-movement/.

373. Bill Combs, Is the Preface to the King James Version Really an Embarrassment to the Kjv-only Movement?, May 16, 2012, https://dbts.edu/2012/05/16/is-the-preface-to-the-king-james-version-really-an-embarrassment-to-the-kjv-only-movement/.

374. Alan James O'Reilly, supra.

375. D.A. Waite, http://textus-receptus.com/wiki/D._A._Waite (last updated November 11, 2023).

376. D. A. Waite, A Warning!! On Gail Riplinger's KJB & Multiple Inspiration HERESY, https://biblefortoday.org/PDF/heresy.pdf (last visited on November 11, 2023).

377. D. A. Waite, A Warning!! On Gail Riplinger's KJB & Multiple Inspiration HERESY, https://biblefortoday.org/PDF/heresy.pdf (last visited on November 11, 2023).

378. D.A. Waite, Defending The King James Bible: A Fourfold Superiority: God's Words Kept Intact in English.

379. Alan James O'Reilly, Flotsam Flush, Re: Cleaning-Up Hazardous Materials by Kirk DiVietro, at 3. https://d3hgrlq6yacptf.cloudfront.net/5f4766d57c3ad/content/pages/documents/1570644312.pdf (last visited on November 11, 2023).

380. Inspire, American Dictionary of the English Language, https://webstersdictionary1828.com/Dictionary/inspire (last visited on November 11, 2023).

381. Inspire, American Dictionary of the English Language, https://webstersdictionary1828.com/Dictionary/inspire (last visited on November 11, 2023).

382. Inspire, American Dictionary of the English Language, https://webstersdictionary1828.com/Dictionary/inspire (last visited on November 11, 2023).

383. Alan James O'Reilly, Flotsam Flush, Re: Cleaning-Up Hazardous Materials by Kirk DiVietro, at 750. https://d3hgrlq6yacptf.cloudfront.net/5f4766d57c3ad/content/pages/documents/1570644312.pdf (last visited on November 11, 2023).

384. MICHAEL BUNKER, SWARMS OF LOCUSTS, *The Jesuit Attack on the Faith,* pg. 44 (2002).

385. D.A. Waite, *Calvin's Error of Limited Atonement,* http://www.biblebelievers.net/calvinism/kjcalvn4.htm#Terms_John112 (last visited on November 8, 2011).

386. D.A. Waite, *Calvin's Error of Limited Atonement,* http://www.biblebelievers.net/calvinism/kjcalvn4.htm#Terms_John112 (last visited on November 8, 2011).

387. D.A. Waite, *Calvin's Error of Limited Atonement,* http://www.biblebelievers.net/calvinism/kjcalvn4.htm#Terms_John112 (last visited on November 8, 2011).

388. COUNCIL OF TRENT, SESSION VI, DECREE ON JUSTIFICATION, Canon XVII, January 13, 1547.

389. Perdition, Noah Webster's American Dictionary of the English Language, https://webstersdictionary1828.com/Dictionary/perdition (last visited on January 28, 2024).

390. ORDERED BY THE COUNCIL OF TRENT, EDITED UNDER ST. CHARLES BORROMEO, PUBLISHED BY DECREE OF POPE ST. PIUS V,

1566, TAN Books, p. 331, 1982.

391. *Id.* at p. 6.

392. *E.g.,* W. GRINTON BERRY, FOXE'S BOOK OF MARTYRS, p. 357.

393. CATECHISM OF THE CATHOLIC CHURCH, § 2034-2035, 1994.

394. ALBERTO RIVERA, FOUR HORSEMEN, Chick Publications, p. 25, 1985 (quoting AVRO MANHATTAN, VATICAN IMPERIALISM IN THE 20th CENTURY, p. 76.). *See also,* JOHN W. ROBBINS, ECCLESIASTICAL MEGALOMANIA, at p. 132 (1999).

395. ALBERTO RIVERA, THE GODFATHERS, Chick Publications, p. 32, 1982 (quoting The Registers of Boniface VIII, The Vatican Archives, L. Fol. 387 and THE CATHOLIC ENCYCLOPEDIA, Encyclopedia Press (1913)).

396. ALBERTO RIVERA, DOUBLE CROSS, Chick publications, p. 27, 1981(quoting THE GREAT ENCYCLICAL LETTERS OF POPE LEO XIII, p. 304, Benziger Brothers (1903).

397. G.A. RIPLER, NEW AGE BIBLE VERSIONS, p. 134 (1993).

398. *Id.*

399. Tim Gilmore, Hope for Life Baptist Church, October 29, 2018, https://jaxpsychogeo.com/west/hope-for-life-baptist-church/.

400. http://www.bookschristian.com/sys/product.php?PRODUCT=145708 (web address current as of October 16, 2005).

401. Heterodoxy Hall of Shame, http://www.outsidethecamp.org/heterodoxy52.htm (web address current as of October 16, 2005).

402. http://www.cuttingedge.org/n1082.html (site active as of July 17, 2001).

403. DES GRIFFIN, THE FOURTH REICH OF THE RICH, p. 70 (1993).

404. Gary Hudson's wrong accusations exposed, https://www.youtube.com/watch?v=25uT0_P7sJQ (last visited on December 5, 2023).

405. Peter Ruckman vs Gary Hudson Are there errors in the KJV?, https://www.facebook.com/100079172964374/videos/peter-ruckman-vs-gary-hudson-are-there-errors-in-the-kjv/5592032064237026/ (last visited on December 5, 2023).

406. Peter Ruckman vs Gary Hudson Are there errors in the KJV?, https://www.facebook.com/100079172964374/videos/peter-ruckman-vs-gary-hudson-are-there-errors-in-the-kjv/5592032064237026/ (last visited on December 5, 2023).

407. Peter Ruckman vs Gary Hudson Are there errors in the KJV?, at 12:44, https://www.facebook.com/100079172964374/videos/peter-ruckman-vs-gary-hudson-are-there-errors-in-the-kjv/5592032064237026/ (last visited on December 5, 2023).

408. Tacit Criminal Admissions, University of Pennsylvania Law Review, Vol. 112:210, 1963, https://scholarship.law.upenn.edu/cgi/viewcontent.cgi?article=6481&context=penn_law_review.

409. Surrender to Reason: An Ex-Pastor's Journey of Deconversion (with Gary Hudson), May 24, 2023, https://mindshiftpodcast.co.uk/?p=3430.

410. Surrender to Reason: An Ex-Pastor's Journey of Deconversion (with Gary Hudson), May 24, 2023, https://mindshiftpodcast.co.uk/?p=3430.

411. Surrender to Reason: An Ex-Pastor's Journey of Deconversion (with Gary Hudson), May 24, 2023, https://mindshiftpodcast.co.uk/?p=3430.

412. Time Gilmore, Hope for Life Baptist Church, October 29, 2008, https://jaxpsychogeo.com/west/hope-for-life-baptist-church/.

413. Stephen Tomkins, John Wesley, A Biography, at 168 (2003) (emphasis added).

414. Time Gilmore, Hope for Life Baptist Church, October 29, 2008, https://jaxpsychogeo.com/west/hope-for-life-baptist-church/.

415. Time Gilmore, Hope for Life Baptist Church, October 29, 2008, https://jaxpsychogeo.com/west/hope-for-life-baptist-church/.

416. Surrender to Reason: An Ex-Pastor's Journey of Deconversion (with Gary Hudson), May 24, 2023, https://mindshiftpodcast.co.uk/?p=3430.

417. Saved from Ruckmanism!, Catholic Answers, February 1, 1990, https://www.catholic.com/magazine/print-edition/saved-from-ruckmanism.

418. Jim McGuiggan, *Hebrews 6 & 10 and Falling Away*, Spending Time With Jim McGuiggan, http://www.jimmcguiggan.com/reflections3.asp?status=Hebrews&id=472 (last visited on November 12, 2011).

419. For, Webster's American Dictionary of the English Language, https://webstersdictionary1828.com/Dictionary/for (last visited on November 27, 2023).

420. Atonement, Webster's American Dictionary of the English Language, https://webstersdictionary1828.com/Dictionary/atonement (last visited on November 27, 2023).

421. Propitiation, Webster's American Dictionary of the English Language, https://webstersdictionary1828.com/Dictionary/propitiation (last visited on November 27, 2023).

422. Redemption, Webster's American Dictionary of the English Language, https://webstersdictionary1828.com/Dictionary/redemption (last visite no November 27, 2023).

423. Because, Online Etymology Dictionary, https://www.etymonline.com/word/because (last visited on November 27, 2023).

424. The Translators to the Reader, https://www.bible-researcher.com/kjvpref.html (last

visited on November 11, 2023).

425. Nicolaitans Meaning and Etymology, http://www.abarim-publications.com/Meaning/Nicolaitans.html#.XE4HRIgvz9c (last visited on January 27, 2019).

426. Nicolaitans Meaning and Etymology, http://www.abarim-publications.com/Meaning/Nicolaitans.html#.XE4HRIgvz9c (last visited on January 27, 2019).

427. Nicolaitans Meaning and Etymology, http://www.abarim-publications.com/Meaning/Nicolaitans.html#.XE4HRIgvz9c (last visited on January 27, 2019).

428. Nick Sayers, Revelation 16:5 and the Triadic Declaration, A defense of the reading of "shalt be" in the Authorized Version, at 52, October 2016.

429. Nick Sayers, Revelation 16:5 and the Triadic Declaration, A defense of the reading of "shalt be" in the Authorized Version, at 71, October 2016.

430. Theodore Beza, Notes to Revelation 1:4, 1599 Geneva Bible, https://www.biblegateway.com/passage/?search=Revelation%201%3A4&version=GNV (last visited on November 20, 2023).

431. Nick Sayers, Revelation 16:5 and the Triadic Declaration, A defense of the reading of "shalt be" in the Authorized Version, at 8, October 2016.

432. The Meaning of God's Name, Nehemia Gordon Clips, September 15, 2023, https://www.youtube.com/watch?v=4vgXMmBst8w&l

ist=WL&index=9.

433.Nick Sayers, Revelation 16:5 and the Triadic Declaration, A defense of the reading of "shalt be" in the Authorized Version, at 12, October 2016.

434.Theodore Beza, Nouum Sive Nouum Foedus Iesu Christi, 1588. Translated into English from the Latin footnote, quoted in Nick Sayers, Revelation 16:5 and the Triadic Declaration, A defense of the reading of "shalt be" in the Authorized Version, at 71, October 2016.

435.Nick Sayers, Revelation 16:5 and the Triadic Declaration, A defense of the reading of "shalt be" in the Authorized Version, at 72, October 2016.

436.Is the Original New Testament Lost? Ehrman vs Wallace (Debate Transcript), http://www.credocourses.com/blog/2016/original-new-testament-lost-ehrman-vs-wallace-debate-transcript/ (last visited on May 18, 2024), quoted in Nick Sayers, Revelation 16:5 and the Triadic Declaration, A defense of the reading of "shalt be" in the Authorized Version, at 73, October 2016.

437.Jack McElroy, Which Bible Would Jesus Use?, at 299 (2013), quoting R. B. Y. Scott, The Original Language of the Apocalypse, at 6 (1928).

438.Jack McElroy, Which Bible Would Jesus Use?, at 299 (2013), quoting Charles Cutler Torrey, Documents of the Primitive Church (1941).

439.Jack McElroy, Which Bible Would Jesus Use?, at 301 (2013)

440. John Hinton, Ridiculous KJV Bible Corrections: Psalm 12 Part 2, verse 7, https://av1611.com/kjbp/ridiculous-kjv-bible-corrections/Psalm-12-Part-2-verse-7.html (last visited on November 18, 2023).

441. John Hinton, Ridiculous KJV Bible Corrections: Psalm 12 Part 2, verse 7, https://av1611.com/kjbp/ridiculous-kjv-bible-corrections/Psalm-12-Part-2-verse-7.html (last visited on November 18, 2023).

442. John Hinton, Ridiculous KJV Bible Corrections: Psalm 12 Part 2, verse 7, https://av1611.com/kjbp/ridiculous-kjv-bible-corrections/Psalm-12-Part-2-verse-7.html (last visited on November 18, 2023).

443. John Hinton, Ridiculous KJV Bible Corrections: Psalm 12 Part 2, verse 7, https://av1611.com/kjbp/ridiculous-kjv-bible-corrections/Psalm-12-Part-2-verse-7.html (last visited on November 18, 2023).

444. John Hinton, Ridiculous KJV Bible Corrections: Psalm 12 Part 2, verse 7, https://av1611.com/kjbp/ridiculous-kjv-bible-corrections/Psalm-12-Part-2-verse-7.html (last visited on November 18, 2023).

445. ALEXANDER HISLOP, THE TWO BABYLONS, pp. 103-113 (1916).

446. *Id*.

447. Nick Sayers, Revelation 16:5 and the Triadic Declaration, A defense of the reading of "shalt be" in

the Authorized Version, at 12, October 2016. See also Should יהוה be Translated as Yahweh or LORD? - Psalm 110:1 | Dr. James White, Ocotber 5, 2020, https://www.youtube.com/watch?v=fDgogzOrxis.

448.KJV Debate: James White & Thomas Ross: King James Bible Only & Textus Receptus Modern Versions & LSB, KJB1611, March 10, 2023, https://www.youtube.com/watch?v=9RgZ-mUh3LM.

449.KJV Debate: James White & Thomas Ross: King James Bible Only & Textus Receptus Modern Versions & LSB, KJB1611, March 10, 2023, https://www.youtube.com/watch?v=9RgZ-mUh3LM.

450.Legacy Standard Bible Exposed (Full Video), January 27, 2022, https://www.youtube.com/watch?v=X-V9zuHqRyA.

451.Legacy Standard Bible Exposed (Full Video), January 27, 2022, https://www.youtube.com/watch?v=X-V9zuHqRyA.

452.Gail Riplinger, In Awe of Thy Word, at 806 (2003).

453.Chris R. Armstrong, Master of language: Lancelot Andrewes, https://christianhistoryinstitute.org/magazine/article/master-of-language-lancelot-andrewes (last visited on December 28, 2023).

454.The King James Bible Translators, https://thekingsbible.com/Library/KJVTranslators (last visited on December 28, 2023).

455.The King James Translators, https://kingjamesbibletranslators.org/ (last visited on

December 28, 2023).

456. John Hinton, Ridiculous KJV Bible Corrections: Who is Yahweh?, https://av1611.com/kjbp/ridiculous-kjv-bible-corrections/Yahweh-Jehova-YHVH.html (last visited on November 16, 2023).

457. The Divine Names and Titles, Appendix 4 To The Companion Bible, https://www.therain.org/appendixes/app4.html (last visited in November 19, 2023).

458. Nick Sayers, Revelation 16:5 and the Triadic Declaration, A defense of the reading of "shalt be" in the Authorized Version, at 13, October 2016.

459. Schaff-Herzog Enclyclopedia, Yahweh, at 472, https://ccel.org/ccel/schaff/encyc12/encyc12.y.html (last visited on November 14, 2023).

460. Schaff-Herzog Enclyclopedia, Yahweh, at 472, https://ccel.org/ccel/schaff/encyc12/encyc12.y.html (last visited on November 14, 2023).

461. Schaff-Herzog Enclyclopedia, Yahweh, at 470, https://ccel.org/ccel/schaff/encyc12/encyc12.y.html (last visited on November 14, 2023).

462. Schaff-Herzog Enclyclopedia, Yahweh, at 472, https://ccel.org/ccel/schaff/encyc12/encyc12.y.html (last visited on November 14, 2023).

463. Miller, James M.; Hayes, John H. A History of Ancient Israel and Judah. Westminster John Knox Press, at 109-110 (1986). ISBN 978-0-664-21262-9. https://www.google.com/books/edition/A_History_of_Ancient_Israel_and_Judah/uDijjc_D5P0C?hl=en&gbp

v=1&pg=PA110&printsec=frontcover.

464. Betz, Arnold Gottfried (2000). "Monotheism". In Freedman, David Noel; Myer, Allen C. (eds.). Eerdmans Dictionary of the Bible. Eerdmans. ISBN 978-90-5356-503-2. https://www.google.com/books/edition/Eerdmans_Dictionary_of_the_Bible/qRtUqxkB7wkC?hl=en&gbpv=1&bsq=bible+monotheism+Betz&pg=PA917&printsec=frontcover.

465. Calvin's Commentaries, Vol. 1: Genesis, Part I, tr. by John King, [1847-50], https://sacred-texts.com/chr/calvin/cc01/cc01007.htm#fr_108. (last visited on November 20, 2023).

466. Nehemia Gordon, The Vowels of Yehovah and Yahweh, June 30, 2023, https://www.youtube.com/watch?v=JYBqEjt1iiU.

467. Nehemia Gordon, The Vowels of Yehovah and Yahweh, June 30, 2023, https://www.youtube.com/watch?v=JYBqEjt1iiU.

468. Nehemia Gordon, The Vowels of Yehovah and Yahweh, June 30, 2023, https://www.youtube.com/watch?v=JYBqEjt1iiU.

469. The Historical Origins of Yahweh, Nehemia Gordon Clips, September 15, 2023, https://www.youtube.com/watch?v=gG5jeuPyxBs&t=80s.

470. The Historical Origins of Yahweh, Nehemia Gordon Clips, September 15, 2023, https://www.youtube.com/watch?v=gG5jeuPyxBs&t=80s.

471. Gesenius' Hebrew and Chaldee Lexicon of the Old Testament Scriptures, at CCCXX XVII.

472. Gesenius' Hebrew and Chaldee Lexicon of the Old Testament Scriptures, at CCCXX XVII.

473. The Historical Origins of Yahweh, Nehemia Gordon Clips, September 15, 2023, https://www.youtube.com/watch?v=gG5jeuPyxBs&t=80s.

474. Daniel E. Fleming, Yahweh before Israel: Glimpses of History in a Divine Name, Cambridge University Press, at 230, 2020.

475. Israel Knohl, Hovav the Midianite: Why Was the End of the Story Cut?, https://www.thetorah.com/article/hovav-the-midianite-why-was-the-end-of-the-story-cut (last visited on December 2, 2023).

476. Israel Knohl, Hovav the Midianite: Why Was the End of the Story Cut?, https://www.thetorah.com/article/hovav-the-midianite-why-was-the-end-of-the-story-cut (last visited on December 2, 2023), citing Rainer Albertz, A History of Israelite Religion in the Old Testament Period, vol. 1 (trans. J. Bowden; London: OTL, 1994), 49-55. The aversion to the Midianites apparent in some of the biblical traditions stems, it seems, from the tensions between priestly houses; see Frank. M. Cross, From Epic to Canon (Baltimore: Johns Hopkins Press, 1998), 59-63.

477. What is the Meaning of the Divine Name Yahweh?, New International Version, https://www.thenivbible.com/blog/what-does-yahweh-

mean-in-the-bible/ (last visited on December 2, 2023).

478. The Meaning of God's Name, Nehemia Gordon Clips, September 15, 2023, https://www.youtube.com/watch?v=4vgXMmBst8w&list=WL&index=9.

479. Israel Knohl, YHWH: The Original Arabic Meaning of the Name, https://www.thetorah.com/article/yhwh-the-original-arabic-meaning-of-the-name (last visited on December 2, 2023)..

480. John Hinton, Ridiculous KJV Bible Corrections: Who is Yahweh?, https://av1611.com/kjbp/ridiculous-kjv-bible-corrections/Yahweh-Jehova-YHVH.html (last visited on November 16, 2023).

481. Gail Riplinger, In Awe of Thy Word, at 421 (2003).

482. Gail Riplinger, In Awe of Thy Word, at 415 (2003).

483. Gail Riplinger, In Awe of Thy Word, at 416 (2003).

484. Gail Riplinger, In Awe of Thy Word, at 417 (2003).

485. John Hinton, Ridiculous KJV Bible Corrections: Who is Yahweh?, https://av1611.com/kjbp/ridiculous-kjv-bible-corrections/Yahweh-Jehova-YHVH.html (last visited on November 16, 2023).

486. About Dr. Nehemia Gordon, PhD, Nehemia's Wall, https://www.nehemiaswall.com/about-nehemia-gordon (last visited on November 18, 2023).

487. Nehemia Gordon, Hebrew Voices #66 – The Historical Pronunciation of Vav, February 28, 2018, https://www.nehemiaswall.com/historical-pronunciation-vav. Also found at: The Pronunciation of the Hebrew Letter Vav (Nehemia Gordon), September 16, 2016, https://www.youtube.com/watch?v=0td4d2UGP0k&t=524s.

488. Is Jeff A. Benner in the "Gunsights" of The LORD ?, November 20, 2022, https://aramaicjudaizers.blogspot.com/2018/07/is-jeff-benner-in-gunsights-of-lord.html.

489. The Way of Yahweh (Part1 of 5), April 28, 2010, https://www.youtube.com/watch?v=rfP6yNbU61A.

490. Nehemia Gordon, Hebrew Voices #66 – The Historical Pronunciation of Vav, February 28, 2018, https://www.nehemiaswall.com/historical-pronunciation-vav. Also found at: The Pronunciation of the Hebrew Letter Vav (Nehemia Gordon), September 16, 2016, https://www.youtube.com/watch?v=0td4d2UGP0k&t=524s.

491. Nehemia Gordon, Hebrew Voices #66 – The Historical Pronunciation of Vav, February 28, 2018, https://www.nehemiaswall.com/historical-pronunciation-vav. Also found at: The Pronunciation of the Hebrew Letter Vav (Nehemia Gordon), September 16, 2016, https://www.youtube.com/watch?v=0td4d2UGP0k&t=524s.

492. See, e.g., Nehemia Gordon on the Pronunciation of the Letter Vav, https://ancient-hebrew.org/ancient-alphabet/vav-discussion.htm (last visited on November 18, 2023).

493. Bible and a Bicycle, Understanding the Hebrew language featuring Jeff Benner, August 15, 2023, https://www.youtube.com/watch?v=XWc6Q5RAeAM. The Way of Yahweh (Part1 of 5), April 28, 2010, https://www.youtube.com/watch?v=rfP6yNbU61A.

494. See Vav, https://ancient-hebrew.org/ancient-alphabet/vav.htm (last visited on November 14, 2023). Jeff A. Benner, Ancient Hebrew Alphabet - Lesson 6 - Vav, April 10, 2013, https://www.youtube.com/watch?v=Ota0EAf2iQM.

495. Thomas Ross, The Battle Over the Inspiration of the Hebrew Vowel Points, Examined Particularly As Waged in England, https://faithsaves.net/history-hebrew-vowel-points/ (last visited on December 26, 2023).

496. God's name is not Yahweh – Proof from Jewish Rabbis, A Rood Awakening, October 31, 2017, https://www.youtube.com/watch?v=yeeA_Abd5Nk.

497. Nehemia Gordon, 1,000 Manuscripts with Yehovah, January 25, 2018, https://www.youtube.com/watch?v=DA3VKpVP17U.

498. John Gill, A Dissertation Concerning the Antiquity of the Hebrew Language, Letters, Vowel Points, and Accents, 1767. https://www.areopage.net/Gill.pdf.

499. Jot, Online Etymology Dictionary, https://www.etymonline.com/search?q=jot (last visited on November 16, 2023).

500. Tittle, Online Etymology Dictionary, https://www.etymonline.com/search?q=tittle (last visited on November 16, 2013).

501. Tittle, YourDictionary, https://www.yourdictionary.com/tittle (last visited on November 16, 2023).

502. Diacritic, Collins English Dictionary, https://www.collinsdictionary.com/dictionary/english/diacritic (last visited on November 16, 2023).

503. John Gill, A Dissertation Concerning the Antiquity of the Hebrew Language, Letters, Vowel Points, and Accents, 1767, at 89. https://www.areopage.net/Gill.pdf.

504. Thomas Ross, The Battle Over the Inspiration of the Hebrew Vowel Points, Examined Particularly As Waged in England, https://faithsaves.net/history-hebrew-vowel-points/ (last visited on December 26, 2023).

505. Thomas Ross, The Battle Over the Inspiration of the Hebrew Vowel Points, Examined Particularly As Waged in England, https://faithsaves.net/history-hebrew-vowel-points/ (last visited on December 26, 2023).

506. Whitfiield, Peter, A Dissertation on the Hebrew Vowel-Points, showing that they are an original and essential part of the Language. Liverpool, 1748, https://kjvgalatians220.files.wordpress.com/2012/03/a-

dissertation-on-the-hebrew-vowel-points-etc.pdf.

507.Dr. Thomas M. Strouse, A Review of and Observations about Peter Whitfield's "A Dissertation on the Hebrew Vowel-Points," Emmanuel Baptist Theological Seminary, https://studylib.net/doc/7593895/strouse-on-peter-whitfield--vowel-points (last visited on December 28, 2023).

508.Dr. Thomas M. Strouse, A Review of and Observations about Peter Whitfield's "A Dissertation on the Hebrew Vowel-Points," Emmanuel Baptist Theological Seminary, https://studylib.net/doc/7593895/strouse-on-peter-whitfield--vowel-points (last visited on December 28, 2023).

509.Dr. Thomas M. Strouse, A Review of and Observations about Peter Whitfield's "A Dissertation on the Hebrew Vowel-Points," Emmanuel Baptist Theological Seminary, https://studylib.net/doc/7593895/strouse-on-peter-whitfield--vowel-points (last visited on December 28, 2023).

510.Paul Henebury, Autographa & Apographa: John Owen on Inspiration and Preservation, 20 January 2013, https://drreluctant.wordpress.com/2013/01/20/autographa-apographa-john-owen-on-inspiration-and-preservation/.

511.The Works of John Owen, D.D., Volume 1X, Divine Original of Scripture. The Integrity and Purity of the Hebrew and Greek Text, Edited by William M. Goold and Charles W. Quick (1865).

512.The Works of John Owen, D.D., Volume 1X, Divine Original of Scripture. The Integrity and Purity of the Hebrew and Greek Text, Edited by William M. Goold and Charles W. Quick, at 90 (1865).

513. The Works of John Owen, D.D., Volume 1X, Divine Original of Scripture. The Integrity and Purity of the Hebrew and Greek Text, Edited by William M. Goold and Charles W. Quick, at 89 (1865).

514. The Works of John Owen, D.D., Volume 1X, Divine Original of Scripture. The Integrity and Purity of the Hebrew and Greek Text, Edited by William M. Goold and Charles W. Quick, at 89 (1865).

515. Scott Clark, Helvetic Consensus Formula (1675), Translated by Martin I. Klauber, September 1, 2022, https://heidelblog.net/2012/09/helvetic-consensus-formula-1675/.

516. Legacy Standard Bible Exposed (Full Video), January 27, 2022, https://www.youtube.com/watch?v=X-V9zuHqRyA.

517. John Hinton, Ridiculous KJV Bible Corrections: Who is Yahweh?, https://av1611.com/kjbp/ridiculous-kjv-bible-corrections/Yahweh-Jehova-YHVH.html (last visited on November 16, 2023).

518. Nehemia Gordon, Hebrew Voices #66 – The Historical Pronunciation of Vav, February 28, 2018, https://www.nehemiaswall.com/historical-pronunciation-vav. Also found at: The Pronunciation of the Hebrew Letter Vav (Nehemia Gordon), September 16, 2016, https://www.youtube.com/watch?v=0td4d2UGP0k&t=524s. Jeff A. Benner knows Dr. Gordon's opinion. Benner maintains that *vav* originally took on the "waw" sound. He states that the "v" sound is a modern

Hebrew form. Benner is unwilling to budge on his opinin that *vav* originally had a "w" sound even when faced with proof that he is wrong. See, e.g., Nehemia Gordon on the Pronunciation of the Letter Vav, https://ancient-hebrew.org/ancient-alphabet/vav-discussion.htm (last visited on November 18, 2023). Benner's opinion is skewed by his belief that God's name is Yahweh. The Way of Yahweh (Part1 of 5), April 28, 2010, https://www.youtube.com/watch?v=rfP6yNbU61A. It seems that Benner has an agenda to maintain the myth that the original pronunciation for vav is "w." See Vav, https://ancient-hebrew.org/ancient-alphabet/vav.htm (last visited on November 14, 2023). Jeff A. Benner, Ancient Hebrew Alphabet - Lesson 6 - Vav, April 10, 2013, https://www.youtube.com/watch?v=Ota0EAf2iQM.

519. John Hinton, Ridiculous KJV Bible Corrections: Who is Yahweh?, https://av1611.com/kjbp/ridiculous-kjv-bible-corrections/Yahweh-Jehova-YHVH.html (last visited on November 16, 2023).

520. Theophoric Names, https://www.putoffthyshoes.com/seminary (last visited on December 27, 2023).

521. Theophoric Names, https://www.putoffthyshoes.com/seminary (last visited on December 27, 2023).

522. Doublemindedness in the Hebrew Roots Movement – The Use of Kabbalah and Gematria, October 24, 2008, https://joyfullygrowingingrace.wordpress.com/2008/10/24/doublemindedness-in-the-hebrew-roots-movement-

the-use-of-kabbalah-and-gematria/. Esoteric Hebrew Names of God, https://www.hebrew4christians.com/Names_of_G-d/Esoteric/esoteric.html (last visited on November 16, 2023).

523. Esoteric Hebrew Names of God, https://www.hebrew4christians.com/Names_of_G-d/Esoteric/esoteric.html (last visited on November 16, 2023).

524. Michael Hoffman, *Judaism Discovered*, at 785 (2008).

525. Lawrence Fine, Chapter on Kabbalistic Texts, From: *Back to the Sources: Reading the Classic Jewish Texts* ("The First Complete Modern Guide to the Great Books of the Jewish Tradition: What They Are and How to Read Them"), at p. 337 (2006) (bold emphasis added, italics in original).

526. Lawrence Fine, Chapter on Kabbalistic Texts, From: *Back to the Sources: Reading the Classic Jewish Texts* ("The First Complete Modern Guide to the Great Books of the Jewish Tradition: What They Are and How to Read Them"), at p. 337 (2006) (quoting Zohar III, 152a).

527. Blavatsky, Theosophical Glossary, p. 168 (quoted by Barbara Aho, Mystery, Babylon the Great Catholic or Jewish?, at http://watch.pair.com/mystery-babylon.html#cabala (last visited on April 17, 2010)).

528. Jewish Encyclopedia, Cabala, at http://www.jewishencyclopedia.com/view.jsp?artid=1&letter=C#4 (last visited on April 18, 2010).

529. MICHAEL A. HOFFMAN, JUDAISM'S STRANGE GODS, at p. 88, (2000).

530. MICHAEL A. HOFFMAN, JUDAISM'S STRANGE GODS, at p. 88, (2000). See also Michael Hoffman, *Judaism Discovered*, at 779 (2008) (quoting Gershom Scholem, *Kabbalah* pp.183-84).

531. MICHAEL A. HOFFMAN, JUDAISM'S STRANGE GODS, at p. 91, (2000).

532. Michael Hoffman, *Judaism Discovered*, at 780 (2008) (quoting Helen Jacaobus, *Eye Jinx*, Jewish Chronicle, May 7, 1999).

533. MICHAEL A. HOFFMAN, JUDAISM'S STRANGE GODS, at p. 92, (2000).

534. What is the real name of the Messiah, http://hiddenbible.com/jesuszeus/jesuszeus.html (last visited on November 17, 2023).

535. James A. Robinson, Jesus means "Hail Zeus" and is a pagan, that is, Demonic name -- his name is Yahooshua, December 3, 2022, https://www.eti-ministries.org/jesus-means-hail-zeus-and-is-a-pagan-that-is-demonic-name-his-name-is-yahooshua.

536. Does 'Jesus' really mean 'Hail, Zeus'?, https://www.compellingtruth.org/Jesus-Hail-Zeus.html (last visited on November 16, 2023).

537. Kepha, Servant of YaHVaH, The Lies About Jesus Christ, http://assemblyofthekingdomofheaven.org/messages/LiesAboutJesusChrist.aspx (last visited on November 16, 2023).

538. Kepha, Servant of YaHVaH, The Lies About Jesus Christ, http://assemblyofthekingdomofheaven.org/messages/LiesAboutJesusChrist.aspx (last visited on November 16, 2023).

539. YAHSHUA – The True Name Of Our Savior And It's Importance For Use, http://yahweh.com/the-name-of-yahshua.html (last visited on November 16, 2023).

540. YAHSHUA – The True Name Of Our Savior And It's Importance For Use, http://yahweh.com/the-name-of-yahshua.html (last visited on November 16, 2023).

541. YAHSHUA – The True Name Of Our Savior And It's Importance For Use, http://yahweh.com/the-name-of-yahshua.html (last visited on November 16, 2023).

542. YAHSHUA – The True Name Of Our Savior And It's Importance For Use, http://yahweh.com/the-name-of-yahshua.html (last visited on November 16, 2023).

543. Altar of Zeus at Pergamon, Turkey: the Throne of Satan, https://voyageturkey.net/temple-altar-of-zeus-in-pergamon/ (last visited on November 16, 2023).

544. Michael Brown, What is the Original Hebrew Name for Jesus? And is it True that the Name Jesus is Really a Pagan Corruption of the Name Zeus?, January 3, 2013, https://askdrbrown.org/article/what-is-the-original-hebrew-name-for-jesus.

545. Michael Brown, What is the Original Hebrew Name for Jesus? And is it True that the Name Jesus is Really a Pagan Corruption of the Name Zeus?, January 3, 2013, https://askdrbrown.org/article/what-is-the-original-hebrew-name-for-jesus.

546. Michael Brown, What is the Original Hebrew Name for Jesus? And is it True that the Name Jesus is Really a Pagan Corruption of the Name Zeus?, January 3, 2013, https://askdrbrown.org/article/what-is-the-original-hebrew-name-for-jesus.

547. Tuvia Pollack, Why do Israelis call Jesus "Yeshu"?, Kehila News, November 23, 2021, https://news.kehila.org/why-do-israelis-call-jesus-yeshu/. Jesus vs. Yeshua?, One For Israel, https://www.oneforisrael.org/bible-based-teaching-from-israel/jesus-vs-yeshua/.

548. Tuvia Pollack, Why do Israelis call Jesus "Yeshu"?, Kehila News, November 23, 2021, https://news.kehila.org/why-do-israelis-call-jesus-yeshu/.

549. Babylonian Talmud: Tractate Sanhedrin, Folio 43a, wherein the name "Yeshu" is used as the name for Jesus, http://www.come-and-hear.com/sanhedrin/sanhedrin_43.html#43a_34 (last visited on November 15, 2023). Compare to Talmud: Tractate Sanhedrin, Folio 43a, on the Sarian website wherein the name "Jesus" is used to refer to Christ, https://www.sefaria.org/Sanhedrin.43a.20?lang=bi (last visited on November 11, 2023).

550. The Jewish Life of Christ, Being the Sepher Toldoth Jeshu or Book of the Generation of Jesus, Translated From the Hebrew, Edited by G.W. Foote & J.M. Wheeler, http://www.ftarchives.net/foote/toldoth/tjtitle.htm (last visited on November 15, 2023).

551. Nesta Webster, Secret Societies and Subversive Movements, https://www.gutenberg.org/files/19104/19104-h/19104-h.htm#fna82 (last visited on November 16, 2023). The Jewish Life of Christ, Being the Sepher Toldoth Jeshu or Book of the Generation of Jesus, Translated From the Hebrew, Edited by G.W. Foote & J.M. Wheeler, http://www.ftarchives.net/foote/toldoth/tjtitle.htm (last visited on November 15, 2023).

552. Michael L. Rodkinson: The History of the Talmud; http://www.come-and-hear.com/talmud/rodkin_ii3.html#E27 (web address current as of February 8, 2004).

553. Michael Hoffman & Alan R. Critchley, The Truth About the Talmud, http://www.hoffman-info.com/talmudtruth.html (current as of September 12, 2001).

554. Michael Hoffman & Alan R. Critchley, The Truth About the Talmud, http://www.hoffman-info.com/talmudtruth.html (current as of September 12, 2001).

555. Michael Hoffman & Alan R. Critchley, The Truth About the Talmud, http://www.hoffman-info.com/talmudtruth.html (current as of September 12, 2001).

556. Michael Hoffman, *Judaism Discovered*, at 534 (2008).

557. Michael Hoffman, *Judaism Discovered*, at 196 (2008).

558. Babylonian Talmud: *Tractate Sanhedrin, Folio 90a*, Sanhedrin Translated into English with Notes, Glossary and Indices Chapters I - VI by Jacob Shachter, Chapters VII - XI by H. Freedman, B.A., Ph.D., Under the Editorship of Rabbi Dr I. Epstein B.A., Ph.D., D. Lit. (1961), *available at* http://www.come-and-hear.com/sanhedrin/sanhedrin_90.html.

559. Michael Hoffman, *Judaism Discovered*, at 534 (2008).

560. Tim Kelley, Ami Yisrael, Circumcision According to Paul, January 29, 2019, https://www.amiyisrael.org/articles/CircumcisionAccordingToPaul/CircumcisionAccordingtoPaul.html.

561. About Us, 119 Ministries, https://www.119ministries.com/about-us/ (last visited on November 17, 2023).

562. Circumcision, The Eternal Sign, Part 2, 119 Ministries, https://www.119ministries.com/teachings/video-teachings/detail/circumcision-the-eternal-sign-part-2/. But see Paul Parsons, Brit Milah, Should a Christian Be Cricumcised?, https://www.hebrew4christians.com/Articles/Circumcision/circumcision.html (last visited on November 17, 2023).

563. Tree of Life Bible Society, https://tlvbiblesociety.org/ (last visited on February 1, 2024).

564. Tongue, American Dictionary of the English Language, https://webstersdictionary1828.com/Dictionary/tongue (last visited on January 26, 2024).

565. Tongue, American Dictionary of the English Language, https://webstersdictionary1828.com/Dictionary/tongue (last visited on January 26, 2024).

566. Hebrew Wod of the Day, Yosef, Joseph, Jerusalem Prayer Team, https://hebrew.jerusalemprayerteam.org/joseph/ (last visited on February 3, 2024). See also Julien Miquel, Yosef: How to Pronounce Joseph?, February 27, 2021, https://www.youtube.com/watch?v=wfYlm-DylKE.

567. Jacob, Behind the Name, https://www.behindthename.com/name/jacob (last visited on February 3, 2024). See also Yaakov: How to Pronounce Jacob in Hebrew?, February 27, 2021, https://www.youtube.com/watch?v=XViI1d-JINs.

568. Jesus vs. Yeshua: Are They Really the Same Messiah??, Lapid Judaism, November 10, 2022, https://www.youtube.com/watch?v=Dt5WzZXhomw.

569. Lapid, Our Mission & Vision, https://www.lapidjudaism.org/about-lapid-judasim/mission-vision (last visited on January 20, 2024).

570. Is Lapid Judaism "Orthodox?", https://www.lapidjudaism.org/about-lapid-judasim

(last visited on January 20, 2024).

571. Yeshua Centered Judasim, https://www.lapidjudaism.org/about-lapid-judasim (last visited on January 20, 2024).

572. Yeshua the Pharisee! This Changes Everything, Lapid Judaism, August 25, 2022, https://www.youtube.com/watch?v=nBFl-TWqFzA&t=981s.

573. March 18, 2024, email from Edward Hendrie to _____ _____.

574. March 18, 2024, email from _____ _____ to Edward Hendrie.

575. March 18, 2024, email from Edward Hendrie to _____ _____.

576. The Fig Tree Generation, https://thefigtreegeneration.net/ (last visited on July 22, 2024).

577. Fortescue, A. (1910). Liturgy. In The Catholic Encyclopedia. New York: Robert Appleton Company. Retrieved February 19, 2010 from New Advent: http://www.newadvent.org/cathen/09306a.htm.

578. The Presence of God, Missionary Priests of the Blessed Sacrament, Winter/Spring 2001, at http://www.perpetualadoration.org/ws2001.htm.

579. Joseph Cardinal Ratzinger, The Reservation of the Blessed Sacrament, Institute for Sacred Architecture, Volume 12, Fall/Winter 2006, *available at* http://www.sacredarchitecture.org/articles/reservation_of_the_blessed_sacrament/.

580. Michael Hoffman, *Judaism Discovered*, at 266-67 (2008).

581. Michael Hoffman, *Judaism Discovered*, at 268 (2008).

582. Terry Watkins, TNIV & THE LORD JESUS, Dial-The-Truth-Ministries, at http://www.av1611.org/kjv/tniv_jesus.html (last visited on April 6, 2010).

583. To Embrace Hebrew Roots: Part IV, The Talmud & Demonology, The Talmudic Myth of Lillith, Seek God, *at* http://www.seekgod.ca/embracnotal.htm (last visited at April 6, 2010).

584. Lawrence Fine, Chapter on Kabbalistic Texts, From: *Back to the Sources: Reading the Classic Jewish Texts* ("The First Complete Modern Guide to the Great Books of the Jewish Tradition: What They Are and How to Read Them"), at p. 337 (2006).

585. Lawrence Fine, Chapter on Kabbalistic Texts, From: *Back to the Sources: Reading the Classic Jewish Texts* ("The First Complete Modern Guide to the Great Books of the Jewish Tradition: What They Are and How to Read Them"), at p. 337 (2006).

586. Lawrence Fine, Chapter on Kabbalistic Texts, From: *Back to the Sources: Reading the Classic Jewish Texts* ("The First Complete Modern Guide to the Great Books of the Jewish Tradition: What They Are and How to Read Them"), at p. 337 (2006).

587. Athol Bloomer, *The Eucharist and The Jewish Mystical Tradition • Part 1*, Association of Hebrew Catholics, *at*

http://hebrewcatholic.org/PrayerandSpirituality/eucharistjewishm.html (originally published in The Hebrew Catholic #77, pp 15-18 (Summer-Fall 2002)).

588.Athol Bloomer, *The Eucharist and The Jewish Mystical Tradition • Part 1*, Association of Hebrew Catholics, *at* http://hebrewcatholic.org/PrayerandSpirituality/eucharistjewishm.html (originally published in The Hebrew Catholic #77, pp 15-18 (Summer-Fall 2002)).

589.Athol Bloomer, *The Eucharist and The Jewish Mystical Tradition • Part 1*, Association of Hebrew Catholics, *at* http://hebrewcatholic.org/PrayerandSpirituality/eucharistjewishm.html (originally published in The Hebrew Catholic #77, pp 15-18 (Summer-Fall 2002)).

590.Rabbi Geoffrey W. Dennis, *The Encyclopedia of Jewish Myth, Magic, and Mysticism*, at 199 (2007), quoted by Michael Hoffman in *Judaism Discovered*, at 239-40 (2008).

591.Dennis, at 199.

592.Michael Hoffman, *Judaism Discovered*, at 239 (2008).

593.Michael Hoffman, *Judaism Discovered*, at 240 (2008).

594.Michael Hoffman, *Judaism Discovered*, at 240 (2008).

595.Moshe Idel, *Hasidism Between Ecstacy and Magic*, at 103.

596. Ithmar Gruenwald, *Israel Oriental Studies* 1 (1971); pp. 132-177 and *Temerin*, vol. 7 (Jerusalem, 1972) pp. 101-139. Gershom Scholem, *Jewish Gnosticism, Merkabah Mysticism and Talmudic Tradition* (Jewish Theological Seminary of America, 1965) cited by Michael Hoffman in *Judaism Discovered*, at 241 (2008).

597. Michael Hoffman, *Judaism Discovered*, at 241 (2008).

598. Tiferet, Jewish Virtual Library, *at* http://www.jewishvirtuallibrary.org/jsource/Judaism/Tiferet.html (last visited on March 2, 2010).

599. Tree of Life created by Friedhelm Wessel (25 October 2008), at http://commons.wikimedia.org/wiki/File:Tree_of_Life_%28Sephiroth%29.svg.

600. Laura Ellen Shulman, Judaism, Jewish *Mysticism Kabbalah and the Sefirot* (March 13, 2007), *at* http://www.nvcc.edu/home/lshulman/Rel232/resource/sefirot.htm.

Other books available from Great Mountain Publishing®

Vaccine Danger: Quackery and Sin
Edward Hendrie
ISBN: 978-1-943056-17-0

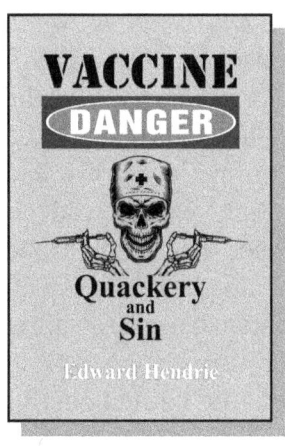

This book reveals the most significant medical fraud in history. The theory that you can prevent illness by injecting poisons into the bodies of healthy people is dangerous quackery and sin. All true science has proven the practice of vaccination to be ineffective and unsafe. But the medical establishment has been lured into the superstitious practice, hook, line, and sinker. It is not merely a matter of ignorance that the debilitating practice flourishes. It is, at its core, being promoted by those who know it is unsafe and ineffective. There is a malevolent spirit behind the practice. It is part of a conspiracy against God and man. While most doctors are unwitting, some are willing minions of that old serpent, called the Devil, and Satan, who are quite happy to kill people for profit. Jesus describes such men: "Ye are of your father the devil, and the lusts of your father ye will do. He was a murderer from the beginning, and abode not in the truth, because there is no truth in him. When he speaketh a lie, he speaketh of his own: for he is a liar, and the father of it." John 8:44.

The Sphere of Influence: The Heliocentric Perversion of the Gospel
Edward Hendrie
ISBN: 978-1-943056-06-4

This book is a sequel to *The Greatest Lie on Earth (Expanded Edition): Proof That Our World Is Not a Moving Globe.* It will primarily focus on the infiltration into the church of the superstitious myth of heliocentrism and how that infiltration has served to undermine the gospel. The gospel is the entire Holy Bible, not just some of it. Matthew 4:4. Christian belief is an all or nothing proposition. "All scripture is given by inspiration of God, and is profitable for doctrine, for reproof, for correction, for instruction in righteousness." 2 Timothy 3:16. God's account of his creation is part and parcel of the gospel. A person with genuine faith believes what Jesus said about both heavenly and earthly things. "If I have told you earthly things, and ye believe not, how shall ye believe, if I tell you of heavenly things?" John 3:12. Jesus is God. Jesus created all things in heaven and on earth. See Colossians 1:16-18. God has revealed himself through his creation. "[T]hat which may be known of God is manifest in them; for God hath shewed it unto them. For the invisible things of him from the creation of the world are clearly seen, being understood by the things that are made, even his eternal power and Godhead; so that they are without excuse." Romans 1:19-20. If men have a misunderstanding of God's creation, they will also have a misunderstanding of who God is. If people believe in a creation that does not exist, they consequently also believe in a creator that does not exist. It is essential, therefore, to have an accurate understanding of God's creation. God did not make a movable, spherical earth. If men believe in a heliocentric creation, they will necessarily believe in a heliocentric creator. A heliocentric creation does not exist. So also, a heliocentric creator does not exist. A heliocentric creator is a false god. We have been warned to avoid the preaching of a false gospel, which presents a false Jesus. "For if he that cometh preacheth another Jesus, whom we have not preached, or if ye receive another spirit, which ye have not received, or another gospel, which ye have not accepted, ye might well bear with him." 2 Corinthians 11:4.

The Greatest Lie on Earth
Proof That Our World Is Not a Moving Globe
Edward Hendrie
ISBN-13: 978-1-943056-01-9

This book reveals the mother of all conspiracies. It sets forth biblical proof and irrefutable evidence that will cause the scales to fall from your eyes and reveal that the world you thought existed is a myth. The most universally accepted scientific belief today is that the earth is a globe, spinning on its axis at a speed of approximately 1,000 miles per hour at the equator, while at the same time it is orbiting the sun at approximately 66,600 miles per hour. All of this is happening as the sun, in turn, is supposed to be hurtling through the Milky Way galaxy at approximately 500,000 miles per hour. The Milky Way galaxy, itself, is alleged to be racing through space at a speed ranging from 300,000 to 1,340,000 miles per hour. What most people are not told is that the purported spinning, orbiting, and speeding through space has never been proven. In fact, every scientific experiment that has ever been performed to determine the motion of the earth has proven that the earth is stationary. Yet, textbooks ignore the scientific proof that contradicts the myth of a spinning and orbiting globe. Christian schools have been hoodwinked into teaching heliocentrism, despite the clear teaching in the Bible that the earth is not a sphere and does not move. This book reveals the evil forces behind the heliocentric deception, and why scientists and the Christian churches have gone along with it.

**The Greatest Lie on Earth (Expanded Edition)
Proof That Our World Is Not a Moving Globe**
Edward Hendrie
ISBN-13: 978-1943056-03-3

This book is an expanded edition of *The Greatest Lie on Earth*. It contains more than 1,000 pages of authoritative evidence with more than 1,300 endnotes that document proof beyond any doubt that the earth is flat and stationary. The book reveals the mother of all conspiracies. It sets forth biblical proof and irrefutable evidence that will cause the scales to fall from your eyes and reveal that the world you thought existed is a myth. The most universally accepted scientific belief today is that the earth is a globe, spinning on its axis at a speed of approximately 1,000 miles per hour at the equator, while at the same time it is orbiting the sun at approximately 66,600 miles per hour. All of this is happening as the sun, in turn, is supposed to be hurtling through the Milky Way galaxy at approximately 500,000 miles per hour. The Milky Way galaxy, itself, is alleged to be racing through space at a speed ranging from 300,000 to 1,340,000 miles per hour. What most people are not told is that the purported spinning, orbiting, and speeding through space has never been proven. In fact, every scientific experiment that has ever been performed to determine the motion of the earth has proven that the earth is stationary. Yet, textbooks ignore the scientific proof that contradicts the myth of a spinning and orbiting globe. Christian schools have been hoodwinked into teaching heliocentrism, despite the clear teaching in the Bible that the earth is not a sphere and does not move. This book reveals the evil forces behind the heliocentric deception, and why scientists and the Christian churches have gone along with it.

Antichrist: The Beast Revealed
Edward Hendrie
ISBN-13: 978-0-9832627-8-7

The antichrist is among us, here and now. This book proves it by comparing the biblical prophecies about the antichrist with the evidence that those prophecies have been fulfilled. This book documents the man of sin's esoteric confession that he is the antichrist. You will learn how the antichrist has changed times and laws as prophesied by Daniel, and how he is today sitting in the temple of God, "shewing himself that he is God," in fulfillment of Paul's prophecy in 2 Thessalonians 2:4. The beast of Revelation has come into the world, "after the working of Satan with all power and signs and lying wonders, and with all deceivableness of unrighteousness," as prophesied in 2 Thessalonians 2:10. The antichrist's adeptness as a hypocrite is the reason for his evil success. Indeed, to be the antichrist, his evil character must be concealed beneath a facade of piety. "And no marvel; for Satan himself is transformed into an angel of light. Therefore it is no great thing if his ministers also be transformed as the ministers of righteousness; whose end shall be according to their works." 2 Corinthians 11:14-15. The key to revealing the identity of the antichrist is to uncover his hypocrisy. Because the hypocrisy of the antichrist is so extreme, those who have been hoodwinked by his religious doctrines will be shocked to learn of it. This book exposes the concealed iniquity of the antichrist and juxtaposes it against his publicly proclaimed false persona of righteousness, thus bringing into clear relief that man of sin, the son of perdition, who is truly a ravening wolf in sheep's clothing, speaking lies in hypocrisy. See Matthew 7:15 and 1 Timothy 4:1-3.

9/11-Enemies Foreign and Domestic
Edward Hendrie
ISBN-13: 978-0983262732

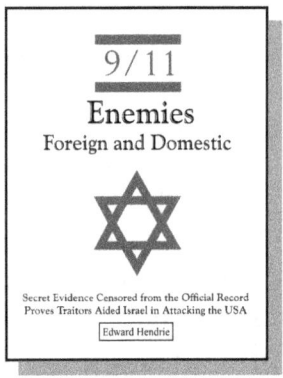

9/11-Enemies Foreign and Domestic proves beyond a reasonable doubt that the U.S. Government's conspiracy theory of the attacks on September 11, 2001, is a preposterous cover story. The evidence in 9/11-Enemies Foreign and Domestic has been suppressed from the official government reports and censored from the mass media. The evidence proves that powerful Zionists ordered the 9/11 attacks, which were perpetrated by Israel's Mossad, aided and abetted by treacherous high officials in the U.S. Government. 9/11-Enemies Foreign and Domestic identifies the traitors by name and details their subversive crimes. There is sufficient evidence in 9/11-Enemies Foreign and Domestic to indict important officials of the U.S. Government for high treason. The reader will understand how the U.S. Government really works and what Sir John Harrington (1561-1612) meant when he said: "Treason doth never prosper: what's the reason? Why if it prosper, none dare call it treason." There are millions of Americans who have taken an oath to defend the U.S. Constitution against all enemies foreign and domestic. The mass media, which is under the control of a disloyal cabal, keeps those patriotic Americans ignorant of the traitors among them. J. Edgar Hoover, former Director of the FBI, explained: "The individual is handicapped by coming face-to-face with a conspiracy so monstrous-he simply cannot believe it exists." 9/11-

Enemies Foreign and Domestic erases any doubt about the existence of the monstrous conspiracy described by Hoover and arms the reader with the knowledge required to save our great nation. "My people are destroyed for lack of knowledge." Hosea 4:6.

Solving the Mystery of BABYLON THE GREAT
Edward Hendrie
ISBN-13: 978-0983262701

"Attorney and Christian researcher Edward Hendrie investigates and reveals one of the greatest exposés of all time. . . . a book you don't want to miss. Solving the Mystery of Babylon the Great is packed with documentation. Never before have the crypto-Jews who seized the reins of power in Rome been put under such intense scrutiny." Texe Marrs, Power of Prophecy. The evidence presented in this book leads to the ineluctable conclusion that the Roman Catholic Church was established by crypto-Jews as a false "Christian" front for a Judaic/Babylonian religion. That religion is the core of a world conspiracy against man and God. That is not a conspiracy theory based upon speculation, but rather the hard truth based upon authoritative evidence, which is documented in this book. Texe Marrs explains in his foreword to the book: "Who is Mystery Babylon? What is the meaning of the sinister symbols found in these passages? Which city is being described as the 'great city' so full of sin and decadence, and who are its citizens? Why do the woman and beast of Revelation seek the destruction of the holy people, the saints and martyrs of Jesus? What does it all mean for you and me today? Solving the Mystery of Babylon the Great answers these questions and more. Edward Hendrie's discoveries are not based on prejudice but on solid evidence aligned forthrightly with the 'whole counsel of God.' He does not condone nor will he be a part of any project in which Bible verses are taken out of context, or in which scriptures are twisted to mean what they do not say. Again and again you will find that Mr. Hendrie documents his assertions, backing up what he says with historical facts and proofs. Most important is that he buttresses his findings with scriptural understanding. The foundation for his research is sturdy because it is based on the bedrock of God's unshakeable Word."

The Anti-Gospel
Edward Hendrie
ISBN-13: 978-0983262749

Edward Hendrie uses God's word to strip the sheep's clothing from false Christian ministers and expose them as ravening wolves preaching an anti-gospel. The anti-gospel is based on a myth that all men have a will that is free from the bondage of sin to choose whether to believe in Jesus. The Holy Bible, however, states that all men are spiritually dead and cannot believe in Jesus unless they are born again of the Holy Spirit. Ephesians 2:1-7; John 3:3-8. God has chosen his elect to be saved by his grace through faith in Jesus Christ. Ephesians 1:3-9; 2:8-10. God imbues his elect with the faith needed to believe in Jesus. Hebrews 12:2; John 1:12-13. The devil's false gospel contradicts the word of God and reverses the order of things. Under the anti-gospel, instead of a sovereign God choosing his elect, sovereign man decides whether to choose God. The calling of the Lord Jesus Christ is effectual; all who are chosen for salvation will believe in Jesus. John 6:37-44. The anti-gospel has a false Jesus, who only offers the possibility of salvation, with no assurance. The anti-gospel blasphemously makes God out to be a liar by denying the total depravity of man and the sovereign election of God. All who preach that false gospel are under a curse from God. Galatians 1:6-9.

Bloody Zion
Edward Hendrie
ISBN-13: 978-0983262763

Jesus told Pontius Pilate: "My kingdom is not of this world." John 18:36. God has a spiritual Zion that is in a heavenly Jerusalem. Hebrews 12:22; Revelation 21:10. Jesus Christ is the chief corner stone laid by God in Zion. 1 Peter 2:6. Those who believe in Jesus Christ are living stones in the spiritual house of God. 1 Peter 2:5; Ephesians 2:20-22. Believers are in Jesus and Jesus is in believers. John 14:20; 17:20-23. All who are elected by God to believe in Jesus Christ are part of the heavenly Zion, without regard to whether they are Jews or Gentiles. Romans 10:12. Satan is a great adversary of God, who has created his own mystery religions. During the Babylonian captivity (2 Chronicles 36:20), an occult society of Jews replaced God's commands with Satan's Babylonian dogma. Their new religion became Judaism. Jesus explained the corruption of the Judaic religion: "Howbeit in vain do they worship me, teaching for doctrines the commandments of men." Mark 7:7. Jesus revealed the Satanic origin of Judaism when he stated: "Ye are of your father the devil, and the lusts of your father ye will do." John 8:44. Babylonian Judaism remains the religion of the Jews today. Satan has infected many nominal "Christian" denominations with his Babylonian occultism, which has given rise to "Christian" Zionism. "Christian" Zionism advocates a counterfeit, earthly Zion, within which fleshly

Jews take primacy over the spiritual church of Jesus Christ. This book exposes "Christian" Zionism as a false gospel and subversive political movement that sustains Israel's war against God and man.

Murder, Rape, and Torture in a Catholic Nunnery
Edward Hendrie
ISBN-13: 978-1-943056-00-2

There has probably not been a person more maligned by the powerful forces of the Roman Catholic Church than Maria Monk. In 1836 she published the famous book, *Awful Disclosures of the Hotel Dieu Nunnery of Montreal*. In that book, she told of murder, rape, and torture behind the walls of the cloistered nunnery. Because the evidence was verifiably true, the Catholic hierarchy found it necessary to fabricate evidence and suborn perjury in an attempt to destroy the credibility of Maria Monk. The Catholic Church has kept up the character assassination of Maria Monk now for over 175 years. Even today, there can be found on the internet websites devoted to libeling Maria Monk. Edward Hendrie has examined the evidence and set it forth for the readers to decide for themselves whether Maria Monk was an impostor, as claimed by the Roman Catholic Church, or whether she was a brave victim. An objective view of the evidence leads to the ineluctable conclusion that Maria Monk told the truth about what happened behind the walls of the Hotel Dieu Nunnery of Montreal. The Roman Catholic Church, which is the most powerful religious and political organization in the world, has engaged in an unceasing campaign of vilification against Maria Monk. Their crusade against Maria Monk, however, can only affect the opinion of the uninformed. It cannot change the evidence. The evidence speaks clearly to those who will look at the case objectively. The evidence reveals that the much maligned Maria Monk was a reliable witness who made awful but accurate disclosures about life in a cloistered nunnery.

What Shall I Do to Inherit Eternal Life?
Edward Hendrie
ISBN-13: 978-0983262770

A certain ruler posed to Jesus the most important question ever asked: "Good Master, what shall I do to inherit eternal life?" (Luke 18:18) The man came to the right person. Jesus is God, and therefore his answer to that question is authoritative. This book examines Jesus' surprising answer and definitively explains how one inherits eternal life. This is a book about God's revelation to man. Except for the Holy Bible, this is the most important book you will ever read.

The Damnable Heresy Of Salvation by Dead Faith (Expanded Edition)
Edward Hendrie
ISBN 13: 978-1943056118

Good works follow salvation; they do not earn salvation. Good works do not save us. The works of faith are those works ordained and performed by God through the believer. They are the result of faith. It is that perfect faith that justifies the believer. "For by grace are ye saved through faith; and that not of yourselves: it is the gift of God: Not of works, lest any man should boast. For we are his workmanship, created in Christ Jesus unto good works, which God hath before ordained that we should walk in them. For we are his workmanship, created in Christ Jesus unto good works, which God hath before ordained that we should walk in them." Ephesians 2:8-10. In Romans, chapters 6 and 8, Paul explains faith without good works cannot save. Paul says that God's elect "walk not after the flesh, but after the Spirit." Romans 8:1. He states that those who do not walk in the Spirit but instead walk in the flesh "shall not inherit the kingdom of God." Galatians 5:15-25. John explains: "If we say that we have fellowship with him, and walk in darkness, we lie, and do not the truth: But if we walk in the light, as he is in the light, we have fellowship one with another, and the blood of Jesus Christ his Son cleanseth us from all sin." 1 John 1:6-7. James asks a rhetorical question: "What doth it profit, my brethren, though a man say he hath faith, and have not works? can faith save him?" James 2:14. James succinctly explains that "faith without works is dead." James 2:20. The pronouncement in James that true faith bears the fruit of good works is a theme found in the gospel. But some perniciously preach that God saves a person by faith that has no good works.

That is one of the "damnable heresies" about which Peter warned. See 2 Peter 2:1-22.

Rome's Responsibility for the Assassination of Abraham Lincoln, With an Appendix Containing Conversations Between Abraham Lincoln and Charles Chiniquy
Thomas M. Harris
ISBN-13: 978-0983262794

The author of this book, General Thomas Maley Harris, was a medical doctor, who recruited and served as commander of the Tenth West Virginia Volunteers during the Civil War. He rose in rank through meritorious service to become a brigadier general in the Union Army. General Harris established a reputation for faithfulness, industriousness, intelligence, and efficiency. He was noted for his leadership in preparing his troops and leading them in battle. He was brevetted a major general for "gallant conduct in the assault on Petersburg." After the Civil War, General Harris served one term as a representative in the West Virginia legislature, and was West Virginia's Adjutant General from 1869 to 1870. General Harris was a member of the Military Commission that tried and convicted the conspirators who assassinated President Abraham Lincoln. He had first hand knowledge of the sworn testimony of the witnesses in that trial. This book summarizes the salient evidence brought out during the military trial and adds information from other sources to present before the public the ineluctable conclusion that the assassination of Abraham Lincoln was the work of the Roman Catholic Church. The Roman Catholic Church has been largely successful in suppressing the circulation of this book. This book has never been given a place on bookstore shelves, as it exposed too much for the Roman Catholic hierarchy to tolerate. Any display of this book would bring an instant boycott of the bookstore. It is only now, in the age of the internet, where the marketplace of ideas has been opened wide, that this book can be found by those searching for the truth of who was behind the assassination of Abraham Lincoln.

The above books can be ordered from bookstores and from internet sites, including, but not limited to:

https://greatmountainpublishing.com
www.antichristconspiracy.com
www.911enemies.com
www.mysterybabylonthegreat.net
www.antigospel.com
https://play.google.com
www.barnesandnoble.com
www.amazon.com

Edward Hendrie
edwardhendrie@gmail.com

www.ingramcontent.com/pod-product-compliance
Lightning Source LLC
Chambersburg PA
CBHW051531230426
43669CB00015B/2565